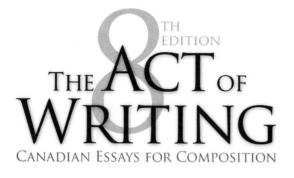

THE ACT OF WRITING
8TH EDITION

CANADIAN ESSAYS FOR COMPOSITION

THE ACT OF WRITING

8TH EDITION

CANADIAN ESSAYS FOR COMPOSITION

RONALD CONRAD

McGraw-Hill Ryerson

Toronto Montréal Boston Burr Ridge, IL Dubuque, IA
Madison, WI New York San Francisco St. Louis
Bangkok Bogotá Caracas Kuala Lumpur Lisbon London
Madrid Mexico City Milan New Delhi Santiago
Seoul Singapore Sydney Taipei

The McGraw-Hill Companies

McGraw-Hill
Ryerson

The Act of Writing: Canadian Essays for Composition
Eighth Edition

Copyright © 2009, 2006, 2003, 1999, 1995, 1993, 1990, 1987, 1983 by McGraw-Hill Ryerson Limited, a Subsidiary of The McGraw-Hill Companies. All rights reserved. No part of this publication may be reproduced or transmitted in any form or by any means, or stored in a data base or retrieval system, without the prior written permission of McGraw-Hill Ryerson Limited, or in the case of photocopying or other reprographic copying, a license from The Canadian Copyright Licensing Agency (Access Copyright). For an Access Copyright licence, visit www.accesscopyright.ca or call toll free to 1-800-893-5777.

ISBN-13: 978-0-07-096929-2
ISBN-10: 0-07-096929-9

1 2 3 4 5 6 7 8 9 10 QPF 0 9

Printed and bound in the United States of America

Care has been taken to trace ownership of copyright material contained in this text; however, the publisher will welcome any information that enables them to rectify any reference or credit for subsequent editions.

Vice-President and Editor in Chief: Joanna Cotton
Sponsoring Editor: Lisa Rahn
Managing Editor: Kelly Dickson
Developmental Editors: Sara Braithwaite/Jennifer Oliver
Marketing Manager: Michele Peach
Editorial Associate: Marina Seguin
Copy Editor: Rodney Rawlings
Team Lead, Production: Jennifer Hall
Composition: Greg Devitt
Interior Design: Greg Devitt
Cover Design: Greg Devitt
Cover Image Credit: Emily Carr/The Bridgeman Art Library/Getty Images
Printer: Quebecor Printing Fairfield

National Library of Canada Cataloguing in Publication
Conrad, Ronald, 1941–
    The act of writing / Ronald Conrad.—8th ed.
Includes bibliographical references.
ISBN 978-0-07-096929-2
    1. English language—Rhetoric—Textbooks. 2. Canadian essays (English).
I. Title.
PE1429.C66 2009   808'.0427   C2008-906657-X

CONTENTS

AND THEN....

"There were cheers and laughter as Tivadar hit me in the nose before I got my jacket off. It was not the first time I had tasted my own blood, but it was the first time a Christian had made it flow."

"I had hoped for more; what traveller doesn't?"

"She is suddenly pure energy, swift and sure. She grabs hold of one of his long legs. He twists and falls away beneath her, leaving his leg behind in her jaws."

"She yelled at me to read and when I didn't she smashed her pointing stick on the desk to frighten me."

"Acrid smoke bites the throat, parches the mouth. I am beyond mere fright. I am frozen with an insane fear that keeps me cowering in the bottom of the trench. I lie flat on my belly, waiting…."

"I went back, and, sitting in front of the image, gave stare for stare. But her stare so over-powered mine, that I could scarcely wrench my eyes away from the clutch of those empty sockets. The power that I felt was not in the thing itself, but in some tremendous force behind it, that the carver had believed in."

HERE'S WHY….

CHAPTER 4: CAUSE AND EFFECT 129

"Live life modestly—except during the holidays and when you've been dumped by your boyfriend—and hope for the best. It's all you can do."

"Once you see Earth from space, you can never again think of it in the same way."

"Like so many things in life, I know now what I should have done then. I should have thrown caution to the winds and done the right thing. Not the big-city thing. The right thing."

"I get the whole gamut of strange looks, stares and covert glances. You see, I wear the *hijab*…."

"When an SUV hits a car from the side, it can ride up over the car's door frame and right into the passenger compartment. (Well, hello there!)"

"The ability to forgive is a central tenet of every major religion in the world—Christian, Judaic, Hindu, Buddhist, and Islamic. Those faiths urge followers to forgive their enemies and, indeed, even to find a way to love those who wrong them. As the twenty-first century dawns, however, the world is making a spectacular mess of such pious admonitions. Instead of goodwill, this is the age of anger…."

IT'S JUST THE OPPOSITE OF….

CHAPTER 5: COMPARISON AND CONTRAST 187

IN A WAY, IT'S LIKE....

CHAPTER 6:
ANALOGY AND RELATED DEVICES   249

THERE ARE THREE KINDS OF THEM....

CHAPTER 7: CLASSIFICATION   281

HERE'S HOW IT'S DONE....

CHAPTER 8: PROCESS ANALYSIS   307

"Now, I believe, he stayed because he loved her. He may not have loved what was left of her, but he loved the essence of who she still was, and he could see that person still; he could see past the alcoholism and the years of damage it had done to them both."

"Jiggins is dead. He was, of course, a pioneer, but the fact that he dumb-belled himself to death at an early age does not prevent a whole generation of young men from following in his path."

THEREFORE....

CHAPTER 9:
ARGUMENTATION AND PERSUASION   345

"One paper cup consumes about 12 times as much steam, 36 times as much electricity, and twice as much cooling water as one polystyrene foam cup, while producing 58 times the volume of waste water."

"All around her the maimed survivors were running and stumbling away from the roaring furnace that had been a city. She ran with them toward the mountains that ring the landward side of Hiroshima."

"Facts about evacuees in Alberta? The fact is I never got used to it and I cannot, I cannot bear the memory. There are some nightmares from which there is no waking, only deeper and deeper sleep."

"There are people who think of the prairie as boring, and it is hard not to pity them. We see them on the highways, trapped inside their cars, propelled by a burning desire to be somewhere else."

"You stood up for freedom, honesty, and justice; you protected the innocent. I believed most of that. I think you did, too. It seemed true at the time."

"As the hip-hop started playing and the first kids bounded down the runway in Nike shoes and workout wear, the assembly broke into cheers and applause."

"He required numerous stitches to his forehead, temple and face but your boots didn't knock one tooth out—thank you."

"… I was popular in the community and at school, received high grades through working hard and exercising an agile mind, and did everything other kids my age did. Yet a close relative thought I should have been 'destroyed at birth,' because of my condition."

"The warmth of his tiny body snuggled against mine filled me with a peace and serenity that elevated me above the chaos. This child was alive yet terribly hungry, beautiful but covered in dirt, bewildered but not fearful. I made up my mind: this boy would be the fourth child in the Dallaire family. I couldn't save Rwanda, but I could save this child."

GLOSSARY

Contents by Subject

ACKNOWLEDGMENTS

Blatchford, Christie; "Mother's Milk," from *The First Man in My Life: Daughters Write About their Fathers,* ed. Sandra Martin, 2007, Penguin Group (Canada). Reprinted with permission of the author.

Callwood, June: "Forgiveness," first published in *The Walrus,* June 2007. June Callwood, Canadian author, journalist, social activist died in April 2007.

Crummey, Michael: "The Fish, the Fish," from *Writing Life,* ed. Constance Rooke, 2006, McClelland and Stewart. Reprinted with permission of the author.

Evans, Jon: "Apocalypse Soon," from *The Walrus,* September 2007. Jon Evans is a Canadian author, journalist and scriptwriter. Visit www.jonevans. ca. Reprinted with permission of the author.

Fiorito, Joe: Excerpted from *Union Station* by Joe Fiorito © 2006. Published by McClelland & Stewart. Used with permission of the publisher.

Ford, Catherine: "Yahoo, It's Calgary," excerpted from *Against the Grain* by Catherine Ford © 2005. Published by McClelland & Stewart. Used with permission of the publisher.

Garneau, Marc: "Canada Must Put the Planet's Interests First," from the Toronto *Globe and Mail,* December 14, 2007, p. A25. Reprinted with permission of the author.

Lam, Dr. Vincent, and Dr. Colin Lee: "Dr. Lam's Perspective: Go on a Canoe Trip," from *The Flu Pandemic and You: A Canadian Guide* by Vincent

Lam, M.D. and Colin Lee, M.D. © 2006 Vincent Lam and Colin Lee. Reprinted by permission of Doubleday Canada, a division of Random House of Canada Ltd.

Lane, Patrick: Excerpted from *There Is a Season: A Memoir in a Garden* by Patrick Lane © 2004. Published by McClelland & Stewart. Used with permission of the publisher.

Mackintosh, C. B.: "Moss Campion" from *Dropped Threads 3: Beyond the Small Circle,* ed. Marjorie Anderson, 2006, Vintage Canada. Reprinted with permission of the author.

MacLennan, Hugh: "A Sound Beyond Hearing" from *Barometer Rising.* Permission granted by McGill-Queens University Press for Hugh MacLennan. First published in 1941.

Nolen, Stephanie: "Regine Mamba," excerpted from *28 Stories of AIDS in Africa* by Stephanie Nolen © 2007 Stephanie Nolen. Reprinted by permission of Knopf Canada.

Rosenthal, Jeffrey: "Poker Power," excerpted from *Struck by Lightning: The Curious World of Probabilities* © 2005 Jeffrey S. Rosenthal. Published by HarperCollins Publishers Ltd. All rights reserved.

Sampang, Crisanta: "Trading Motherhood for Dollars," from *Between Interruptions: Thirty Women Tell the Truth About Motherhood,* published 2007 by Key Porter. Reprinted with permission of the author.

Savage, Candace: "Stuck on the Prairies: Where Is Here?" from *Curious by Nature* by Candace Savage, published 2005 by Greystone Books, a division of Douglas & McIntyre Ltd. Reprinted by permission of the publisher.

Von Hahn, Karen: "Self-Serving Propaganda," from the Toronto *Globe and Mail,* August 11, 2007. Reprinted with permission of the author.

Wiebe, Rudy: "The Bull," excerpted from *Of This Earth: A Mennonite Boyhood in the Boreal Forest* by Rudy Wiebe © 2006 Jackpine House Ltd. Reprinted by permission of Knopf Canada.

To the Student

We hope you like *The Act of Writing*. In our eight editions so far, we've put real effort into collecting material that is fun to read, that provides issues to debate in class, that inspires you to write about significant things, and that suggests good books to keep you reading after the course is done.

The 50 selections between these covers provide some good reading right now. Notice, though, how the introduction to each author also lists more works by that person. And the "Explorations" feature after each selection suggests which of those books are probably most worth reading. Circle the most likely ones to try over the holidays, or next summer, or whenever else you have time. (Then keep this book, so you have a record of those choices!)

If our selection by Jeffrey Rosenthal or Linda McQuaig or Stephanie Nolen or Margaret Atwood or Naomi Klein especially appeals to you, then treat it like a movie trailer: go on to a full-length feature as soon as you can. Remember that in addition to the fun you may have and the insights you may get, the act of opening a book is probably the most direct path to improving your own writing. Every time you read good writing, your mind is forming patterns that will help you produce your own.

"Explorations," the feature following each essay, also suggests several websites about this author and this subject. Check them out. You can read a poem by Goran Simic or Michael Crummey, or view Emily Carr's best paintings, or see a video interview with June Callwood on her social views, Stephanie Nolen on her reporting about AIDS in Africa, or Christie Blatchford about what she saw with Canadian troops on the battlefields of Afghanistan. Or after reading astronaut Marc Garneau on global warming, you can view a site that calculates your own carbon footprint.

Finally, *The Act of Writing* teaches a philosophy of composition. We hope you consider carefully this book's advice about how good writing is produced in the real world: not just through blueprinting an essay before you write the first word, but through a process of discovery, of "thinking by writing." Do read our overview of the writing process, on pages 1 through 19, with close attention. Free yourself up to try the techniques it suggests, and free yourself from some of the inefficient or even harmful practices of the past. The methods we suggest are based on today's research, but they are also the same ones that most good writers have always used.

R.C.

TO THE TEACHER

The essay as a form of writing has never been more important than now. It is true that our nation has long focussed on facts: the early Jesuit martyrs issued detailed reports of their work; the factors of the Hudson's Bay Company penned exact records of their trade with trappers; and explorers such as Captain Thomas James and Samuel Hearne wrote clear and even polished accounts of their discoveries and adventures. Today, if anything, we see a resurgence of that factual impulse. Never have so many film documentaries been seen in so many theatres by so many people. Never have events such as Toronto's Hot Docs been so popular.

And what about the nonfiction essay today? Anthologies such as *The Act of Writing* abound, competing for the honour of educating students. Also, recently in Canada a flood of essay anthologies for the general reader has appeared, with titles such as *Between Interruptions: Thirty Women Tell the Truth About Motherhood; Writing Life; Dropped Threads 1, 2 and 3; Utopia: Towards a New Toronto; Canada's Young Activists: A Generation Stands Up for Change; What I Meant to Say: The Private Lives of Men; The First Man in My Life: Daughters Write About Their Fathers;* and *What Is a Canadian?: Forty-Three Thought-Provoking Responses.*

Fine new periodicals such as *The Walrus*, with significant and arresting essays, are also being founded. Even newspapers devote space to essays, on every conceivable topic, by their readers.

What does all this mean? It certainly does not mean that Canadians lack imagination, for a flood of good fiction is also coming out. No, what I take this to mean is that the essay and its cousins satisfy a great need in the public. After the stasis of the Cold War and more recently the paralysis of 9/11, Canadians are ready to explore and learn. They want to know how others live. They want to understand how everything works. And in pursuing these desires, they are becoming better citizens of Canada and of the world.

It is with real hope, then, that an anthologist launches a new edition. Welcome to our eighth!

CONTINUITY

One aspect of designing a new edition is to conserve what readers have liked so far. Many reviewers have helped us in this task. We have stayed very close to their wishes, and we trust this means we have stayed close to your wishes too. In this eighth edition a core of proven and familiar pieces stays in place, which we hope will provide many of your own favourites as you design your course.

In the core structure of the book, as well, we are not pursuing change for the sake of change. In earlier editions we have dropped and added chapters, in response to readers' wishes. This time we are maintaining the overall outlines of the book, because of the good degree of user satisfaction shown in the reviews. Note that our most-used chapters (determined by review results) contain the largest numbers of essays, so that students and teachers will have the greatest de facto choice of readings. (Also see that at the end of each chapter introduction appears a list of essays in *other* chapters that also make use of the present means of organization—to give a still larger choice.)

EXPLORATION

Of the 50 selections in *The Act of Writing*, eighth edition, about a third are new. But the newness lies even more in the selection of writers than in their number. We have many fresh voices this time—such as Jeffrey Rosenthal, Marc Garneau, Crisanta Sampang, Stephanie Nolen, Michael Crummey, Jon Evans, Drs. Vincent Lam and Colin Lee, C. B. Mackintosh, Catherine Ford, Christie Blatchford and Candace Savage—as a new generation of writers continues to take its place in Canada. Many of our new contributors are from Western Canada, to better balance our contents geographically. There is representation from Quebec and from the First Nations population, and an ever-larger number of our contributors are new Canadians. As for gender, we offer a balanced proportion of 25 selections by women and 25 by men.

In addition, we resolutely maintain *The Act of Writing* as an anthology of all-Canadian essays, to provide an alternative for teachers and students who want more than a token selection of our own materials in the classroom. Yet at the same time you will find a strong international focus through Canadian eyes: astronaut Marc Garneau tells how his world changed when he saw it from space; Crisanta Sampang describes the experience of so many mothers working in Canada to support their children elsewhere; Stephanie Nolen shows us an African grandmother who, amid the AIDS epidemic, fights to save her grandchildren;

Catherine Pigott learns new body image in Gambia; Margaret Atwood sees new directions in America; Naomi Klein investigates the sweatshop origins of clothes worn by Canadians; and Lt.-Gen. Roméo Dallaire takes us to Rwanda, a paradise made hell by politics both local and international.

As times change, controversy keeps on emerging. A great many *Act of Writing* selections explore issues: globalization, war, racism, homelessness, sexism, SUVs and their effects; technology changing the ways we read and write; protecting ourselves against pandemics; prejudice against the disabled; and the challenges of being an immigrant. To reflect our strong emphasis on issues, the feature "Ideas for Discussion and Writing," which appears after each selection, is on the average fairly extensive, while "Structure" and "Style" are on the average more compact.

Finally, the feature "Explorations," at the end of each selection, has grown, to offer students a larger choice of books, websites and other sources that relate to the author and/or subject of that selection. We like to think of *The Act of Writing* as an index to independent readings students may wish to do: when they have been stimulated by a selection, they are given paths to continue on their own.

The book's website at www.mcgrawhill.ca/olc/conrad contains the "Topics for Writing" that formerly appeared at the end of each chapter.

IF YOU ARE NEW TO THIS BOOK

The Act of Writing, eighth edition, encourages flexibility and individualization. The combination of three to nine essays per chapter, with several more identified in cross-references, will yield more selections per unit than you are likely to use. Thus you can individualize, choosing readings that best suit the needs and interests of your particular class. This book also offers a range of difficulty, from essays that are very accessible to others that are challenging.

Note: **The "Table of Contents and Difficulty Ranking" of your Instructor's Manual rates all selections at one of three levels of difficulty, so if you are new to this book you can more quickly tailor a syllabus to your class.**

The discussion topics after each selection offer themes for analysis and debate. "Explorations," as described earlier, suggests books and websites for independent investigation. And finally, the "Process in Writing" topic after each essay and the process "Guidelines" tailored for each chapter offer some latitude of choice for the individual teacher, the individual class, the individual student.

See the two tables of contents. The first lists all selections in their chapters arranged by *form of organization* (you can choose from eight essays, for example, that all demonstrate organization through comparison and contrast). The second table of contents lists all essays by general *subject,* to help you choose selections of interest to your particular students, especially in a theme-based course.

An introductory essay, "The Act of Writing," starts the book off by putting to rest several common misconceptions about writing that plague students, then describes what it is that an essayist actually does. It emphasizes the individuality of the writer, the importance of motivation, the role of intuition as well as logic, and a balance of spontaneity and revision of the process of writing.

As we have seen, the essays are arranged in chapters that each demonstrate a fundamental pattern of thought—and therefore of organization. "Narration" starts the book off, because no approach is easier or more motivating for a first assignment than writing a story, in chronological order, about oneself. "Example" and "Description" follow, because these tools of development are used to some degree in almost all writing. "Cause and Effect" and its following chapter, "Comparison and Contrast," are at the centre of the essayist's organizational repertoire. "Analogy and Related Devices" and "Classification" follow "Comparison and Contrast," for they are both varieties of comparison. "Process Analysis," an approach used widely across the curriculum, follows. After all these *forms,* our largest chapter, "Argumentation and Persuasion," explores more fully the writer's most basic *purpose:* to make a point. It examines the dualities of deduction and induction, and of argumentation and persuasion, then illustrates their application with nine model essays.

Throughout the book each selection is prefaced by an introduction to the author, designed to interest the student, often to present the author as a role model, and to encourage further reading of his or her works. Then each selection is followed by pedagogical material entitled "Explorations," "Structure," "Style," "Ideas for Discussion and Writing," and in Chapter 9 "Argumentation and Persuasion." Note that in this material different questions serve different purposes. Some are directive, calling attention to major features of the essay. Some are technical, for example focussing on a specific point of language that illustrates a technique. Still others are exploratory, encouraging open-ended response.

The Instructor's Manual answers those questions that are not open-ended and suggests responses to some that are. (Be sure to go to the text's Online Learning Centre at www.mcgrawhill.ca/olc/conrad to download.) Read the Manual's introduction: it gives more suggestions for using *The Act of Writing*. For each essay, the Manual also lists vocabulary that may need attention.

Each of the nine chapters begins with a discussion of how and why to use the form at hand. Then each chapter ends with a generous number of essay topics (now to be downloaded from the Online Learning Centre, mentioned just above). These topics have been chosen with care, to tap some of the students' deepest concerns and channel them into motivation for writing. The reason for this attention to topics is that no one problem is more destructive to the performance of both student and teacher than dull or superficial subject matter. How can writing be important if its content is not? And how can a teacher enjoy or even tolerate marking without an interest in what the students are saying?

A further "Process in Writing" topic is given after each essay. If class members have had a good discussion about the selection, their motivation and writing performance may be greatest if they explore these topics, which draw upon both the subject and the underlying form of the essay preceding them. Then at the end of each chapter are the process guidelines mentioned earlier, individualized for the specific pattern of development in that unit.

Finally, a glossary at the book's end defines literary terms often used in the discussion questions; when one of these words is a key part of a passage in the chapter itself, it appears in SMALL CAPITALS.

In Appreciation

Here I would like to recognize two of our long-time authors whose words are still with us in *The Act of Writing* but who in the past months have left this world: Doris Anderson, whose "The 51-Per-Cent Minority" first appeared in *Maclean's* and then in all eight of our editions since 1983; and June Callwood, who now appears in the third of her essays that over time we have republished: the wise and benevolent "Forgiveness," which she wrote in the last weeks of her life and first published in *The Walrus*.

I would also like to thank the many instructors who made suggestions from their experiences in the classroom, and the many who reviewed both our previous edition and our new selections:

Graeme Abernethy, *University of the Fraser Valley*
Amy Airhart, *University of Toronto*
Jason Bermiller, *Thompson Rivers University*
Wilhelm Emilsson, *Douglas College*
Derek Hanebury, *North Island College*
Ingrid Hutchinson, *Fanshawe College*
Carolyn Ives, *Thompson Rivers University*
Heidi L. M. Jacobs, *University of Windsor*
Christine Kirchner, *Camosun College*
Rita S. Matlock, *University of Saskatchewan*
Peter C. Miller, *Seneca College*
Andrew Murray, *University of Victoria*
Declan Neary, *Humber College*
Norma-Jean Nielsen, *Canadore College*
Diana Patterson, *Mount Royal College*
Kelly Pitman, *Camosun College*
Pavlina Radia, *University of Toronto, Scarborough*
Gillian Schell, *Laurentian University*
Sandra Slade, *Langara College*
Timothy Walters, *Okanagan College*

Thanks to my daughter Suzanne (herself a teacher) for her valuable suggestions, and for introducing me to her colleague Miroslaw Lalas, who has developed his own special way of using *The Act of Writing* in the classroom. Thanks to my daughter Katherine, who, as a lawyer, brought her keen judgement to bear on the final choice of new selections. Thanks also to my son Charles, who with a decade of IT experience solved every computer problem. Also thanks to many others, too numerous to name, who gave suggestions of all kinds. Most of all, I sincerely thank my wife, Mary, who in fact is co-author of this book, though she declines to be named on the cover. Her hard work, lively interest and unerring judgement have helped shape every edition so far, especially this one.

R. C.

INTRODUCTION: THE ACT OF WRITING

Writing is one of the most misunderstood of human activities. It is strange that after all the years we've spent in school, after all the hours we've spent reading other people's writing and producing our own, most of us can't say what really happens when we write. We can describe other complex tasks—driving a car, producing a spreadsheet, casting for trout, or searching the Web. But to many people the act of writing is a mystery. Not that we don't have theories, either those told us in school or those we have arrived at ourselves. But many of these theories are misconceptions that actually hinder our efforts to write. Let's look at some of them.

MISCONCEPTION: *Writing is like following a blueprint: I figure it all out in advance and then just fill in the details.* Of course an outline, used sensibly, will help. But a generation or two ago, many students were taught that their best thinking should go into a logical and detailed

1

outline—and that the writing itself was secondary. Thus they were reduced to carpenters or plumbers of the written word, who merely sawed, cut and fit pieces in place once the master plan was established. The problem with this reassuringly logical approach (which even today is taught in some places) is that it views writing as a technology, not as the art that all our practical experience tells us it is. How many of us have given up on a required outline, done our thinking mostly as we wrote the essay itself, then later produced the outline by seeing what we wrote? Or how many of us have painfully constructed a detailed outline in advance, only to find while writing the essay that our real message does not fit the plan?

Writing is exploring! We know which way we are headed and the main landmarks we hope to pass, but not every twist and turn of the path. What a dull trip that would be! Let's leave room for discovery, because our best ideas may occur in the act of writing. The Quebec poet Hector de St.-Denys Garneau actually said, "I cannot think except when writing." Some teachers reflect this fact of writing as discovery by calling a first version the *discovery draft*.

But while avoiding the rigor mortis of overplanning, let's not go to the opposite extreme, like Stephen Leacock's famous horseman who "rode madly off in all directions." We do work best with an outline, five or ten or fifteen lines that define the main point and how we intend to support it. But the outline should be a compass on a journey, not the blueprint of a construction project.

MISCONCEPTION: *If I don't hit it right the first time, I've failed.* It's not hard to see where this idea came from: in school we write so many essays and tests within the limits of one class period that writing in a hurry begins to seem normal. But under such conditions, merely producing enough is hard; seriously revising it is even harder. Few people can "hit it right the first time." Professional writers know this; most of them take longer to write than we do. They tinker with words and sentences, they delete and replace sections, they go through two or three or even five or ten versions—and sometimes they throw the whole thing out and start over. These writers know by experience that writing is not a hit-or-miss affair with only one try allowed, but a *process*. They know that revision can yield amazing results.

MISCONCEPTION: *When I write, I am speaking on paper.* If you've heard a recording of yourself speaking, you were no doubt surprised at all the filler words you used. "Uh," "um," "well" and "hmmm" may fill the gaps between your thoughts very conveniently, but they hardly help to carry the message. And if you listened closely, you may have been surprised at the number of incomplete statements—fragments that by themselves made little or no sense. Fillers and fragments are accepted in speech because, after all, we're making up our message on the spot. There is no chance to plan, revise, edit or proofread.

But in writing there is, and this fact increases the expectations of your reader far beyond those of your listener. Language in written form can be planned. It is complete. It is precise and concise. It uses standard words. It has punctuation. It follows the rules. In short, it is a product of the time that its written form allows you to give it, not a spur-of-the-moment, hope-for-the-best effort like the speech that comes so easily from your mouth.

MISCONCEPTION: *The best words are the biggest words.* Variations on this theme are *If my writing looks scholarly it will impress the reader,* and even *If I make my essay so difficult that no one knows what I'm saying, everyone will believe me.* At the roots of these widespread ideas is a notion that writing is a kind of competition between writer and reader. A writer who is obscure enough will make the reader feel like a dummy and will thus win the game. But ask yourself: In real life do you *ambulate* or *walk? Expectorate* or *spit? Interdigitate* or *hold hands? Cogitate* or *think?*

Avoiding this game of writer vs. reader is not easy when so many leaders in business, education and government play it. The first step toward open communication, though, is to think of your reader not as an opponent but as a teammate. You are both moving toward the same goal, which is the reader's clear understanding of your ideas.

Another step is to admit that words small in size can be large in meaning. The best-loved writings in our language (think of the lines from Shakespeare you may have memorized for school) are filled with short words. Writing made of them is more concise, more vivid, and usually more profound than writing made of the elephantine words that some of us ransack the dictionary or thesaurus for. If a long word—like "elephantine" above—conveys your meaning best, by all means use it. But often the writer, like the architect, finds that *less is more.*

MISCONCEPTION: *I don't like to write.* For some unfortunate people this statement is true. But for most who say it, the truth is really "I don't like to *begin* writing." Who does? Staring at that blank page or screen is like staring from a diving board at the cold water below. But a swimmer and a writer both gather the courage to plunge in, and soon they both feel a new sensation: they don't want to come out. Teachers whose students write journals in class see the process at work every day. As class begins, the writers are filled with stress: they chew their pens and frown as they stare at the page to be filled. But in a while they are scribbling furiously, recording in an almost trance-like state their latest experiences, feelings and insights. When the teacher asks them to stop, in order to begin the next activity, they are annoyed: they sigh and *keep on writing* till asked a second or third time to stop.

Let's admit that most writers—and that includes professionals—dread the beginning. Let's also admit that most writers can enjoy the rest of it, hard work though it may be.

With some of the most widespread misconceptions behind us now, let's take a fresh look at the act of writing. First, allow for personal differences. *Know yourself.* If you are a person whose desk is piled high with papers and books, whose closet is an avalanche waiting to happen, and whose shoes have not been shined in two years, you may write best by planning little and relying on your spontaneity. But if you are a person who plans an August holiday in January, keeps a budget right down to the penny, and washes the car every Wednesday and Saturday whether it needs it or not, you may write best by planning fully.

On the other hand, your natural tendencies may have caused you problems and so may need to be controlled. If your spontaneity has produced writings that wander off topic, plan more: make a careful outline. If overorganizing has sucked the life out of your writing, free yourself up: leave more room for discovery as you write. Whatever the case, try to determine and use the approach that works for *you.*

Let's allow also for differences in writing tasks. If you are dashing off a short personal sketch, your planning may be no more than an idea and a few moments of thought. If you are writing a long research paper, the product of days in the library, you may need an outline two pages long. No single approach works for every person and every assignment. Keep in mind, then, that the process we are about to examine is a *starting point*, a basis but not a blueprint, for your own writing.

BEFORE YOU START THE ESSAY, TRY ANSWERING THESE QUESTIONS:

1. WHY AM I WRITING? Today most of us are writing more than ever before. In Margaret Wente's essay "Busy, Busy, Busy" (Chapter 2), someone says: "I took three days off and when I got back to the office I had six hundred e-mails." Another person replies: "That's nothing.... I had two thousand...." Mobile communication devices add to the flurry, with text messaging throughout the day. Even while in school, we exchange written digital messages to plan our social events, organize our activities or just to entertain each other with our comments. We know why we are writing. But in an academic sense, when we begin to imagine and write an essay, do we know why we are writing? This basic question too often goes unasked. If the answer is "to fill up five pages," "to impress" or "to get an A," you begin with a severe handicap. The immediate reason to write may be a class assignment, but the real reason must be to communicate something of value. Otherwise your motivation is lost and so is your performance. So, from a list of topics, choose the one that means the most to you. If no topic seems significant, devise a way to *make* one significant. Probe the topic through the exercise of freewriting, explained later. Look at your topic from a new view-point or approach it in some unusual way.

If that fails, and if your teacher is approachable, voice your concern and ask for an alternative topic. One teacher always made students analyze the relative merits of chocolate and vanilla ice cream, on the theory that a dull subject will not distract a writer from the real goals: grammar and style. He was wrong. Research shows motivation to be the single greatest factor in writing performance—and motivation comes from writing about things that matter.

When you write on your own, as in a personal journal, you may still need to answer the question *Why am I writing?* Just recording events may not be enough. Add your feelings, your perceptions and your conclusions about those events. If you have problems, as most people do, confront them on the page. The more you discover yourself and your world through writing, the more important the writing becomes.

2. WHO IS MY AUDIENCE? Do you talk the same way to a friend and a stranger? To an old person and a child? Probably not. Neither would you write the same way to all readers. In a personal journal you can write as freely as you think, for you are your own reader: omissions and excesses of all kinds will be understood and forgiven. In messages to a close friend you are nearly as free, because the reader knows you well enough to supply missing explanations or interpret remarks in the light of your personality. But your freedom shrinks when you write for others: a business person, a public official, a teacher. Now you must fight a misconception shared by many people: *Everyone is like me.*

This idea is seldom articulated but may lurk as a natural assumption in the back of our minds. It is a form of egotism. If you assume everyone is like you, many readers will not accept or even understand your message—because they are *not* like you. They did not grow up in your family, neighbourhood or even country. They are older or younger, or of the opposite sex. They have had different life experiences, so now they have different knowledge and temperaments and values.

Accept these differences as you write. You will never prove your point by quoting Marx to a banker, the Bible to an atheist, or Margaret Atwood to a male supremacist. Any argument built on a partisan foundation will collapse if the reader does not accept that foundation. Instead, build from facts or ideas that your reader probably *does* accept: killing is bad, government is necessary, women are human beings, and so on. Is your subject controversial? Then avoid an open display of bias. Calling police "pigs" or intellectuals "eggheads" or abortionists "hired killers" will appeal only to those who shared your view in the first place. (For more on these matters, read the introduction to Chapter 9, "Argumentation and Persuasion.")

Does the reader know what you know? If you write about statistics for a statistics teacher, use any technical terms customary to the field, and avoid the insult of explaining elementary points. But if you write on the same subject for a class exercise in English or a letter to the editor of your hometown newspaper, your reader will be very different: avoid most technical terms, define those you do use, and explain more fully each step of your argument.

The more open you become to the individuality of your reader, the more open your reader becomes to your message. It's a matter of mutual respect.

3. HOW BIG IS MY TOPIC? Classroom essays are shorter than most people realize. A book may contain 100,000 words; a magazine article 2000 or 5000; a classroom essay as few as 500 or even 250. So narrowing the essay topic is more important than most people realize.

One student, who had been a political prisoner before coming to Canada, chose to write about economic systems. He knew the subject well, as his teacher found out talking with him, and he was committed to it. But what he attempted was an analysis of communism, socialism and capitalism, all in two pages! A lack of focus spread his very short essay so thin that it approached the state of saying nothing about everything. It was the barest scratching of the surface, a summary of basic facts everyone already knows.

If the same person had focussed on his arrest and imprisonment—or even on one day in his cell—he might have said far more about the system he opposed. He could have told his readers about the rotten food, the noise, the open bucket latrine, the insulting guards, and the patriotic slogans on the walls. He could have described the other prisoners who had been arrested for showing up at political protests. It is in specifics that we best see generalities. Think of writing as photography. Putting aside the wide-angle view that includes too much at a distance, let the zoom bring you up close to a small part of the subject. Select the part most meaningful to you, the part most characteristic of the whole, then take the picture.

Nearly all the essays in this book are closeups: they explore one situation, one incident, one person or one process. Yet many of them are longer than the essays you will write. So when you choose a topic, judge its size. And if you have to, *change* its size to fit your writing task.

4. WHAT MESSAGE AM I SENDING? *(Or: What is my* THESIS STATEMENT*?)* You may know your topic well. But unless you send a message concerning it, your reader will think *What's the point?* A message is often a value judgement: Are robots dangerous? Will they take away our jobs or someday even rule over us? Or do they help us? Will they free us at last from the dehumanizing tyranny of manual labour? Most of the essays in this book take such a stance, either pro or con, toward their subjects. Some avoid judging their subjects directly, but send other messages: what it's like to be homeless, or what it's like to operate on someone's brain.

If you have chosen a topic because it seems meaningful, you will probably have a message to send. So what do you most feel like saying about the topic? Try the techniques of brainstorming and freewriting described in the next section, "Prewriting," to help you find out. Once you know, get your message down in writing. This THESIS STATEMENT, as it is called, is normally a single sentence that occurs at or near the beginning of an essay. But it doesn't just announce the subject; it also clearly conveys the writer's message, the writer's *opinion,* about some aspect of that subject.

For example, the sentence *"Many people have credit cards"* does announce an overall subject, but could never be a thesis statement because it is too general. It tells us something we already know. How could we spend several pages arguing that many people have credit cards? But certainly there are other messages about this important subject that could be sent. Let's look at some potential thesis statements. Which ones focus their subject down to a closeup? Which ones take into account their audience? Which ones announce a message, a point of view, that is worth supporting?

- *Many students have credit cards.* (Forget it: this is almost as general as "Many people have credit cards.")
- *I once lost my credit card.* (This is more specific, but how could it be argued when it's merely an incident? Where is the opinion we need?)

- *The fastest way to gain control over your finances is to cut up your credit card.* (Now we're getting somewhere: the topic is very specific, and the statement is an opinion that needs support so that readers will accept it. All kinds of evidence might be given: the high credit card interest rates, the risk of identity theft and other fraud, the ease of spending more with a card, etc.)

- *In order to keep the working class enslaved in debt, the greedy masters of our capitalist system promote more and more use of credit cards.* (This writer forgot to ask "Who is my audience?" Any reader who does like our economic system will probably reject the argument that follows. That argument might still succeed, though, with more tactful language and with enough factual examples (such as the interest rate of many cards nearing 20% annually).

- *A credit card is a good financial tool if the balance is paid off each month.* (Here again is a worthwhile potential thesis statement: it is well focussed, and it has an idea that requires support so the reader will accept it.)

Prewriting

So how do we begin the act of writing? By putting those first words on a page? The philosopher Lao-Tze said, "A journey of a thousand miles begins with a single step." In a way he was right: if we never take that official first step, we'll certainly never arrive at our destination. But how much daydreaming and planning do we do beforehand? Do we set out on a journey without consulting the map or the calendar or the tourist brochure or the travel guide—not to mention our wallet? And do we write an essay without somehow answering the questions we have just asked:

Why am I writing?

Who is my audience?

How big is my topic?

What message am I sending?

The process of writing, then, begins in thought. But thoughts do not come on command. Like the person on the diving board, we look down at the cold water and dread the plunge. Some writers like to break the ice by manipulating their environment: finding a quiet spot, going to a favourite chair with good lighting, or listening to music. Others fortify themselves with a good night's sleep, junk food or coffee. Any of these tricks may help, but they all skirt the real issue: How do we begin to *think*?

One direct approach, a variation on the old technique of out-lining, is **brainstorming**. Once you have roughly identified your sub-ject, just write down words or phrases that relate in any way to it, in a list going down a page. Put down anything that comes, letting one thought lead to another. Some entries will seem off-topic, trivial or even crazy, but others may be just what you need: the keys to your essay. Circle them. Put them in order. As crude as this primitive out-line may seem, it has served a purpose: your thoughts have begun to arrive. The process is in motion. You have taken that first "step" before even starting the first draft.

A similar but even more powerful icebreaker is *freewriting*. Put a blank page on the desk with your watch beside it. Think of your topic. Now write! Put down anything that comes: sentences, phrases, words—logical thoughts, hasty impressions, even pure garbage. Do not cease the physical act of writing, do not even lift the pen from the page, or your fingers from the keyboard, for at least five minutes. If your next thought doesn't come, write the last one over and over till the next one does come. What emerges may surprise you.

Like brainstorming, freewriting is an exercise in free association: the flow of your thoughts, the sudden leaps of your intuition, will break the ice so you can write. They may do even more: as in brainstorming, you may end up with a page of scribbling that contains the main points of your essay. Try to find them. Circle them. Put them in order. See if your intuition has led the way in answering the questions: *Why am I writing? Who is my audience? How big is my topic? What message am I send-ing?* If all goes well, you have already begun your journey.

THE FIRST WORDS

Once your thoughts are flowing comes the next step, the opening pas-sage of your essay. In a very short composition your THESIS STATEMENT may serve also as the first words. But in most essays of medium to long length, it comes at the end of an introduction. Only about one-fourth of the selections in this book start right off with what could be called a thesis statement. What do the others start with?

BACKGROUND INFORMATION: About half the essays in this book lead off by telling the circumstances in which the topic is set. For examples, see the beginnings of our selections by Gabori (p. 26), Simic (p. 84), Wiebe (p. 101), Garneau (p. 138), McQuaig (p. 154), Hocking (p. 354), Dobbs (p. 361), Schindler (p. 404), Atwood (p. 392) and Christy (p. 409).

ANECDOTE: A brief story, usually of a humorous or dramatic incident, can lead into the topic. See Wente (p. 61), Pearson (p. 133), Callwood (p. 161), Pigott (p. 196), Taylor (p. 216), Bernstein (p. 311) and Leacock (p. 338).

QUOTATION OR ALLUSION: The words of a philosopher, of a news report, of a recognized specialist in the subject, or of anyone with close experience of it can be used to break the ice. See Pearson (p. 133), Taylor (p. 216), Dobbs (p. 361) and Kogawa (p. 373).

SENSE IMAGES: Vivid description can attract a reader's interest to the topic. See Lane (p. 37), Geddes (p. 45), Fiorito (p. 77), McLaren (p. 96), Wiebe (p. 101), Harrison (p. 108), Mackintosh (p. 270), Klein (p. 398) and Dallaire (p. 414).

A STRIKING COMPARISON OR CONTRAST: Showing how things are like or unlike each other is a dramatic way to introduce a topic. See Shields (p. 31), Gabori (p. 26), Rosenthal (p. 71), Garneau (p. 138), Anderson (p. 191), Nolen (p. 202), Pigott (p. 196), Koehl (p. 318) and Hocking (p. 354).

NARRATIVE: Several selections in this book begin by telling a story upon which the essay is based. See Carr (p. 117), D'Angelo (p. 144), Pigott (p. 196), Dobbs (p. 361), Klein (p. 398) and Dallaire (p. 414).

AN UNUSUAL OR PUZZLING STATEMENT: Such an opening appeals to the reader's curiosity. See Simic (p. 84), Carr (p. 117), Pearson (p. 133) and Evans (p. 238).

FIGURES OF SPEECH: A striking METAPHOR, SIMILE or PERSONIFICATION can spark the opening. See Hill (p. 228) and Bennett (p. 264).

Most of these introductions are short: a couple of sentences or a paragraph or two at the most. And all are designed to *interest* the reader, for a bored reader may not even finish the essay, let alone like or understand it. Writing is fishing. You throw in the line. Your reader tastes the bait (your introduction), bites, is pulled through the stream of your argument, and—if the line of thought doesn't break—lands in your net.

You, the writer, may also be hooked. Once you have hit upon a strong introduction, one that shows off the drama or importance of your topic, the beginning may carry you along. And once you get going, the idea embodied in your thesis statement may pull you through the essay, enabling you to write freely as one page leads to another. You may become less and less aware of your surroundings as you become more and more immersed in your subject. By the time you develop a good beginning, you may experience the act of writing the way one student described it: "At first I couldn't start, but then I couldn't stop."

THE BODY

An introduction to an essay is like your head: it may decide to go somewhere but it needs your body to take it there. The "body" of your essay has the main work to do: following the direction set by your introduction, and especially by your thesis statement, the body explains, illustrates and sometimes attempts to prove your point. But if it ever ignores the direction set by the head, it ceases to do its job. Even the best of explanations, without a purpose, is like one of those unfortunate football players who completes a spectacular run to the wrong goal. On the other hand, we know that writing is discovery. The acts of writing and revising will sometimes take us in a direction better than the old one decided by the introduction. When that happens, correct not the body but the head—so the two can move together in the new direction.

One of the easiest ways to keep a direction is to choose a pattern for your essay—and that is what much of this book is about. As you read and discuss the essays that follow, and as you write your own essays, trying out the patterns other writers use, you will explore a range of choices:

NARRATION: In simple time order, from the first event to the last event, tell a story that illustrates the point. (See pages 26 to 52.)

EXAMPLE: Give one in-depth example that explains the point, or a number of shorter examples. (See pages 61 to 87.)

DESCRIPTION: Recreate for your reader, through vivid language, your own or someone else's experience with the subject. (See pages 96 to 124.)

CAUSE AND EFFECT: Explain by showing how one situation or event causes another. (See pages 133 to 182.)

COMPARISON AND CONTRAST: Explain by showing how two things are like or unlike each other. (See pages 191 to 244.)

ANALOGY AND RELATED DEVICES: In comparing two things, use the one to explain the other. (See pages 253 to 275.)

CLASSIFICATION: Make a point by dividing your subject into parts, then explaining each in turn. (See pages 284 to 302.)

PROCESS ANALYSIS: Show how something is done or how something happens. (See pages 311 to 341.)

ARGUMENTATION AND PERSUASION: Using any pattern that works, make your point through logic and/or emotion. (See pages 354 to 421.)

Seldom does one of these methods appear alone. A *process analysis*, for example, is usually told as a *narrative*. Here and there it may use *examples*, *description* or any of the other patterns to help make its point, but these combinations occur naturally, often without the writer's knowing it. In most cases the only form actually chosen by a writer is the main one that organizes the whole essay.

How do you choose the right form? Let the subject be your guide. In architecture, form follows function. Rather than cram an office into a preselected structure, a designer likes to begin with the function of that office. How much space does it need? What shape? What barriers and passageways between one section and another? What front to present to the world?

An essay is much the same: the needs of its subject, if you are open to them, can suggest a form. If the main idea is to explain what something is like, you will tend to choose *examples* and *description*. If the subject is unusual or little known, you may *compare or contrast*, or make an *analogy* with something the reader does know. If its parts seem important, you may examine them one by one through *classification*. When some other need is greater, you may use still another form. If you stay open to the subject, whatever it is, this process can be so natural that you *recognize* a form rather than *choose* it.

If the process is natural, then why study these forms at all? Well, architecture students certainly study different kinds of building design, so their future condominiums or shopping centres don't collapse and kill people. Fortunately, readers are not killed by poorly organized essays, but the idea is similar: if the writer has a conscious knowledge of all the possibilities, his or her arguments will be easier to build and will be less likely to collapse.

Consider the longer essay—say, a major report or research paper. A jumble of notes sits on your desk. They are in chaos. Even with brainstorming or freewriting, knowing your purpose, having the facts and completing a thesis statement, you don't know how to coordinate all those facts. First give the natural process its best chance: *sort all your notes into groups of related material,* using a pair of scissors if necessary to divide unrelated points. When everything is in two stacks, or three stacks or five, let your mind work freely. How do these groups relate to each other? Does one contradict another? Are they all steps in a process or parts of a whole? Now add your conscious knowledge of the forms: Do you see *narration, example, description, cause and effect, comparison and contrast, analogy, classification* or *process analysis?* It is the rare case when one of these forms cannot supply a structure to support your argument.

Right now you are practising them one by one, as the students in architecture school study different structures one by one—so that in all your future writing you will have choices. And for now, you may be using the topics at the end of the readings, or the larger list of Topics for Writing on the Online Learning Centre at www.mcgrawhill.ca/olc/conrad, because they are coordinated to go with the form you have just read and discussed. But in your future writing you will go a step further, making the match yourself between topic and form.

Yet, even when you are looking over 30 options, you are exercising choice: spend a good long time to pick the topic that strikes you as most interesting, most significant—and therefore most motivating. It is writing about things that matter that will most increase your performance—now and always.

TRANSITIONS

We have mentioned the passageways inside a building. Without them an office would be useless: no one could move from one room to another to have meetings. Yet some essays are built without passage-ways. One point ends where another begins, without even a "then" or "therefore" or "however" or "finally" to join them. Readers then have to break down walls to follow thoughts from one room to the next.

Help your readers. *You* know why one point follows another, but do *they*? Make sure by supplying plenty of transition words. They come in many kinds: to show *contrast* say "although" or "but" or "on the other hand" or "instead." To show *causality* say "because" or "there-fore" or "as a result" or "since." To show *progression in time*, say "first" or "next" or "finally" or "last" or "in conclusion." And when you are moving readers from one main part of your essay to the next, devote a full sentence or even a paragraph of transition to the job (one good example is paragraph 10 of Doris Anderson's essay).

It is a little-known fact that one of the quickest and easiest ways for most students to make their writing stronger is to use many more of these transition words. Look for places where they are needed. In fact, when you are proofing and checking, devote one complete read-through of your manuscript to adding transition words. Make sure they are the right ones, too, so that each will help convey the logic of the passage.

Your overall essay plan may already be the right one, arranging your points in their most logical order. But now let that logic show: through use of transitions, give your readers a door between every room.

THE CLOSING

A recent piece of e-mail humour says that a conclusion is "the place where you got tired of thinking." Well, if you got some sleep last night and had your coffee, that doesn't have to happen. Every essay does have an ending—the place where the writing stops. But just halting the words is not enough. A closing in some way has to be deliberate, has to achieve a worthwhile purpose, has to let your reader know that this is where you have chosen to stop. If you quit at just any convenient spot, without engineering an effect to fit your ending, the essay may trail off or even fall flat. But as preachers, com-posers, playwrights and film directors know, a good closing can be even stronger than a good opening. How do the essays in this book come to a close? They use a variety of devices:

REFERENCE TO THE OPENING: Repeating or restating something from the opening gives a sense of culmination, of having come full circle. See the openings and closings by Wente (pp. 61 and 63), Rosenthal (pp. 71 and 73), Fiorito (pp. 77 and 81), Simic (pp. 84 and 87), Nolen (pp. 202 and 207), Evans (pp. 238 and 244), Lam (pp. 285 and 287), Kogawa (pp. 374 and 377) and Christy (pp. 410 and 411).

CONTRAST OR REVERSAL: This ironic device exploits the dramatic potential of the closing. See the opening and closing by Wente (pp. 61 and 63), Fiorito (pp. 77 and 81) and Sampang (pp. 176 and 182).

QUESTION: A question and its answer, or a question calling for the reader's answer, is a common means of closing. See Leacock (p. 341) and Christy (p. 411).

QUOTATION: A good quotation, of either prose or poetry, can add authority and interest to a closing.

TRANSITION SIGNALS: Words, phrases or sentences of transition commonly signal the closing. See Gabori (p. 28), Sampang (p. 182), Pigott (p. 199), Evans (p. 244) and Johnston (p. 261).

REVEALING THE SIGNIFICANCE: Showing the implications or importance of the subject makes for a strong closing. See Gabori (p. 28), Shields (p. 34), Lane (p. 41), Garneau (p. 140), Petrowski (p. 172), Callwood (p. 165), Johnston (p. 261), Dobbs (p. 369), Atwood (p. 395) and Dallaire (p. 421).

SUMMARY: About a fourth of the essays in this book give a summary, either alone or in combination with other closing techniques, but one that is always short. See McQuaig (p. 158), Anderson (p. 193), Bennett (p. 267), Koehl (p. 320) and Hocking (p. 358).

CONCLUSION: Although "conclusion" is often a label for the closing in general, more accurately it is only one of many closing techniques— the drawing of a conclusion from the discussion in the essay. See Geddes (p. 52), Rosenthal (p. 73), Pearson (p. 135), Garneau (p. 140), Mustafa (p. 151), Callwood (p. 165), Traill (p. 225), Lam and Lee (p. 254), Ford (p. 325), Atwood (p. 395) and Klein (p. 401).

PREDICTION: A short look at the subject's future can very logically close a discussion of that subject's past or present. See Geddes (p. 52), Petrowski (p. 172), Evans (p. 244) and Savage (p. 389). Sometimes discussing the future takes the form of a call to action.

You have probably noticed that some authors are named here more than once; closings, like openings, can exploit more than one technique. In fact, the more the better. Stay open to techniques that appear while you write, even as you construct a closing using a technique you have deliberately chosen.

Any of these choices will be stronger, though, when used with the most fundamental technique of all: building your whole essay toward a high point or *climax*. Put your points in order from least important to most important, from least useful to most useful, or from least dramatic to most dramatic. (Sometimes you will not know this order till late in the writing. Just use your software to cut and paste.) When everything leads up to that climax, you have set the stage for a closing that applies all the dramatic power of the final position.

When you get there, apply the force of that closing to a real message. Techniques used just for their own sake are cheap tricks. Do not waste them. Instead, use them to underline your basic message, to impress upon your audience one last and most convincing time that what you have to say is significant. Your closing, more than any other part of your essay, can send the reader away disappointed—or moved.

THE PROCESS: HOW MUCH REVISION?

We have discussed the act of writing as a process in which, rather than trying to "hit it right the first time," we follow a number of steps in the journey toward a good essay. The rest of this book develops that approach. After each selection you'll find an assignment called "Process in Writing" that draws on the essay you've just read, suggesting a related topic for an essay of your own. The main steps of the process are given, individualized for each topic.

At the end of each chapter are sections called "Process in Writing: Guidelines" that give the steps of a process designed for the organizational form you've just studied. Also, in the online Topics for Writing at www.mcgrawhill.ca/olc/conrad, you'll find a whole page of essay topics designed for such practice. Whether you write on an end-of-essay or an online topic, remember that these steps are only *guidelines* to the process; choose the ones that seem best for each case.

Our process of writing is flexible; it is not a blueprint like the elaborate outlines students have in the past been made to construct.

Above all, the process is "recursive"—that is, while you may begin with brainstorming or freewriting, go on to a discovery draft, revise your argument in further versions, and finally edit for spelling and punctuation, you may also double back or jump ahead at any time. Studies show that professionals writing all kinds of documents in all kinds of fields do this. While generating their first version they may stop here and there to improve a word choice or fix punctuation— changes that normally are made later. Or, while they are in the middle of editing or even proofreading, a fine new idea may come thundering out of their mind; so they may back up a few steps, write it out, and add it to their argument, maybe dropping something else they had thought was good. All this is consistent with the reality that *we think while writing.*

Do feel free to transgress the process "guidelines" in these ways, but not so often that you undercut the advantages of the process itself. For example, in writing your first version you may detect some weak sentence structure. If you must, stop here to edit. But better yet, why not just mark the spot (at the keyboard, insert something easy to see, such as several asterisks), then come back to fix things later? For now, let the material keep rolling out uninterrupted. Then later on, while you are editing or even proofreading, a whole new idea may arrive. You could go back even now to fit it in—but this means work, maybe even reorganization. Proceed only if it is a real improvement and if you have the time.

WHEN YOU DO GET TO THE MAIN PROOFREADING, THE FINAL QUALITY CONTROL, TRY THESE TECHNIQUES:

- Whenever possible, leave some time between the writing and the checking, so that you can see text with new eyes, and more easily catch errors.
- Try reading your manuscript backwards, sentence by sentence. This will isolate each sentence from its context, so that you can more easily see if it makes sense on its own.
- Lay a straight edge, such as a ruler, under each line of print as you check it. This will prevent visual confusion.

- Read your manuscript aloud, slowly, because your ear will hear things that your eye will not see. For example, you may have used one word too many times in the same passage; when you hear this repetition, you will recognize it and can then look for replacement words.
- Keep in mind the tools of your computer, and their limitations. When using your thesaurus (digital or paper), don't choose and add any word whose meaning you don't really know. Use the paper dictionary to make sure. Spelling is another matter: of course your software will signal right away when you have misspelled a word. Make the corrections, either then or later, but keep in mind that computer spelling programs cannot detect a correctly spelled word that is in the wrong place (for example, "there" for "their," or "to" for "too.") So there is still work to do of your own. Don't trust your grammar checking program either. It is better to keep a book of usage and grammar on your desk, and consult it often.

Finally, how much revision is enough? Gone are the days when students would write on paper, insert a mass of corrections between the lines or in the margin, then copy the whole thing over into draft two, make more corrections, then go on to draft three or even four or five. This whole labour-intensive system has of course been changed by the computer. Now most of us compose our first version right onto the screen. Later we make changes—anything from adding a comma to seriously revising the whole argument. Then whenever we are done, for the moment, we save. Later we return as often as we want, making further improvements. Finally we apply proofing techniques such as those listed above, and save again. The important thing is not calculating how many "drafts" we are producing, but just getting down to work and spending serious time refining our argument, our organization, our style, our correctness.

When do you reach the journey's end? You will probably know when you get there. It is the point where your response to a significant topic has become so direct, so exact, so forceful, that at last you know exactly what you think. It is clear that you were writing for others, but at this moment it is even clearer that you were writing for yourself.

Geostock/Getty Images

"Her eyes are bright with a cold, steady patience. I have stared into them and tried to see into her arachnid mind but what stared back at me was nothing I knew or understood."

—Patrick Lane, *"There Is a Season"*

NARRATION

1

AND THEN....

Telling a story, or *narrating*, is an appealing and natural way to convey information. Every time you tell a joke, trade gossip, invent a ghost story or tell a friend what you did on the weekend, you are narrating. In both speech and writing, telling a story can also be the most direct way to make a point. If your idea or opinion was formed by an experience, a clear account of that experience can help others understand and believe your point.

For example, in this chapter George Gabori narrates his experience of a schoolyard fight. At age nine, the Jewish boy has just moved to a public school in his village in Hungary. A new friend, Tivadar, asks him one day whether it was the Jews who killed Jesus. They had not, young George's father informs him that night. But the next day when George relates this information to his friend, Tivadar hits him and bloodies his nose. A crowd gathers, shouting to "kill the Jew," but in fact it is young George who gets in a blow that sends Tivadar sprawling and helpless. Later, he assumes his father will be angry,

21

especially when the father muses, "Jews don't fight." George asks, outraged, "Then why did you put me in a Christian school?"

"That's why I put you there, my son," the father replies, then kisses him and adds, "You're learning fast; only next time don't hit him quite so hard."

So why did George Gabori, years later living in Canada and writing his autobiography, retell this event? Why, in fact, did he use it as the opening passage to his whole life's story? The answer is clear: this was the day he learned what racism is, and that knowledge would be central to his later life. It turned him into a scrapper who blew up German trains in the Resistance, and who survived both Nazi and communist concentration camps.

Notice that nowhere in this passage does Gabori editorialize on what it was he learned that day. There is no official thesis statement, as there normally is in the essays we write. But there is what could be called an *"implied" thesis statement.* It is simply the fact that this short reading, like all effective narratives, has a point.

In "There Is a Season," later in this chapter, Patrick Lane offers another kind of implied thesis statement. After reporting on the whole mating ceremony of the orb-weaver spider, after showing us the male strumming on the web, the female charging to make a meal of him, then his escaping as she tears off one of his legs, Lane ends the passage with his own resolve to give the food gift of a moth or a fly to "one of the great mothers of the garden." In this envisioned act, Lane "implies" his sense of respect and wonder at the lives of these spiders.

Of course narratives don't have to be violent or tragic or even dramatic. When Carol Shields in "Encounter" tells of her memorable walk in the rain, sharing an umbrella with a total stranger in Tokyo, we quickly grasp her underlying point that communication is a universal desire.

Narration is such an all-purpose tool that many authors in other chapters of this book use it too. Emily Carr narrates three painting expeditions to coastal native villages. Paul D'Angelo narrates a personal encounter in an elevator. Both Hugh MacLennan and Kildare Dobbs narrate the details of dramatic human-made explosions. Dr. Mark Bernstein narrates a brain operation, and General Roméo

Dallaire narrates an incident that, for him and for us, sums up the tragedy of genocide in Rwanda. (See below for page numbers.)

(By the way, the term "narration" can also refer to pieces of speech quoted in an essay or in fiction. In this chapter, though, we are using it mostly in its larger sense of telling a story.)

Many *examples* given by writers are really bits of *narrative*. To show how Canadians love risky water sports (in "This Boat Is My Boat," p. 216), Drew Hayden Taylor takes us out on the waves of the Georgian Bay, briefly narrating an experience that makes the point very clear.

In some ways narrating is easy. For example, the only research Shields required was her own experience; and her basic plan of organization was no more complicated than the chronological order in which the events occurred. (A flashback to the past or a glance at the future may intervene, but basically a narrative is the easiest of all writing to organize.) Yet a narrative, like any form of writing, is built on choices:

CHOICE OF SCOPE: Time stretches infinitely toward both the past and future—but where does your narrative most logically begin and end? Include only parts that develop your point. Do you need to dwell on getting dressed, eating breakfast, brushing your teeth and catching the bus, on the day you became a Canadian citizen? Or did the event really begin when you opened the courthouse door? When facts about the past or future are needed, sketch them in briefly so you interrupt the least you can.

Note that different narratives can have different time spans: while Shields shares maybe half an hour of her life story with us, Lane shares several hours, Gabori shares two days and Carole Geddes ("Growing Up Native") shares her whole lifetime so far. Of course the challenge increases with the span of time: Geddes is very careful to choose details that convey her main life experiences without consuming too many words.

CHOICE OF DETAILS: Which details count? Reject random or trivial ones and seek those that convey your main impression or idea. When on that school playground young Gabori experiences racist violence, he tells us how he tastes his own blood. What could more clearly convey his experience that day? Choose details that are vivid. Reject weak ones and select those that help the reader *see, hear, feel, smell* or *taste*—in other words those which, by appealing to the senses, help readers live the event.

CHOICE OF CONNECTIONS: Readers love to be "swept along" by narrative. How is this effect achieved? Partly just through a good story. Time signals, though, increase the impact of any narrative. Like road signs for the driver, terms like "at first," "next," "then," "immediately," "suddenly," "later," "finally" and "at last" show the way and encourage progress. Use these road signs, and others like them, at every curve. Choose carefully, so signals speed the reader to your chosen destination.

So far we have been discussing mostly the first-person narrative. There are many advantages to writing about yourself. You know your subject well (in fact, is there any subject you know better?), yet in writing about yourself you may better understand your own ideas and actions. Your vital interest in your subject will motivate the writing. And finally, readers appreciate the authenticity of a story told by the very person who lived the event.

But of course writing in third person opens up many more possibilities. Only by writing about others can one discuss past eras, places one has never visited, and events one has never experienced. Kildare Dobbs does this masterfully in his narrative "The Scar," in Chapter 9. He was not in Hiroshima the day it crumbled beneath an atomic blast, but his research and his imagination almost make it seem so; more importantly, reading his narrative almost makes us feel we were there too.

Note: Many authors in later chapters combine narration with other ways to develop their material. For more examples, see these selections:

Margaret Wente, "Busy, Busy, Busy," p. 61
Rudy Wiebe, "The Bull," p. 101
Emily Carr, "D'Sonoqua," p. 117
Charles Yale Harrison, "In the Trenches," p. 108

GEORGE GABORI

Coming of Age in Putnok

Translated from the Hungarian by Eric Johnson with George Faludy

For much of his life George Gabori (1924–1997) drove taxi and ran a cab company in Toronto. Like many immigrants to this country, though, he had a past he would never forget. Gabori (pronounced Gábori) was born to a Jewish family in the village of Putnok, Hungary. His childhood was happy but short, for when the Germans overran Hungary and threatened the existence of the Jews, he joined the resistance. He led daring sabotage raids, blowing up German trains, till the Gestapo sent him, still a teenager, to a concentration camp. When later the Russians drove out the Germans, Gabori was as troublesome for the communists as he had been for the Nazis: soon after his release from Dachau, he was breaking rocks in a notorious Soviet labour camp. Always outspoken in favour of democracy, Gabori played a part in the 1956 Revolution, then escaped from Hungary to Canada, a "decent land," where years later he wrote his memoirs in Hungarian. With the help of Hungarian poet George Faludy, Eric Johnson condensed and translated the enormous manuscript, and in 1981 it was published. Since then, When Evils Were Most Free *has become a minor Canadian classic and has been translated into many other languages. Our selection is its opening passage.*

1   When I was nine years old my father, victorious after a long argument with my grandfather, took me out of our town's only *cheder* and enrolled me in its only public school. Overnight I was transported from the world of Hebrew letters and

monotonously repeated texts to the still stranger world of Hungarian letters, patriotic slogans and walls covered with maps.

Grandfather rolled his eyes and predicted trouble, but it seemed he was wrong. I sat beside a boy my own age named Tivadar, a gentile—everybody was a gentile in that school except me. Tivadar and I got along famously until, after two or three weeks, he approached me in the schoolyard one day and asked me if it was true what the others were saying, that "we" had murdered Jesus. 2

Strange to tell—for this was 1933 and we were in Hungary—I had never heard about this historical episode, and I left Tivadar amicably enough, promising to ask my father about it. We met again the next morning and I told him what I had learned: that the Romans had killed Jesus, and that anyway Jesus had been a Jew, like me, so what did it matter to the Christians? 3

"That's not true," said Tivadar menacingly. 4

"My father does not lie," I replied. 5

By now a crowd had gathered around us and there was nothing for it but to fight it out. There were cheers and laughter as Tivadar hit me in the nose before I got my jacket off. It was not the first time I had tasted my own blood, but it was the first time a Christian had made it flow. Tivadar was flushed with pleasure and excitement at the applause and not at all expecting it when I lashed out with my fist and sent him sprawling backward on the cobbles. The crowd of boys groaned and shouted to Tivadar to get up and kill the Jew, but poor Tivadar did not move. Frightened, I grabbed my jacket and shoved my way through the crowd stunned into silence by this overturning of the laws of nature. 6

They were silent at home too when I told them what had happened. My father sent for me from his office in the afternoon, and I entered cap in hand. He always wore a braided Slovak jacket at work and looked more like a peasant than a Jewish wine merchant. 7

"Well, who started it?" asked my father, wearing an expression I had never seen on his face before. I was not at all frightened. 8

"He did. I told him what you said about Jesus and he challenged me." 9

My father clamped his teeth on his cigar and nodded, looking right through me. 10

11   "Jews don't fight," he finally said.

12   "Then why did you put me in a Christian school?" I asked in a loud, outraged whine.

13   "That's why I put you there, my son," he said at last, then swept me up and kissed me on the forehead. "You're learning fast; only next time don't hit him quite so hard."

14   Then he sent me out quickly and I stopped on the landing, startled to hear loud, whooping, solitary laughter coming out of my father's office.

EXPLORATIONS:

George Gabori, *When Evils Were Most Free*
George Faludy, *My Happy Days in Hell*
Adam Horvath, "Lives Lived: George Gabori," Toronto *Globe and Mail,* December 7, 1997
Anne Frank, *The Diary of Anne Frank*
Anne Michaels, *Fugitive Pieces*
Barbara Coloroso,
     The Bully, the Bullied and the Bystander
     Extraordinary Evil: A Brief History of Genocide
http://www.bullying.org
http://www.cyberbullying.org
http://en.wikipedia.org/wiki/1956_Hungarian_Revolution
http://ftp.nizkor.org/ftp.py?bibliographies/biblio.04

STRUCTURE:

1. What overall pattern organizes this selection?
2. Point out at least ten words or phrases in this *narrative* that signal the flow of time.
3. Scrutinize Gabori's opening paragraph: has he prepared us for the selection? Name every fact revealed about the setting and about the author.

STYLE:

1. How economical of words is this opening passage of Gabori's life story? How clearly does it reveal the author and his times? Would you predict with any confidence his character or fate as an adult? Do these pages tempt you to read the whole book? Why or why not?

2. *When Evils Were Most Free* is translated and condensed from the Hungarian original. Does this act separate us from Gabori's thoughts? How exact can translations be? If you are bilingual or multilingual, how precisely can you put sayings from one language into another? Can translator Eric Johnson even be seen as a co-author of these pages?

3. In paragraph 6 Gabori states, "It was not the first time I had tasted my own blood...." What makes this image strong?

IDEAS FOR DISCUSSION AND WRITING:

1. What exactly is the "overturning of the laws of nature" at the end of paragraph 6?

2. Was Gabori's father right to move the boy from a Hebrew *cheder* to a public school? In disproving the STEREOTYPE that "Jews don't fight" (par. 11), has the boy learned a worthy lesson? Or does he merely copy the worst traits of his opponents, thereby becoming like them?

3. Every ethnic group in Canada—including English Canadians—is a minority. Has your minority been persecuted here? If you have been a victim, *narrate* an actual incident, including your own reaction. Like Gabori, give many specifics.

4. In taunting and hitting his Jewish classmate, Tivadar is a bully. Have you seen bullying in your own school years? Visit the http://www.bullying.org and http://www.cyberbullying.org websites above, and report to the class if these materials bring to mind experiences of your own.

5. What are autobiographies for? What do you think writing your own life story would do for you? For others?

6. **PROCESS IN WRITING:** *Write a chapter of your own autobiography. Select one key incident in your life, then freewrite on it for a few minutes. Look*

over what you have produced, keep the best of it, and from this write your first draft. Have you begun and ended at just the right places, narrating *the event itself but omitting parts that don't matter? Enrich the next draft with more* IMAGES *and* examples, *following Gabori's lead. Now share your* narrative *with a group of classmates, and adjust whatever does not communicate with this* AUDIENCE. *Finally, read your narrative aloud, with expression, to the whole class.*

Note: See also the Topics for Writing on the Online Learning Centre at www. mcgrawhill.ca/olc/conrad.

CAROL SHIELDS

Encounter

American by birth, Carol Shields came at age 22 to Canada and went on to be one of our nation's best-loved authors. Though she taught at several universities, notably the University of Manitoba, and though she often wrote on academic subjects—as in her acclaimed 2001 biography of Jane Austen—Shields also became a novelist gifted in showing the mysteries of everyday life. Drawing richly on her own experience as wife and as mother of five children, and beginning to publish only after the children were all in school, Shields had a gift for uncovering what The Guardian *called "the dramatic in the domestic." Believing there is no such thing as "ordinary" life, Shields breathed such force into her everyday characters that to thousands of readers they came alive on the page. She also wrote and published poetry, but it is her fiction that raised her to the first rank of our authors. Her first novel,* Small Ceremonies, *appeared in 1976, then in 1987 her novel* Swann. *But it was in 1993 that she stunned the critics and won both the Pulitzer Prize in America and the Governor General's Award in Canada with* The Stone Diaries. *Many thousands of readers in 17 languages around the world followed its main character, Daisy Goodwill, through each stage of life as a woman in her society. Then in 1997 Shields depicted another "ordinary" character, this time a man, in her best-selling novel* Larry's Party. *The last novel before her untimely death in 2003 was* Unless. *Then in 2005 appeared her* Collected Stories, *introduced and edited by Margaret Atwood. Our own selection, from Katherine Govier's anthology* Without a Guide: Contemporary Women's Travel Adventures, *is autobiography—and, as always, examines the ordinary things of life, which in the vision of Carol Shields become remarkable.*

1   I was in Tokyo to attend a conference, one of a thousand or so delegates—and that probably was my problem: the plasticized name card and the logo of my organization marked me as someone who desired only to be cheerfully accommodated.

2   The allotted two weeks had passed. A single day in Japan remained, and at last I admitted to myself that I was disappointed. The terrible banality of tourist desire invaded me like a kind of flu. Walking the broad, busy boulevards, I caught myself looking too eagerly, too preciously, for minor cultural manifestations—the charming way the bank teller bowed when presenting me with my bundle of cash, the colourful plastic food in the windows of restaurants; these were items I was able to record in my travel journal, touching them up in the way of desperate travellers, shaping them into humorous or appreciative annotation on the Japanese people and the exotic city they inhabited.

3   But Tokyo with its hotels and subways and department stores was a modern industrial complex. Its citizens went to work in the morning, earned money, and travelled home again at night. These homes, to be sure, were impenetrable to me, but the busy working days bore the same rhythms as those found in any large North American city. The traffic noises, the scent of pollution, and the civility of people in the street made me think of—home.

4   I had hoped for more; what traveller doesn't? Travelling is expensive, exhausting, and often lonely—the cultural confusion, the acres of concrete, the bitter coffee, the unreadable maps, and the rates of exchange that are almost always unfavourable. And then, like a punishment at the end of the traveller's day, there waits a solitary room, and a bed that, however comfortable, is not your bed. What makes all this worth the effort is the shock of otherness that arrives from time to time, rattling loose your bearings and making you suddenly alert to an altered world. But Tokyo was determinedly polite, fulsomely western, a city with a bland, smiling face, ready to welcome me not on its terms but on my own.

5   I already know that the banquet that was to conclude the conference would be a model of French cuisine. Seven courses, seven different wines. No rice, no noodles, no sushi, no hot radish. It was to be held at the famous Imperial Hotel, which was fifteen or twenty minutes' walk from the somewhat less expensive hotel where I was staying.

I started out in good time. It was a soft spring evening, and the 6
thought of a leisurely stroll was appealing. I would be able to look
around one last time, breathe in a final impression that I could perhaps test against my accumulated disappointment, acquiring some
fresh point of perception with which to colour and preserve my
Japanese sojourn.

At that moment it began to rain. A few drops at first, then it came 7
down in earnest, spotting the silk dinner suit I was wearing and threatening to flatten my carefully arranged hair. I looked about for a taxi or
a roof to shelter under, but neither presented itself. The only thing to
do, I decided, was to run as quickly as I could the rest of the way.

But a tall man was standing directly in front of me, a man with an 8
umbrella. He was smiling tentatively, and gesturing, and his mouth
was moving. But what was he saying? I wasn't sure, since the accent
was unfamiliar, but it sounded like "Imperial Hotel?" With a question
mark behind it. "Yes," I said, nodding and speaking with great delib-
eration, "Imperial Hotel," and at that he lifted his umbrella slightly,
and invited me under.

The umbrella was large and black, resolutely standard, the sort of 9
umbrella found in every city or backwater of the world. "Thank you,"
I said in Japanese—the only phrase I had mastered—but he only
repeated what he had said earlier: "Imperial Hotel?" And tipped his
head quizzically in an eastward direction. "Yes," I said again. And we
began walking.

It seemed only polite to make an effort at conversation. Where was 10
he from? Was he with the conference? Was he a stranger in Japan
like myself? He shook his head, uncomprehending, and released a
shower of words in an unidentifiable language. Now it was my turn
to shake my head. After that, smiling, we continued our walk in a
contained silence, as though we had each admitted to the other that
language was absurd, that rhetoric was a laughable formality that
could be set aside for this brief interval.

Suddenly careless of social taboos, and because it's difficult for a 11
short woman to walk with a tall man under an umbrella, I took the
stranger's arm. (Thinking about this later, I theorized that he must
have gestured minutely with his elbow, inviting my intimacy.) Now,
arms linked, we were able to walk together smoothly, stepping over

and around the puddles without losing our stride, pausing at traffic lights, stepping down from curbs.

12   Wë had arrived quickly at our congenial gliding pace, left foot, right foot, left foot again, a forward rhythm with a very slight sideways roll like a kind of swimming. Our mutually constrained tongues, the sound of the pelting rain, and our random possession of a random moment in time, seemed to seal us in a temporary vacuum that had nothing to do with Japan, nor with gender or age or with Hollywood notions about men and women walking in the rain. This was good walking, though, I knew that much—walking that transcended mere movement. Hypnotic walking. Walking toward the unimaginable. And I found myself wanting it to go on and on.

13   But there we suddenly were, at the brilliantly lit entrance of the Imperial Hotel, caught in a throng of people arriving and departing, people who had come from every corner of the globe, and trailing after them their separate languages, their lives, their ribbons of chance connection. The stranger with the umbrella abruptly disappeared. I looked around for him but was unable to recall his face, how he had been dressed. One minute he was there and the next minute he'd vanished, leaving me alone with that primary shiver of mystery that travellers, if they're lucky, hope to hang on to: the shock of the known and the unknown colliding in space.

EXPLORATIONS:

Carol Shields,
> *The Stone Diaries*
> *Larry's Party*
> *Swann*
> *Coming to Canada (poems)*

Marta Dvorak, ed., *Carol Shields and the Extra-Ordinary* (literary criticism)

http://oprf.com/Shields

http://en.wikipedia.org/wiki/Carol_Shields

http://www.uwinnipeg.ca/~morton/Telecourse/Stone_Diaries/ eb_on_carol_shields.htm

http://www.nwpassages.com/author_profile.asp?au_id=1234
http://www.bookreporter.com/authors/au-shields-carol.asp
http://www.cbc.ca/news/obit/shields_carol

STRUCTURE:

1. This *narrative* is really two in one: a summary of the author's stay in Tokyo so far, then a real-time narrative of her "encounter" with the stranger. How does the first prepare us for the second? Where does the first end and the second begin? Which of the two phases of *narrative* is more powerful, and why?
2. How does Shields' two-part structure of *narrative* exploit the device of *contrast?*

STYLE:

1. Carol Shields has been one of the nation's best-loved novelists. Does this nonfiction selection seem at all in the vein of fiction? If so, how?
2. Does Shields' STYLE excite admiration, or is it more like a clear window that shows us the events? Which approach do you prefer when you read? When you write? Why?
3. Point out the best FIGURES OF SPEECH in paragraph 12. Also analyze the power of the images that close this selection.

IDEAS FOR DISCUSSION AND WRITING:

1. "Encounter" narrates a small event, two strangers sharing an umbrella. In what ways, though, may this event be larger than it seems? What truths may it reveal about our lives in general?
2. Many writers seek sensational topics such as disaster, murder, adventure and romance. Were you attracted, though, by Shields' modest tale of "walking toward the unimaginable" (par. 12) with a stranger? If so, what does this show about focus and development in writing?
3. The two strangers of "Encounter" are thrown together by rain. When have you had close communication with strangers through

events such as floods or earthquakes; ice, rain or snow storms; accidents; or power blackouts? *Narrate* an incident to the class. What does it show about life?

4. Shields discovers "the terrible banality of tourist desire" (par. 2) in a far place that turns out to be "fulsomely western, a city with a bland, smiling face, ready to welcome me not on its terms but on my own" (par. 4). Why do we become tourists? Why do we seek far away places? Are they disappearing? If so, why?

5. Can you communicate, as Shields did, with people who do not speak your language? If your family has immigrated, can your own grandparents speak your language? Suggest communication techniques to the class.

6. PROCESS IN WRITING: *Shields' closing words describe the mystery that travellers seek, "the shock of the known and the unknown colliding in space." Freewrite on this topic for at least five minutes, never stopping the movement of your pen or keyboard, remembering a time when you felt this "shock." Now write the quick discovery draft of a narrative based on this material. Let your words cool off for a day, then take stock: Does your introduction prepare us for the story? If not, add. Have you described the persons and the place well enough to help us live the story too? If not, add SENSE IMAGES. Do TRANSITIONS speed us on? If not, add. And does the action sweep us towards a CLIMAX? If not, rearrange. Last of all, check for spelling and punctuation before you print off your best version.*

Note: See also the Topics for Writing on the Online Learning Centre at www. mcgrawhill.ca/olc/conrad.

PATRICK LANE

There Is a Season[*]

Patrick Lane had always loved gardening, in the mild climate of Vancouver Island. But in 1999 when his worsening drug and alcohol habits threatened to kill him, he took a new step: he would spend a whole year of rehab in his garden, tending the plants, observing the birds and animals and insects, putting his life in order. It worked: the garden saved his life. Then in 2004 he published an account of that beautiful year, There Is a Season: A Memoir in a Garden. *From it comes our selection.*

Lane had many issues to work on during the therapy of his garden year. Born in 1939 in Nelson, British Columbia, he grew up suffering the anger of a brutal father, who was himself later murdered. After high school Lane worked in the logging industry, as a choker, Cat skinner, first aid officer, trucker and sawmill worker, jobs that convinced him working people are exploited cogs in the industrial machine. When in the sixties Lane began to write poetry, readers noticed his dark vision of solitude, violence and death, informed by his early experiences. For decades Lane was a rolling stone, living in places as far away as South America, and serving as writer in residence and teacher at many universities, such as Concordia, Victoria, Toronto and York. By now he has published over 20 books, including Poems New and Selected *(Governor General's Award, 1978),* Selected Poems *(1987),* Syllable of Stone: Selected Poems *(2005) and* Last Water Song *(2007).*

---

*We have given this free-standing but untitled selection the title of the book it came from, *There Is a Season*.

1   A small, thin spider peers over the lip of a Mexican orange bush leaf. He wants to pluck the dream-catcher's° strings. Below him is a cluster of fragrant white blossoms. Their scent is citrus, a slice of orange perfume that cuts the air. Attached to one of the petals is a single strand of webbing. It is tied to the leaf by six tiny anchors of thread. The main filament stretches over a gap, an opening the light breeze moves through. The small spider's long legs touch the leaf's glossy surface for a moment and then he pulls himself up out of his hiding and crosses the leaf to the flower and places the tip of one of his long legs on the string of web.

2   He is a male orb-weaver spider and across from him in space is the dream-catcher of a female. She is huge, her body swollen from months of steady feeding. She has moved her web around the front garden, sometimes among the bright, thorned leaves of the holly, sometimes in the lilac or the ivy that shoots out from the walls of the house, its berries slowly turning purple in the fall sun, anywhere insects gather to feed or dance in the bright air. For the last week, her web has floated here, anchored by the Mexican orange, the laurel, and the holly. It hangs at just the right height to catch the last bees, flies, and other tiny flying things of the season. She rebuilds her web once a day, usually in early evening after the sun has set, but sometimes in the morning if some passing creature has torn it in the night. It takes her an hour.

3   Each web has been a little larger as she has grown larger, and now it is almost fifty centimetres in diameter. It is a spiral nebula, a swirl that is a massive killing ground. In its lower left quadrant hang the rolled-up carapaces of a wasp and a crane fly. She injected a killing poison into them earlier in the day and it has turned their internal organs to liquid. She will drink them dry when she gets hungry again. Right now she hangs in the centre of the web from her two back legs. Deep in her abdomen lie hundreds of unfertilized eggs. The female and her unborn offspring are waiting for male sperm to bring them to life. Her front legs rest on walking strings, the long filaments of web that radiate from the centre. Only the circling strands are sticky.

°dream-catcher: In the Ojibwa tradition, a small willow hoop enclosing a loose net. Sometimes called a "dream snare," it hangs on the wall over the beds of children, to catch and deter nightmares. Dream-catchers resemble the spiral wheel-shaped web of a spider, and in fact, in Ojibwa are called *asabikeshiinh*, meaning "spider."

The straight support strings are what she walks and runs on when prey crashes into her aerial trap.

Her huge abdomen is beautiful with shades of grey and brown and there are two pale stripes that arch up from her head and over the high curve of her back. They are shocks of light, a pale yellow-white against the deeper browns and tans. She has survived the wind, the drought, and the rare rains. She has also survived the birds of spring who eat young spiders. No bird would touch her now. She too large, too formidable. Her eyes are bright with a cold, steady patience. I have stared into them and tried to see into her arachnid mind but what stared back at me was nothing I knew or understood.

The male spider's body is small, one-tenth the size of the female's. His legs are much longer than his abdomen and they move in front of him, constantly testing the surfaces and textures that confront him. As I watch, he places one of his two longest legs on the thin strand of web and, bracing himself, plucks the string. The bit of webbing vibrates and he plucks it again like a guitar or violin that has one pure note.

The vibrations travel up the anchor string to the web and when they reach her the female tenses. She comes fully alive in a startled vigilance. She turns quickly to face the direction his message comes from. It *is* a message. It is unlike the thrashing struggle of an insect caught in her web. She knows this song. It is one buried deep inside her, passed on to her by her mother and all the mothers before her.

The male plucks intermittently for a full five minutes or more and then, not feeling a response, climbs out on the anchor string and slowly, carefully begins to walk along it toward the far dream-catcher. As he gets closer to the perimeter the female rushes to where the anchor string leaves the last circle and stops. The male, feeling her dash, backs away down the anchor and stops as well. He turns to face the female and then plucks the string again. She races toward him and he drops on his own filament and hangs below.

He has carried his escape webbing in a gathered ball beneath him. As she came toward him he stuck it to her anchor and dropped. He swings now below her. She stares down and then retreats to the edge of her web where she waits for five minutes before walking back to its centre. She hangs there upside down but she is tense for a long time. Finally she relaxes and the male spider climbs up his rope to the anchor string, his escape web gathered in a frizzy ball under his body.

9   He walks slowly up the strand and almost touches the outer perimeter when she attacks. The male drops down again, this time only a hand's breadth from the edge. She squats above him. This time she stays longer. Below her the male swings like a living pendulum in the warm, autumn air. She rises up and moves her body about as if uncomfortable, as if the muscles in her legs are stiff. Then, turning, she makes her way back to her perch.

10   Again, the male climbs back up and walks the anchor to the perimeter. Once there he reaches out with his long leg and plucks the string again. The vibrations are stronger now and it only takes two or three plucks for the female to return. Once again he drops away.

11   This goes on for almost an hour. Each time the male returns he advances a little farther down the gossamer string, and now he is inside the dream-catcher. Each time she rushes at him she moves more slowly and now he doesn't drop away but only retreats to the outside edge until she has returned to her perch.

12   Inside the female are her eggs and inside the male is a small package of sperm. His job, his life's purpose, is to deposit the sperm package into a vent on the side of her abdomen and so fertilize her eggs. It is a difficult and dangerous procedure for she sees him as the source of two things, food and sperm. His job is to get her to sit absolutely still so he can deposit his sperm and then escape. This is not so simple as it sounds. She will poison him in a millisecond once the sperm is delivered. He knows that. It's why he's been so careful, but he is implacable. He knows what he has to do.

13   He sits very close to her now and begins his music in earnest. He plays her a tune, his longest legs alternating on two strings. The whole of this long courtship has been like an opera, a complex and beautiful ballet. This last musical interlude takes place just before his last advance. She has become quieter where she hangs. Her legs have relaxed. Perhaps she is entranced by his playing.

14   Now I understand why his legs are so long. He comes up to her and touches her legs. They tense and then, under his repeated, alternating drumming and stroking, they relax again. His legs are

long in order to allow him to escape if she attacks. The male continues touching her until he can reach past her legs and head to her abdomen. He strokes her flanks, her huge, distended belly. His legs caress her. He is close now, close enough for her to kill him but she is stilled by his stroking, stilled by his gentle touch, his long caresses. She has fallen into a reverie, some place of quiet beauty all her own. Her many eyes stare into his with perfect stillness.

His penis is at the end of his longest leg and as he strokes her he comes closer and closer to her vent. He strokes and strokes and then, deftly, quickly, he slips the tip of his penis-leg into her. 15

Instantly, he withdraws all of his legs. He is going to drop down his escape line. As he pulls back, she transforms from the benign and sleepy female into a killer. Both things happen at once. She is suddenly pure energy, swift and sure. She grabs hold of one of his long legs. He twists and falls away beneath her, leaving his leg behind in her jaws. As he falls she stares down at him, then she drops the leg. 16

The male has only seven legs instead of eight, but he has successfully placed his sperm in her and has done so without becoming a meal. He swings a moment or two longer, then strings out more filament from his spinners and drops down to a laurel berry. There he sits as if exhausted from the long ordeal he has just gone through. It has taken almost two hours. His dance is done and he has his life. Above him the female sits in her web. She too is tired. He waits a moment and then, just before moving away from the huge dreamcatcher above him, he plucks the filament of web that still attaches him to the female above. He plucks it three times, but there is no response. This last plucking seems a kind of farewell song. He cuts himself away from his falling string and climbs off the laurel berry onto a glossy green leaf and then under it. 17

I peer under the leaf and see him hanging there in the shade. Then I peer in close at the huge female. Her eyes stare out from above her slowly moving jaws. Soon, she will attach her fertilized egg sac to a nearby leaf. Perhaps a dozen or so of the hundreds of their spiderlings will survive next year to grow as formidable as their mother, as wily and quick as their father. I will watch for them and if I catch a fly or moth I will toss it living into one of their webs. It will be my gift to one of the great mothers of the garden. 18

EXPLORATIONS:

Patrick Lane,
>*There Is a Season: A Memoir in a Garden*
>*Poems, New and Selected*
>*What the Stones Remember*

Annie Dillard, *Pilgrim at Tinker Creek*

David Thoreau, *Walden*

http://patricklane.ca

http://www.canadianarachnology.org

http://www.ojibway.ca/spiders.htm

http://en.wikipedia.org/wiki/Orb-weaver_spider

http://amonline.net.au/spiders/culture/history.htm

STRUCTURE:

1. Although Patrick Lane presents his account of mating spiders in mostly chronological order, there are places where he looks briefly backward (flashbacks) or briefly forward (flashforwards). Point out five such examples in his *narrative*.

2. Readers like to be "swept away" by a strong *narrative*. One way writers achieve this effect is to use many TRANSITION words and expressions. Find at least ten places in this narrative where time signals such as "then," "soon," "right now" or "suddenly" speed the reader on.

3. Read Lane's final paragraph aloud in class. What technique of closing does he use here to underline the importance of his subject?

STYLE:

1. Hold your book at arm's length, and look at Lane's *narrative*. Is it made mostly of big words or little words? In Shakespeare's best-known passages do we see mostly big words or little words? In your own essays do you try for mostly big words or little words? Which way is best? Which is used more by poets such as Patrick Lane? Which is used more by bureaucrats? And why?

2. Would you expect an essay on spiders to be FORMAL and OBJECTIVE, as in a scientific article? What is your reaction when in paragraph 14 the male spider "strokes her flanks, her huge, distended belly. His legs caress her. He is close now, close enough for her to kill him but she is stilled by his stroking, stilled by his gentle touch, his long caresses"? Or when in paragraph 16 "She grabs hold of one of his long legs. He twists and falls away beneath her, leaving his leg behind in her jaws. As he falls she stares down at him, then she drops the leg." Can nature writing be racy, scary, erotic and even violent? Would this express the realities of life in the garden? Or should it be more like the essay about paper and foam cups, by scientist Martin Hocking, in Chapter 9 of this book? Or does it all depend on who is the intended reader? Describe the AUDIENCE that poet Patrick Lane was probably writing for.

3. Why does Lane write in the present tense, when the events he *narrates* happened at some time in the past?

4. Paragraph 2 refers to a "dance," 5 to "a guitar or violin," paragraph 13 to "music" and "opera" and paragraph 17 to a "farewell song." What FIGURES OF SPEECH are at work in these comparisons? And how do they enrich Lane's view of life in the garden?

IDEAS FOR DISCUSSION AND WRITING:

1. As a recovering alcoholic and cocaine addict, Patrick Lane chose his Vancouver Island garden as the place to reclaim his life. Why do so many other people garden as well? Are the reasons economic? Recreational? Spiritual? Give examples.

2. Lane chooses what seems like a very small subject: the mating dance of two spiders. In what ways, though, may this subject be larger than it seems?

3. Do you dread spiders and insects in general? Why? Look at the other side: give at least five examples of insects helping us.

4. PROCESS IN WRITING: *Is the outdoors a healer, as well as a place of fear and danger? Tell of a time when nature healed you. Close your eyes to recall the event, then take a page of quick notes. Now choose the right place to begin the story, and the right place to end it.* Narrate *the event, moving quickly, not stopping now to fix little things. The next day look your*

narrative *over. Have you tried present tense, like Lane, to make things seem to happen right now? Have you used* TRANSITION *signals, like Lane, to speed the action on? Have you described how things looked, felt, sounded, smelled and maybe even tasted? Edit for all this. Then after checking your punctuation and spelling, read your best version to the class.*

Note: See also the Topics for Writing on the Online Learning Centre at www. mcgrawhill.ca/olc/conrad.

CAROL GEDDES

Growing Up Native

Since Carol Geddes tells her own life story in the narrative that follows, we will not repeat it all here. Born into the security of her Tlingit First Nations family in the wilds of the Yukon, she was six when she first knew her country's majority culture and began to see the problems it causes for Native people. Since then she has spent her life integrating these two worlds. She celebrates the current "renaissance" of interest in Native culture, yet also values the rest of North American life. "We need our culture," she writes, "but there's no reason why we can't preserve it and have an automatic washing machine and a holiday in Mexico, as well." Hers is a success story. Despite the obstacles, she completed a university degree in English and philosophy (Carleton, 1978), did graduate studies in communications at McGill, and is today a successful filmmaker and spokesperson for her people. In addition to her films Place for Our People *(1981),* Doctor, Lawyer, Indian Chief *(National Film Board, 1986) and* Picturing a People: George Johnston, Tlingit Photographer *(NFB, 1997), she has produced some 25 videos on the lives and culture of aboriginal people in Canada. Geddes is a producer at Studio One of the National Film Board, and has taught other filmmakers at the Banff Centre for the Arts. She has also been a Director of the Yukon Human Rights Commission, the Yukon Heritage Resources Board and the Women's Television Network Foundation, and is the first Northerner and first Native Person to be a Director of the Canada Council. In her spare time she does wilderness hiking and fishing in the Yukon, where she lives. Our selection, from* homemakers *magazine of October 1990, won the National Magazine Awards Foundation Silver Award.*

1   I remember it was cold. We were walking through a swamp near our home in the Yukon bush. Maybe it was fall and moose-hunting season. I don't know. I think I was about four years old at the time. The muskeg was too springy to walk on, so people were taking turns carrying me—passing me from one set of arms to another. The details about where we were are vague, but the memory of those arms and the feeling of acceptance I had is one of the most vivid memories of my childhood. It didn't matter who was carrying me—there was security in every pair of arms. That response to children is typical of the native community. It's the first thing I think of when I cast my mind back to the Yukon bush, where I was born and lived with my family.

2   I was six years old when we moved out of the bush, first to Teslin, where I had a hint of the problems native people face, then to Whitehorse, where there was unimaginable racism. Eventually I moved to Ottawa and Montreal, where I further discovered that to grow up native in Canada is to feel the sting of humiliation and the boot of discrimination. But it is also to experience the enviable security of an extended family and to learn to appreciate the richness of the heritage and traditions of a culture most North Americans have never been lucky enough to know. As a film-maker, I have tried to explore these contradictions, and our triumph over them, for the half-million aboriginals who are part of the tide of swelling independence of the First Nations today.

3   But I'm getting ahead of myself. If I'm to tell the story of what it's like to grow up native in northern Canada, I have to go back to the bush where I was born, because there's more to my story than the hurtful stereotyping that depicts Indian people as drunken welfare cases. Our area was known as 12-mile (it was 12 miles from another tiny village). There were about 40 people living there—including 25 kids, eight of them my brothers and sisters—in a sort of family compound. Each family had its own timber plank house for sleeping, and there was one large common kitchen area with gravel on the ground and a tent frame over it. Everybody would go there and cook meals together. In summer, my grandmother always had a smudge fire going to smoke fish and tan moose hides. I can remember the cosy warmth of the fire, the smell of good food, and always having

someone to talk to. We kids had built-in playmates and would spend hours running in the bush, picking berries, building rafts on the lake and playing in abandoned mink cages.

One of the people in my village tells a story about the day the old lifestyle began to change. He had been away hunting in the bush for about a month. On his way back, he heard a strange sound coming from far away. He ran up to the crest of a hill, looked over the top of it and saw a bulldozer. He had never seen or heard of such a thing before and he couldn't imagine what it was. We didn't have magazines or newspapers in our village, and the people didn't know that the Alaska Highway was being built as a defence against a presumed Japanese invasion during the Second World War. That was the beginning of the end of the Teslin Tlingit people's way of life. From that moment on, nothing turned back to the way it was. Although there were employment opportunities for my father and uncles, who were young men at the time, the speed and force with which the Alaska Highway was rammed through the wilderness caused tremendous upheaval for Yukon native people.

It wasn't as though we'd never experienced change before. The Tlingit Nation, which I belong to, arrived in the Yukon from the Alaskan coast around the turn of the century. They were the middlemen and women between the Russian traders and the Yukon inland Indians. The Tlingit gained power and prestige by trading European products such as metal goods and cloth for the rich and varied furs so much in fashion in Europe. The Tlingit controlled Yukon trading because they controlled the trading routes through the high mountain passes. When trading ceased to be an effective means of survival, my grandparents began raising wild mink in cages. Mink prices were really high before and during the war, but afterwards the prices went plunging down. So, although the mink pens were still there when I was a little girl, my father mainly worked on highway construction and hunted in the bush. The Yukon was then, and still is in some ways, in a transitional period—from living off the land to getting into a European wage-based economy.

As a young child, I didn't see the full extent of the upheaval. I remember a lot of togetherness, a lot of happiness while we lived in the bush. There's a very strong sense of family in the native community, and a fondness for children, especially young children. Even today, it's like a special form of entertainment if someone brings a baby to visit. That sense of family is the one thing that has survived all the incredible difficulties native people have had. Throughout a time of tremendous problems, the extended family system has somehow lasted, providing a strong circle for people to survive in. When parents were struggling with alcoholism or had to go away to find work, when one of the many epidemics swept through the community, or when a marriage broke up and one parent left, aunts, uncles and grandparents would try to fill those roles. It's been very important to me in terms of emotional support to be able to rely on my extended family. There are still times when such support keeps me going.

7   Life was much simpler when we lived in the bush. Although we were poor and wore the same clothes all year, we were warm enough and had plenty to eat. But even as a youngster, I began to be aware of some of the problems we would face later on. Travelling missionaries would come and impose themselves on us, for example. They'd sit at our campfire and read the Bible to us and lecture us about how we had to live a Christian life. I remember being very frightened by stories we heard about parents sending their kids away to live with white people who didn't have any children. We thought those people were mean and that if we were bad, we'd be sent away, too. Of course, that was when social workers were scooping up native children and adopting them out to white families in the south. The consequences were usually disastrous for the children who were taken away—alienation, alcoholism and suicide, among other things. I knew some of those kids. The survivors are still struggling to recover.

8   The residential schools were another source of misery for the kids. Although I didn't have to go, my brothers and sisters were there. They told stories about having their hair cut off in case they were carrying head lice, and of being forced to do hard chores without enough food to eat. They were told that the Indian culture was evil, that Indian people were bad, that their only hope was to be Christian. They had to stand up and say things like "I've found the Lord," when a teacher told them to speak. Sexual abuse was rampant in the residential school system.

By the time we moved to Whitehorse, I was excited about the idea   9
of living in what I thought of as a big town. I'd had a taste of the
outside world from books at school in Teslin (a town of 250 people),
and I was tremendously curious about what life was like. I was hungry
for experiences such as going to the circus. In fact, for a while, I was
obsessed with stories and pictures about the circus, but then when I
was 12 and saw my first one, I was put off by the condition and treatment of the animals.

Going to school in Whitehorse was a shock. The clash of native and   10
white values was confusing and frightening. Let me tell you a story.
The older boys in our community were already accomplished hunters
and fishermen, but since they had to trap beaver in the spring and
hunt moose in the fall, and go out trapping in the winter as well, they
missed a lot of school. We were all in one classroom and some of my
very large teenage cousins had to sit squeezed into little desks. These
guys couldn't read very well. We girls had been in school all along,
so, of course, we were better readers. One day the teacher was trying
to get one of the older boys to read. She was typical of the teachers
at that time, insensitive and ignorant of cultural complexities. In an
increasingly loud voice, she kept commanding him to "Read it, read
it." He couldn't. He sat there completely still, but I could see that he
was breaking into a sweat. The teacher then said, "Look, she can read
it," and she pointed to me, indicating that I should stand up and read.
For a young child to try to show up an older boy is wrong and totally
contrary to native cultural values, so I refused. She told me to stand up
and I did. My hands were trembling as I held my reader. She yelled at
me to read and when I didn't she smashed her pointing stick on the
desk to frighten me. In terror, I wet my pants. As I stood there fighting my tears of shame, she said I was disgusting and sent me home. I
had to walk a long distance through the bush by myself to get home.
I remember feeling this tremendous confusion, on top of my humiliation. We were always told the white teachers knew best, and so we had
to do whatever they said at school. And yet I had a really strong sense
of receiving mixed messages about what I was supposed to do in the
community and what I was supposed to do at school.

Pretty soon I hated school. Moving to a predominantly white high   11
school was even worse. We weren't allowed to join anything the white

kids started. We were the butt of jokes because of our secondhand clothes and moose meat sandwiches. We were constantly being rejected. The prevailing attitude was that Indians were stupid. When it was time to make course choices in class—between typing and science, for example—they didn't even ask the native kids, they just put us all in typing. You get a really bad image of yourself in a situation like that. I bought into it. I thought we were awful. The whole experience was terribly undermining. Once, my grandmother gave me a pretty little pencil box. I walked into the classroom one day to find the word "squaw" carved on it. That night I burned it in the wood stove. I joined the tough crowd and by the time I was 15 years old, I was more likely to be leaning against the school smoking a cigarette than trying to join in. I was burned out from trying to join the system. The principal told my father there was no point in sending me back to school so, with a Grade 9 education, I started to work at a series of menial jobs.

12   Seven years later something happened to me that would change my life forever. I had moved to Ottawa with a man and was working as a waitress in a restaurant. One day, a friend invited me to her place for coffee. While I was there, she told me she was going to university in the fall and showed me her reading list. I'll never forget the minutes that followed. I was feeling vaguely envious of her and, once again, inferior. I remember taking the paper in my hand, seeing the books on it and realizing, Oh, my God, I've read these books! It hit me like a thunderclap. I was stunned that books I had read were being read in university. University was for white kids, not native kids. We were too stupid, we didn't have the kind of mind it took to do those things. My eyes moved down the list, and my heart started beating faster and faster as I suddenly realized I could go to university, too!

13   My partner at the time was a loving supportive man who helped me in every way. I applied to the university immediately as a mature student but when I had to write Grade 9 on the application, I was sure they'd turn me down. They didn't. I graduated five years later, earning a bachelor of arts in English and philosophy (with distinction).

14   It was while I was studying for a master's degree in communications at McGill a few years later that I was approached to direct my

second film (the first was a student film). *Doctor, Lawyer, Indian Chief* (a National Film Board production) depicts the struggle of a number of native women—one who began her adult life on welfare, a government minister, a chief, a fisherwoman and Canada's first native woman lawyer. The film is about overcoming obstacles and surviving. It's the story of most native people.

Today, there's a glimmer of hope that more of us native people will overcome the obstacles that have tripped us up ever since we began sharing this land. Some say our cultures are going through a renaissance. Maybe that's true. Certainly there's a renewed interest in native dancing, acting and singing, and in other cultural traditions. Even indigenous forms of government are becoming strong again. But we can't forget that the majority of native people live in urban areas and continue to suffer from alcohol and drug abuse and the plagues of a people who have lost their culture and have become lost themselves. And the welfare system is the insidious glue that holds together the machine of oppression of native people.

Too many non-native people have refused to try to understand the issues behind our land claims. They make complacent pronouncements such as "Go back to your bows and arrows and fish with spears if you want aboriginal rights. If not, give it up and assimilate into white Canadian culture." I don't agree with that. We need our culture, but there's no reason why we can't preserve it and have an automatic washing machine and a holiday in Mexico, as well.

The time has come for native people to make our own decisions. We need to have self-government. I have no illusions that it will be smooth sailing—there will be trial and error and further struggle. And if that means crawling before we can stand up and walk, so be it. We'll have to learn through experience.

While we're learning, we have a lot to teach and give to the world— a holistic philosophy, a way of living with the earth, not disposing of it. It is critical that we all learn from the elders that an individual is not more important than a forest; we know that we're here to live on and with the earth, not to subdue it.

The wheels are in motion for a revival, for change in the way native people are taking their place in Canada. I can see that we're equipped, we have the tools to do the work. We have an enormous number of smart, talented, moral Indian people. It's thrilling to be a part of this movement.

20   Someday, when I'm an elder, I'll tell the children the stories: about the bush, about the hard times, about the renaissance, and especially about the importance of knowing your place in your nation.

EXPLORATIONS:

Carol Geddes, *Doctor, Lawyer, Indian Chief* (NFB film, 29 min.)
Daniel David Moses and Terry Goldie, eds., *An Anthology of Canadian Native Writers in English*
Penny Petrone, ed., *First People, First Voices* (anthology of writings by First Nations people in Canada)
Julie Cruikshank, *Life Lived Like a Story* (interviews with Native Canadian women)
Brian Maracle, *Back on the Rez: Finding the Way Home* (memoir)
Basil Johnston, *Indian School Days* (memoir)
Hugh Brody, *Maps and Dreams* (anthropology)
Tomson Highway, *Kiss of the Fur Queen* (novel)
http://www.nfb.ca/portraits/carol_geddes/en
http://users.ap.net/~chenae/natlink.html
http://www.nativeweb.org
http://www.collectionscanada.ca/02/02012001_e.html

STRUCTURE:

1. "I remember it was cold," says Geddes in her opening sentence, and "Someday, when I'm an elder," she says in her closing sentence. Most *narratives* in this chapter relate one incident, but "Growing Up Native" tells the highs and lows of a whole life. Has Geddes attempted too much? Or has she got her message across by focussing on the right moments of her life? Cite examples to defend your answer.

2. Did you have the impression of being *told* a story, rather than reading it on the page? Cite passages where "Growing Up Native"

comes across as oral history, as a tale told in person. Why do you think Geddes may have taken this approach?

3. Does Geddes *narrate* in straight chronological order? Point out any flashbacks or other departures from the pattern.

4. Read paragraph 12 aloud. Analyze its power as a TRANSITION between Geddes' past and present.

STYLE:

1. Geddes' paragraphs are well organized: most begin with a topic sentence, then clearly develop it with examples. Identify five paragraphs that follow this pattern.

2. Why are paragraph 10 and several others so long? Why is paragraph 20 so short?

3. In paragraph 2 Geddes tells of "the sting of humiliation and the boot of discrimination." Find other good FIGURES OF SPEECH in paragraphs 9, 12 and 15.

IDEAS FOR DISCUSSION AND WRITING:

1. Despite the hardships of living in the bush, does Geddes' childhood sound like a good one? If so, why? Give *examples*.

2. Geddes exposes various ways in which First Nations people have been STEREOTYPED. Point out the worst of these.

3. The white high school of paragraph 11 routinely put native students in typing instead of science. How do the high schools of your province advise minority students as to course selection and career? Is a minority or working-class student shut out from opportunity, or encouraged to try? Give *examples* from your own observation.

4. Geddes envisions First Nations people keeping their culture, yet also having washing machines and holidays in Mexico (par. 16). Discuss techniques for achieving such goals in the urban setting where most Native people now live.

5. PROCESS IN WRITING: *Interview someone who either grew up long ago, or who is from a culture very different from yours, to hear her or his life story. Tape the interview, then at home play it back, taking notes. Now choose either one main event of this* narrative *(such as the scene in which Geddes realizes she too can go to university), OR choose to give the overall sweep*

of the story. Also choose whether to just assemble the best excerpts from the tape to put in writing, OR to summarize the key events in your own words. Load your first draft with the best examples *you have. Stay mainly in time order, but do use a flashback or flashforward if they enhance the story. Finally edit your version for things like spelling and punctuation. Read it aloud to the class. If there is time, also play the interview so the class can see how you chose and arranged the material of your* narrative.

Note: See also the Topics for Writing on the Online Learning Centre at www. mcgrawhill.ca/olc/conrad.

PROCESS IN WRITING: GUIDELINES

Follow at least some of these steps in the act of writing your narrative (your teacher may suggest which ones).

1. Search your memory, or search any diary or journal that you keep, for an incident that might develop one of our topics.
2. When you have chosen an incident, test it by freewriting nonstop for at least five minutes. If the results are good, use the best parts in your first draft. If the results are weak, try another topic.
3. Write your discovery draft rapidly, letting the story just flow out onto the paper or the computer screen. Do not stop now to fix things like spelling and punctuation, for you will lose momentum. Consider narrating in the *present* tense, making the action seem to happen *now*.
4. Look this draft over: Does it begin and end at just the right places, narrating the event itself but omitting parts that don't matter? If you see deadwood, chop it out.
5. Now add more SENSE IMAGES to heighten realism. Add more time signals, such as "first," "next," "then," "suddenly" and "at last," to speed the action.
6. Read your narrative to friends, family members or classmates. Does it sound good? Revise awkward passages. Does it communicate with your AUDIENCE? Revise any part that does not.
7. Finally, edit for spelling, punctuation and other aspects of correctness before printing off your best version.

Thinkstock/Index Stock

"*A fire truck can sometimes arrive on the scene faster than an ambulance, and while paramedics don't put out fires, every fireman knows how to use a defibrillator.*"

—*Joe Fiorito, "The Fire Hall down the Street"*

EXAMPLE 2

FOR EXAMPLE....

Many an audience, after struggling to grasp a speaker's message, has been saved from boredom or even sleep by the powerful words *"for example...."* Heads lift up, eyes return to the front, bodies shift in their chairs, and suddenly the message is clear to all.

Writers, like speakers, use examples. Do you enjoy reading pages of abstract reasoning, generalizations, theory without application? You have probably heard the Chinese proverb "A picture is worth a thousand words." When the writer's words never form "pictures," how can you "see" the point? Of course generalizations have their place. For example your thesis statement is one, and so are subpoints, summaries and conclusions. These and others are needed, but cannot do the job alone. If you do not "show" as well as "tell," your reader will be like the people in the audience sinking into their seats—until you, like the speaker, say "for example...."

Why not try for at least 50% example content in every essay, to avoid the hot-air approach to writing? This means, though, that you need to know the subject. Two suggestions:

- If you cannot think of examples, then you may have chosen the wrong topic. Try another, before investing too much time in a topic that will not work for you. The best essays are like icebergs: only a tenth of what you know shows above the surface, but it is supported by the other nine-tenths below.
- If examples do not come to mind, take action. Go to the library. Use the online catalogue and periodical indexes. Consult reference works such as the almanac or the encyclopedia. Check the more reliable sources on the Internet (ones belonging to well-known governmental or educational organizations). If you are quoting, make sure to use quotation marks and attribute each source.

Examples take many forms:

PERSONAL EXPERIENCE: To illustrate your point, narrate an incident you have experienced. Did an earthquake or tornado or ice storm or heat wave or flood or tsunami show you the power of nature? Did your car accident illustrate the dangers of drinking and driving, or did your fire show the dangers of smoking in bed? Did a major success or failure demonstrate the importance of your work or planning or persistence?

THE EXPERIENCE OF OTHERS: To illustrate the point, narrate an incident you saw in person or heard about from others. Did your neighbour's unloved child run away from home or rob a milk store or get married at age 16? Did your cousin lose her job because of automation or downsizing or outsourcing or a corporate merger? Did a famous person succeed despite a physical disability or a deprived childhood?

HYPOTHETICAL EXAMPLES: In a future-oriented society like ours, many arguments speculate about what might happen *if....* Since the event or situation has not yet come to pass, use your best judgement to imagine the results. What would happen if street drugs were

EXAMPLE   **59**

legalized? If the forests were all cut? If Quebec separated? If the national debt were paid off? If the polar ice cap melted? If our electricity came from wind turbines? If a world government were adopted?

QUOTATIONS: If the words of a poet, politician, scientist or other prominent person illustrate your point clearly and authoritatively, quote them (using quotation marks) and of course state who said them. What did Aristotle, Shakespeare, Marx, Einstein, Jane Jacobs, Warren Buffet, Nelson Mandela, Mordecai Richler or Margaret Atwood say about love or power or sex or money or old age or war? Start with the index of *Colombo's Canadian Quotations* or *Bartlett's Familiar Quotations* to find an apt statement on almost any important topic. Or go online to check out *Bartlett* at http://www.bartleby.com/100, entering keywords for a search. Another good source is *Wikiquote* at http://en.wikiquote.org/wiki/Main_Page.

STATISTICS: These numerical examples lend a scientific, objective quality to your argument. Tell what percentage of marriages will end in divorce or how many minutes each cigarette takes off one's life or how much energy a person consumes travelling by car as opposed to train, bus or airplane. Good places to find statistics are *The World Almanac and Book of Facts, Canada Year Book* and any good atlas. Be scrupulously honest, because everyone knows how statistics can lie (remember the statistician who drowned in the river that averaged two feet deep!).

OTHER DEVICES: Later chapters in this book discuss cause and effect, comparison and contrast, and analogy. These devices may be used not only to plan the structure of an entire essay, but also to construct short and vivid examples within the essay.

Almost all good writing has examples, but is there an upper limit? Some writers, such as Karen Von Hahn and Jeffrey Rosenthal in this chapter, go far beyond the 50% level suggested above. Von Hahn reaches probably 80% and Rosenthal 90% or more. Some readers of Rosenthal may tune out during his succession of poker hand examples, but probably more because of the mathematics involved than the sheer number of cases. As for Von Hahn, many of her examples are very short bits of narrative, which are easy to digest and have a high degree of human interest. So are those of

Margaret Wente, Joe Fiorito and Goran Simic, all in this chapter. Among the authors in other chapters who also make massive and skilful use of examples are Patricia Pearson in Chapter 4 and Doris Anderson in Chapter 5. You may want to look ahead and see their techniques and arguments now. Though it is very possible to disagree with the arguments of any of these prolific example users, it would be astonishing if you did not at least understand their views after "seeing" them so clearly in action.

Another way to use examples is to let one long one make the point. On page 170 of Chapter 4, Nathalie Petrowski develops one extended example of one young man who became a mass murderer. Yet through the single case of Marc Lépine, she helps us "see" the situation of many other Canadian youth who may also explode into violence if we do not reduce the pressures our society puts on them. Of course one example—or a hundred—will prove nothing. Statistics come close to proof, especially when based on a large and carefully designed study. But in general an example is not proof; it is a device of illustration and therefore an aid to both understanding and enjoyment.

Note: Authors in other chapters also use many examples, as well as other ways to develop their point. See especially these selections:

Patricia Pearson, "Avoiding the Big C: A Little Simple Advice," p. 133
June Callwood, "Forgiveness," p. 161
Doris Anderson, "The 51-Per-Cent Minority," p. 191
Drew Hayden Taylor, "This Boat Is My Boat," p. 216
Catharine Parr Trail, "Remarks of Security of Person and Property in Canada," p. 222
Lawrence Hill, "Black + White = Black," p. 228
Samantha Bennett, "It's Not Just the Weather That's Cooler in Canada," p. 264
Margaret Atwood, "Letter to America," p. 392

MARGARET WENTE

Busy, Busy, Busy

An "accidental Canadian," as she puts it in the title of her book, Margaret Wente did not immigrate to Canada till her teens. She grew up in the fifties in a conservative suburb of Chicago, then, when her divorced mother married a Canadian, moved with the family to Toronto. She found the city conservative as well, but was charmed by signs of change, such as the Yorkville espresso bars and the new music. After a B.A. from the University of Michigan and an M.A. in English literature from the University of Toronto, she began a career in journalism that led her to be editor of Canadian Business, ROB Magazine *and the* Globe and Mail*'s business section. And from 1992 she has become known to a much larger audience, writing a quirky, humorous, brash and controversial column for the* Globe. *Not everyone is a fan. She steps on toes easily, for example in 2005 infuriating the whole province of Newfoundland with unflattering comments. And while she is often progressive on social issues, she is conservative on political ones, deflating Canadian cultural icons and often supporting American actions unpopular in Canada. Then in 2004 Wente collected many of her best columns in* An Accidental Canadian: Reflections on My Home and (Not) Native Land. *From it comes our selection.*

N ot long ago, I phoned up an old friend of mine, a high-powered career woman who is usually on the road two or three days a week.

"How about lunch?" I said. "How does your calendar look for June?"

"How about today?" she said. "I'm totally free."

61

4   I was shocked. Nobody I know is free for lunch today. A person of average busyness is sometimes free the week after next. If you're trying to book a higher-status person, four to six weeks is normal, by which time you will be lucky to remember what it is you wanted to have lunch about anyway. This lunch will probably be rearranged a few times by various executive assistants, who will spend more time talking to each other, coordinating your respective calendars, than you will spend talking to your lunchee. If you are higher status (i.e., busier) than the other person, you will be allowed to reschedule at least twice.

5   That is, if you still do lunch. Busy people don't, and when they do, they tell you, "I really don't do lunch anymore," implying that you ought to be immensely honoured that they have broken the rule for you. And you'd better eat in a hurry. An hour and ten minutes is the most anyone spends on a business lunch now.

6   Whenever I run into someone I haven't seen for a while and ask how they are, they always say the same thing: "I'm really busy."

7   Want to get together for dinner some Saturday with another busy couple? Two months, minimum, before you can fit it in.

8   And when you do get together, you'll all brag about how much e-mail you get. "It's horrible," someone will say. "I took three days off and when I got back to the office I had six hundred e-mails!"

9   "That's nothing," the next person will say. "I had two thousand, and I had forty-seven voice mails."

10   The truly busy person, of course, will have answered all these voice mails and e-mails while on vacation so that she can get right back down to work.

11   Then comes the discussion about how early people get up in the morning. If you sleep in after 5:30 on a weekday, your best strategy is to lie about it so your friends don't think you're a slacker.

12   Recently, I took a few days off from work between assignments. It was pleasant to spend all day reading the papers at my kitchen table, with the sun streaming in, no places to go, no people to see. Pleasant—for about five minutes. Then I started to get nervous. What if they had forgotten all about me? So I got on the phone and called a few friends. The first person I called had to take a call on his cellphone while he was speaking to me. The second and third persons were in meetings and would call me back just as soon as they were free.

Everyone was so busy! I recalled that just the day before I had been   13
that busy too, and in a few days' time I would be that busy again.
Meantime, I had the odd sensation that I was fading away. I quickly
invented a ridiculously complicated project that involved a great deal
of Internet searching and faxing things overseas at all hours of the
day and night, and immediately felt much better.

How did we get so busy? That's not too hard to figure out. The   14
work world has become a far more Darwinian° place in the past decade. Plenty of middle managers with middling incomes are obligated
to put in sixty or seventy hours a week on the job. Workaholism? It's
a condition of employment. Job flexibility? Puh-lease. New technology? Fabulous. It lets us work all the time. To be is to do. And the
more there is on your to-do list, the more reassured you are that you
must count for something.

Of course, you don't get work overload without work stress, and   15
everyone I know has plenty of that. But people who suddenly aren't
busy have more.

One man told me what happened to him after he had accepted a   16
gigantic buyout. He took his bag of money and set up a little office
to figure out what to do next. He showed up on Monday morning
at eight. His appointment book was blank. The phone didn't ring.
Nobody needed him. He says it was the worst moment of his life.

When I met my friend for lunch, I asked her what had happened   17
to her ultra-busy schedule. She told me that she had put herself on
a strict new regimen. She was turning down at least three assignments a week. She was practising being a slacker. She had sworn off
multitasking and was trying unitasking, though she confessed it was
incredibly difficult. Then she invited me to go to the garden centre
with her after lunch.

It would have been fun, I said. But I really had to get back to   18
work.

°Darwinian: Referring to Charles Darwin (1809–82) who in 1859 published *The Origin of Species*, a work arguing that stronger individuals and species survived and propagated themselves through "natural selection," while the weaker died off.

EXPLORATIONS:

Margaret Wente, *An Accidental Canadian: Reflections on My Home and (Not) Native Land*

Carl Honoré, *In Praise of Slow: How a Worldwide Movement Is Challenging the Cult of Speed*

http://en.wikipedia.org/wiki/Karoshi

http://www.statcan.ca/english/studies/11-008/feature/star2002064000s1a01.pdf

http://www.nsb.com/speakerbio.asp?name=Margaret+Wente

STRUCTURE:

1. What well-known technique does Wente choose to open her argument?
2. Roughly what proportion of her argument does Wente fill with *examples?* Have you ever used this many? Do you find it hard to think of them? Why? What is the solution?
3. Why does Wente choose to end her entire essay on the word "work"?

STYLE:

1. What is Wente doing when she uses the terms "lunchee" in paragraph 4 and "puh-lease" in paragraph 14? Are these usages appropriate for her topic and her treatment of it?
2. If overwork is a serious problem for Wente and the rest of us, why does she joke about it? Does her humorous TONE undermine the significance of her argument? Or can it be a valid approach to a real topic?
3. Explain the IRONY that in paragraph 18 powers Wente's closing: "It would have been fun, I said. But I really had to get back to work."

IDEAS FOR DISCUSSION AND WRITING:

1. Wente sums up the pressures to work with the words "To be is to do" (par. 14). Is this what our society believes? Is it what you believe? Are there alternative ways to "be"? Back your view with reasons and *examples.*

2. Is work addictive? (See the examples in pars. 12, 13, 15 and 16.) Are Wente and her friends hooked? Are you? If so, how does addiction begin? How serious does it get? How can it be beaten? What is withdrawal like?

3. In paragraphs 8–9, Wente's dinner companions say that when they took time off, they came back to 600 to 2000 e-mails, and as many as 47 voice mails. How many e-mails do you receive per day? Share your best techniques for dealing with them. Does digital communication increase or decrease our workload? Give *examples*.

4. The Japanese have a word for working oneself to death: *Karoshi*. Key the term into a search engine and visit some of the many websites on this topic. Report your findings to the class: How frequent and widespread is this problem? Does it happen only in Japan?

5. "The work world has become a far more Darwinian place in the past decade," reports Wente in paragraph 14. Explore this point. Draw an ANALOGY between humans competing in the workplace and animals competing in the wild.

6. One high-ranking employee of the World Bank says that if she leaves work before 7:30 p.m. she goes out the back door, to avoid being seen going home early. And in paragraph 11 Wente says that on weekdays one gets up at 5:30 a.m. to avoid being a slacker. How many hours do you think make a reasonable work week? And why? Give your best techniques for "having a life" while being an employee.

7. PROCESS IN WRITING: *You are probably among the majority of today's students who also have a part-time job. How busy is the combination of your studies and work? Write your own version of "Busy, Busy, Busy," giving large numbers of* examples *to illustrate your point. First freewrite or brainstorm to get ideas and examples safely down on paper, then look over these notes to make a short outline with a* thesis statement. *Write the draft quickly, not stopping now for corrections. Later look it over: Is there at least 50% of* example *content? Is the* TONE *consistent, whether serious or humorous? Have you used* logic signals *to speed your argument on? Are the words short and strong, or big and flabby? Edit for all these things. Finally, check the sentence structure and punctuation before printing off your best version.*

Note: See also the Topics for Writing on the Online Learning Centre at www. mcgrawhill.ca/olc/conrad.

KAREN VON HAHN

Self-Serving Propaganda

Karen von Hahn has been called "Canada's leading voice on lifestyle and trends in the art of consumption." She writes a weekly column, "Noticed," in the Toronto Globe and Mail, *on style and lifestyle. She also writes for* EnRoute, Toronto Life, Fashion, Flare, House & Home, Town & Country, *and* Report on Business, *and in 1996 published a book, the* Hip Guide to Toronto. *Von Hahn also hosts seminars on fashion-related topics, and is host of* The Goods *on BBC Canada. In all this writing and speaking she focuses mostly on ephemeral topics such as clothing trends, but from time to time her other role of social critic takes the forefront as she deals with broader issues of society. Such was the case with our selection, an attack on the "self-serve" way of doing business which companies force on consumers (for example, through promotion of airport check-in kiosks, self-serve check-outs, automated phone systems, etc.). The essay appeared in the* Globe and Mail *of August 11, 2007.*

1   I finally figured out why I'm so crabby and exhausted. Not only am I busy juggling my many, admittedly self-imposed jobs (columnist/wife/mother of two), but more and more, everywhere I go, people want me to do their work for them.

2   I don't know about you, but when I travel, I do not particularly look forward to struggling in a long queue with my bags at the airport for the opportunity of playing ticketing agent at the new self-serve check-in kiosks.

Moreover, when stressed by frequent departure announcements   3
over the loudspeaker, I find I'm not particularly well-qualified to
punch in all the passport numbers of each of my family members
with sufficient accuracy to prevent having to enter the whole thing
over again and bursting into tears.

Frankly, I already have a job or three. Why is it that I have to pay   4
for the pleasure of taking on yet another one? Yet thanks to the "self-
serve" movement, which has now spread like a virus from big-box
discount retailers to airports and even government services, almost
everything that was once somebody's full-time job is being offloaded
onto the already overburdened shoulders of consumers.

To my mind, the biggest deception in this mass, self-serve phenom-   5
enon is that somehow it's empowering.

At a gas station, I not only have to fill the tank, check the oil and   6
clean the windows, but now I also have to process the payment. At
a bank (now an ATM machine, as all the historic bank buildings
have become restaurants), it's me who's the teller. If I stop for a $3
Americano, I'm the one who has to find the right lid for the cup and
add the milk.

Similarly, the fact that while attempting to contact the customer   7
service wing of any commercial establishment or enterprise, I am
permitted to enter my nine-digit telephone number/customer
account code before speaking to a live customer-care representa-
tive who will then immediately ask me for my nine-digit telephone
number/customer account code, does not really make me feel like a
contributing part of such organization.

And this may be news to Staples and Best Buy, but even though I   8
use a personal computer every day, I have not yet developed sufficient experience in the field of computer engineering to determine
which cable is compatible with which brand of wireless routing technology simply by examining the exteriors of the cardboard boxes
from China on the store shelves.

Now that the Ontario government is permitting me (for a small   9
additional fee) to renew my own driver's licence and register for my
own social insurance number at their new public online kiosks, I am
starting to wonder if this whole offloading thing has gone too far. I

mean, can I handle even the relative security and stress-free lifestyle of a government desk job on top of all my other daily responsibilities?

10   The other day I was at Home Depot, when a voice from a loud-speaker sounded like a word of warning: "When reaching for larger products located on our higher shelves, please ask one of our sales representatives for assistance."

11   At the new, self-serve checkout, where the auto-cashier was so apparently exasperated with my poor attempts to scan a mop that I had to flag down one of the few remaining living salespeople on the vast floor to help, I felt forced to inquire whether self-service had ever resulted in any serious accidents.

12   "Oh, yeah," said my sales associate (who, incidentally, seemed much more adroit than me at scanning in my mop). "It happens all the time. I heard some guy in Florida was climbing up on the shelves to get some sheets of wood or something and he fell and smashed his head open."

13   It's interesting to note that all this moonlighting we're doing isn't only infuriating, it's also dangerous. But please, please, just stop telling us while you're offloading all the work—and its risks—that we're the ones being empowered.

EXPLORATIONS:

George Orwell, *1984*
http://en.wikipedia.org/wiki/Self_checkout
http://en.wikipedia.org/wiki/Automated_teller_machine

STRUCTURE:

1. Von Hahn uses a classic technique in introducing her topic. What is it? And where does it lead into her THESIS STATEMENT?
2. Roughly what proportion of this essay is devoted to *examples*? What proportion of your own essays is usually given to them? Why are von Hahn's all taken from her own personal experience? Should she have done research to find examples experienced by others? Why or why not?

3. Which of von Hahn's *examples* can you most strongly relate to? Tell why.

4. Why does von Hahn wait till her closing paragraph to directly address the businesses that create the "self-serving propaganda"? And why does she end the entire selection on the word "empowered"?

5. Von Hahn also uses a classic technique of closing when she makes her final sentence refer back to the THESIS STATEMENT in paragraph 5. What effects does this create?

STYLE:

1. How FORMAL or INFORMAL is the style of this essay (length of words, sentences and paragraphs; level of vocabulary; complexity of thought)? Create a profile of the AUDIENCE von Hahn is probably aiming for.

2. In paragraph 4 the "self-serve" movement has spread "like a virus." Think of at least five other SIMILES that might express this same thought (see "Figures of Speech" in the Glossary to this book).

IDEAS FOR DISCUSSION AND WRITING:

1. Is von Hahn angry? Is this piece a rant, like those of Canadian humourist Rick Mercer? Is it a whine? Or does she merely share with us a normal human reaction to the self-serve culture? And can anger be a good starting point for writing an essay?

2. Do you indeed feel "empowered" by self-serve transactions (at the gas pump, in the airport, at the bank, on the phone, at the store, etc.)? Are they faster and do they give more choice, as the companies tell us? Or do you agree with Karen von Hahn that they merely profit companies by offloading work onto customers? Give *examples* from your own experience.

3. Do you prefer the bank machine or the teller? Do you care that bank machines replace tellers? Or is that just business today? Does it just mean that better jobs are opening up in new areas? Defend your view with *examples*.

4. PROCESS IN WRITING: *One kind of self-serve transaction von Hahn does not mention is shopping online. Do you do it? Is it fast or slow?*

Safe or risky? Pleasant or unpleasant? Fill a page with notes, especially examples. *Then put your main point into a* THESIS STATEMENT, *and follow it up either with a long string of* examples *(like von Hahn's), or with one* example *explained in depth. The next day look it over, and revise: Is your* example *content at least 50%? Do all the* examples *support your argument? Now read aloud to detect weakness in style, such as repeated words, lack of* TRANSITIONS, *wordiness, and unclear passages. Print off your best version, and share it with the class.*

Note: See also the Topics for Writing on the Online Learning Centre at www. mcgrawhill.ca/olc/conrad.

JEFFREY ROSENTHAL

Poker Power

Born in 1967 in Toronto, at age 20 Jeffrey Rosenthal graduated from the University of Toronto in math, physics and computer science. Then at the startlingly young age of 24 he earned his Ph.D. in mathematics from Harvard. Since then he has received many honours and awards, has taught at Harvard and at the University of Minnesota and is now a full professor of statistics at the University of Toronto. Numbers have been kind to this statistician, who likes to point out that he was born on a Friday the thirteenth. He has authored textbooks on probability at both the undergraduate and graduate levels, has published over 50 research papers in the field and has worked as a programmer of computer games. Rosenthal's lively and humorous style has made him popular with students, and has led him to such activities as improvisational comedy performance. In 2005 it also powered his bestselling book, Struck by Lightning: The Curious World of Probabilities, *in which he sheds the scholarly style of his academic work and shows the average person the extent to which probabilities determine one's fate. From this lively book comes our selection.*

No game of chance has captured the popular imagination 1
quite like poker. Poker showdowns feature in numerous
movies about the Wild West, from *Butch Cassidy and the
Sundance Kid* to *Maverick*. Psychological manipulation, macho posturing, tough talk, and the occasional six-shooter all combine to give
poker its entertainment value. Such depictions of poker emphasize
the competitive, psychological, and financial aspects of the game,

71

all of which are significant. Unfortunately, they leave out the most important part: probabilities.

2   In many a movie scene, the final hand is won by the hero when he is dealt a Royal Flush: the 10, Jack, Queen, King, and Ace all of the same suit. Is this really a plausible outcome? In reality, there are nearly 2.6 million different five-card hands that can be dealt. Of these, just four are Royal Flushes (one for each suit). So, the probability of the hero's actually being dealt a Royal Flush on the final hand is four chances in 2.6 million, or about one chance in 650,000. It is extremely rare. And, popular entertainment aside, no amount of tough talk or intimidation (short of outright cheating) will change this probability. From the strongest cowboy to the cleverest card shark to the greenest novice, we all have exactly the same chance of being dealt a Royal Flush in five cards.

3   Of course, there are many different versions of poker, including some with wild cards, extra cards to choose from, opportunities to exchange cards, and so on. Each of these modifications changes all the probabilities and, with enough wild cards, even a Royal Flush isn't so unlikely. Nevertheless, the probabilities are the same for everyone. And the way to succeed at poker is not by magically getting a Royal Flush every time, but rather by understanding probabilities and making good decisions once the cards are dealt.

4   Suppose you're playing five-card stud poker, where each player is dealt a total of five cards (with no extra or wild cards). Suppose you have been dealt four Spades, with the fifth card still to come. If the fifth card ends up being a Spade, then you will have a Flush (all five cards of the same suit), which is a very good hand that will likely win the pot. On the other hand, if the fifth card is not a Spade, then your hand will be very weak (at best, one pair) and will probably lose. Everything comes down to whether or not your fifth card will be a Spade.

5   What is your probability of success? If the deck is well shuffled and nobody cheats, every unseen card is equally likely to be dealt next. You have already seen four cards, all Spades. So, there are 48 cards remaining, of which nine are Spades. This means that the probability that the next card will be a Spade is equal to 9/48, or about 19%. Those odds are pretty low, so perhaps you should fold at this point (though that decision also depends on the pot odds, discussed below).

Is that all there is to it? No. In many poker games, some of the   6
cards are dealt face up, for everyone to see. For example, in the usual
version of five-card stud, all but the first of each player's cards are
viewable by all. Consider again the Flush example, where you have
been dealt four Spades and are waiting for a fifth. Suppose you are at
a table with nine opponents, each of whom already has three face-up
cards showing. That makes an extra 27 cards that you already know
about, leaving just 21 unseen. If none of your opponents' face-up
cards are Spades, then there are still nine unseen Spades. So, in this
case, the probability that your fifth card will be a Spade increases to
9/21, or 43%—far more than the 19% it was before. By contrast, if
seven of those other 27 cards are Spades, then there are only two
Spades left, so your probability reduces to 2/21, or 9.5%, which is
far worse.

For another example, suppose you have been dealt a 5, a 6, an 8,   7
and a 9. If your next card is a 7, then you will have a Straight (five
cards in succession), a good hand that will probably win. What is the
probability that your fifth card will be a 7? Well, there are only four
7's in the deck. So, if you haven't seen any other cards, then your
chances are 4/48, or about 8%, quite small. Even if you have seen
27 other cards, and none of them are 7's, then your chances are still
just 4/21, or 19%. You are "drawing to an Inside Straight," and your
chances are not good.

On the other hand, if you were instead dealt a 5, a 6, a 7, and an 8,   8
then either a 4 or a 9 would complete your Straight. This time, your
chances of success are twice as good. This is called "drawing to an
Outside Straight," which, as all good poker players know, is twice as
likely to succeed as drawing to an Inside Straight.

So, while the poker players in movies are busy snarling and threat-   9
ening and chewing tobacco, real poker players are carefully examining every card they can see, including opponents' "unimportant"
discards. They are using this information to compute and update
their probabilities of success, to make better decisions. It's true that
psychological factors—things like bluffing and "tells" and keeping a
"poker face"—are important, too. But probability is central to serious
poker games, and players ignore it at their peril.

EXPLORATIONS:

Jeffrey S. Rosenthal, *Struck by Lightning: The Curious World of Probabilities*

M. J. Evans and J. S. Rosenthal, *Probability and Statistics: The Science of Uncertainty*

Olav Kallenberg, *Foundations of Modern Probability* (2nd ed.)

http://probability.ca/jeff

http://probability.ca/sbl

http://en.wikipedia.org/wiki/Poker

STRUCTURE:

1. Do you like the title of the book from which this selection comes: *Struck by Lightning: The Curious World of Probabilities*? What are titles for? What makes a good one?

2. Rosenthal's introductory paragraph is powerfully organized. How does he first attract our attention? How does he begin to show the significance of the topic? What common device does he use to introduce his THESIS STATEMENT? And why does he place the word "probabilities" at the very end of the paragraph?

3. How does Rosenthal's final paragraph complete the strategies of his first?

4. What proportion of Rosenthal's argument is devoted to *examples* of probability in poker? Are they clear? Do they all support his main idea that winning comes from mathematics? Could the argument have stood without them?

STYLE:

1. Jeffrey Rosenthal is a Harvard Ph.D. and a University of Toronto professor of statistics. His scholarly articles have titles like "Extremal Indices, Geometric Ergodicity of Markov Chains, and MCMC" or "Quantitative bounds on convergence of time-in homogenous Markov Chains." Contrast the STYLE he employs in "Poker Power." Why is it so different? Who is the intended AUDIENCE?

2. What are the benefits of popularizing math and science for the masses? Name some famous scientists who do so. What would happen if the average person knew nothing about the latest technical developments?

3. In designing his book for the average person, Rosenthal is careful to define each important new term or concept. Point out at least three places where he does so.

Ideas for Discussion and Writing:

1. Do you play poker? Give all the reasons why or why not. Why has poker become so popular? Why does it appear so much on television and on the Internet?

2. Why do people flock to casinos, even when the odds are stacked in favour of the house? Why do millions of people buy lottery tickets? What are the motivations for all this gambling? Is greed exciting? Or are people just looking for hope?

3. Rosenthal's suggestions for how to win at poker all involve remembering which cards have been shown so far. Are most people's memories up to the task? Can memory be trained and improved?

4. When people buy stocks or mutual funds, are they investing or gambling? If you know something about this field, name some common ways to invest more safely or more aggressively.

5. How important to our lives is knowledge of probabilities? Would your actions change if you knew that air travel is safer or less safe than car travel? If you knew whether crime is increasing or decreasing? If you knew whether life insurance is statistically worth its cost or not worth its cost? Read Rosenthal's book *Struck by Lightning*, from which "Poker Power" comes. Report to the class on at least three of its analyses that have opened your eyes.

6. PROCESS IN WRITING: *Are lotteries a "tax on idiots," as a former prime minister of Italy once stated, or are they a worthwhile approach to solving one's financial problems? Fill a page with notes on examples you have witnessed, or experienced yourself. Then compose a THESIS STATEMENT that defines your point of view. Now write a quick draft of your argument, not stopping now to fix things like sentence structure, punctuation or spelling. Then look it over. Have you used a great number of examples,*

as Rosenthal does? If not, think more and add. Have you defined difficult terms, as he does? If not, revise. Have you used expressions of TRANSITION, as he does? If not, add. Finally, read your draft aloud, to detect rough spots in style, then edit and print out your best version.

Note: See also the Topics for Writing on the Online Learning Centre at www. mcgrawhill.ca/olc/conrad.

JOE FIORITO

The Fire Hall down the Street

As a child in Fort William (now Thunder Bay), Ontario, Joe Fiorito grew up hearing a wealth of family stories from his father, a notorious local character who delivered mail and played in dance-hall bands. "Who are we if not our stories?" Fiorito would ask years later as a much-loved newspaper columnist, repeating history by continuing to tell stories about characters in the neighbourhood, about people he met around town, about local heroes like the firefighters of our selection. Fiorito has lived in Montreal and written for the Montreal Gazette, *the* National Post *and the* Globe and Mail. *He now lives in Toronto where he is a city columnist for the* Toronto Star. *He also publishes books. In 1994 appeared* Comfort Me with Apples *and in 1996* Tango on the Main, *selections of his columns from the* Montreal Gazette. *In 1999 he published* The Closer We Are to Dying, *a bestselling memoir of 21 nights spent at his father's deathbed, and the harsh but beautiful family stories he heard there one last time. In 2003 appeared his Toronto-Book-Award-winning novel* The Song Beneath the Ice, *and then in 2006 another collection of his columns,* Union Station: Love, Madness, Sex and Survival on the Streets of the New Toronto. *From it comes our selection. "The Fire Hall down the Street" is typical of Fiorito's writing: direct, clear, stripped down, concrete, evocative.*

One block east of my house is Fire Station 15, the biggest and busiest fire hall in the city. I fall asleep to the sound of sirens, and far too often sirens wake me in the middle of the night. Once, instead of fighting sleep, I wandered over and hung around on full alert with the crew of Pumper Truck 15.

1

2   The night shift began at 4 p.m. with the placement of boots in overalls. And then the placement of boots-in-overalls by trucks, a timesaver, this: you run to your truck, you step in your boots, you pull up your overalls and off you go. Mostly you don't go anywhere. Mostly you sit and wait.

3   On this evening, Shaw is the captain, Galante is the driver and Lacey and Stawarek are the crew of the big red pumper truck. They are thick-wristed, strong-armed, short-haired guys, as easy in each other's company as ballplayers between innings. They wait and they drink coffee. They eat sweet buns and watch TV. They read the paper, crack jokes and plan vacations. In the summer, they wash their cars. In winter, they pump a little iron. They check their equipment— hoses, oxygen tanks, fire axes—every day of the year.

4   They eat supper together in the station every night, alongside the crews of two other trucks. They are a dozen men in total. How do they decide who cooks? Those who can, do.

5   On this evening, Shaw made fettucine with red sauce: he used tomatoes, tomato paste, onions, garlic, mushrooms, hot sausage, green peppers, zucchini and, he said, Al Pacinos. Al Pacinos?

6   "We used to have a captain here who couldn't say 'jalapenos.'"

7   Before the red sauce could come to a boil, they heard the familiar scritch and whirr of a computer printer. An incoming call; the corner of Howard Park and Dundas West. Plates down, everybody out, the Linh Son Buddhist temple is burning. Shaw took an extra moment to shut off, and then to double-check, each burner; it wouldn't be the first time a stove was left on in a fire hall.

8   Let's go, let's go, let's go, lights flashing, sirens wailing, cop cars blocking traffic when we arrived; there was a crowd in the street, the sky was dark, the night was cold and the flames were shooting upward. It looked bad. Four of the firemen scampered up ladders.

9   On the street, a small crowd surrounded three Buddhist nuns. The nuns wore yellow robes. Their heads were shaved. A woman in the crowd put her arm around the oldest nun to keep her warm. By now, the police had all the traffic under control. I asked the littlest nun a question. She smiled; she doesn't speak English.

10   A man stepped forward. He said, "I can translate."

11   Okay, is anyone still in the building?

The little nun smiled broadly and said nothing. Did you see any-   12
one start the fire? Smiled broadly, said nothing. Did you call? Smiled
broadly.

And then someone else stepped forward and whispered in the   13
translator's ear. He turned to me. "This nun doesn't speak."

Oh, you mean she's mute? More whispering. "No, she's a Buddhist   14
nun; she doesn't speak." Ah, I get it; she was mute for religious
reasons. Which posed a koan:° Who shouts "Fire!" in a Buddhist
temple?

No one, apparently. In any case, there was no need: a couple of   15
passersby noticed the flames and knocked on the door; when they
got no answer, they ran into the building and made sure all the nuns
escaped.

The Linh Son Buddhist temple is a gaudy red and yellow building;   16
the flames which leapt from the roof were also red and yellow.

Temple and flame, is there a difference?   17

Not to a firefighter. The blaze seemed isolated to a metre-square   18
black wooden box which housed an exhaust fan; the firefighters
prised apart the wooden box and doused the flames.

White smoke, rising like an offering to the heavens.   19

The firefighters checked the temple from top to bottom, to make   20
sure there was no more fire lurking. What's it like inside? "There's a
little water damage to one of the ceiling tiles, but the only smoke in
there is from incense." In other words, a good fire. Not much damage, not much danger, no lives lost, no men hurt; the building was
saved, the nuns were smiling and the men were clear to head home
for supper.

Fettucine with Al Pacinos.   21

The mood was good; the tension of the start of the shift had been   22
released. Captain Shaw reheated his red sauce and boiled water for
the fettucine. The sauce was sweet and thick, nippy from the jalapenos. Every man ate his fill. An old boy from the neighbourhood—
he is in the habit of dropping by at suppertime—was sitting in the

°koan: In Zen Buddhism, a story or statement that may not be understood logically, but that conveys
meaning, and perhaps a lesson, through intuition. "What is the sound of one hand clapping?" is a well-known
example.

office. Shaw looked at him, and he mimed dishing up a serving. "Oh, well; if there's plenty, I won't say no." The old man got a big bowl, no questions asked.

23 And after supper the firefighters washed his dishes with their own. All twelve men lent a hand scrubbing pots, drying plates and wiping tables. Everything was done in unison; intuitive, masculine, efficient. The leftover red sauce went into the freezer for a future pot of chili.

24 "Let me fill your cup," said Lacey. The coffee was weakly offensive, as if someone had been painting a watercolour of coffee and had dipped the brushes in water and had served that to drink. I was about to fend off his generosity when every man froze in mid-gesture: the scritch of the printer again. Wait for it, wait for the call: 55 Rankin Crescent. Oh-oh, that's a high-rise.

25 Boots on, in the truck, out the door; go, go, go again, again, again. Galante drove, Shaw rode shotgun; Lacey and Stawarek sat in back. The siren was sharp as a knife and the streets ran red with flashing lights. The temple was a good fire. No one likes a high-rise.

26 Halfway there, the pumper yielded the right of way to a pair of trucks from another station. Galante muttered, "Yeah, yeah, yeah; but they know we were here first."

27 In the lobby of 55 Rankin, the building super, a skinny man in a T-shirt, shifted his weight from one foot to another. It was all he could do; he waited, and by his side a salaryman with a cellphone waited, and near the door a woman in a green dress waited.

28 The fire alarm was deafening.

29 The captains of all three trucks stood alert, poised for action. A pair of firefighters headed up the stairs for the fourth floor, armed with pry bars. They returned after a few minutes, strolling casually. A faulty smoke detector; no sign of smoke. The super reset the alarm.

30 The building was silent once more.

31 Back at the station, most of the men turned in before midnight but some sat up, cracking their knuckles, tapping their fingers, flipping the soft pages of yesterday's papers; waiting, waiting.

32 Station 15 has taken calls as terrible as the rooming-house fire on Dowling Avenue in which three people died; and calls as absurd as the flaming toilet on the corner of Lisgar and Queen.

You never know; you wait. 33

Nearly half the calls are medical emergencies. A fire truck can 34
sometimes arrive on the scene faster than an ambulance, and while
paramedics don't put out fires, every fireman knows how to use a
defibrillator. Suddenly, three quick calls in succession:

1:25 a.m. A forty-year-old man in a rooming house, having trouble 35
breathing. He was also smoking a cigarette; he smelled vaguely of
solvents. He'll be fine; that is to say, he will be fine for a while.

2:44 a.m. An elderly woman with chest pains in a nursing home. She 36
is little more than a whisper in a nightgown; she takes oxygen from an
ambulance crew. She'll be fine; that, too, is a short-term call.

3:25 a.m. An alarm at the CNE. No traffic, no siren, no matter. 37
Gremlins or raccoons have tripped a security panel; another false
alarm. And so to bed.

Leaves blew past the station in the chill air, and weak sunlight 38
began to leak onto the street. No more fires now, no false alarms.
The day shift, smelling of cinnamon buns, rolled in. Shaw and
Galante, Lacey and Stawarek went home to get some rest.

I have trouble sleeping at night because I live within earshot of 39
Fire Station 15. Not true, not true. I sleep a little better.

EXPLORATIONS:

Joe Fiorito,
> *Union Station: Love, Madness, Sex and Survival on the Streets of the*
> *New Toronto*
> *The Song Beneath the Ice* (novel)
> *The Closer We Are to Dying* (family memoir)

http://www.thestar.com/comment/columnists/94546
http://en.wikipedia.org/wiki/Fire_department

STRUCTURE:

1. Read aloud in class the opening (par. 1) and the closing (par. 39)
   of Fiorito's essay. How are they coordinated? What effects do they

achieve together? And why does his THESIS STATEMENT not appear until the very last sentence of the essay?

2. To what extent is "The Fire Hall down the Street" a *narrative?* To what extent is it a *description?* Cite *examples* to support your answers.

3. In showing us a night in the life of the firefighters, Fiorito provides a large number of *examples* so we "see" his point that the actions and skills of the crew help him to "sleep a little better." Identify the most vivid of these *examples,* and tell how they support his argument.

STYLE:

1. "The Fire Hall down the Street" has one of the most INFORMAL styles of any piece in this book. Point out *examples* (such as the term "cop cars" in par. 8) where the author seems to be talking more than writing. Does this informal TONE work with his readers? Why would we not use it in an academic essay? Describe the audience you believe Fiorito is writing for.

2. "The Fire Hall down the Street" contains several partial sentences, such as "White smoke, rising like an offering to the heavens." Locate five more. Are these accidental, or are they deliberate, forming part of Fiorito's conversational, informal STYLE?

3. In paragraph 25 Fiorito writes that "The siren was sharp as a knife and the streets ran red with flashing lights." Find at least five more SENSE IMAGES. To what extent are they poetry? How do they increase the impact of this selection?

IDEAS FOR DISCUSSION AND WRITING:

1. Tell how the tragic events of 9/11 elevated firefighters, in the public eye, to the status of heroes. Name one other profession whose members, in your opinion, should be considered heroes. Tell why.

2. What are the main dangers that confront firefighters?

3. In his hundreds of columns about life in Montreal and, more recently, life in Toronto, Fiorito has reported much more good

than bad. People help one another. They may be down on their luck, but they keep trying. Their neighbourhood is a community, and everyone has a role to play there. In your own experience, is this an accurate view of life in the city? Gives *examples* to defend your answer.

4. Elsewhere in his book *Union Station,* Joe Fiorito asks "Who are we if not our stories?" He takes the time to observe the many "stories" all around him, then passes them on to us in his own columns. Why do stories fascinate us? Recall a human-interest "story" you recently observed in your own neighbourhood. Tell it to the class, and include *examples* that clearly convey the information.

5. PROCESS IN WRITING: *Joe Fiorito believes that people are basically good, and in his columns gives a multitude of examples to make his point. If you share his belief, do the same. Think of one big* example *(or several small examples) you have recently observed, that support a positive view of humankind. Take notes. Develop a* THESIS STATEMENT *(possibly at the end, like Fiorito's, or more likely near the beginning) that identifies your point and your view of it. Now write a quick draft of your argument, developing your point with the highest proportion of* example *content you can achieve. Later look it over. Is there an opening and a closing? Does everything support the main point? Is your draft concise? Do transition signals speed it on? Finally, check the spelling and punctuation before printing out your best version.*

Note: See also the Topics for Writing on the Online Learning Centre at www. mcgrawhill.ca/olc/conrad.

Goodbye Muse, Hello Prada

Born in Bosnia in 1952, Goran Simic had become a leading writer and intellectual of his country by the early 90s, when civil war broke out in Yugoslavia. With his Muslim wife and two young children, he spent a harrowing three years in the siege of Sarajevo, living the appalling events he would later describe so vividly in his poems. Then when in 1996 he and his family immigrated to this country, with the help of PEN Canada, he had a rude awakening: as he relates in this selection, what his new employers wanted was not his brain but his muscles. Yet despite the drudgery he so wittily depicts on these pages, Simic found time to resume his real career. In Yugoslavia he had edited several literary magazines, and published many books of short stories, plays, radio dramas and lyrics for opera. Then in 1997 Oxford Press published a collection of his powerful Sarajevo poems, Sprinting from the Graveyard, *translated by David Harsent. More poems followed:* Peace and War *in 1998,* Immigrant Blues *in 2003,* From Sarajevo with Sorrow *in 2005, and also in 2005 a book of short stories,* Yesterday's People. *By now Simic has published a dozen books, and has been translated into almost a dozen languages. He also writes essays, such as our lively and ironic selection from the February 24, 2000 Toronto* Globe and Mail.

1   "Y ou shouldn't have gone to another continent just to be a slave. You could get a better job here in Bosnia," my father told me bitterly last month when we met.

2   It was his honest reaction to my honest need to inform him, which I'd avoided for three years, about my job in Canada. I hadn't

84

expected he'd easily swallow the fact that I was no longer a bookshop owner or a book columnist, as I'd been in Sarajevo, but just a worker in a Holt Renfrew warehouse.

But I hadn't bargained with the words "labourer" and "North America" summoning to his mind historical images of black slaves in the American South toiling in the cotton fields, with me in the middle of them.

My brother was still a general in the army, my other brother was still a professor, but I'd switched from being a respectable poet to being a slave. What a disgrace to the family!

That moment I realized how much I'd erred in being honest with my father. At his age—almost 80—he accepted only good news. He'd had enough bad news the past few years. After having fought as a partisan during the Second World War and celebrated victory over fascism, he experienced the Bosnian war, which finished like a bad football game: 0-0, with 200,000 killed, and nothing to celebrate.

Instead of enjoying retirement in his own flat or in our family house in Sarajevo, he lives in a rented house in the middle of a nowhere village because a rural refugee family squatted in his flat and because our family home was plundered and destroyed by his former neighbours.

"You know why our neighbours will never invite me again to their homes?" he asked me sadly. "Because I would recognize some of my own furniture."

I didn't let him say all this happened just because he was a Serb, since I don't think there's a difference between Muslim and Serb thieves. They all have the same religion: robbery.

Then I tried to make him smile by putting all my effort into describing a Canada that is not the American South, and where there are no slaves.

After I came to Canada, it didn't take long to realize that poetry would not pay my bills. Moreover, judging by the public attention it received, poetry seemed like an unwanted pregnancy in the marriage between publishers and readers. "You're a poet, fine, but what's your real job?" I heard.

In my first Canadian job, I came to realize that the load of ideas and words I carried in my head was worth less than what I could lug on my back. At first I didn't understand this, not because of vanity or the feeling that a job labouring in a warehouse could ruin my poet's image, but because it didn't dawn on me that for $1,100 a month my muscles were going to be rented along with just 10 per cent of my brain. With the rest I could do whatever I wanted—but only at lunch break and after 4 p.m. Good-bye, muse. Hello, boss. I now understood that I was a replaceable wheel in a machine someone else made.

12   I got precious advice on how to save my soul from my old friend Sasha Bukvic, one of the best sculptors in the former Yugoslavia, who now worked at a job like mine. "Since you have to spend three hours on the commute, don't sleep on the buses or subway cars," he told me. "This is the time for who you are."

13   It wasn't easy to keep my eyelids open, but soon my favoured travelling companions were Milan Kundera, Jung Chang and Joseph Brodsky—all of them writers who lived outside their homelands. But the books didn't keep me from noticing how, at 6 a.m., the bus driving to Mississauga carried almost entirely first-generation immigrants. Only the driver was Canadian-born.

14   Alone among the 20 workers who came from all over the world—India, Iraq, Ethiopia—and who mostly worked scanning or marking down prices, I was the one who moved merchandise from world-famous clothing designers. Loading trucks, moving suits from one line to another, carting boxes, I soon realized how closely the prices of coats matched their weights.

15   On the one hand, I felt some designers had good fun searching for the quickest way to get money out of rich people's pockets. (Once I saw a Jamaican employee staring in disgust at the price tag of a Prada suit. The price was higher than his entire year's earnings.) On the other hand, it was a pleasure to handle a wardrobe I imagined myself wearing.

16   After a while I could recognize designers by their styles, the same way I would notice the difference between French surrealism and German symbolism, but I avoided saying this. Somebody might wickedly note that the difference between poetry and haute couture amounted to quite a few more zeros on the price tag.

The painter Johnny Cadiz, who worked with me for almost [17] two years, commented that our communication could be weirdly ambiguous:

"Where is Armani?" [18]

"He's in the room with Donna Karan." [19]

"Who hung up Calvin Klein on the rolling rack?" [20]

"What's Prada doing in the same box as the Boss?" [21]

I didn't spot any workers who weren't reading the horoscope in [22] the morning and weren't certain that next Friday they'd be Lotto 649 millionaires. It was amusing to listen to what they'd do with the money, but at the top of everybody's wish list was always: Quit this job immediately. What they'd say as a farewell to the managers was not generally to be found in dictionaries. But I heard worse cursing before Christmas when the managers announced that everyone would be laid off till the first week of the New Year.

To be honest, I didn't learn as much about the job as I learned [23] about my co-workers. You can learn quickly about a job, but you learn about people all your life. Some of them had lost everything, some had lost relatives, some held two jobs just to earn enough to bring their children here, or to feed their families. I asked myself who I was to think that my struggles were more important than theirs.

Once, at a PEN Canada° social gathering, I was introduced to [24] Hilary Weston, a nice woman who is Lieutenant-Governor of Ontario and married to the man who owns Holt Renfrew and many other enterprises. When I told her I worked in the Holt Renfrew warehouse she said, "Great! I hope one day you'll be manager." I didn't tell her I wanted to remain a writer.

As it happened, I met her again, two years later, this time on [25] Canada Book Day. After I told her I was quitting the job, she said, "Pity. But good luck."

I didn't tell my father any of this. He would have said, "What did I [26] tell you. There are still slaves in America!"

°PEN Canada: The Canadian branch of International PEN, a world association of writers that defends freedom of opinion and "campaigns on behalf of writers around the world persecuted for the expression of their thoughts." See http://www.pencanada.ca.

EXPLORATIONS:

Goran Simic,

> *Sprinting from the Graveyard* (poems, translated by David Harsent)
> *Immigrant Blues* (poems, translated by Amela Simic)
> *Selected Sorrows* (CD of his selected poems, set to music by Miro Brcic)

André Aciman, ed., *Letters of Transit: Reflections on Exile, Identity, Language, and Loss*

http://www.angelfire.com/poetry/goransimic
http://www.brickbooks.ca/BL-Simic.htm
http://www.sentinelpoetry.org.uk/online0805/index_files/page0002.htm
http://www.cbc.ca/wordsatlarge/blog/2007/10/goran_simic_interview.html

STRUCTURE:

1. A good opening attracts the reader's attention. Does this one? Point out every technique Simic uses in paragraph 1 to get us reading.
2. How far does the rest of Simic's introduction extend? What does the rest of it achieve?
3. Identify the THESIS STATEMENT.
4. The body of the argument (starting in par. 11) appears in *chronological* order. Point out several time signals that move us on to each new part of the author's Canadian experience.
5. It is *examples* that do the main work of supporting Simic's argument. Point out two or three of your favourites. Has Simic reached the recommended 50% of *example* content for effective essays? Have you? Calculate this percentage for your own most recent essay, and report it to the class.

STYLE:

1. When in paragraph 11 Simic says, "the load of ideas and words I carried in my head was worth less than what I could lug on my

back," he uses the power of IRONY. Point out five more strong ironies in this essay.

2. If the subject of "Goodbye Muse, Hello Prada" is loss and hard
   times, why does Simic use so much humour? Does this strengthen
   or weaken his message?

3. Read paragraphs 17 through 21 aloud. What is so weird about this
   conversation, and why?

IDEAS FOR DISCUSSION AND WRITING:

1. Why does society pay Goran Simic more for lugging suits and coats
   around a warehouse than for writing poetry? Which activity do you
   see as having more value? Defend your answer with reasons.

2. Have you or your family, like Simic, risked your profession by
   immigrating to Canada? Give every reason you can think of why
   a doctor, lawyer, teacher or writer would come here if it means
   going to work as a labourer, security guard or janitor.

3. Have you, like Simic, been a "slave" renting your muscles and 10%
   of your brain? Tell the techniques you have found for coping with
   such a job.

4. Simic reports that he earns $1100 a month. In your own town or
   city, how much must you make to rent housing? To buy a condo or
   house? To support a family? To buy the kinds of clothes our author
   lugs around the Holt Renfrew warehouse? Have you bought lottery tickets, like all Simic's co-workers, to solve these problems?
   Why or why not?

5. Like more and more employees, our author commutes three
   hours a day (par. 12). How long is your own trip to school or work?
   Tell what you do to make it more pleasant or productive. Sleep?
   Read? How serious a problem is traffic and commuting time in the
   place where you live? What can individuals do about it? What can
   government do?

6. PROCESS IN WRITING: *Close your eyes, and think of the worst job you
   have ever had. Now taking notes, fill a page with colourful examples of
   what it was like. Looking these over, put your overall point into a THESIS
   STATEMENT, then write a discovery draft, packing the argument with your
   examples. The next day, look again. Have you reached at least a 50%*

content of examples? *If not, add. Does each* example *support the overall point? If not, cut or revise. Is your* TONE *consistent (either humorous and ironic, like Simic's tone, or serious)? If not, revise. Finally, hone the spelling and punctuation before printing your best version to show the class.*

Note: See also the Topics for Writing on the Online Learning Centre at www. mcgrawhill.ca/olc/conrad.

Process in Writing: Guidelines

Follow at least some of these steps in developing your essay through examples (your teacher may suggest which ones).

1. Take time choosing your topic, then try it out through brainstorming or freewriting. Do you have something to say? Can you supply examples? If not, try another topic.
2. Visualize your AUDIENCE: What level of language, what TONE, what examples, will communicate with this person or persons? (Remember the kinds of examples listed in our chapter introduction.)
3. Do a rapid discovery draft. Do not stop now to fix things like spelling and punctuation; just get the material safely out on paper.
4. The next day, look this draft over. Do your examples make up at least 50% of the content? Or if you give one long example, do you explain in enough depth? If not, add. Does every example support your main point? If not, revise. Are examples in order of increasing importance? If not, consider rearranging to build a climax.
5. Now check for TRANSITIONS, and if necessary add. Test your prose by reading aloud, then revise awkward or unclear passages. Now use the dictionary and style guide if you need them.
6. Proofread your final copy slowly, word by word (if your eyes move too fast, they will "see" what should be there, not necessarily what is there).

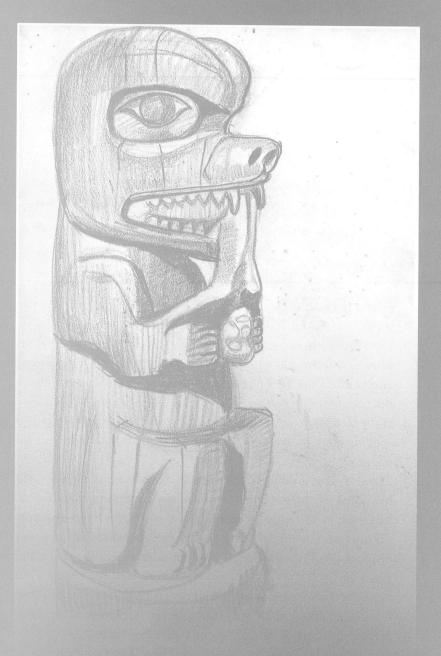

Image PDP00903. Courtesy of Royal BC Museum, BC Archives

The eyes were two rounds of black, set in wider rounds of white, and placed in deep sockets under wide, black eyebrows. Their fixed stare bored into me as if the very life of the old cedar looked out....

—Emily Carr, "D'Sonoqua"

DESCRIPTION

IT'S LARGE AND PURPLE AND....

Consider the writer's tools: words in rows on a page. The writer cannot use gestures, facial expression or voice, as the public speaker does. The writer cannot use colour, shape, motion or sound, as the filmmaker does. Yet words on a page can be powerful. We've all seen readers so involved in the words of a book that they fail to hear their own name called for dinner, or pass their own stop on the bus. These people have entered another world, living at second hand what a writer has lived or at least imagined at first hand.

How does writing do this to us? How does it make experience come alive? There are many ways, and one of the best is description. In simulating real life, description makes frequent appeals to our senses:

    sight   hearing   touch   smell   taste

In "D'Sonoqua," in this chapter, Emily Carr appeals to our senses of smell and sight together when she writes, "Smell and blurred light oozed thickly out of the engine room, and except for one lantern on the wharf everything else was dark." Then in the next paragraph she moves on to hearing and touch: "Every gasp of the engine shook us like a great sob."

In her first sentence alone, Christie McLaren shows us the "red hair and the purple dress" of her "Suitcase Lady" who sits "night after night" in the "harsh light of a 24-hour doughnut shop on Queen Street West." These details have already begun to "show" us one particular homeless person and her life.

In his selection, Rudy Wiebe makes sure we see, hear and even smell the escaped bull: the "body solid and thick as a steamer smoking across our yard," and the lips "twisting back above his gigantic teeth as he roared the smell [of manure] into the sky...." Wiebe makes it easy, indeed, for readers to share the terror of the three-year-old that Wiebe was when he witnessed this event.

Similarly, behind every descriptive choice you make, behind every image you give your reader, should be your own overall purpose. In a warmup exercise such as freewriting, or even as you begin a discovery draft, you may not yet know that purpose. But the act of writing should soon make it clear: Is your subject scary, inspiring, pitiful, exasperating, ugly, beautiful, calm or violent? Once you know, help your audience to know as well. In some pieces of descriptive writing, a thesis statement helps readers to grasp the point; other times, as is often the case in narratives, an "implied thesis statement" does the job (review the chapter introduction to "Narration," where this point is discussed).

Figures of speech—such as the similes and metaphors discussed in Chapter 6—are powerful tools of description. When Emily Carr writes that a person's face is "greeny-brown and wrinkled like a baked apple," we see old age clearly. In other places she uses onomatopoetic terms—words like "scuttled," "slithered," "grated" and "ooze"—that describe by sounding like what they mean. (See FIGURES OF SPEECH in the glossary.)

In a description some words are better than others. Use short and strong ones from everyday life, not the long and flabby ones that some would-be writers think are eloquent. Do we really "perspire" or do we "sweat"? "Ambulate" or "walk"? "Altercate" or "argue"?

"Masticate" or "chew"? "Expectorate" or "spit"? It is obvious that the second term in each case is stronger, more vivid, more descriptive. So why would we use the first?

Choose words that convey the right *feeling* as well as the right dictionary meaning. One student closed a pretty description of the ocean by saying "the water was as still as a pan full of oil." The image of water as oil may imply stillness, but this water is not exactly something we would want to dive into or even watch at sunset—we'd be too busy thinking of pollution! Another person described forest trees in autumn as being the colour of a fire engine. The colour may be right, but will the image of a large truck perched in the tree branches really give us that autumn feeling?

Take the time, then, to *feel*, as well as *think*, your words. Search drafts for weak or inexact or inappropriate terms, and replace them. If the right word doesn't come, find it in a dictionary or thesaurus. And realize that your electronic thesaurus may be fast, but a desk-size book version offers far more choices to help your overall idea or feeling, whatever it may be, come through clearly. One more thing: Do not let your search lead to wordiness. A paragraph of mostly small, strong, well-chosen words (what some writers have called "noun and verb language") can say more than a page of large and vague ones.

Note: Many authors in other chapters use description to help make their point. See especially these examples:

Patrick Lane, "There Is a Season," p. 37
Catherine Pigott, "Chicken-Hips," p. 196
Hugh MacLennan, "A Sound Beyond Hearing," p. 296
Dr. Mark Bernstein, "Yes, It Is Brain Surgery," p. 311
Candace Savage, "Stuck on the Prairies: Where Is Here?," p. 381
Joy Kogawa, "Grinning and Happy," p. 373
Lt.-Gen. Roméo Dallaire, "*Cri de coeur*," p. 414

CHRISTIE McLAREN

Suitcase Lady*

Christie McLaren lives in Canmore, Alberta, where she does freelance writing and editing. But it was in 1981, as a student at the University of Waterloo, that she spent a term reporting for the Toronto Globe and Mail *as part of her English co-op work experience: after spending several evenings with "the Vicomtesse," she heard the story that she reports in this selection. After graduating, McLaren spent a year and a half at the* Winnipeg Free Press, *then returned to the* Globe, *where she continued to report on many issues. An avid hiker, backpacker, skier and canoeist, McLaren channelled her love of the outdoors into several years of investigating forestry, energy and other environmental topics, as well as writing on national health policy and Ontario politics. Her articles have appeared also in* Nature Canada, Equinox *and* Explore Magazine. *Then in 2002 appeared her book on the Canadian forestry industry,* The Last Stand. *Though a professional journalist, McLaren says that "writing is nothing but pain while you're doing it and nothing but relief when it's done. Any joy or satisfaction, I think, is a bit of fleeting luck."*

1   Night after night, the woman with the red hair and the purple dress sits in the harsh light of a 24-hour doughnut shop on Queen Street West.

2   Somewhere in her bleary eyes and in the deep lines of her face is a story that probably no one will ever really know. She is taking pains to write something on a notepad and crying steadily.

*Editor's title.

96

She calls herself Vicomtesse Antonia The Linds'ays. She's the suitcase lady of Queen Street. 3

No one knows how many women there are like her in Toronto. 4
They carry their belongings in shopping bags and spend their days and nights scrounging for food. They have no one and nowhere to go.

This night, in a warm corner with a pot of tea and a pack of 5
Player's, the Vicomtesse is in a mood to talk.

Out of her past come a few scraps: a mother named Savaria; the 6
child of a poor family in Montreal; a brief marriage when she was 20; a son in Toronto who is now 40. "We never got along well because I didn't bring him up. I was too poor. He never call me mama."

She looks out the window. She's 60 years old. 7

With her words she spins herself a cocoon. She talks about drapes 8
and carpets, castles and kings. She often lapses into French. She lets her tea get cold. Her hands are big, rough, farmer's hands. How she ended up in the doughnut shop remains a mystery, maybe even to her.

"Before, I had a kitchen and a room and my own furniture. I had 9
to leave everything and go."

It's two years that she's been on the go, since the rooming houses 10
stopped taking her. "I don't have no place to stay."

So she walks. A sturdy coat covers her dress and worn leather boots 11
are on her feet. But her big legs are bare and chapped and she has a ragged cough.

Yes, she says, her legs get tired. She has swollen ankles and, with 12
no socks in her boots, she has blisters. She says she has socks—in the suitcase—but they make her feet itch.

As for money, "I bum on the street. I don't like it, but I have to. 13
I have to survive. The only pleasure I got is my cigaret." She lights another one. "It's not a life."

She recalls the Saturday, a long time ago, when she made $27, and 14
laughs when she tells about how she had to make the money last through Sunday, too. Now she gets "maybe $7 or $8," and eats "very poor."

When she is asked how people treat her, the answer is very matter-of- 15
fact: "Some give money. Some are very polite and some are rude."

16   In warm weather, she passes her time at the big square in front of City Hall. When it's cold she takes her suitcase west to the doughnut shop.

17   The waitresses who bring food to the woman look upon her with compassion. They persuaded their boss that her sitting does no harm.

18   Where does she sleep? "Any place I can find a place to sleep. In the park, in stores—like here I stay and sit, on Yonge Street." She shrugs. Sometimes she goes into an underground parking garage.

19   She doesn't look like she knows what sleep is. "This week I sleep three hours in four days. I feel tired but I wash my face with cold water and I feel okay." Some questions make her eyes turn from the window and stare hard. Then they well over with tears. Like the one about loneliness. "I don't talk much to people," she answers. "Just the elderly, sometimes, in the park."

20   Her suitcase is full of dreams.

21   Carefully, she unzips it and pulls out a sheaf of papers—"my concertos."

22   Each page is crammed with neatly written musical notes—the careful writing she does on the doughnut shop table—but the bar lines are missing. Questions about missing bar lines she tosses aside. Each "concerto" has a French name—Tresor, La Tempete, Le Retour—and each one bears the signature of the Vicomtesse. She smiles and points to one. "A very lovely piece of music. I like it."

23   She digs in her suitcase again, almost shyly, and produces a round plastic box. Out of it emerges a tiara. Like a little girl, she smooths back her dirty hair and proudly puts it on. No one in the doughnut shop seems to notice.

24   She cares passionately about the young, the old and the ones who suffer. So who takes care of the suitcase lady?

25   "God takes care of me, that's for sure," she says, nodding thoughtfully. "But I'm not what you call crazy about religion. I believe always try to do the best to help people—the elderly, and kids, and my country, and my city of Toronto, Ontario."

EXPLORATIONS:

Jack Layton, *Homelessness: The Making and Unmaking of a Crisis*
Marlene Webber, *Street Kids: The Tragedy of Canada's Runaways*
George Orwell, *Down and Out in Paris and London*
Rohinton Mistry, *A Fine Balance*
Susan Scott, *All Our Sisters: Stories of Homeless Women in Canada*
http://ryandale.org/ryanlinks.html
http://www.nationalhomeless.org
http://aspin.asu.edu/hpn
http://www.homelessness.gc.ca
http://www.parl.gc.ca/information/library/prbpubs/prb991-e.htm

STRUCTURE:

1. "Suitcase Lady" was a feature article in the Toronto *Globe and Mail*. As newspaper journalism, how does it differ from a typical ESSAY?
2. What does the opening *description* achieve?
3. How do the many quotations help the *description*?
4. Explain the IRONY of the closing.

STYLE:

1. Why is the vocabulary of "Suitcase Lady" so easy?
2. "With her words she spins herself a cocoon," states McLaren in paragraph 8. How appropriate is this METAPHOR?
3. Point out at least five concrete details that help you picture this homeless woman's life. Now think about your own writing: do you also give details, or do you hide behind GENERALIZATIONS?

IDEAS FOR DISCUSSION AND WRITING:

1. "It's not a life," says "the Vicomtesse" in paragraph 13. Is your province or city currently making life easier or harder for homeless people? Give *examples*.

2. How do you react to people who, like the suitcase lady, "bum on the street"? How often do you give? What makes you give to one person but not another?

3. In paragraph 6 the suitcase lady speaks of her son in Toronto: "We never got along well because I didn't bring him up. I was too poor. He never call me mama." In the area where you live, how much money does a family need to stay together? To avoid quarrels over money? To be hopeful about the future?

4. PROCESS IN WRITING: *Tape an interview with someone who in economic status, age, values or some other respect is very different from you. Then write a profile. Like McLaren, portray your subject through her or his best comments. Now add many* IMAGES *of physical appearance to build your* description. *Edit for conciseness and finally correctness. Then read your best version, with feeling, to the class.*

Note: See also the Topics for Writing on the Online Learning Centre at www. mcgrawhill.ca/olc/conrad.

RUDY WIEBE

The Bull*

The parents of Rudy Wiebe had fled the Soviet Union in 1930, escaping the anarchy that had brought persecution of their Mennonite community. Once in Canada they settled in an isolated farm village near Fairholme, Saskatchewan, where at the edge of the boreal forest they carved out their bush farm, spoke their ancestral language of Low German, and practised their Anabaptist religion in freedom. Here Rudy was born in 1934. Though he never spoke English until he began school, Wiebe was an eager student, devouring shelves of books, and eventually earning a B.A. from the University of Alberta, studying in Germany, and teaching at Goshen College in Indiana and then at the University of Alberta until his retirement. Meanwhile he has published many significant and original books, mostly novels. Some of the best have been his early controversial work, And Peace Shall Destroy Many *(1962), about the deep but sometimes rigid religious life of his childhood village;* The Temptations of Big Bear *(Governor General's Award, 1973), about the Christ-like struggles of the legendary Cree leader;* A Discovery of Strangers *(Governor General's Award, 1994), about the ill-fated Franklin expedition and the Native people it encountered in the Arctic; and* Of This Earth: A Mennonite Boyhood in the Boreal Forest *(2006), the autobiography from which our selection comes.*

The light and dark I lived in as a boy were the day and night of the sun; it was changed very little by barn lanterns or the solitary kerosene lamp with its elegant glass chimney on   1

*Editor's title.

our kitchen table. But wherever I was, I was inside family, and the kitchen, lit or unlit, shifted its shadows however I moved, behind the stove or the wood piled there, in the corners by the curtained cupboards and under the benches and table or beside the waterpail and washstand by the door: the light and the dark of the house, inside or out, held no fear. Not even the startling *crack!* of a wall log splitting as it dried in the winter cold. Wherever I walked or sat, whatever happened I had already seen or heard it before, smelled, or at the very least touched.

2   But every child, no matter how beloved, discovers some unknown to fear, and the earliest I remember was not the dark, or the wild weather of thunderstorms or blizzards, and certainly not the rustling boreal forest; it was fear of the bull. On a thirties homestead where no electricity or engines existed, the work and food animals can be as much fun and chaseable as a dog or squawky, scolding chickens, as frisky as calves sucking your fingers for milk or a mousing cat curled around your leg, but some farm animals are squat, thick, immovable as pigs, or enormous like cows and horses. One slight movement of their huge legs or heads, to say nothing of their gigantic bodies, can be unexpected and disastrous for a child. The horses I first became aware of were usually harnessed, attached to a wagon or farming machine, always haltered and bridled for control and you learned before you knew it from the very movements of adults, from the way father or brother handled them, your mother and sisters walked wide to climb into the wagon far from the huge heads tossing themselves against flies and mosquitoes and bulldogs (as we called biting horseflies), stomping hooves and the endless slash of tails, you understood these bodies had such immense, startling power that you would never climb through the barbed-wire fence into a pasture where they were grazing loose. Even at three you were not that stupid.

3   Nevertheless, farm animals were not necessarily easy to control. We lived on the outermost edge of the community and in summer anyone could herd their cattle on the unsettled free range west of us, wherever they found a hay slough or open clearing. Some even let their animals graze unattended for days because there were sloughs for watering everywhere, no large wild animals to fear and no possible thieves. So we're CPR lucky again, Pah said, forever optimistic,

a quarter right beside empty land, no need to chase our cattle for miles, all the free range we want right beside us. Nah yoh, well yes, our Mam was inclined by nature and grim experience to anticipate the worst, and so we also have the endless trample of neighbours' cattle across our land to and from the free range. And they were both right.

Individual farm herds were small, at most fifteen animals in the general poverty of the Depression, and each herd was belled for identification. Every morning my mother and sister milked our two or three cows, and then we would open the rails of the corral and our entire little herd would file away to graze for the day. We all knew the distinctive sound of our several bells and throughout the day we listened, tracking the distance they wandered to find grass. At times those sounds would vanish, sometimes when wavering summer heat lay over the wooded hills, when mosquitoes and bulldogs swarmed them, the cattle would lie motionless among thick willows to escape those pests and chew their cud. Then not a sound could be heard, and by early afternoon Mam would pull on her canvas shoes, slit to fit her painful bunions, and walk the cattle trails west with a saskatoon stick, taking Mary or perhaps even Helen along to help her listen to find them. And sometimes, in that wild land, it became a question of who was lost, the cattle or the searchers?

In our family, our mother did what needed to be done, always. For us small children the thought of Mam not knowing what to do on the farm was incredible; that she would not do whatever was necessary we could not imagine. But she had lived the first thirty-five years of her life in a Mennonite row village on the immense steppes sloping up to the wide Romanovka hills; she often could not recognize the features of this Canadian boreal landscape: it was empty in a way, yes, but also wildly endless and crowded, you could see nothing for bush! Walking, listening, straining to see while struggling over deadfall and through muskeg and around water sloughs and up the repeated rolls of hills, she lost any sense of where our house clearing might be. The search for cows became desperate then: they had to be found so they could lead her home. Where her children waited.

But a bull was coming! Mam and Mary and Carlo were searching for cattle again and only we three youngest were in our yard, playing tag and laughing and often standing still, listening for the cowbells we knew were ours, listening them closer, come, come home. And suddenly we heard a bull bellow, and saw it, and we ran into the house terrified.

7   The bull came across Louis Ulmer's field and through the willow fence beside our house as if it wasn't there, bellowing, his enormous head, his horns curled forward above his wiry, white face, red body solid and thick as a steamer smoking across our yard, snuffling at the barn and manure pile, tossing chunks high with his horns and lifting his head, lips twisting back above his gigantic teeth as he roared the smell into the sky; we could see the steel ring in his nose flip upwards as we peered through the useless glass of windows. If he saw us move he'd charge the house, the kitchen door would crumple with one heave of his head, we'd have to be up the stairs like lightning before— but Mam! Mary!—if they came home with the cows he'd trample and horn them into dust, we were all three crying and trying not to move to attract the bull's attention, but we had to look out to know where he was, to see what that wille Tiea, wild beast was doing—Pah was there!

8   Walking straight from where our wagon trail bent out of the trees and across the yard to the barn, a long poplar in his hand. The bull turned, stared, hooked up a sod of rage with his left hoof and Pah hit him smash on the ring in his nose so hard we could hear the *thud*! in the house and the bull wheeled and Pah sliced him one across both flanks and the bull galumphed away, kicking up his heels as if he was doing exactly what he wanted but he was running—towards us staring from the window!—past the corner of the kitchen, crashing through the fence back into Louis Ulmer's field again, his tail up and bucking high, the thin green summer shit squirting from his smeared buttocks. We ran out the door, Pah was home and Mam and Mary were coming waving poplar branches to fend off mosquitoes, we could hear the cowbells just beyond the barn and Carlo barking, we were laughing and crying at the same time.

9   "You don't have to be scared," Pah said. "Just Loewen's scrub Mejchel."

Mejchel, prejchel, loht mie läwe
Dee baste Koo woa etj die gäwe....

Michael, prichael, let me live
The best cow to you I'll give....

That Low German skipping song goes on for as many verses as you   10
can invent, but we were running wildly down the slope of the yard
towards the cattle corral, shouting, swinging the empty milk pails
over our heads.

EXPLORATIONS:

Rudy Wiebe,
>   *Of This Earth: A Mennonite Boyhood in the Boreal Forest* (memoir)
>   *A Discovery of Strangers* (novel)
>   *The Temptations of Big Bear* (novel)
>   *And Peace Shall Destroy Many* (novel)

Arthur Kroeger, *Hard Passage: A Mennonite Family's Long Journey from Russia to Canada*

Miriam Toews, *A Complicated Kindness* (novel)

Sinclair Ross, *As for Me and My House* (novel)

http://en.wikipedia.org/wiki/Rudy_Wiebe

http://www.enotes.com/contemporary-literary-criticism/wiebe-rudy-vol-137

STRUCTURE:

1. This passage is a self-contained section of Wiebe's childhood memoir. To what extent is it a *narrative* as well as a *description?* Does it begin and end at the right places? Is there any unnecessary content, or does everything contribute toward the overall meanings?

2. Point out Wiebe's THESIS STATEMENT.

3. If the reason for *description* is to show what something was like, where does Wiebe most strongly succeed in this goal? Point out five of the most vividly *descriptive* passages in this selection.

4. Though *Of This Earth* is nonfiction, Rudy Wiebe is best known as a novelist. Have you noticed any novelistic liberties he has taken

with structural elements such as paragraph lengths, sentence lengths and grammatical structure? If so, point out examples.

5. Read aloud the final sentence of this piece. How does the image of children swinging empty milk pails over their heads bring the story of the bull to a meaningful conclusion?

STYLE:

1. Growing up on a prairie homestead among Mennonite refugees from the chaos of Russia, young Wiebe never learned English till he began school. Do you like his technique of quoting rhymes about the bull in his native tongue of Low German (par. 9)? Can a tiny artifact like this help *describe* a culture? And why learn about other cultures?

2. Can you read the second sentence of paragraph 8 all in one breath? Try. Or do its 107 words leave you "breathless"? Is this sentence too much, or do its onrushing clauses, and all of its "and"s, build some desired effect? If so, what is that effect?

3. Describing the interior of the family cabin, Wiebe writes in paragraph 1, "Wherever I walked or sat, whatever happened I had already seen or heard it before, smelled, or at the very least touched." Look this whole section over again. Find one example each of SENSE IMAGES appealing to hearing, sight, smell, touch, and taste.

IDEAS FOR DISCUSSION AND WRITING:

1. *Of This Earth*, the book from which our selection comes, is the story of Rudy Wiebe's early life. Why write autobiography? What can it do for the author? For the readers? Which other selections, up to this point in our book, are mostly autobiographical? Which of these do you like most, and why?

2. Wiebe writes in his introduction that, as a young child, he feared very little on the farm—except for the bull. What were your main fears as a child? And did you overcome them? Now what are your main fears as an adult? Did you notice places in Wiebe's description where, as a three-year-old, his fears of the bull went beyond

reason (for example, his thought that the beast could break into the house, and the children would have to escape by going upstairs)? Did the father, "Pah," also experience fear, or was subduing the animal just part of a day's work on the farm?

3. Statistically, farming is one of the most dangerous of all occupations. Did you grow up on a farm? If so, give examples of what can happen.

4. Why is the bull such an IMAGE of power and danger? Have you seen *corridas* in the bullring or bull-riding events in rodeos? How did you react? Do humans need to fear something? Why have Godzilla, King Kong, Dracula, Frankenstein's creation and other monsters been the subjects of so many horror movies?

5. How much do you know about the Mennonites? (Visit some websites on this topic.) How has this group, like so many other groups of immigrants to Canada, kept its culture relatively intact for so long? Why keep and cherish one's original culture, beliefs and language? Are you from a background of immigration? To what extent has your family preserved its own heritage? And why?

6. PROCESS IN WRITING: *Wiebe powerfully* describes *the environment of his early childhood. Now do the same for yours. Start by* describing *the interior and exterior of the family house or apartment, as Wiebe does, and from there move to a major event that occurred there. Did the event produce fear, as in the appearance of the bull, or did it involve pride, love or some other emotion? You decide. Take a page of notes. Choose a* thesis statement *(like Wiebe's in the first sentence of paragraph 2), which announces your main subject and your view of it. Now draft a quick version of the event, filling it with* descriptions *that make it come alive. (If possible, include* images *of hearing, sight, smell, touch and taste.) Later look it all over. Does everything contribute to the same overall effect? Do TRANSITIONS speed the action? Now read the* description *aloud to detect wordiness or rough sentence structure. Finally, print out your best version, and bring it to class prepared to share.*

Note: See also the Topics for Writing on the Online Learning Centre at www. mcgrawhill.ca/olc/conrad.

CHARLES YALE HARRISON

In the Trenches

Charles Yale Harrison (1898–1954) was born in Philadelphia and grew up in Montreal. His independent spirit revealed itself early: in grade four he condemned Shakespeare's The Merchant of Venice *as anti-Semitic, and when his teacher beat him he quit school. At 16 he went to work for the* Montreal Star *and at 18 joined the Canadian army. As a machine gunner in France and Belgium during 1917 and 1918, Harrison witnessed the gruesome front-line scenes he was later to describe in fiction. He was wounded at Amiens and decorated for bravery in action. After the war Harrison returned to Montreal but soon left for New York, where he began a career in public relations for the labour movement and for numerous humanitarian causes. He also wrote several books, both nonfiction and fiction. By far the best is* Generals Die in Bed, *an account of trench warfare that shocked the public and became the best seller of 1930. Spare in style, biting and vivid, this autobiographical novel was described by the* New York Evening Post *as "the best of the war books." From it comes our selection.*

1   We leave the piles of rubble that was once a little Flemish peasant town and wind our way, in Indian file, up through the muddy communication trench. In the dark we stumble against the sides of the trench and tear our hands and clothing on the bits of embedded barbed wire that runs through the earth here as though it were a geological deposit.

2   Fry, who is suffering with his feet, keeps slipping into holes and crawling out, all the way up. I can hear him coughing and panting behind me.

I hear him slither into a water-filled hole. It has a green scum on it. Brown and I fish him out.   3

"I can't go any farther," he wheezes. "Let me lie here, I'll come on later."   4

We block the narrow trench and the oncoming men stumble on us, banging their equipment and mess tins on the sides of the ditch. Some trip over us. They curse under their breaths.   5

Our captain, Clark, pushes his way through the mess. He is an Imperial, an Englishman, and glories in his authority.   6

"So it's you again," he shouts. "Come on, get up. Cold feet, eh, getting near the line?"   7

Fry mumbles something indistinctly. I, too, offer an explanation. Clark ignores me.   8

"Get up, you're holding up the line," he says to Fry.   9

Fry does not move.   10

"No wonder we're losing the bloody war," Clark says loudly. The men standing near-by laugh. Encouraged by his success, the captain continues: 11

"Here, sergeant, stick a bayonet up his behind—that'll make him move." A few of us help Fry to his feet, and somehow we manage to keep him going.   12

We proceed cautiously, heeding the warnings of those ahead of us. At last we reach our positions.   13

It is midnight when we arrive at our positions. The men we are relieving give us a few instructions and leave quickly, glad to get out.   14

It is September and the night is warm. Not a sound disturbs the quiet. Somewhere away far to our right we hear the faint sound of continuous thunder. The exertion of the trip up the line has made us sweaty and tired. We slip most of our accouterments off and lean against the parados. We have been warned that the enemy is but a few hundred yards off, so we speak in whispers. It is perfectly still. I remember nights like this in the Laurentians. The harvest moon rides overhead.   15

Our sergeant, Johnson, appears around the corner of the bay, stealthily like a ghost. He gives us instructions: 16

17   "One man up on sentry duty! Keep your gun covered with the rubber sheet! No smoking!"

18   He hurries on to the next bay. Fry mounts the step and peers into No Man's Land. He is rested now and says that if he can only get a good pair of boots he will be happy. He has taken his boots off and stands in his stockinged feet. He shows us where his heel is cut. His boots do not fit. The sock is wet with blood. He wants to take his turn at sentry duty first so that he can rest later on. We agree.

19   Cleary and I sit on the firing-step and talk quietly.

20   "So this is war."

21   "Quiet."

22   "Yes, just like the country back home, eh?"

23   We talk of the trench; how we can make it more comfortable.

24   We light cigarettes against orders and cup our hands around them to hide the glow. We sit thinking. Fry stands motionless with his steel helmet shoved down almost over his eyes. He leans against the parapet motionless. There is a quiet dignity about his posture. I remember what we were told at the base about falling asleep on sentry duty. I nudge his leg. He grunts.

25   "Asleep?" I whisper.

26   "No," he answers, "I'm all right."

27   "What do you see?"

28   "Nothing. Wire and posts."

29   "Tired?"

30   "I'm all right."

31   The sergeant reappears after a while. We squinch our cigarettes.

32   "Everything O.K. here?"

33   I nod.

34   "Look out over there. They got the range on us. Watch out."

35   We light another cigarette. We continue our aimless talk.

36   "I wonder what St. Catherine Street looks like—"

37   "Same old thing, I suppose—stores, whores, theaters—"

38   "Like to be there just the same—"

39   "Me too."

40   We sit and puff our fags for half a minute or so.

41   I try to imagine what Montreal looks like. The images are murky. All that is unreality. The trench, Cleary, Fry, the moon overhead— this is real.

In his corner of the bay Fry is beginning to move from one foot to   42
another. It is time to relieve him. He steps down and I take his place.
I look into the wilderness of posts and wire in front of me.

After a while my eyes begin to water. I see the whole army of wire   43
posts begin to move like a silent host towards me.

I blink my eyes and they halt.   44

I doze a little and come to with a jerk.   45

So this is war, I say to myself again for the hundredth time. Down   46
on the firing-step the boys are sitting like dead men. The thunder to
the right has died down. There is absolutely no sound.

I try to imagine how an action would start. I try to fancy the pre-   47
liminary bombardment. I remember all the precautions one has
to take to protect one's life. Fall flat on your belly, we had been
told time and time again. The shriek of the shell, the instructor
in trench warfare said, was no warning because the shell traveled
faster than its sound. First, he had said, came the explosion of the
shell—then came the shriek and then you hear the firing of the
gun....

From the stories I heard from veterans and from newspaper   48
reports I conjure up a picture of an imaginary action. I see myself
getting the Lewis gun in position. I see it spurting darts of flame into
the night. I hear the roar of battle. I feel elated. Then I try to fancy
the horrors of the battle. I see Cleary, Fry and Brown stretched out
on the firing-step. They are stiff and their faces are white and set in
the stillness of death. Only I remain alive.

An inaudible movement in front of me pulls me out of the dream.   49
I look down and see Fry massaging his feet. All is still. The moon sets
slowly and everything becomes dark.

The sergeant comes into the bay again and whispers to me: 50

"Keep your eyes open now—they might come over on a raid now   51
that it's dark. The wire's cut over there—" He points a little to my
right.

I stand staring into the darkness. Everything moves rapidly again as   52
I stare. I look away for a moment and the illusion ceases.

Something leaps towards my face.   53

I jerk back, afraid.   54

Instinctively I feel for my rifle in the corner of the bay.   55

It is a rat.   56

57   It is as large as a tom-cat. It is three feet away from my face and it looks steadily at me with its two staring, beady eyes. It is fat. Its long tapering tail curves away from its padded hindquarters. There is still a little light from the stars and this light shines faintly on its sleek skin. With a darting movement it disappears. I remember with a cold feeling that it was fat, and why.

58   Cleary taps my shoulder. It is time to be relieved.

59   Over in the German lines I hear quick, sharp reports. Then the red-tailed comets of the *minenwerfer*° sail high in the air, making parabolas of red light as they come towards us. They look pretty, like the fireworks when we left Montreal. The sergeant rushes into the bay of the trench, breathless. "Minnies," he shouts, and dashes on.

60   In that instant there is a terrific roar directly behind us.

61   The night whistles and flashes red.

62   The trench rocks and sways.

63   Mud and earth leap into the air, come down upon us in heaps.

64   We throw ourselves upon our faces, clawing our nails into the soft earth in the bottom of the trench.

65   Another!

66   This one crashes to splinters about twenty feet in front of the bay.

67   Part of the parapet caves in.

68   We try to burrow into the ground like frightened rats.

69   The shattering explosions splinter the air in a million fragments. I taste salty liquid on my lips. My nose is bleeding from the force of the detonations.

70   SOS flares go up along our front calling for help from our artillery. The signals sail into the air and explode, giving forth showers of red, white and blue lights held aloft by a silken parachute.

71   The sky is lit by hundreds of fancy fireworks like a night carnival.

72   The air shrieks and cat-calls.

73   Still they come.

74   I am terrified. I hug the earth, digging my fingers into every crevice, every hole.

°*minenwerfer*: Mine-throwing trench mortars.

A blinding flash and an exploding howl a few feet in front of the   75
trench.

My bowels liquefy.   76

Acrid smoke bites the throat, parches the mouth. I am beyond   77
mere fright. I am frozen with an insane fear that keeps me cowering
in the bottom of the trench. I lie flat on my belly, waiting....

Suddenly it stops.   78

The fire lifts and passes over us to the trenches in the rear.   79

We lie still, unable to move. Fear has robbed us of the power to   80
act. I hear Fry whimpering near me. I crawl over to him with great
effort. He is half covered with earth and débris. We begin to dig
him out.

To our right they have started to shell the front lines. It is about   81
half a mile away. We do not care. We are safe.

Without warning it starts again.   82

The air screams and howls like an insane woman.   83

We are getting it in earnest now. Again we throw ourselves face   84
downward on the bottom of the trench and grovel like savages
before this demoniac frenzy.

The concussion of the explosions batters against us.   85

I am knocked breathless.   86

I recover and hear the roar of the bombardment.   87

It screams and rages and boils like an angry sea. I feel a prickly   88
sensation behind my eyeballs.

A shell lands with a monster shriek in the next bay. The concussion   89
rolls me over on my back. I see the stars shining serenely above us.
Another lands in the same place. Suddenly the stars revolve. I land
on my shoulder. I have been tossed into the air.

I begin to pray.   90

"God—God—please ..."   91

I remember that I do not believe in God. Insane thoughts race   92
through my brain. I want to catch hold of something, something that
will explain this mad fury, this maniacal congealed hatred that pours
down on our heads. I can find nothing to console me, nothing to
appease my terror. I know that hundreds of men are standing a mile
or two from me pulling gun-lanyards, blowing us to smithereens. I
know that and nothing else.

93   I begin to cough. The smoke is thick. It rolls in heavy clouds over the trench, blurring the stabbing lights of the explosions.

94   A shell bursts near the parapet.

95   Fragments smack the sandbags like a merciless shower of steel hail.

96   A piece of mud flies into my mouth. It is cool and refreshing. It tastes earthy.

97   Suddenly it stops again.

98   I bury my face in the cool, damp earth. I want to weep. But I am too weak and shaken for tears.

99   We lie still, waiting....

EXPLORATIONS:

Charles Yale Harrison, *Generals Die in Bed*

Erich Maria Remarque, *All Quiet on the Western Front* (novel)

Ernest Hemingway, *A Farewell to Arms* (novel)

Timothy Findley, *The Wars* (novel)

Heather Robertson, ed., *A Terrible Beauty: The Art of Canada at War*

Tim Cook, *At the Sharp End: Canadians Fighting the Great War 1914–1916*

http://en.wikipedia.org/wiki/World_War_1

http://www.rootsweb.com/~ww1can/index.html

http://www.firstworldwar.com

http://www.worldwar1.com

http://gutenberg.net.au/ebooks05/0500061h.html

http://www.collectionscanada.gc.ca/firstworldwar/index-e.html

STRUCTURE:

1. In *narrating* his description of trench warfare, does Harrison ever deviate from straight chronological order? If so, where and how?

2. Harrison uses SENSE IMAGES so often that throughout this passage *description* carries the main weight of development. Find one example each of a strong appeal to our senses of sight, hearing, touch, taste and smell.

3. Many of the paragraphs are small, some only a word or two long. Examine paragraphs 25–30, 53–56, and 60–68, determining in each passage why the paragraphs are so short.

4. This account of an artillery attack ends with the words "We lie still, waiting...." Is the ending effective, and if so, how?

STYLE:

1. What degree of CONCISENESS has Harrison achieved in this selection?

2. Harrison tells of the rat: "I remember with a cold feeling that it was fat, and why" (par. 57). How does he convey so much horror in so few words?

3. Analyze the power of the deceptively simple events of paragraph 89: "A shell lands with a monster shriek in the next bay. The concussion rolls me over on my back. I see the stars shining serenely above us. Another lands in the same place. Suddenly the stars revolve. I land on my shoulder. I have been tossed into the air."

4. In describing, Harrison exploits FIGURES OF SPEECH. Point out at least one good SIMILE and one good METAPHOR.

5. Why is "In the Trenches" told in present tense, even though the book was published years after the war?

IDEAS FOR DISCUSSION AND WRITING:

1. Our narrator relates his first experience of war. What has it taught him?

2. Have you read books or seen films that show war in a positive light? Name them. In what ways does "In the Trenches" differ from those accounts?

3. "In the Trenches" is part of a book entitled *Generals Die in Bed.* Discuss the implications of this title.

4. If you have read "Coming of Age in Putnok," compare the conflict described by George Gabori with that described by Harrison. Does hostility between individuals contribute to hostility between nations?

5. **PROCESS IN WRITING:** *Have you lived through a violent or even life-threatening experience, as Harrison did? Close your eyes and remember it. Then in a rapid first draft,* describe *to your audience what it was really like. How did things look, sound, feel, smell or even taste? Use SENSE IMAGES, as Harrison does, to help your reader know too. The next day look your* description *over. Does it begin and end at the right spots, to emphasize the important things? If not, chop or add. Are there unimportant details? If so, chop. Are some parts "thin"? If so, add. Are paragraphs longer in the slower parts and shorter in the tenser parts, like Harrison's? If not, adjust them. Finally, edit for correctness and style before producing your final version.*

Note: See also the Topics for Writing on the Online Learning Centre at www. mcgrawhill.ca/olc/conrad.

EMILY CARR

D'Sonoqua

Although Emily Carr (1871–1945) was born to a conservative family in the confined atmosphere of 19th-century Victoria, British Columbia, she emerged as one of the nation's most original painters and writers. Strong-willed and independent, she turned down several offers of marriage because she believed men "demanded worship" and would only hold her back. Instead she pursued her goal to San Francisco, London and Paris, studying art. Home again, with a new way of seeing inspired by postimpressionist artists in France, she set out on solo expeditions to remote Indian villages along the coast and in the Queen Charlotte Islands, where she put on canvas the power she felt in the ruins of ancient cultures. Our selection describes three such trips. The public laughed at her bold and free art, but she kept on. Around 1929 Carr shifted focus to the paintings she is best known for now, her looming, explosive visions of the coastal rainforest itself. Emily Carr lived for years in poverty, because recognition came late. For years she managed a rooming house, and would often paint on cardboard because canvas cost too much. In her last years, plagued by ill health, she abandoned painting for writing. Our selection comes from her first and best book, published in 1941, Klee Wyck *(the title is her name, "Laughing One," given her by the Nootka people).* Klee Wyck *is an extension of her painting: a collection of word sketches in language rich and suggestive, yet pared to the bone. During her lifetime she published two more volumes,* The Book of Small *(1942) and* The House of All Sorts *(1944). Others appeared after her death:* Growing Pains *(autobiography, 1946),* The Heart of a Peacock *(1953),* Pause: A Sketch Book *(1953), and finally her journals, published as* Hundreds and Thousands *(1966).*

1 I was sketching in a remote Indian village when I first saw her. The village was one of those that the Indians use only for a few months in each year; the rest of the time it stands empty and desolate. I went there in one of its empty times, in a drizzling dusk.

2 When the Indian agent dumped me on the beach in front of the village, he said "There is not a soul here. I will come back for you in two days." Then he went away.

3 I had a small Griffon dog with me, and also a little Indian girl, who, when she saw the boat go away, clung to my sleeve and wailed, "I'm 'fraid."

4 We went up to the old deserted Mission House. At the sound of the key in the rusty lock, rats scuttled away. The stove was broken, the wood wet. I had forgotten to bring candles. We spread our blankets on the floor, and spent a poor night. Perhaps my lack of sleep played its part in the shock that I got, when I saw her for the first time.

5 Water was in the air, half mist, half rain. The stinging nettles, higher than my head, left their nervy smart on my ears and forehead, as I beat my way through them, trying all the while to keep my feet on the plank walk which they hid. Big yellow slugs crawled on the walk and slimed it. My feet slipped, and I shot headlong to her very base, for she had no feet. The nettles that were above my head reached only to her knee.

6 It was not the fall alone that jerked the "Oh's" out of me, for the great wooden image towering above me was indeed terrifying.

7 The nettle-bed ended a few yards beyond her, and then a rocky bluff jutted out, with waves battering it below. I scrambled up and went out on the bluff, so that I could see the creature above the nettles. The forest was behind her, the sea in front.

8 Her head and trunk were carved out of, or rather into, the bole of a great red cedar. She seemed to be part of the tree itself, as if she had grown there at its heart, and the carver had only chipped away the outer wood so that you could see her. Her arms were spliced and socketed to the trunk, and were flung wide in a circling, compelling movement. Her breasts were two eagle heads, fiercely carved. That much, and the column of her great neck, and her strong chin, I had seen when I slithered to the ground beneath her. Now I saw her face.

9 The eyes were two rounds of black, set in wider rounds of white, and placed in deep sockets under wide, black eyebrows. Their fixed

stare bored into me as if the very life of the old cedar looked out, and it seemed that the voice of the tree itself might have burst from that great round cavity, with projecting lips, that was her mouth. Her ears were round, and stuck out to catch all sounds. The salt air had not dimmed the heavy red of her trunk and arms and thighs. Her hands were black, with blunt finger-tips painted a dazzling white. I stood looking at her for a long, long time.

The rain stopped, and white mist came up from the sea, gradually 10 paling her back into the forest. It was as if she belonged there, and the mist were carrying her home. Presently the mist took the forest too, and, wrapping them both together, hid them away.

"Who is that image?" I asked the little Indian girl, when I got back 11 to the house.

She knew which one I meant, but to gain time, she said, "What 12 image?"

"The terrible one, out there on the bluff." The girl had been to 13 Mission School, and fear of the old, fear of the new, struggled in her eyes. "I dunno," she lied.

I never went to that village again, but the fierce wooden image 14 often came to me, both in my waking and in my sleeping.

Several years passed, and I was once more sketching in an Indian vil- 15 lage. There were Indians in this village, and in a mild backward way it was "going modern." That is, the Indians had pushed the forest back a little to let the sun touch the new buildings that were replacing the old community houses. Small houses, primitive enough to a white man's thinking, pushed here and there between the old. Where some of the big community houses had been torn down, for the sake of the lumber, the great corner posts and massive roof-beams of the old structure were often left, standing naked against the sky, and the new little house was built inside, on the spot where the old one had been.

It was in one of these empty skeletons that I found her again. She 16 had once been a supporting post for the great centre beam. Her pole-mate, representing the Raven, stood opposite her, but the beam that had rested on their heads was gone. The two poles faced in, and one judged the great size of the house by the distance between them. The corner posts were still in place, and the earth floor, once beaten to the hardness of rock by naked feet, was carpeted now with rich lush grass.

17 I knew her by the stuck-out ears, shouting mouth, and deep eye-sockets. These sockets had no eye-balls, but were empty holes, filled with stare. The stare, though not so fierce as that of the former image, was more intense. The whole figure expressed power, weight, domination, rather than ferocity. Her feet were planted heavily on the head of the squatting bear, carved beneath them. A man could have sat on either huge shoulder. She was unpainted, weather-worn, sun-cracked, and the arms and hands seemed to hang loosely. The fingers were thrust into the carven mouths of two human heads, held crowns down. From behind, the sun made unfathomable shadows in eye, cheek and mouth. Horror tumbled out of them.

18 I saw [...] Tom on the beach, and went to him.

19 "Who is she?"

20 The Indian's eyes, coming slowly from across the sea, followed my pointing finger. Resentment showed in his face, greeny-brown and wrinkled like a baked apple,—resentment that white folks should pry into matters wholly Indian.

21 "Who is that big carved woman?" I repeated.

22 "D'Sonoqua." No white tongue could have fondled the name as he did.

23 "Who is D'Sonoqua?"

24 "She is the wild woman of the woods."

25 "What does she do?"

26 "She steals children."

27 "To eat them?"

28 "No, she carries them to her caves; that," pointing to a purple scar on the mountain across the bay, "is one of her caves. When she cries 'OO-oo-oo-oeo,' Indian mothers are too frightened to move. They stand like trees, and the children go with D'Sonoqua."

29 "Then she is bad?"

30 "Sometimes bad ... sometimes good," Tom replied, glancing furtively at those stuck-out ears. Then he got up and walked away.

31 I went back, and, sitting in front of the image, gave stare for stare. But her stare so over-powered mine, that I could scarcely wrench my

eyes away from the clutch of those empty sockets. The power that I felt was not in the thing itself, but in some tremendous force behind it, that the carver had believed in.

A shadow passed across her hands and their gruesome holdings.   32
A little bird, with its beak full of nesting material, flew into the cavity of her mouth, right in the pathway of that terrible OO-oo-oo-oeo. Then my eye caught something that I had missed—a tabby cat asleep between her feet.

This was D'Sonoqua, and she was a supernatural being, who   33
belonged to these Indians.

"Of course," I said to myself, "I do not believe in supernatural   34
beings. Still—who understands the mysteries behind the forest? What would one do if one did meet a supernatural being?" Half of me wished that I could meet her, and half of me hoped I would not.

Chug—chug—the little boat had come into the bay to take me to   35
another village, more lonely and deserted than this. Who knew what I should see there? But soon supernatural beings went clean out of my mind, because I was wholly absorbed in being naturally seasick.

When you have been tossed and wracked and chilled, any wharf   36
looks good, even a rickety one, with its crooked legs stockinged in barnacles. Our boat nosed under its clammy darkness, and I crawled up the straight slimy ladder, wondering which was worse, natural seasickness, or supernatural "creeps." The trees crowded to the very edge of the water, and the outer ones, hanging over it, shadowed the shoreline into a velvet smudge. D'Sonoqua might walk in places like this. I sat for a long time on the damp, dusky beach, waiting for the stage. One by one dots of light popped from the scattered cabins, and made the dark seem darker. Finally the stage came.

We drove through the forest over a long straight road, with black   37
pine trees marching on both sides. When we came to the wharf the little gas mail-boat was waiting for us. Smell and blurred light oozed thickly out of the engine room, and except for one lantern on the wharf everything else was dark. Clutching my little dog, I sat on the mail sacks which had been tossed on to the deck.

38   The ropes were loosed, and we slid out into the oily black water. The moon that had gone with us through the forest was away now. Black pine-covered mountains jagged up on both sides of the inlet like teeth. Every gasp of the engine shook us like a great sob. There was no rail round the deck, and the edge of the boat lay level with the black slithering horror below. It was like being swallowed again and again by some terrible monster, but never going down. As we slid through the water, hour after hour, I found myself listening for the OO-oo-oo-oeo.

39   Midnight brought us to a knob of land, lapped by the water on three sides, with the forest threatening to gobble it up on the fourth. There was a rude landing, a rooming-house, an eating-place, and a store, all for the convenience of fishermen and loggers. I was given a room, but after I had blown out my candle, the stillness and the darkness would not let me sleep.

40   In the brilliant sparkle of the morning when everything that was not superlatively blue was superlatively green, I dickered with a man who was taking a party up the inlet that he should drop me off at the village I was headed for.

41   "But," he protested, "there is nobody there."

42   To myself I said, "There is D'Sonoqua."

43   From the shore, as we rowed to it, came a thin feminine cry—the mewing of a cat. The keel of the boat had barely grated in the pebbles, when the cat sprang aboard, passed the man shipping his oars, and crouched for a spring into my lap. Leaning forward, the man seized the creature roughly, and with a cry of "Dirty […] vermin!" flung her out into the sea.

44   I jumped ashore, refusing his help, and with a curt "Call for me at sundown," strode up the beach; the cat followed me.

45   When we had crossed the beach and come to a steep bank, the cat ran ahead. Then I saw that she was no lean, ill-favoured Indian cat, but a sleek aristocratic Persian. My snobbish little Griffon dog, who usually refused to let an Indian cat come near me, surprised me by trudging beside her in comradely fashion.

The village was typical of the villages of these Indians. It had only one   46
street, and that had only one side, because all the houses faced the
beach. The two community houses were very old, dilapidated and
bleached, and the handful of other shanties seemed never to have
been young; they had grown so old before they were finished, that it
was then not worth while finishing them.

Rusty padlocks carefully protected the gaping walls. There was the   47
usual broad plank in front of the houses, the general sitting and sun-
ning place for Indians. Little streams ran under it, and weeds poked
up through every crack, half hiding the companies of tins, kettles, and
rags, which patiently waited for the next gale and their next move.

In front of the Chief's house was a high, carved totem pole, sur-   48
mounted by a large wooden eagle. Storms had robbed him of both
wings, and his head had a resentful twist, as if he blamed somebody.
The heavy wooden heads of two squatting bears peered over the
nettle-tops. The windows were too high for peeping in or out. "But,
save D'Sonoqua, who is there to peep?" I said aloud, just to break
the silence. A fierce sun burned down as if it wanted to expose every
ugliness and forlornness. It drew the noxious smell out of the skunk
cabbages, growing in the rich black ooze of the stream, scummed
the water-barrels with green slime, and branded the desolation into
my very soul.

The cat kept very close, rubbing and bumping itself and purring   49
ecstatically; and although I had not seen them come, two more cats
had joined us. When I sat down they curled into my lap, and then
the strangeness of the place did not bite into me so deeply. I got up,
determined to look behind the houses.

Nettles grew in the narrow spaces between the houses. I beat them   50
down, and made my way over the bruised dank-smelling mass into a
space of low jungle.

Long ago the trees had been felled and left lying. Young forest had   51
burst through the slash, making an impregnable barrier, and sealing
up the secrets which lay behind it. An eagle flew out of the forest,
circled the village, and flew back again.

Once again I broke silence, calling after him, "Tell D'Sonoqua—"   52
and turning, saw her close, towering above me in the jungle.

53 Like the D'Sonoqua of the other villages she was carved into the bole of a red cedar tree. Sun and storm had bleached the wood, moss here and there softened the crudeness of the modelling; sincerity underlay every stroke.

54 She appeared to be neither wooden nor stationary, but a singing spirit, young and fresh, passing through the jungle. No violence coarsened her; no power domineered to wither her. She was graciously feminine. Across her forehead her creator had fashioned the Sistheutl, or mythical two-headed sea-serpent. One of its heads fell to either shoulder, hiding the stuck-out ears, and framing her face from a central parting on her forehead which seemed to increase its womanliness.

55 She caught your breath, this D'Sonoqua, alive in the dead bole of the cedar. She summed up the depth and charm of the whole forest, driving away its menace.

56 I sat down to sketch. What was this noise of purring and rubbing going on about my feet? Cats. I rubbed my eyes to make sure I was seeing right, and counted a dozen of them. They jumped into my lap and sprang to my shoulders. They were real—and very feminine.

57 There we were—D'Sonoqua, the cats and I—the woman who only a few moments ago had forced herself to come behind the houses in trembling fear of the "wild woman of the woods"—wild in the sense that forest-creatures are wild—shy, untouchable.

EXPLORATIONS:

Emily Carr,
>   *Klee Wyck*
>   *The Book of Small*
Maria Tippett, *Emily Carr: A Biography*
Doris Shadbolt, *The Art of Emily Carr*
Susan Crean,
>   *The Laughing One*
>   *Opposite Contraries*
http://www.emilycarr.ca
http://en.wikipedia.org/wiki/Emily_Carr
http://www.geocities.com/michaelpeterson12000/carr.html

STRUCTURE:

1. Carr's opening words are, "I was sketching in a remote Indian village when I first saw her." Why are we not shown "her" identity till paragraph 6?

2. Where do the three parts of this selection each begin and end? How do the three images of D'Sonoqua form a progression?

3. A voyage by water precedes Carr's visit to each image. Beyond its structural function, does it have a symbolic role? Consider this passage from paragraph 38:

> There was no rail round the deck, and the edge of the boat lay level with the black slithering horror below. It was like being swallowed again and again by some terrible monster, but never going down. As we slid through the water, hour after hour, I found myself listening for the OO-oo-oo-oeo.

STYLE:

1. Although Carr is esteemed as a writer, she is better known as a painter. What aspects of her PROSE remind you of the visual arts? Point out passages that illustrate your answers.

2. What does Carr gain by using words such as "scuttled" (par. 4), "slithered" (par. 8), "grated" (par. 43) and "ooze" (par. 48)?

3. Carr plays with words. Rather than describe the walk as "slimy," she writes that slugs "slimed" the walk. Find other words she uses in fresh ways.

4. What FIGURE OF SPEECH depicts the wharf's "crooked legs stockinged in barnacles" (par. 36)? Where else does it occur? How does it further the *description*?

5. The term "Indian," current when Carr published *Klee Wyck* in 1941, is now seldom used. Why? Name all the reasons you can think of why now the preferred term is often "First Nations People."

IDEAS FOR DISCUSSION AND WRITING:

1. In paragraph 31 Carr states of the second D'Sonoqua, "The power that I felt was not in the thing itself, but in some tremendous force

behind it, that the carver had believed in." Is skill itself enough to create art, or must the artist believe in some "tremendous force"?

2. What is art for? Think of these:
   - Monumental architecture, as in banks, cathedrals, train stations and airports
   - Pretty paintings and photographs on living-room walls
   - Statues of generals on horseback or politicians orating
   - Nonrepresentational art in its many forms: impressionism, cubism, surrealism, expressionism, etc.
   - The images of D'Sonoqua carved in cedar

3. The narrator and others fear D'Sonoqua. Why have humans always imagined monsters such as the Minotaur, Grendel, Dracula, Frankenstein, King Kong, Godzilla and the Boogeyman, not to mention the traditional witches and ghosts? Do we in some way need them?

4. In what ways can "D'Sonoqua" be considered a feminist essay?

5. PROCESS IN WRITING: *Visit the first Emily Carr website listed in "Explorations" above, and choose your favourite among the paintings that it shows. Take notes on the appearance of your favourite (as to colour, texture, form, etc.), and on your reactions to it. Now in a rapid first draft, write your own* description *of this painting. Use frequent sense images, as Carr does in "D'Sonoqua." Later when you edit, remember Carr's advice from her book* Growing Pains: *"get to the point as directly as you can; never use a big word if a little one will do."*

Note: See also the Topics for Writing on the Online Learning Centre at www. mcgrawhill.ca/olc/conrad.

PROCESS IN WRITING: GUIDELINES

Follow at least some of these steps in the act of writing your description (your teacher may suggest which ones).

1. If you can, take fresh eyewitness notes for your description. If you cannot, choose a topic you know well enough to make good notes from memory.

2. Look these notes over. What is your main impression, feeling or idea of the subject? Put it into a sentence (this will be your THESIS STATEMENT, whether or not you will actually state it in the description).

3. With your notes and thesis statement before you, write a rapid first draft, getting your subject safely out on paper or on the computer screen, not stopping now to revise.

4. When your first draft has cooled off, look it over. Does every line of your description contribute to the main overall effect? If not, revise. Does each word feel right? When one does not, consult your computer or paper thesaurus for another.

5. Now add more SENSE IMAGES—appeals to sight, hearing, touch, smell and maybe even taste. Add more TRANSITIONS. Read aloud to hear flaws you did not see. Then revise.

6. Finally, look over the spelling and punctuation before printing off your best version.

Royalty-Free/CORBIS

"Once you see Earth from space, you can never again think of it in the same way."

—Marc Garneau, *"Canada Must Put the Planet's Interests First"*

CAUSE AND EFFECT

HERE'S WHY....

H ave you heard the true story—and aren't they all supposed to be true?—of the philosophy prof who walked into class to give the final exam? He went to the blackboard and wrote one word: *Why?*

He knew that one of our most human traits is a desire to make sense of things by asking *Why?* If something good happens, we want to know *why* so we can repeat it. If something bad happens, we want to know *why* so in future we can avoid it. On news reports of earthquakes, hurricanes, fires, floods, accidents, crimes and terrorist attacks, victims are always shaking their heads and asking "*Why?*"

In the financial world investors bite their nails guessing what makes stocks go up or down. Will a growing economy push stocks up? Or will it cause inflation, which will cause us to stop buying things we can't afford, which in turn will lower company profits and cause stocks to fall? Will a controversial election send stocks crashing? Or will it just clear the air of uncertainty, making stocks soar?

Will a devastating earthquake harm the economy and the stock market? Or will the cleanup just create employment, sending stocks up? Using the same data, hundreds of experts reason that stocks will rise, while hundreds of others reason that they will fall. Do these experts, or do we, think cause and effect logic is easy?

Yet it is important. We use it in everyday life, and therefore many of our essays are based on it. So when you investigate causes and effects, think hard to get them right.

One of the most common sources of faulty cause-and-effect reasoning in everyday life is superstitions. Many students put a good-luck object on the desk in front of them while writing an exam, and may wear a good-luck item of clothing such as an old baseball hat or a certain pair of old shoes. Speaking of shoes, Canadian finance ministers customarily buy a new good-luck pair for every federal budget speech. Then there are the hockey players who observe lucky rituals such as letting their beards grow during playoffs. It is "bad luck" to wish an actor well before a theatre performance, so instead friends will say "break a leg," aiming for good luck through a reverse method. Many people, when realizing they have bragged or even expressed satisfaction, will knock on wood, to show their humility by touching an everyday object. Thus they will not be struck down by fate. Some superstitions are downright scary. It is said that the spouse who goes to sleep first on the wedding day will be the first to die. Even worse, it is said that "A green Christmas makes for full graveyards." In the vast majority of these and other superstitions, there is actually zero cause and effect, a deficiency that is called the *Post hoc, ergo propter hoc* fallacy ("After this, therefore because of this"). Only in the case of the graveyard may there be actual causality: if grass is green at Christmas, it means the weather has been milder than usual; and if the weather has been mild, then more microbes have survived to attack us. Of course, it could be equally argued that if the weather is warmer, we will suffer fewer chills and be healthier. As in the example of predicting stock market behaviour, does anyone think cause-and-effect logic is easy?

In summary, when you trace causes and effects, consider these principles:

JUST BECAUSE ONE EVENT FOLLOWS ANOTHER, DON'T ASSUME THE FIRST CAUSES THE SECOND. (As we have seen above, try to avoid the *Post hoc, ergo propter hoc* fallacy.) If a black cat crosses the road just before your car engine blows up, put the blame where it belongs: not on the cat but on the mechanic who forgot to replace your crankcase oil.

CONTROL YOUR PREJUDICES. If the bank manager refuses to give you a loan, is it because bankers are capitalist exploiters who like to keep the rest of us down? Or is it because this one had to call the collection agency the last time you took out a loan?

EXPLORE CAUSES BEHIND CAUSES. Your employer fired you because you didn't work hard enough. But *why* didn't you work hard enough? Because the job was a bore and the employer was a jerk? Or because you have two other jobs as well, and sleep only three hours a night? And if so, do you work these hours because the car you bought consumes every cent you earn? Finally, the real question may be *why did you buy the car?*

Many events have multiple causes and multiple effects:

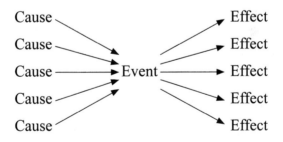

In addition, each cause may have one or more causes behind it, and each effect may produce further effects, leading to an infinite chain of causality receding into the past and reaching into the future.

Where, then, do you draw the boundaries as you plan an essay of cause and effect? The answer lies in your own common sense: include enough to make the point clearly and fairly, then stop. If your parents are workaholics, a description of their behaviour may help a reader understand your own. But do we need to hear about your grandparents as well? If we do, would a quick summary be enough, since we've already heard the details in your parents' case?

All the essays in this chapter show at least one clear-cut cause and at least one clear-cut effect. But while it is possible to give equal attention to both, constructing an essay may be easier if you concentrate *mostly* on cause or *mostly* on effect. Thus your attention can be focussed further, so you can delve deeper and end up with a more satisfying argument, saying more about less—rather than less about more.

Note also that while some essays in this chapter focus on one major cause or one major effect, others show several causes or several effects. For example, Patricia Pearson examines many possible causes of "the big C," while Linda McQuaig traces many effects of driving SUVs. As you choose your own approach to the organization of a cause-and-effect essay, remember above all your purpose: What kind of focus will most strongly explain and support your main point? Once you know, use it.

Note: Many essays in other chapters use cause and effect logic to help make their point. See especially these examples:

Karen Von Hahn, "Self-Serving Propaganda," p. 66
Stephanie Nolen, "Regine Mamba," p. 202
Catherine Pigott, "Chicken Hips," p. 196
Catharine Parr Traill, "Remarks of Security of Person and Property in Canada," p. 222
Lt.-Gen. Roméo Dallaire, with Major Brent Beardsley, "*Cri de coeur*," p. 414

PATRICIA PEARSON

Avoiding the Big C:
A Little Simple Advice

Patricia Pearson is the granddaughter of Lester B. Pearson, prime minister of Canada from 1963 to 1968, who won the Nobel Peace Prize for resolving the Suez Crisis of 1956 with his proposal to create a United Nations peacekeeping force. When Pierre Trudeau died in 2001, Patricia Pearson wrote a moving column in the National Post, *recalling how at age eight she was devastated by the death of her beloved grandfather, and how, like Trudeau's family, hers had to hear the events broadcast on the public media, and share the state funeral with the nation. Later she lived and wrote for several years in New York City. She has also lived in Mexico, and now resides with her husband and two children in the boreal forest north of Montreal. Pearson has written for the* National Post, USA Today, Maclean's, *the* New York Times, *the* Guardian, *and the* Times of London. *Her article on the notorious Canadian killer Karla Homolka, "Behind Every Successful Psychopath," won a National Magazine Award, and in 1997 appeared her widely read book* When She Was Bad: Violent Women and the Myth of Innocence, *which demolished the myth that women, unlike men, are incapable of violence. Then in 2003 was published her comic novel* Playing House, *in 2005 its sequel* Believe Me, *and also in 2005 a book of comic essays,* Area Woman Blows Gasket and Other Tales from the Domestic Frontier. *In 2008 she published* A Brief History of Anxiety (Yours and Mine). *Our own selection, a* National Post *column of August 28, 1999, showcases Pearson's witty and personal approach to journalism.*

1 The *New England Journal of Medicine* recently reported that "longer-legged people are significantly more prone to certain types of cancer." Indeed. Well, that's a huge relief for me. I can never see over anybody's head in a crowd. Guess I'll snicker at the supermodels and fry myself another burger.

2 What else, exactly, am I supposed to do with this information? Science, you may have noticed, pelts us daily with new studies on everything that causes cancer, everything that prevents it—and everything that they thought caused cancer before but they now realize actually prevents it.

3 At the moment, for example, I know that if I stay short, drink red wine, eat tomatoes and olive oil, avoid working in a coke foundry, avoid cigars, sleep more, take Aspirin, swallow Vitamin E, alter my estrogen levels, sip green tea, shun charcoal briquettes, dine on fish—but not from the Great Lakes—reduce my stress level and stay clear of Eastern Europe, my chances of dying from cancer will be reduced for the time being.

4 But it turns out that the sunblock that I've been slopping all over myself for five years may be carcinogenic, whereas sunburn is now thought to act as a cancer preventive. Meanwhile, the spinach and apples I've been eating all these years to bust cancer are laden with cancer-causing residues.

5 Likewise, Vitamin C, long touted as an antioxidant par excellence in megadoses, may actually change the structure of our DNA in such a way that … guess what? It makes us more susceptible to cancer.

6 And those soft plastic dishes I've been using to microwave my anti-cancer vegetable recipes? They cause cancer.

7 You may recall that a cancer-fighting diet book came out a while back. After chumps like me went out and bought it, an army of doctors charged forth and repudiated its findings.

8 Well, isn't that just great. I wanted to phone my mom to tell her how I've had it up to here (writer's hand slicing sideways at chin level) with trying to keep track of every eensy-weensy obscure bit of research on health dangers. But I'd just read that cell phones were being implicated in brain tumours.

9 It seems to me, the more I think about it, that what this whole explosion in medical research is actually discovering is that sooner

or later people die. Of course, scientists are finding out other things that are useful to them, but they are not very useful to me. What all this research is generating in people is the expectation that somehow they don't have to die—that if they can only get *all the information* they can beat the odds.

If you talk to an insurance actuary, you'll be told what people   10
actually die of, cancer-wise: smoking. Smoking is way, way up there with automobile accidents and heart attacks. And you don't need to read any more studies to know what to do about that one. Every other prevention strategy, in my opinion, is a crapshoot.

From now on, I follow the only recipe for longevity that's ever   11
actually made sense to me: moderation in all things. A little wine, a nice walk, a good dish of pasta, a minimal amount of microwaving in Tupperware containers, a dash of olive oil, a soupçon of Vitamin C, a very brief visit to a foundry. Live life modestly—except during the holidays and when you've been dumped by your boyfriend—and hope for the best. It's all you can do.

EXPLORATIONS:

Patricia Pearson,
> *When She Was Bad: Violent Women and the Myth of Innocence*
> *Area Woman Blows Gasket* (humorous essays)

http://www.pearsonspost.com/bio2.html
http://www.randomhouse.ca/author/results.pperl?authorid=23494
http://www.pearsonspost.com

STRUCTURE:

1. Pearson starts right off with the odd idea that "longer-legged people are significantly more prone to certain types of cancer." What does this opening do for her readers?
2. Though Pearson informs us early as to her subject and point of view, her actual THESIS STATEMENT is kept in reserve till the first sentence of the last paragraph, where she advises "moderation in

all things." Name one advantage of placing it at the end. Name one potential disadvantage. Why in most essays does it come at or near the beginning?

3. Roughly what percentage of her essay space does Pearson devote to *examples?* Tell two or three of your favourites. Has she reached the recommended 50% level? Point out which paragraphs are built entirely or mostly of examples.

4. In this essay of *cause and effect*, Pearson first questions current medical views on what does or does not *cause* cancer, before going on to her own advice. Have you tried to follow any of the popularly believed techniques in paragraph 3? Do her exposés of once-accepted but now rejected beliefs in paragraphs 4–7 seem to question the validity of the beliefs in paragraph 3? Finally, does the fact that she has made fun of formerly accepted beliefs help us to accept her own points that (in par. 10) smoking is the most obvious *cause* of cancer, and (in her closing paragraph) that "moderation in all things" is the main *cause* of longevity?

STYLE:

1. Does Pearson's humorous TONE work with the very serious topic of cancer?

2. In paragraph 10 Pearson calls most cancer prevention strategies "a crapshoot." Where else does she use very informal, COLLOQUIAL language? Does it work in her argument, or does it make us doubt her seriousness?

IDEAS FOR DISCUSSION AND WRITING:

1. Do you try to follow all the latest techniques to achieve the *effect* of good health, or do you just enjoy life and hope for the best? Argue for one of these points of view, giving reasons.

2. If you have read Stephen Leacock's essay "How to Live to Be 200" (in Chapter 8), compare the attitude of Jiggins, who "dumb-belled himself to death," with that of modern health seekers who try to reach the ideal diet and lifestyle.

3. Who in your extended family has reached a very old age? Do you think this longevity was *caused* by the person's lifestyle, or was the cause genetic? Give *examples*.

4. PROCESS IN WRITING: *Patricia Pearson's basic message is "moderation," but in our time we are more likely to encounter the "extreme." Why do so many of us seek extreme lifestyles, in areas such as food and drink, drugs, financial life, career, relationships, or in risky outdoor adventures? Fill a page with notes on this question, then narrow your focus down to one item—such as an "extreme sport" that you practise yourself. Analyze all the causes you can think of, or all the effects, and explain them in a first draft filled with examples. Examine it the next day. Does the THESIS STATEMENT unify your argument? Have you reached at least 50% example content? Do your points rise up to the most important at the end? After editing for content, polish the style, then bring your argument to class to read aloud.*

Note: See also the Topics for Writing on the Online Learning Centre at www. mcgrawhill.ca/olc/conrad.

MARC GARNEAU

Canada Must Put the Planet's Interests First

Born 1949 in Quebec City, Marc Garneau has become a well-known figure in Canada, an astronaut who has gone to space three times and spent almost 700 hours there. After his graduation in 1970 from the Engineering Physics program of Royal Military College in Kingston, he went on in 1973 to complete a doctorate in Electrical Engineering from the Imperial College of Science and Technology, London, England. From there he began to design hardware and instruct Canadian naval personnel in weapons systems. In 1982 he was promoted to commander, and in 1986 to captain. Meanwhile in 1983 Garneau was chosen for astronaut training. The next year he became the first Canadian to fly in space, and flew missions again in 1996 and 2000. Named deputy director of the Canadian Astronaut Program, he designed program support for experiments to be done in space, and served as capsule communicator in Mission Control during space shuttle flights. Then in 2001 he became president of the Canadian Space Agency. In his long and distinguished career, Marc Garneau has received many awards and honours, including numerous doctorates. In 2007, as a scientist and as one of the few people who have seen Earth from space, Garneau addressed the Canadian public in the Toronto Globe and Mail *essay that follows, urging idealism and generosity in the fight against global climate change.*

1   One of the consequences of going to space is that it changes the way you view our planet. It's unavoidable. Once you see Earth from space, you can never again think of it in the

same way. It's one thing to view small bits and pieces of it from below over time. It's another to gaze on it from above as you go around it once every 90 minutes, 16 times a day.

The Earth from that perspective strikes you as rather small and 2 fragile as more than six and a half billion of us scramble below, trying to live our lives as best we can. One look at its atmosphere, that thin layer of air that makes life possible, and you are struck by the thought that our existence on Earth is more tenuous than we realize.

It's no longer an abstract notion to speak of global environmental 3 change, to speak of large-scale human engineering gone wrong, of deforestation, of desertification, of soil erosion, of glaciers melting. It smacks you in the face.

The consequences of global warming affect *every* single country in 4 the world. There are no exceptions. It is the single most important issue facing humanity.

To be sure, it's a breathtakingly beautiful planet, a warm and 5 inviting oasis of life, particularly when viewed against the stark and infinite backdrop of space.

But it is also in the process of being damaged by both visible and 6 invisible forces, often as a result of well-intentioned decisions. Those invisible forces are, of course, the greenhouse gases that we collectively emit into the atmosphere. We all need to know that the course of history is already set for decades to come, no matter what.

What should a country like Canada do? Should it encourage all 7 countries to take action? Yes, absolutely. Should it act by itself even if others refuse? Absolutely. In fact, Canada needs to do something that has never been done before by any country: It needs to put the planet's interests before its own. Let me explain.

Canada, the second-largest country in the world, is blessed with 8 huge resources, an abundance of fresh water and vast open spaces. It has a great deal going for it, and its successful future is assured. It is the most fortunate country on this planet. It can and should take a position of leadership on the issue of the environment. It is the right thing to do. The world would like to see Canada assume that leadership, and Canada can afford to assume it.

That's a radical approach when you know that countries always 9 put their own interests first and only then those of others. We can easily summon excuses to avoid action: Our contribution to the world's total greenhouse gases is only 2 per cent, we are an important energy-producing country and, besides, what good we do will be swamped by the bad that others do. That's the traditional approach, but is it the right one for a truly global issue such as environmental change? No, it is not.

10   Can Canada afford to do this without crippling its economy? It certainly can. To make the point, Canada's most recently available total figure of 747 megatons of carbon dioxide equivalent (for 2005) is 187 megatons over its Kyoto target of 560 megatons (6 per cent below the 1990 total). At a high cost of $30 per ton on one of the climate exchanges (carbon trading), that would represent about $5.6-billion, which equates roughly to a cut of 1 per cent in the GST.

11   Of course, this is not the way that Canada should deal with its surplus emissions, but it is certainly proof that the country would not fall apart economically or be put at a significant disadvantage.

12   The course of action for Canada is obviously to reduce its emissions and, in the process, actually generate new wealth, particularly if it follows the example of certain European countries with a deliberate strategy to profit from the development of environmentally sustainable technologies. There is an irony at work here. Canada can put the planet first and, in the process, serve its own self-interest if it aggressively joins the emerging industrial revolution focused on environmental sustainability.

13   Most important, we as Canadians can begin to think in a whole new way, an enlightened approach to global challenges, not the current "I'll get serious if you get serious." Rather: I will put the planet first because it is the right thing to do, because it demonstrates leadership and, ultimately, because it will serve the country's interests as well.

14   I know the great majority of Canadians are willing to sign on to such an approach.

EXPLORATIONS:

Roberta Bondar,
Touching the Earth

Canada in Space: 25 Years and Counting (video, 12 min.,
     featuring Marc Garneau)
Al Gore, *An Inconvenient Truth* (book and documentary film)
Edward Burtynsky, *Manufactured Landscapes* (documentary film)
http://www.jsc.nasa.gov/Bios/htmlbios/garneau.html
http://www.space.gc.ca/asc/eng/astronauts/biogarneau.asp
http://en.wikipedia.org/wiki/Kyoto_Protocol
http://www.environmentaldefence.ca/reports/pdf/TarSands_
   TheReport.pdf
http://www.davidsuzuki.org
http://www.ecojustice.ca
http://zerofootprint.net

STRUCTURE:

1. On his three trips to space, Canadian astronaut Marc Garneau saw
   all of planet Earth from a distance. Why does he choose this IMAGE
   to introduce his argument? How far does he continue developing
   the image, and its significance, in the paragraphs that follow? And
   how does all this exploit the logic of *cause and effect*?
2. Point out Garneau's THESIS STATEMENT.
3. How has Garneau employed more *cause and effect* logic in paragraph 8? In paragraph 12?

STYLE:

1. How FORMAL or INFORMAL is Garneau's STYLE in this essay? Who is his
   AUDIENCE, and is the style appropriate for this group of readers?

IDEAS FOR DISCUSSION AND WRITING:

1. Astronaut Marc Garneau opens this essay with an image that
   makes him think about environmental issues—a view of Earth
   from space. For those who have stayed on Earth, are there equivalent sights that would move us to write our own environmental
   essay? What might yours be?

2. Garneau states that global warming affects "*every* single country in the world" (par. 4) and that it is "the single most important issue facing humanity." Yet he also characterizes Canada as having "huge resources" (par. 8), "an abundance of fresh water," and "vast open spaces." Some people even believe global warming will be good for Canada, since this is a northern country. What is your view? Is global warming our biggest issue? Why or why not?

3. In an unfortunate pattern of *cause and effect*, global warming is caused mostly by the burning of fossil fuels, which causes greenhouse gas emissions, mostly carbon dioxide, which then trap more heat from the sun. Garneau states in paragraph 10 that Canada emits 747 megatons of carbon dioxide, which is 187 megatons over the target of 560 megatons that was established at the 1997 Kyoto Protocol. Why does Canada produce so much greenhouse gas?

4. The Alberta tar sands (one of the world's largest producers of greenhouse gas) have inspired both pride in economic growth and dread of environmental pollution. The project is huge. The Toronto *Globe and Mail* of February 1, 2008 reported that extracting the gooey bitumen requires first removal of the soil and the trees (called "overburden"), then a fleet of giant trucks with tires four metres high. Refining requires 2 tonnes of oil sands for each barrel of oil, 2 to 4 barrels of water for each barrel of oil, and 17 million cubic metres of natural gas each day to heat the bitumen. Then the waste is poured into vast lakes held in place by dams. The future looks bigger still, since the tar sands occupy an area of Alberta the size of Florida. The *Globe* of January 25, 2008 estimated that oil production there may quadruple to 4 million barrels a day by 2020. In fact Canada has now surpassed Saudi Arabia as the largest supplier of crude to the United States. Government officials are now calling Canada an "energy superpower." Are we? Should we be? What is your opinion? Defend or attack this new role of our nation, giving reasons.

5. The oil industry is working on technology to help clean up mining and refining. For example carbon sequestration, the filling of underground spaces with the carbon dioxide generated in refining bitumen, may someday be practical on a large scale. Do

examples like this mean that science and technology will solve our problems? Argue with examples.

6. In 2008, British Columbia became the first province to impose a carbon tax on business and industry. It is being phased in gradually, and the proceeds will be allocated to reducing taxes elsewhere. Is this the model for our future environmental progress? Agree or disagree, giving reasons.

7. Visit the website Zerofootprint (http://zerofootprint.net), sponsored by a nonprofit Canadian organization. Go to the "One Minute Calculator," enter some basic information about your driving, eating, flying and housing habits, then see whether your "carbon footprint" is bigger, or smaller, than that of the average person. Tell your results to the class, analyzing the *causes* of either your good or your bad results.

8. PROCESS IN WRITING: *Explore further the Zerofootprint site given above, or other sites like it, investigating how lifestyle choices affect our carbon footprint. Now think about your own lifestyle. What one or more things could you change to help safeguard our "oasis of life" that Garneau celebrates in paragraph 5? First devise a THESIS STATEMENT that defines your main point, then write a rapid first version, emphasizing the effect or effects of your suggested change or changes. Later look it over. Are there plentiful examples, as in Garneau's essay? If not, add. Is your style concise and clear, like his? If not, edit. Have you used logic signals such as "therefore," "since," "as a result" and "because," to highlight the effects? Finally, check for punctuation and grammar, then print out your best version. Read it to the class, and invite reactions.*

Note: See also the Topics for Writing on the Online Learning Centre at www. mcgrawhill.ca/olc/conrad.

PAUL D'ANGELO

The Step Not Taken

Paul D'Angelo's usual idea of writing is to tell fish stories, and he admits that his, like most, will stretch the truth. But one day the writer and TV critic for Outdoor Canada *magazine stepped into a Toronto elevator, and lived the true and sobering story that follows. When it appeared in the* Globe and Mail *of April 3, 1995, it struck a deep chord: dozens of readers sent replies, one of them 5000 words long. Several recounted tragic experiences they had just had themselves, and told how D'Angelo's confession had helped them face their own trials. The author of this thought-provoking essay has an unusual background for a writer. Born in Toronto, D'Angelo never went to university but always read a lot, an activity that gave him a way with words. After high school he spent seven years in Europe and Africa travelling, working here and there, and just living life. In the meantime, on a visit home he launched a seasonal greeting card business, which still left him seven months a year to roam. For some years, now, he and his family have lived in Toronto, where he thinks of himself mostly as an entrepreneur, but goes north to fish pike and bass for fun, and then writes about it in several columns a year. "Write what you live!" he says. Though D'Angelo usually finds writing to be slow and tough, he felt our selection so strongly that he just wrote it right off, to "get it off his chest." The* Globe *changed only one word. Though he "felt better," his hope that the young man in the elevator would see the article and respond never came true.*

1   A few weeks ago I was followed into an office-building elevator by a well-dressed young man carrying a briefcase. He looked very sharp. Very buttoned-down. Wearing gold wire-frame

glasses, he was of medium height and build with neatly trimmed brown hair and, I would guess, in his mid-20s. Typical junior executive material. There was nothing about him that seemed unusual. Nothing at all to indicate what was about to take place.

The elevator had only one control panel, and I excused myself as I [2] leaned over to his side of the car and pushed the button for the 10th floor. He pushed the button for the 15th. The doors of the elevator closed and we began to ascend. Employing typical Toronto elevator etiquette, I stood staring up at the row of floor numbers above the doors while purposely ignoring my fellow passenger. Then it happened. A sudden strained gasp. Turning toward the noise, I was astonished to see the young man drop his briefcase and burst into tears. Our eyes met for a split second and, as if slapped, he averted his face from me, leaned his head against the wood-panelled wall of the elevator and continued to weep.

And what I did next still shames me. [3]

The elevator stopped at the 10th floor and, without looking back, [4] I stepped out. I stood in the hallway, a bundle of mixed emotions, wondering what to do. A combination of guilt and uncertainty washed over me. Should I go up to the 15th floor and make sure he's okay? Should I search him out from office to office? Should I risk the embarrassment it might cause him? Is he mentally disturbed? A manic depressive, perhaps? Is he a suicide just waiting to happen?

I didn't know what to do. So I did nothing. [5]

And now he haunts me. Not with fear, of course, but with a sense of [6] regret. I see his face crumbling before he turns to the wall. I see his shoulders heave as he sobs in a combination of sorrow and shame. I wonder now what brought him to that moment in time. How long had he been holding his pain inside before he could no longer contain it? What could possibly have overwhelmed him to such an extent that he was unable to keep from crying out?

Had he just visited the doctor and been told that he had an incur- [7] able disease? Was he having marital problems? Was his wife ill? His child? Had someone dear recently died? Was he being laid off? Was he looking for a job and meeting with no success? Was he having financial woes? Was he without friends in the city and crushed by loneliness?

8   The sorrows of this world are endless.

9   The few people I have told about the incident all say I did the proper thing, the best thing, by leaving the young man alone.

10   But they are wrong.

11   Like so many things in life, I know now what I should have done then. I should have thrown caution to the winds and done the right thing. Not the big-city thing. The right thing. The human thing. The thing I would want someone to do if they ever found my son crying in an elevator. I should have given him the opportunity to unload his sadness onto my shoulders. I should have reached out a hand and patted him on the back. I should have said something like, "Why don't you let me buy you a cup of coffee and you can tell me all your problems. There's no reason to feel self-conscious. I'll listen for as long as you want to talk."

12   What would his reaction have been to that? Would he have turned even further to the wall? Or would he have turned on me? Cursing me? Telling me to mind my own damned business? Would he have lashed out at me? Sorrow and insecurity turning to rage? Would he have physically attacked me? Or would he have gone with me for that cup of coffee?

13   I don't know. I'll never know. All I can be certain of is that I left him in that elevator with tears streaming down his face. And that he was alone. All alone.

14   I hope that somehow he gets to read these words, because I want him to know that I'm pulling for him. That I hope things are looking up for him. That I hope his sorrow is in the past. That I hope he is never again burdened with such awful despair. That I am thinking of him. That I said a prayer for him. That I was wrong, dreadfully wrong, not to step forward in his time of need.

15   That I'm sorry.

EXPLORATIONS:

Joseph Hartog et al., eds., *The Anatomy of Loneliness*
John Glassco, trans., *Complete Poems of Saint Denys Garneau*
http://www.depressioncanada.com

http://www.nimh.nih.gov/healthinformation/depressionmenu.cfm
http://www.cfpc.ca/English/cfpc/programs/patient%20education/
  depression/default.asp?s=1

STRUCTURE:

1. D'Angelo begins with an ANECDOTE. Is this a good technique? Do you see it often? How well does this one work as an introduction?
2. In paragraph 1 D'Angelo refers to "what was about to take place"; in paragraph two he says "Then it happened"; and in paragraph 3 he says "And what I did next still shames me." Why does he keep building suspense? What does this do for his AUDIENCE?
3. Identify D'Angelo's THESIS STATEMENT.
4. Tell how paragraph 10 works as a TRANSITION between parts. Why is it only one sentence long?
5. Where does D'Angelo ask himself *why*? Where does he ask *what if*? What *causes* does he imagine? What *effects*? And how important are these to the essay?

STYLE:

1. How CONCISE is this selection? Can you find any wasted words at all?
2. Read paragraphs 14 and 15 aloud in class. Why has D'Angelo given us a series of partial sentences? Why do most begin with "That ..."? Is this repetition accidental or deliberate? What effect does it achieve?
3. Why does D'Angelo's last paragraph contain only three words?

IDEAS FOR DISCUSSION AND WRITING:

1. If you were Paul D'Angelo, what would you have done when the young man on the elevator began to cry? Why do you think he was crying? Do you, like our author, live in the big city? Describe a time when the actions of a stranger made you wonder how to react. Did you take the risk of involvement? Or did you do the

"big-city thing"? Why? And now what do you think you should have done?

2. Did this selection bring tears to your own eyes? If so, in which parts? Is it good for an essayist to seek emotion in the reader?

3. Describe the favourite techniques of subway, streetcar, bus and elevator riders to preserve their solitude in rush hour. Arrange chairs as in a public transit vehicle, and role-play the situation in class.

4. Our essay title, "The Step Not Taken," is probably a reference to "The Road Not Taken," a poem by Robert Frost, in which the poet wonders what his journey would have been like had he taken the other fork in the path. Is this a universal theme? Describe a fork in your own path. Imagine to what destination "the road not taken" might have led you.

5. PROCESS IN WRITING: *You were the young man—or, if you like, a young woman—who was in the elevator that day, and you have just read Paul D'Angelo's article. Now answer him in a letter telling the* causes *of your pain, and responding to his shame at not helping. Look over your first draft: Have you found all the main* causes? *Are there also important* causes *behind* causes? *Have you used* TRANSITION SIGNALS *to highlight the logic (words like "because," "therefore," "as a result of," "so," etc.)? Revise. Now check for punctuation and spelling before printing out your best version.*

Note: See also the Topics for Writing on the Online Learning Centre at www. mcgrawhill.ca/olc/conrad.

NAHEED MUSTAFA

My Body Is My Own Business

Born in England to parents from an Indo-Pakistani background, Naheed Mustafa moved as an infant to Canada. In 1992 she completed an honours degree in political science and philosophy at the University of Toronto, specializing in Third-World development. Then she studied journalism at Ryerson University. Mustafa currently lives in Toronto with her husband, and combines working as an editor and freelance writer with raising her three children. "Almost anybody who's willing to work hard enough can learn to write very well," Mustafa says. It was on July 29, 1993 that "My Body Is My Own Business" appeared in the Toronto Globe and Mail. *Since we first reprinted the essay it has become widely anthologized in print, has been widely circulated on the Internet and is still attracting commentary. Mustafa states, "I see myself as being on something of a journey around this issue...." Ironically, the author of "My Body Is My Own Business" recalls the first edition of a textbook that inspired her in high school: it had a photo of a lightning strike on its cover. Its title was* The Act of Writing.

I often wonder whether people see me as a radical, fundamentalist Muslim terrorist packing an AK-47 assault rifle inside my jean jacket. Or maybe they see me as the poster girl for oppressed womanhood everywhere. I'm not sure which it is. 1

I get the whole gamut of strange looks, stares and covert glances. You see, I wear the *hijab*, a scarf that covers my head, neck and throat. I do this because I am a Muslim woman who believes her body is her own private concern. 2

149

3   Young Muslim women are reclaiming the *hijab*, reinterpreting it in light of its original purpose—to give back to women ultimate control of their own bodies.

4   The Koran teaches us that men and women are equal, that individuals should not be judged according to gender, beauty, wealth or privilege. The only thing that makes one person better than another is her or his character.

5   Nonetheless, people have a difficult time relating to me. After all, I'm young, Canadian born and raised, university-educated—why would I do this to myself, they ask.

6   Strangers speak to me in loud, slow English and often appear to be playing charades. They politely inquire how I like living in Canada and whether or not the cold bothers me. If I'm in the right mood, it can be very amusing.

7   But why would I, a woman with all the advantages of a North American upbringing, suddenly, at 21, want to cover myself so that with the *hijab* and the other clothes I choose to wear, only my face and hands show?

8   Because it gives me freedom.

9   Women are taught from early childhood that their worth is proportional to their attractiveness. We feel compelled to pursue abstract notions of beauty, half realizing that such a pursuit is futile.

10   When women reject this form of oppression, they face ridicule and contempt. Whether it's women who refuse to wear makeup or to shave their legs or to expose their bodies, society, both men and women, have trouble dealing with them.

11   In the Western world, the *hijab* has come to symbolize either forced silence or radical, unconscionable militancy. Actually, it's neither. It is simply a woman's assertion that judgment of her physical person is to play no role whatsoever in social interaction.

12   Wearing the *hijab* has given me freedom from constant attention to my physical self. Because my appearance is not subjected to public scrutiny, my beauty, or perhaps lack of it, has been removed from the realm of what can legitimately be discussed.

13   No one knows whether my hair looks as if I just stepped out of a salon, whether or not I can pinch an inch, or even if I have unsightly stretch marks. And because no one knows, no one cares.

Feeling that one has to meet the impossible male standards of   14
beauty is tiring and often humiliating. I should know, I spent my
entire teenage years trying to do it. I was a borderline bulimic and
spent a lot of money I didn't have on potions and lotions in hopes of
becoming the next Cindy Crawford.

The definition of beauty is ever-changing; waifish is good, waifish   15
is bad, athletic is good—sorry, athletic is bad. Narrow hips? Great.
Narrow hips? Too bad.

Women are not going to achieve equality with the right to bare   16
their breasts in public, as some people would like to have you believe.
That would only make us party to our own objectification. True
equality will be had only when women don't need to display themselves to get attention and won't need to defend their decision to
keep their bodies to themselves.

EXPLORATIONS:

Elizabeth Warnock Fernea, *In Search of Islamic Feminism: One
   Woman's Global Journey*
Richard Gordon, *Eating Disorders: Anatomy of a Social Epidemic*
Naomi Wolf, *The Beauty Myth: How Images of Beauty Are Used Against
   Women*
Bharati Mukherjee, *Jasmine* (novel)
Salman Rushdie, *Shame* (novel)
Under One Sky: Arab Women in North America Talk About the Hijab
   (NFB, 43 min., 1999)
http://en.wikipedia.org/wiki/Hijab
http://en.wikipedia.org/wiki/Burqa
http://www.usc.edu/dept/MSA/othersites

STRUCTURE:

1. Why does Mustafa open with two STEREOTYPES? Do they draw your
   attention? Do they go straight to her topic?
2. In her argument does Mustafa give more attention to *causes* or
   effects? Name the main causes. Name the main effects.

3. Why does Mustafa explore effects *first* and causes *after*, reversing the logical order of the two?
4. Identify the TRANSITION in which Mustafa actually asks "why" and answers with "because ... ," as she moves from *effects* to *causes*.

STYLE:

1. Ending on a key word is a powerful device of emphasis. Note the final word in each half of Mustafa's argument: What makes "freedom" and "themselves" good choices for these positions?
2. Language can speak through rhythm as much as through words. Read aloud the first sentence of paragraph 6, then analyze how its sound reinforces its meaning.

IDEAS FOR DISCUSSION AND WRITING:

1. Mustafa says male standards of beauty for women are "impossible" and that feeling the need to meet them is "humiliating" (par. 14). Is she right? Whatever your own gender, give examples to attack or defend her view.
2. Examine the PARADOX of paragraph 8: that the effect of covering oneself with the *hijab* is "freedom." Do non-Muslims have means of shielding themselves, as well, from the unreasonable scrutiny and expectations of others? Name any such techniques you have used.
3. In news coverage of the Canadian military presence in Afghanistan, we often see images of women wearing another garment that conceals the body, the *burqa*. Describe it. Tell any *effects* that you believe its use has on the wearer and on people observing the wearer. Can it offer "freedom," as Mustafa believes the *hijab* does?
4. Though part of her background is the culture of another country, Mustafa is Canadian. If you too have origins in another culture, to what extent do you see yourself retaining the clothes, the foods, the religion and the language of that culture, here in Canada. Predict the *effects* of your intended course of action.

5. Mustafa confesses that as a teen she was a "borderline bulimic" (par. 14). What do you see as the main *causes* of bulimia and anorexia nervosa? What *causes* women, not men, to be the main victims?

6. At the library look through an illustrated history of art, taking notes on how the ideal of beauty in women has changed through the centuries. Then report your findings to the class, showing illustrations as evidence for your conclusions.

7. Watch your favourite television channel for at least an hour, taking notes on how women are presented both in programs and commercials. Then report to the class on the attitudes, especially any STEREOTYPES, which you detected. What *effects*, in both male and female viewers, do you think these attitudes will *cause*?

8. **PROCESS IN WRITING:** *Do number 6 above, except as an essay. Look over your notes, then choose a THESIS STATEMENT that expresses the main* effect(s) *on viewers of the* examples *you observed. Now write a rapid first draft, supporting your thesis statement with large numbers of these* examples. *When the draft has cooled off, look it over. Do the* causes *and* effects *seem reasonable? Have you tried to be objective, rather than interpret according to your own prejudices? Are there* causes *behind causes, or* effects *of effects, that might enrich your analysis? Do TRANSITIONS such as "since," "because" and "therefore" help the audience follow your logic? If not, add. Finally, edit for things like punctuation and spelling before doing the final version. Read it to the class, and be ready to answer questions from other points of view.*

Note: See also the Topics for Writing on the Online Learning Centre at www. mcgrawhill.ca/olc/conrad.

LINDA McQUAIG

Killing Machines*

Linda McQuaig is one of our nation's most hard-hitting social and economic critics. In her newspaper columns and in her books, she tirelessly battles vested interests such as big oil and other polluters, powerful transnational corporations and governments that favour the wealthy over the poor. Bringing research, wit and a vivid writing style to bear upon her subjects, she excels at tracing webs of cause and effect, such as the corruption and greed for oil that she argues lay behind the American invasion of Iraq. These and other petroleum-related subjects are exposed in her bestselling 2004 book It's the Crude, Dude: War, Big Oil and the Fight for the Planet. *(Our own selection, attacking gas-guzzling SUVs, comes from the same book.) Among McQuaig's many other published volumes have been* Behind Closed Doors: How the Rich Won Control of Canada's Tax System *(1987);* The Quick and the Dead: Brian Mulroney, Big Business and the Seduction of Canada *(1991);* Shooting the Hippo: Death by Deficit and Other Canadian Myths *(1995); and* Holding the Bully's Coat: Canada and the U.S. Empire *(2007). McQuaig has also written regularly for the* Globe and Mail, *the* Toronto Star, Maclean's *magazine, the* National Post *and CBC Radio. She is also a popular speaker, bringing to her audiences the same sharp wit and vivid examples that fill her writings.*

1   Having paid insufficient attention to car advertisements in the 1990s, I somehow didn't get the concept of an SUV. I didn't realize, for instance, that it was a symbol

*Editor's title.

154

of a bold, adventurous, sporty kind of life, driven by people with a tendency to go off-road—just as, elsewhere in their lives, they have a tendency to break with the pack, to do things their way, to think outside the box. To show how far out of the loop I was, I didn't even know there was a difference between an SUV and a minivan. They both just seemed like awkward, bulky, oversized versions of a car—useful, no doubt, for those trips to Price Chopper when one comes home laden with several extra cases of Coke and a year's supply of toilet paper.

Of course, I was dead wrong. I've learned that there's a world 2 of difference between a utilitarian minivan, which is designed for the Price Chopper trip as well as carting around children's soccer equipment, and an SUV, which is not only bold and adventurous but also glamorous, the car of choice these days among Hollywood stars and others with limitless resources. Still, one can appreciate the role advertising has played in making this sort of distinction clear to people, in establishing the SUV as the symbol of everything chic. The sheer brilliance of this advertising coup can perhaps best be measured by the extent of the image transformation the SUV has undergone since its first incarnation as a vehicle with few uses outside the funeral business. As Keith Bradsher has noted in his book *High and Mighty*, the forerunner of the SUV—the Chevy Suburban—dates back to the 1930s, and it managed to survive in the early decades largely because its body was the perfect height and width for the easy loading and unloading of coffins. This feature is retained today but omitted from SUV advertising.

So effective has the advertising campaign been that the public 3 seems largely unaware that SUVs are generally difficult to handle, with poor agility and manoeuvrability—exactly the opposite of the sports car, which of course, used to be the sexy car of choice. While a sports car, with its low-slung body and road-gripping tires, can zip around corners at great speed, the rigid, high-set body of the SUV makes its way around corners with considerably more difficulty, which explains why ads typically show SUVs motionless at the top of a mountain or charging straight ahead (got to get straight home with all that toilet paper), rather than driving on the kind of winding, exotic cliffside roads typically seen in sports car ads.

4   Much of the appeal of today's SUV may have less to do with sporti-
ness and glamour, and more to do with security in an age of fear.
Huge and growing ever larger, the SUV offers its riders a massive,
wraparound steel exterior with the feel of a tank—a mobile version of a gated community. Bradsher reports that this is deliberate,
that the tough, even menacing-looking appearance of many SUVs
is intentionally and consciously designed by automakers for an era
when civility on the roads has been replaced with unabashed hostility, a kind of me-first aggressiveness. In the age of everything from
road rage to anthrax to SARS, you can't have too much steel between
you and the rest of what's driving around out there.

5   And it's true: SUVs *are* a threat to others on the road—a fact that
was appreciated as early as thirty years ago by researchers trying to
draw attention to the dangers of designing vehicles with the sort of
stiff, high front ends that are the hallmark of the SUV. In an accident, an SUV is two and a half times more likely than a mid-size car
to kill the occupants of the other vehicle, due to the fact that SUVs
are heavier (by a thousand pounds on average), stiffer and taller.
These characteristics effectively turn SUVs into "battering rams in
collisions with other vehicles," notes a recent report by the Union
of Concerned Scientists. When an SUV hits a car from behind, it is
more likely to ride up over the car's bumper, leaving the car (and its
occupants) essentially defenseless. When an SUV hits a car from the
side, it can ride up over the car's door frame and right into the passenger compartment. (Well, hello there!) This mismatch of sizes has
been dubbed "vehicle incompatibility," but another possible name
would be "vehicle homicide." And one-on-one against an unarmed
pedestrian, an SUV is more lethal still, hitting the pedestrian higher
up on the body, closer to vital organs, than a regular car does. Yet this
greater height, stiffness and body weight seems to be something of a
selling point, rather than a signal that perhaps something is seriously
wrong with these oversized killing machines.

6   Even if the thought of killing others isn't a deterrent, one would
think the thought of killing oneself and one's loved ones would
count for something. But apparently not. SUV sales have skyrocketed
despite the fact that they are also a danger to their own passengers
because, with their considerable height, they have a tendency to roll

over. More than 51,500 occupants of SUVs (and light trucks) died in rollovers from 1991 to 2001. The overall fatality rate for SUVs was 8 percent worse than for cars in 2000.

But the more far-reaching problem with SUVs—at least in terms of the survival of the planet—is the devastating amount of greenhouse gases they spew out into the air. An SUV produces roughly 40 percent more greenhouse gas emissions than a regular car does, and with SUV sales soaring—sales have increased seventeen-fold in the past two decades—their emissions have become a significant part of the problem of global warming. At a time when the dangers of global warming are blatantly evident and of serious concern to people all over the world, the breezy marketing of SUVs in North America makes a mockery of any claim that we are addressing the problem. While common sense would call for a special effort to move away from these over-emitting vehicles, exactly the opposite has been happening. Both the U.S. and Canadian governments have contributed to the SUV problem by offering SUVs regulatory controls far looser than those applied to regular cars. (The regulations were established in the U.S., but Canada has effectively adopted matching standards, which the automakers have agreed to deliver on a voluntary basis.) The extraordinary growth in SUV sales over the last two decades, then, can be attributed as much to government favouritism as to the massive advertising campaign that has left prospective SUV buyers thinking of off-road adventure rather than the ease of moving coffins.

The story of the SUV is in many ways a microcosm of the human folly that has led us to the brink of a climate change disaster. Perhaps it seems unfair to pick on the SUV. After all, it isn't, by any means, the only source of greenhouse gas emissions. It is, however, one of the fast-growing sources. SUVs now account for an astonishing 24 percent of all new cars sold, up from just 2 percent in 1980. (Overall, the transportation sector accounts for 26 percent of U.S. greenhouse gas emissions. Along with coal-fired power plants, transportation is one of the key sources of the global warming problem.)

I'm picking on the SUV partly because it somehow serves as a metaphor for the absurdity of the situation we find ourselves in, if for no other reason than that these enormous, awkward vehicles seem so ... well ... unnecessary. There's another aspect to this story that makes it emblematic of the saga of global warming: how easily the problem could be corrected if there were any serious political will. The technology exists to make enormous strides in cutting back the greenhouse gas emissions currently spewing out of SUVs (and other vehicles, but particularly SUVs) on highways across North America. I'm not talking about exotic space-age cars that run on hydrogen in some dream scenario (that's likely a couple of decades or so down the road), but about technology that already exists—and currently sits on shelves—in the offices of our big automakers. This, then, is the story of how Luddites° in the auto sector, fearful of risking their dominant market position, have declined to take us to where any sane person can see we must go, hiding behind claims of technological "can't do," hoping the public won't realize that what we have here is, in fact, a tale of technological "won't do."

°Luddites: In 1811 in Nottingham, England, textile workers led by Ned Ludd revolted against factory owners who were replacing craftsmen with new technology. They smashed the weaving machines, to protect their own jobs, until authorities put down the uprising. Since then, those who oppose new technology have often been called "Luddites."

EXPLORATIONS:

Linda McQuaig,
> *It's the Crude, Dude: War, Big Oil and the Fight for the Planet*
> *The Cult of Impotence: Selling the Myth of Powerlessness in the Global Economy*

Keith Bradsher, *High and Mighty: SUVs—The World's Most Dangerous Vehicles and How They Got that Way*

Al Gore, *An Inconvenient Truth* (feature-length documentary, and book)

Who Killed the Electric Car? (feature-length documentary, on DVD)

http://www.rabble.ca/about_us/bios.shtml?x=814

STRUCTURE:

1. Why does McQuaig begin by confessing her former ignorance about sports utility vehicles (SUVs)?

2. Identify McQuaig's THESIS STATEMENT.
3. Point out how in paragraph 3 McQuaig exploits the device of *contrast.*
4. McQuaig explores both *causes* and *effects* of the SUV phenomenon. First point out all the *causes* she gives, then all the *effects.*
5. What technique does McQuaig exploit in closing on the very words "'won't do'"?

STYLE:

1. In places Linda McQuaig uses academic words such as "emblematic," "microcosm" and "Luddites," but in other places more conversational language such as "got to get straight home with all that toilet paper" (par. 3) or, as the SUV is riding up over another car's door frame and into the passenger compartment, "Well, hello there!" (5). Is this mixture of TONE effective? Why or why not?
2. What FIGURES OF SPEECH does McQuaig apply when she likens an SUV to a "tank," a "gated community" (par. 4) and a "battering ram" (5)?

IDEAS FOR DISCUSSION AND WRITING:

1. In our era of consumerism, many people speak of "moving up" to a bigger car or house, rather than making a "lateral move." Do you aspire to drive an SUV? What do you think would be the *effects* on your status level? Your driving habits? Your bankbook?
2. McQuaig argues that SUVs are two and a half times more likely to kill occupants of another vehicle (par. 5), are more lethal to pedestrians (5), are 8% more likely to kill even their own passengers (6) and emit 40 percent more greenhouse gases (7), thus hastening planetary disaster. Why, then, do automakers promote these vehicles so heavily? And why do these "Luddites," as she calls them, refuse to take new technology off the shelf to improve the vehicles?
3. "I'm picking on the SUV," McQuaig openly states in paragraph 9. Has she gone too far in only criticizing and ridiculing? Should she have included positive points, in order to be fair? Or would that just diminish the whole idea of arguing a case?

4. In paragraph 7 McQuaig points out how Canada has followed the United States in adopting the same loose SUV emission standards. What are all the *causes* of this fact? What are the *effects?* Are we a nation of followers, or are there areas of public policy that are all our own?

5. What is the solution: Drive less? Car-pool? Drive a small car? (Are they safe?) Use public transit? Cycle or walk? Give your own conclusions.

6. PROCESS IN WRITING: *Write an essay on the* causes and/or effects *of owning one of the following: a bicycle, a motorcycle, a very small car, a sports car, a pickup truck, a Hummer or a luxury car. First rough out a page or two of notes. Then look to see if you have mentioned mostly* causes, *mostly* effects, *or both. Accordingly, plan your argument, arrive at a* THESIS STATEMENT, *and write a rapid first draft filled with* examples. *The next day look it over. Have you left out any obvious* causes and/ or effects? *If so, add. Do logic signals such as "because," "therefore," "so that" and "as a result" highlight your cause-and-effect argument? If not, add. Finally, look over the punctuation and sentence structure before printing out your best version.*

Note: See also the Topics for Writing on the Online Learning Centre at www. mcgrawhill.ca/olc/conrad.

JUNE CALLWOOD

Forgiveness

Founder or co-founder of some 50 humanitarian organizations, author of over a dozen books and of some 2000 articles and columns, for over six decades a fighter for the rights of women and children and the vulnerable everywhere, June Callwood became the nation's most effective social justice advocate. She was born in 1924 in Chatham, Ontario, grew up in the poverty of the Great Depression, dropped out of high school to help support her family, got her first journalism job at $7.50 a week in Brantford, then in 1942, at age 18, won a post at the Toronto Globe and Mail. *But her celebration of progressive values in journalism was not enough: she also took direct action, creating institutions in response to public need. In the sixties she founded Digger House, a shelter for homeless young people; then in 1974 Nellie's, a shelter for battered women; in 1982 Jessie's Centre for Teenagers; and in 1988 Casey House, a hospice for AIDS victims. Meanwhile she was a founding member of PEN Canada and of the Canadian Civil Liberties Association. Callwood hosted numerous television series, and ghost-wrote some ten autobiographies, as well as authoring her own books on humanitarian themes. Honoured with the Order of Canada and many other civic prizes, and granted 17 honorary degrees, Callwood never slowed down. Late in life she still drove her sports convertible around town, and maintained her pilot's licence. It was in April 2007, while Callwood was 82 and suffering from a long illness, that* The Walrus *published our selection, "Forgiveness." Later that month the nation lost one of its most exemplary citizens.*

1   A small boy in an industrial city in Ontario was beaten severely many times by his father, to the extent that the boy not infrequently required a doctor to stitch up the wounds. His father, a policeman, sincerely believed that if he beat his son with chains, belts, sticks, and his fists, the boy would not grow up to be gay. That boy, now in his thirties and indelibly a gay man, says he will never forgive his father.

2   "What he did is not forgivable," the man says with composure. "How can it ever be all right to abuse a child? But I have let it go."

3   And a woman, raised on the Prairies in a Finnish home, married a black man and had a son. She showed the infant proudly to her mother, whose reaction was a look of naked disgust. Her mother and that son, now a charming and successful adult, have since developed an affectionate relationship, but the daughter has not forgotten or forgiven the expression on her mother's face.

4   "The best I can do," she says, "is that I have stopped hating her."

5   The ability to forgive is a central tenet of every major religion in the world—Christian, Judaic, Hindu, Buddhist, and Islamic. Those faiths urge followers to forgive their enemies and, indeed, even to find a way to love those who wrong them. As the twenty-first century dawns, however, the world is making a spectacular mess of such pious admonitions. Instead of goodwill, this is the age of anger, the polar opposite of forgiveness. Merciless ethnic, tribal, and religious conflicts dominate every corner of the planet, and in North America individuals live with high levels of wrath that explode as domestic brutality, road rage, vile epithets, and acts of random slaughter.

6   Many people, like the gay man or the woman in a biracial marriage, find forgiveness an unreasonable dictate. Some assaults on the body or soul are unconscionable, they feel, and forgiveness is simply out of the question. It satisfies the requirements of their humanity that they gradually ease away from the primitive thoughts of revenge that once obsessed them.

7   When Simon Wiesenthal, the famed Nazi hunter, was in a German concentration camp, he found himself in a strange situation. He was taken to the bedside of a dying SS officer, a youth who had killed many

Jews, and the young man asked him, a Jew, for forgiveness. Wiesenthal was silent and left the room, but was haunted ever after. Thirty years later, he contacted some of the world's great thinkers and asked, what should I have done? Theologians such as Bishop Desmond Tutu and the Dalai Lama gently hinted that he should have been forgiving, for his own sake, but others, notably philosopher Herbert Marcuse, said that great evil should never be forgiven. In *The Sunflower*, a collection of fifty-three responses to Wiesenthal's question, Marcuse wrote sternly that forgiveness condones the crime.

The moral vacuum left by the pervasive disuse and misuse of reli-   8
gious tenets has allowed a secular forgiveness industry to spring into being. People who yearn desperately to rid themselves of an obses-sion for vengeance will seek help in curious places. Since 1985, the University of Wisconsin–Madison has offered forgiveness studies, and an International Forgiveness Institute was founded there. Four years ago, the world's first international conference on forgiveness drew hundreds of delegates to Madison. Stanford University has a forgiveness research project and people in California, a state on the cutting edge of self-absorption, are taking part in studies on the art and science of forgiveness. Self-help shelves in bookstores abound in titles such as *Forgive Your Parents: Heal Yourself.*

An odious US daytime television show, *Forgive or Forget*, features   9
guests who say they owe someone an apology. They describe their offence, and then, *ta-dah*, the injured party appears on the appropri-ately tacky set and either grants or withholds forgiveness. Will the for-mer foes embrace one another? The titillated audience can't wait.

Apologies are iffy because often they are contrived or coerced.   10
Apologies extracted by judges, mediators, and parents are thin gruel for the wronged person. One familiar genre of apology, the one which commences, "I am sorry you are feeling badly," is particularly counterproductive because there is no admission of any responsibil-ity; it is the other person's problem for being thin-skinned. A sincere and remorseful acceptance of blame, however, can close a wound.

Psychologists are engrossed by the topic and so are theologians, phi-   11
losophers, psychiatrists, and—surprise—cardiologists. Unforgiving

people, some studies show, are three times more likely to have heart disease as people who don't carry grudges. These findings raise the suspicion that the researchers may have the cart before the horse. Heart attacks occur more often in blow-top people who have unfortified egos, the very ones most apt to be relentlessly unforgiving. On the other hand, people who hold tolerant views of human nature and don't seem to nurse grievances unduly tend to have blood pressures in the normal range.

12 Clergy, counsellors, and people who lecture and write books about forgiveness all preach reductionism as a strategy for overcoming hot resentment of someone's nasty behaviour. They say that people who have been harmed should see the hurtful as deeply flawed human beings working out nameless aggressions. Pitiable and inferior, they are examples of failure to thrive. Adults still distressed by abuse, neglect, or rejection in childhood are urged to consider what happened in their parents' childhoods—often, bad parenting comes from being badly parented. The theory is that understanding the reasons for their parents' limitations will enable the offspring to acquire a measure of compassion.

13 Maybe it works. Hillary Clinton apparently forgave her sleazy husband because she knows he had an unhappy childhood.

14 This technique can be applied to almost any injustice and falls within the rapists-were-beaten-as-children, *poor them* school of thought, which for some skeptics veers perilously close to non-accountability. The law and commonsense hold that adults are responsible for what they do. While empathy may help people appreciate why others behave badly, the exercise is somewhat patronizing. The offender is reduced to a contemptible hive of neuroses and ungovernable aberrations, which accordingly elevates the injured party to a morally superior person.

15 Demonizing the enemy is a common coping mechanism in times of adversity. In military terms, it captures the high ground.

16 Catastrophes such as divorce, job loss, rape, robbery, infidelity, and slander are all assaults on personal dignity and self-respect. A sense of being intact—*safe*—has been violated, and people are dismayed to find themselves for some time emotionally crippled by anger and grief. Betrayal and loss take big chunks out of people's confidence and leave them feeling excruciatingly vulnerable to random harm.

The starting place, some therapists say, is to accept that some-   17
thing appalling has happened, and it hurts. Denial, a recourse more
favoured by men than by women, won't help. The next step, they say,
is to develop an off switch. When fury threatens to make the brain
reel, people should grasp for distractions. Brooding about revenge
only serves to unhinge reason. If people don't rid themselves of
wrath, personal growth stops cold. The hard part comes at the end
of the process. The choices are to enter a state of forgiveness, which
is a triumph of generosity, or just to put the matter in a box, cover it
with a lid, place a brick on the lid, and move on. In healthy people,
a perverse state of mind eventually wears itself out.

In yoga, they say that it takes six years of regularly practising medi-   18
tation to gain spiritual insight. Forgiveness of a great wrong may take
longer. The process can't even begin until the injured person stops
crying.

Some people are marvellously unbroken by great injustices. Nelson   19
Mandela smiled gently at his adversaries after twenty-seven years of
brutal imprisonment. A worldwide figure of wonder, he even invited
his white jailer to his inauguration as South Africa's president. In
Cambodia, a pastor whose family had been wiped out by the Khmer
Rouge baptized and forgave a notorious Khmer Rouge leader known
as Duch. A university professor in Virginia had an urge to kill the
intruder who beat his mother to death, but stopped himself with
the thought, "Whose heart is darker?" And the father of a young girl
casually murdered in a street encounter with a teenager she didn't
know attended the trial and sat quietly throughout the appalling
testimony. He said he would visit the youth in prison. "I do not think
I can forgive him," he explained, "but perhaps if I know him I will
not hate him."

Forgiveness is hard work. A woman, a devout Roman Catholic who   20
forgave the man who tortured and killed her seven-year-old daughter, said, "Anyone who says forgiveness is for wimps hasn't tried it."
The reward for giving up scalding thoughts of reprisal is peace of
mind. It is worth the candle.

EXPLORATIONS:

June Callwood, *Twelve Weeks in Spring*
Anne Dublin, *June Callwood: A Life of Action*
Simon Wiesenthal, *The Sunflower*
http://www.cbc.ca/thehour/video.php?id=1513
http://en.wikipedia.org/wiki/June_Callwood
http://archives.cbc.ca/arts_entertainment/media/topics/1393
http://www.caseyhouse.com/en/june_callwood/biography/
   march_2007
http://www.mayoclinic.com/health/forgiveness/MH00131

STRUCTURE:

1. This argument of *cause and effect* makes strong use of *examples*. Roughly what percentage of the total argument is devoted to them? In which paragraph do they begin? Which speak most strongly to you?

2. After the two dramatic introductory *examples* in paragraphs 1–4, Callwood's THESIS STATEMENT is all of paragraph 5. Point out how it is built on a *contrast*.

3. In paragraphs 8–10 Callwood criticizes what she calls the "secular forgiveness industry." Why, in her view, are its attempts at forgiveness not very successful? What actually works better?

4. In a particularly concrete example of *cause and effect*, Callwood reports in paragraph 11 that "unforgiving people, some studies show, are three times more likely to have heart disease as people who don't carry grudges." To what extent do you believe good attitudes *cause* good health? Give examples from your own experience or observation.

5. In paragraph 14 Callwood describes what she calls the "rapists-were-beaten-as-children, *poor them* school of thought." Study the rest of this paragraph, then review the essay by Nathalie Petrowski in this chapter, "The Seven-Minute Life of Marc Lépine." In her search for the *causes* of the infamous Montreal Massacre, to what

extent does Petrowski conclude that Lépine was a victim of his own past?

6. Callwood packs paragraph 19 with a succession of dramatic acts of forgiveness. How do these lead to her closing?

STYLE:

1. Some of Callwood's paragraphs are quite long. Is this a flaw, or are there reasons?

2. How CONCISE is this essay? Do you see wasted words, or does everything contribute?

IDEAS FOR DISCUSSION AND WRITING:

1. The greatest hero of our time is widely thought to be Nelson Mandela, who emerged from decades as a political prisoner to lead his country of South Africa to democracy. Analyze his act of forgiveness in paragraph 19: inviting his own white jailer to his inauguration as South Africa's president. What may have *caused* Mandela's ability to forgive? What *effects* do you think the forgiveness may have achieved?

2. As in the opening examples of the gay man (paragraphs 1–2) and of the mother in a biracial marriage (3–4), forgiveness may not always be possible. But at least he has "let it go" and she has "stopped hating" her mother. Is this enough to help the offended persons? Is any step toward forgiveness a good step?

3. In paragraph 7 Callwood tells of the Nazi hunter Simon Wiesenthal, who pondered the question of whether "great evil" should ever be forgiven. What is your view? Could you have forgiven the dying SS officer? Or do you agree with philosopher Herbert Marcuse that "forgiveness condones the crime."

4. Put yourself in the place of June Callwood, whose own son Casey was killed by a drunk driver, while riding his motorcycle to university. Could you ever forgive? And if not, how do you imagine trying to contain your anger so it would not ruin your life? Reflect on the fact that in memory of her son (who did not have

AIDS), Callwood founded Casey House, a hospice for people living with AIDS.

5. **PROCESS IN WRITING:** *Think of the worst offence anyone has ever committed against you: perhaps an act of racism, or sexism, or betrayal, or violence, or even a crime. If the event is something you can share, make a page of notes on your own reactions: How have you responded, and what have been the effects of your response (for example, have you gone for anger, hate and revenge, or have you made attempts at closure, reconciliation or even forgiveness?)? Now develop a THESIS STATEMENT that tells your subject and your viewpoint toward it. Write a quick draft of your cause and effect essay. The next day look it over. Is there an opening and a closing? Have you given plentiful examples, like Callwood? Do TRANSITION SIGNALS move the argument forward? Now cut waste: surplus words, or even whole sections that do not support your main point. Last, check for spelling and punctuation. Now print out your best version. If it's something you cannot share with the class, then share it with a trusted friend.*

Note: See also the Topics for Writing on the Online Learning Centre at www. mcgrawhill.ca/olc/conrad.

NATHALIE PETROWSKI

The Seven-Minute Life of Marc Lépine*

Translated from the French by Ronald Conrad

Born 1954 in Paris and educated in Montreal, Nathalie Petrowski is a radio and TV personality, and one of Quebec's favourite print journalists—quirky, personal, satirical. In 1995 she also published Maman Last Call, *and wrote the script for the book's feature film version released in 2005. In her newspaper column for* Le Devoir *of December 16, 1989 Petrowski had a special challenge: ten days before, 25-year-old Marc Lépine had walked into an engineering class at the University of Montreal's École Polytechnique, shouted at the women students "You're all a bunch of feminists, and I hate feminists," ordered the men to leave—then lifted his rifle and shot the women. Six died. During the next minutes of terror he roamed the building, shooting. Altogether he gunned down 27 students, killing 14, all women. Then Lépine had turned the weapon on himself and died too. Canada felt a shock wave of anger and remorse, for this was the worst one-day mass murder in the nation's history, and its selectivity seemed to express a general sexism in society. In the next days, as the flag over Parliament flew at half-mast, citizens learned that Lépine's father had beat him and divorced the mother, and that the boy, though intelligent, had problems both academically and socially. He loved war movies, and from a paratrooper uncle had learned to handle firearms. His unemployment benefits were running out, the army would not take him, and the Polytechnique had refused him admission to its engineering program.*

*Editor's title.

Now on December 6 of every year, ceremonies across the nation honour the 14 young women, training for a profession still dominated by men, who were killed by a man whose suicide note blamed feminists for ruining his life. The essay that follows (originally entitled "Pitié pour les salauds") has a special poignancy, for Nathalie Petrowski wrote it in shock, as she and the nation first struggled to see meaning in the event.

1   Pardon if I insist, pardon if I don't just mourn and forget, but it's stronger than I am, for a week I can't stop thinking about Marc Lépine. A psychoanalyst would say I'm identifying with the aggressor. But I'd say that inside every aggressor, every villain, there hides a victim.

2   I think of Marc Lépine to block out all the talk that just confuses things: Rambo, television, violence towards women, pornography, abortion, and firearms in display windows.

3   I think of Marc Lépine, still wondering what happened and exactly when the hellish countdown of his act was unleashed. Was it the morning of December 6, was it November 21 when he bought his rifle or September 4 when he applied for the firearm permit? Was it the day of his birth, the first time his father beat him, the day his parents divorced, the week when he suddenly quit all his courses, the night a girl didn't want to dance with him? What about all the hours, the days, the weeks, the years that passed before the bomb inside him went off?

4   Still, journalists have told us everything: where he lived, the schools he went to, the names of teachers and students he knew. We know how much he paid for his rifle and how he loved war movies. But once all this has been said, nothing has been said.

5   We know nothing of the ache that consumed him, of the torture inside him. We know nothing of the evil path he slipped into smiling the cruel smile of the angel of destruction, no longer himself, knowing only that he was put on earth to destroy.

6   I think of Marc Lépine but equally of Nadia,° his sister who was beaten, too, for singing out loud in the morning, Nadia who came

---

°Nadia: Lépine's sister Nadia Garbi later became a drug addict. In 1996 she died of cardiac arrest from an overdose.

from the same family but didn't fall prey to the same madness. Why Marc and not Nadia, why Marc and not another? That's what I ask myself when facts only deepen the mystery, when social criticism only confuses things.

No one remembers him from grade school, or from Sainte-Justine Hospital where he spent a year in therapy with his mother and sister. Until last week Marc Lépine did not exist. He was an unknown quantity, a number, an anonymous face in the crowd, a nobody who no one would even look at or give the least warmth, the slightest affection. In a few moments he went from a nothing to one of a kind, a pathological case who the experts claim in no way represents the society where he was born and grew up. 7

For a week I've been talking with these experts, hoping to understand. For a week all I've seen is that there is no one answer, there are a thousand. For a week I've dealt with the official and professional voices who keep their files under key, who keep repeating that there's no use wanting to know more, that Marc Lépine is dead, that he can no longer be healed or saved, that it's too late to do anything at all. Sometimes their excuses and justifications sound like lies. 8

But I refuse to hear the silence of death that falls like snow, the shameful silence that freezes my blood. Somewhere deep in the ruins of our private space we hide the truth, we try to protect ourselves saying that families—ours, his, the victims'—have been traumatized. 9

Forget about the past, say the authorities, let's move on and not let Marc Lépine's act dictate our choices. Yet the surest way to let this act dictate our choices is to hide it, to let it become a medical, psychological and criminal secret, to push it into the smallest hollow of our collective memory till it's erased and we can say it never existed at all. 10

In this province where memory is reduced to a slogan on a licence plate,° we want to forget Marc Lépine like we forget all events that can disturb us and make us think. Though I know nothing of Marc Lépine's story, I've met enough young people in the high schools and colleges to know that chance as well as reasons, randomness as well as all the wrong conditions in one person's life, caused this act. 11

°a slogan on a licence plate: Quebec licence plates bear the motto *"Je me souviens"* ("I remember"); Quebeckers consider this a reference to their history, and especially the Conquest.

His tragic destiny looks more and more like a tangle of shattered hopes, of frustrated dreams, of hopeless waits on a long and cold road without a single hand extended to help, and no guardrail.

12   Marc Lépine died the evening of December 6, but unlike his victims, he had died long before. In the end his life lasted just seven minutes. Before and after, he was forgotten.

13   So pardon my pessimism, but I cannot help believing that somewhere, at this moment, there are other Marc Lépines who won't ask for anything because they don't even know what to ask for—other children turned into monsters by abusive fathers and impersonal school systems, by a society so intent on excellence that every day it hammers the nail of Defeat further in, and plants seeds of frustration and violence in the fragile spirits of its children.

14   Though nothing can be done now for Marc Lépine, something can still be done for the others, whose inner clock has already begun the terrible countdown. It would be a mistake to forget them.

EXPLORATIONS:

Nathalie Petrowski, *Il Restera toujours le Nébraska* (novel; available only in French)

Louise Malette and Marie Chalouh, eds., *Polytechnique, 6 décembre* (writings on the Montreal Massacre; available only in French)

Elliott Leyton, *Hunting Humans* (book on multiple murders)

Neil Boyd, *The Beast Within: Why Men Are Violent*

Heidi Rathjen and Charles Montpetit, *December 6: From the Montreal Massacre to Gun Control*

After the Montreal Massacre (NFB/CBC video, 27 min.)

Camilo José Cela, *Pascal Duarte's family* (novel, Spain)

Gabriel García Márquez, *Chronicle of a Death Foretold* (novella, Colombia)

Anne Hébert, *The Torrent* (novella)

http://www.whiteribbon.ca

http://www.litterature.org/ile32000.asp?numero=373

http://www.infoculture.ca/?page=5&view=2&numero=5223

http://www.radio-canada.ca/radio/indicatifpresent/
  Chroniques/47790.shtml
http://en.wikipedia.org/wiki/Marc_L%C3%A9pine
http://archives.cbc.ca/IDD-1-70-398/disasters_tragedies/Montreal_
  massacre

STRUCTURE:

1. Identify Nathalie Petrowski's THESIS STATEMENT.
2. Tragic events leave people asking "Why?" Point out all the reasons that Petrowski examines to explain Marc Lépine's acts. How fully is her argument built on *cause-and-effect* reasoning?
3. How does paragraph 6 use *comparison and contrast?*
4. What popular technique of conclusion gives force to the closing?

STYLE:

1. In paragraph 1 and elsewhere, Petrowski groups sentences together with commas. Do you view this as faulty punctuation, or is it a way for Petrowski to express strong feeling? Are we ever justified in breaking rules of punctuation and sentence structure?
2. Identify all the FIGURES OF SPEECH in paragraph 9. What do they contribute?
3. What feeling does paragraph 3 convey in its flurry of questions?

IDEAS FOR DISCUSSION AND WRITING:

1. After murdering 14 engineering students because they were women, Marc Lépine used the last bullet on himself. But in what sense had he "died long before" (par. 12)? In what sense did his life last only "seven minutes" (par. 12)?
2. Petrowski opens her essay with the belief that "inside every aggressor, every villain, there hides a victim." Can we and should we view Marc Lépine, the killer, as himself a victim? If so, a victim of who or what? What might have been done, and by whom, to help Lépine before it was too late?

3. In its issue covering the Montreal Massacre, *Maclean's* reported that in Canada one of every four women is harassed sexually at some time in life, and that a million women are abused each year by their husbands or partners. It also quoted a study by Rosemary Gartner who found that "as women move into non-traditional roles, they run a significantly higher risk of being killed." Do you see a link between this information and the act of Marc Lépine? Explain.

4. By the tenth anniversary of that terrible day, the number of female students in Canadian engineering programs had doubled. Are the problems being solved? Or do you believe women and their goals are still at risk?

5. In a *Fifth Estate* documentary, *Legacy of Pain*, marking the massacre's tenth anniversary, correspondent Francine Pelletier spoke of one survivor, Nathalie Provost, now an engineer and a mother. "The first time her little boy went bang-bang to her, she said she went white," reported Pelletier. "She took him by the arm and said, 'Don't you ever do that to me. Because mommy's been there.'" Would you allow your own children to have toy weapons? To play cops and robbers, or other traditional games of violence? What could be the *effects?* Defend your response with evidence.

6. On that day, Lépine carried one of the most popular rifles in Canada, a .223-calibre Sturm, Ruger semiautomatic, with two 30-clip magazines holding shells with expanding slugs. Are firearms such as this a danger in your city or town? Attack or defend the sale of arms, including handguns, over the counter. Are our gun laws an attack on civil liberties, as many hunters maintain, or are they still too weak to stop the next Marc Lépine?

7. Go to reliable websites and read about other mass murders that have taken place in schools, such as Columbine High School (Colorado, 1999), or Virginia Tech University (2007). What seem to be the main *causes?*

8. PROCESS IN WRITING: *Lépine used a rifle, but handguns are the weapon of choice for shootings. At the library or at reliable websites, gather information on the role of handguns in crime in Canada. Research also our current regulations for their sale and use. Now decide on your* THESIS STATEMENT: *whether Canada should end, more severely limit or continue*

to permit the sale of handguns to civilians. List your reasons. From this short outline write a fast discovery draft of your essay, developed mainly through cause-and-effect *logic, not stopping now to fix things like spelling or punctuation. The next day look it over. Is every point backed by a reason or* example? *Does your* evidence *lead clearly to your* conclusion? *(Remember that many essayists will change a conclusion or even a thesis statement when the act of writing uncovers better ideas.) Finally, edit for correctness as you produce your final version.*

Note: See also the Topics for Writing on the Online Learning Centre at www. mcgrawhill.ca/olc/conrad.

CRISANTA SAMPANG

Trading Motherhood for Dollars

Crisanta Sampang tells much of her life story in the essay that follows. Since her small village in the Philippines, Pagulingin, offered no education past grade four, her parents sent her to a larger village that did. Angry at being "given away," as she perceived it, to relatives there, Sampang dropped out at 18 and by 19 was married. When her husband proved to be an alcoholic, she left him. Now with children and no means of support, Sampang made the tough decision in 1984 to go abroad. In Singapore she worked as a maid, sending cheques home while her mother and "an army of relatives" raised the three girls in Pagulingin. During her four years in Singapore, Sampang also began writing for the Straits Times. *Then she moved to Vancouver and worked as a domestic. She also began to counsel other nannies, took evening courses and started working in film and television. Soon Sampang won an award for a documentary about extreme mountain biking, then in 2005 published a well-received book about the life of a domestic,* Maid in Singapore. *Now she is also Canadian news correspondent for* The Manila Times. *It was in 2007 that our selection, "Trading Motherhood for Dollars," was published in Cori Howard's anthology* Between Interruptions: Thirty Women Tell the Truth About Motherhood. *Though Sampang keeps in close contact with her daughters and grandchildren, they are still in the Philippines while she continues working in her new country of Canada.*

1   After many years of serious underachieving, I found redemption at the age of twenty-one.

2   I saw it in the eyes of my two-year-old daughter as she

looked up at me, face shining with pure devotion, as if I were Imelda Marcos° and an angel from heaven rolled into one, the only person in this world whose kiss could make all her boo-boos disappear and the bedtime "momos" retreat into their caves. Suddenly, all thoughts of sleepless nights and ten thousand diaper changes faded into the mist. I picked her up and held in my arms this miniature version of myself, this extension of my ego, fulfiller of my unachieved dreams, the future doctor or lawyer I'd always wanted to be and never became. She snuggled against me and said in her little baby voice, "Lub you, Mommy." At that very moment, I swore to myself I would never let her down.

When I did, much later, I did it unknowingly.   3

There are very few things in this world that are irreplaceable. One   4
of them is a mother's presence in her children's life. It's a lesson I've had to learn twice now, first as a nine-year-old going to school in the city and living away from my parents, then as a mother when I left my three daughters and went to work as a domestic in Singapore and later in Canada.

When I was nine, I would gladly have forgone studying in the city   5
for the chance to stay with my parents on the farm. I would have been happy to grow up barely literate, get married to a sugar cane farm worker, have six to nine children, lose my teeth one by one, live out my life in that narrow rural world, poor but close to my mother.

I grew up in Pagulingin, a small farming village in the Philippines   6
where school only went up to Grade 4. My parents believed I would benefit from higher education, so they sent me to board with relatives in Lipa, a city thirty minutes away from our village by jeepney. They didn't tell me they were doing this because they loved me. They assumed I already knew. I went, but I held it against my mother for the next eighteen years. I grew up thinking my parents gave me away. I became an angry teenager. I dropped out of college at eighteen, and by nineteen I was married and pregnant. I only forgave my parents years later, after I left my children in my mother's care.

°Imelda Marcos: Former first lady of the Philippines, wife of the dictator Ferdinand Marcos. A former beauty queen. Her spending habits, and especially her shoe collection, were legendary. In 1986 she and her husband fled the country, amid charges of corruption.

7   Motivated by an impoverished childhood, I was determined never to let my daughters experience any poverty. I went away so that I could raise them the way I wanted to. Alone in another country, separated from my little ones, I understood the lengths a mother will go to ensure the welfare of her children.

8   I'll never forget the second time I left my daughters. I had spent a month's holiday with them and, very reluctantly, I was going back to Singapore. On departure day, I hired a jeepney and the whole family came to the airport to see me off. When it was time to leave, we walked together from the parking lot to the immigration gates. I kissed everyone and said goodbye, then walked slowly away without looking back. I heard Maricel start to cry. Maricar and Catherine joined in. My mother called out a blessing. I walked on, faster and faster, farther and farther away from them, my heart beating as if it would explode inside my chest. I thought I would pass out. But I did not stop. Because if I stopped, if I looked back, I knew I would never leave; and I needed to go. My dreams for my little ones were only half-fulfilled.

9   Today, my grown-up daughters tell me they understand why I had to leave. Yet, given a choice, they would have picked poverty and the pleasure of welcoming me home every night after weeding a sugar cane field over dollar remittances. They would've exchanged a truckload of imported goodies and a month's allowance for a week of my presence. My youngest daughter, Catherine, first expressed it when she wrote me, at age eight: "You don't have to buy me a Barbie doll, just come home now!"

10   I wasn't listening properly then. All I heard was the insistent voice of my plans for their future: *I am doing this because I want you all to go to a good school and have a good education. I want you to have everything money can buy. Hang in there. I'll come home soon.* As it turned out, despite spending all my holidays with them, I never really came home for twenty-two years.

11   I hadn't been married long when I decided to leave my husband, a young businessman who loved beer and imported whisky. Drinking is a habit I hate almost pathologically. I'd seen my male relatives drink

themselves under the table as I was growing up, and I wasn't about to condone the same performance from the father of my children. After witnessing another of his all-night drinking sessions with his buddies, I packed my bags and went with my daughters to live with my mother.

I was twenty-seven, jobless, and had three kids to feed. After things settled down I looked for a job, any job, but found nothing. I tried applying for work in a factory and was told I was too short. I had no office skills. I'd never worked on a farm. I didn't know anybody influential who could help me get employed anywhere else. So, later that year, I took the only option available to me. Following the waves of Filipinos going out of the country to find employment abroad, I left my home to work as a maid in Singapore. Like thousands of other mothers who left for the Middle East, Hong Kong and Singapore, I left my children in the care of others. We traded motherhood for dollars. 12

But the family members left behind benefit financially: they will be able to build their own house, start their own small business, send the children to a better school. For this, I willingly lived through tired days and sleepless nights in a foreign country, all by myself, while tallying up every day the kisses and cuddles and hugs and birthdays and Christmases I'd be missing. 13

My daughters belonged to a subculture of students in their school— children whose mothers had gone away to work in another country. Many of these kids looked neglected. Their school uniforms weren't ironed or properly laundered; sometimes they'd attend classes with mismatched socks. These same kids wondered, according to my firstborn, Maricel, why she and her sisters appeared normal, if their own mother wasn't around. Grandma, she told the others, looked after them. I felt buoyed by such stories. In my mind, their being with Grandma was just as good as being under my own care. 14

I worked for three and a half years in Singapore. After that, I went on to Canada, once again as a domestic. The country's Live-In Caregiver program allows a qualified foreign domestic to sponsor her family into the country after working continuously for two years. Like many Filipina mothers before me, I hoped to take advantage of the plan. But after two years, I changed my mind. I watched other 15 women work sixteen hours a day to finance their families' sponsorship applications, then continue working the same number of hours to provide for them after arrival, even when there were fathers to help out. I was a single parent. I got very frightened about raising my daughters without adequate supervision. After a long and painful consideration, I decided to let them grow up in the Philippines, raised by Grandma and an army of relatives.

16   Much later, I regretted that decision. In fact, I'd been mistaken in a lot of ways. I had believed that Maricel, my eldest, was coping better than her sisters. She was very independent. She had taken the role of big sister seriously. She graduated from university with a degree in communications and went on to work full-time for a computer assembly company. Everything seemed fine until recently, when she received a job offer from Vancouver and started getting her papers ready. Then, with no warning, Maricel told me she was pregnant and planning to marry a man fifteen years older than herself. What's more, she intended to leave her baby to work in Vancouver as she had initially planned.

17   After so many years, the shock of this turn of events gave me the courage to confront what I'd always been afraid to face. I asked my middle daughter, Maricar, about my absence in her life. After much prodding and some crying, she told me that despite their grandmother's presence, she felt there was a hole in her life, an indescribable void, that couldn't be filled by my regular visits home or long-distance telephone calls or a regular and generous allowance.

18   Maricar dropped out of school during her first year in engineering and got married early. She succeeded in filling up the emptiness in her life by raising her own family. Today, she is a very protective mother of three small children. She doesn't let her kids out of her sight for more than thirty minutes. Once, Maricar's mother-in-law invited Francis, the oldest boy, to spend a weekend with her back in the village. Maricar refused to let him go. When I asked her why, she said, "I grew up away from you and I know how it felt, not having a mother around. I will never let my children feel the same way, ever."

19   I suspect Maricar is trying to compensate for my absence in her childhood. Maricel is repeating my history. These discoveries make me feel very sad and extremely guilty.

My youngest daughter stopped studying in her third year of [20] computers to work in Singapore. That's where she met Robert, a young sailor from Tacoma, Washington. Tacoma is only a three-hour drive from Vancouver, where I live. They got married within a year. I asked her sisters whether Catherine married Robert because living in Tacoma would bring her closer to me. They assured me that Catherine was in love and very happy with the man she married.

"Proof?" I asked. [21]

"Catherine cried every day after Robert got on his ship and sailed [22] away," I was told, "until the day she left to join him in Tacoma."

That's at least one load off my mind. [23]

Through the years, I've met other absentee mothers in Vancouver [24] and Singapore, all of whom feel guilty and are trying to soften their absence with presents—the latest iPod, cellphones, Game Boys, PlayStations, all the brand-name denim jeans the kids want—a practice that spawns materialistic and brand-conscious children. My own daughters would settle for nothing less than a genuine pair of Levi's 501s, something far removed from my childhood, when my mother made my dresses out of cotton hog-feed sacks, which actually came in many designs and a variety of lovely colours. Yet none of those expensive things are replacement enough. Every long-distance mother knows this deep inside.

Sociologists confirm my experiences. Research I've read on the [25] phenomenon of women's migration shows that kids of mothers like me feel different, unloved and angry, despite being left under the care of devoted relatives. Many of them display tendencies toward materialism, bad school performance, or drug addiction.

I've done my best to avoid these pitfalls. I went home every year. I [26] regularly remind my daughters that they were there and I was here not because I abandoned them but because I wanted them to enjoy things I never had as a child. That I loved them and that one day we would all be together again. I believed that if they weren't told my reasons, they would form their own conclusions, perhaps the wrong ones.

Because I stayed away for too long, my children chose their own [27] paths. I'm still alone in Vancouver. I'm still caught in the same time warp that my friends, other mothers, have successfully left behind. My kids have never grown up in my mind. At forty-eight, I'm still frantically trying to make up for lost time. Whenever I visit my daughters, despite their husbands, kids, and other people being around, they become my little girls again. I'm a young mother again, and they revert to their childhood habits. We cuddle a lot. I cook for them. We go shopping together. I buy them presents. Then I leave to pursue my own life once again, and we're back to replaying the same drama at the Manila International Airport.

28   Afterwards, their husbands jokingly tell me they've had to deal with their wives' "Mommy hangovers" for days. This wasn't what I'd hoped for when I left them in 1984. I may have changed the course of our lives, but not in the way I wanted. I console myself with the fact that I did not fail too badly None of them turned to drugs or ran away from home. They've grown up relatively normal and happy with their choices. They say they have forgiven me for going away because they know I was only trying to do my best for them.

29   And I will keep doing so. On a recent trip home, I gathered my brood together for three weeks. One day, I watched with overwhelming grandmotherly joy as my three older grandchildren—Francis, who is eight, Charles, seven, and Patricia, three, all happy, well-adjusted, and secure in their mother's presence—learned to work together on a computer I bought for them. This is how a family should be, I thought.

30   And as I cuddled my latest grandbaby, Maricel's two-month-old Margaret Sydney, I reiterated everything I vowed to myself as a twenty-one-year-old parent: I'll do my very best to give you everything, I promise. And then I add another thought—another promise—one I wish I'd made in my own life as a mother. I'll make sure your mom never leaves you.

EXPLORATIONS:

http://thetyee.ca/News/2006/03/28/GlobalNanny
http://en.wikipedia.org/wiki/Philippines

STRUCTURE:

1. Point out Crisanta Sampang's THESIS STATEMENT.
2. Sampang's decision to live abroad, leaving her children with family in the Philippines, is rooted in several *causes*. Point them out.
3. Sampang's decision to live abroad, leaving her children in the Philippines, also brings many *effects*. Cite the main ones.
4. Read aloud this selection's closing paragraph. How does Sampang's "promise" to her two-month-old granddaughter serve to cap her whole argument? In what way is it an *effect* of all that has gone before?

STYLE:

1. Hold your book at arm's length. Can you see whether our selection is made mostly of small words or big words? Which would be more appropriate to "Trading Motherhood for Dollars"? Describe the AUDIENCE for which Sampang is writing.
2. Read paragraph 8 aloud, with feeling. Analyze Sampang's STYLE in recounting this harrowing scene at the airport. How does she build suspense? How does she convey tension?

IDEAS FOR DISCUSSION AND WRITING:

1. Sampang has followed "the waves of Filipinos going out of the country to find employment abroad" (par. 12). Journalist Deborah Campbell, in "A Global Nanny's Story" (*The Tyee* of March 28, 2006: http://thetyee.ca/News/2006/03/28/GlobalNanny) specifies the numbers behind this "wave." Some 8 million Filipinos (10% of the population) work abroad as "nannies, housekeepers, nurses and home support workers." They send US$8 billion a year back home. About 30% of Filipino children "live in households where at least one parent works abroad." And in Canada, a domestic worker earns as much in one month as most people in

the Philippines earn in a year: about US$1000. Many other nations are in a similar position, with large numbers of their citizens sending home money from jobs abroad. Is this a worthwhile way for nations to help support their economies? What are the good *effects*? What are the bad *effects*?

2. In the article just mentioned, Sampang tells Deborah Campbell that "the effect of migration on families is a 'two-edged sword.'" On the positive side, she was able to buy a house and land for her mother, and "send one of each of her brothers' children to college with the understanding that they will help their siblings." Was the sacrifice for these advantages worth it?

3. When Crisanta Sampang was young she wore clothes made of hog-feed sacks. But as an absentee mother she was able to shower her children and grandchildren with material gifts: "the latest iPod, cellphones, Game Boys, PlayStations, all the brand-name denim jeans the kids want" (24). Is all this an advantage to the family, or does it just import a foreign lifestyle of greed and materialism?

4. In closing, Sampang cuddles her two-month-old granddaughter. She thinks to herself, "I'll do my very best to give you everything, I promise. And then I add another thought—another promise— one I wish I'd made in my own life as a mother. I'll make sure your mom never leaves you." After all you have read in this selection, do you agree that Sampang should have stayed with her family? Or was she right to leave? Defend your view with reasons.

5. PROCESS IN WRITING: *Can parents become "absentees" without ever leaving home? Think of someone you know, either in your own family or not, who did. Now take two pages of paper. On one write the probable* causes *of this choice, and on the other write down what you see to be the* effects. *Next devise a* THESIS STATEMENT *that specifies your topic and your view of it. Write a quick draft of your argument, probably placing all the* causes *first and the* effects *later. Then look it over. Have you reached a high percentage of example* content, *as Crisanta Sampang has? Do all the* examples *support your overall point? If not, either remove some or modify your point. Finally check for conciseness, for good punctuation, and for spelling, before printing out your best version.*

Note: See also the Topics for Writing on the Online Learning Centre at www. mcgrawhill.ca/olc/conrad.

PROCESS IN WRITING: GUIDELINES

Follow at least some of these steps in writing your essay of cause and effect (your teacher may suggest which ones).

1. *In the middle of a page, write the subject you wish to explore in your essay of* cause and effect. *Now around it write many other words that it brings to mind. Connect related items with lines, then use this cluster outline to discover your argument. Except for the introduction and conclusion, which may give background or look at the subject's future, focus down to EITHER the* causes *OR the* effects.
2. *Now write a quick first draft, getting it all out on the computer screen or the paper without stopping now to revise.*
3. *When this version has "cooled off," analyze it, referring to our chapter introduction: Have you begun and ended at the right places in the chain of causality? If not, cut or add. Have you found the* real causes *or the* real effects*? If not, revise. Do you also need* causes of causes, *or* effects of effects*? If so, add.*
4. *Now sharpen the* TRANSITIONS, *using expressions like "since," "although," "because" and "as a result" to signal each step of your logic.*
5. *Share this version with a group of classmates. Revise any places where this* AUDIENCE *does not follow your logic.*
6. *Finally, edit for things like spelling and punctuation before printing out your best version.*

Mike Constable

"Women workers earn, on an average, only 70 cents for every $1 a man gets—even though on an average, women are better educated than men."

—*Doris Anderson, "The 51-Per-Cent Minority"*

COMPARISON
AND CONTRAST

IT'S JUST THE OPPOSITE OF….

You may have heard the old Chinese proverb "I felt sorry for myself because I had no shoes, until I met a man who had no feet." How much more we suddenly know about both the shoes and the feet, thinking of them together! This is the power of comparison and contrast.

See Mike Constable's cartoon on the opposite page. What is happening? All the runners are in starting position, awaiting the same shot from the same referee, and no doubt aiming for the same finish line. These are the *comparisons* (similarities). Yet at the same time there are *contrasts* (differences). Three of the runners are men, but only one is a woman. The referee holding his gun is also a man, unlike the woman contestant. She will run in skirt and high heels, while the men clearly will not. Worst of all, the men will run straight ahead, while she must race uphill to reach their level. Is there any way the woman can win this race?

Though the cartoon shows both comparisons and contrasts, clearly it is the contrasts that send the message—men have advantages in the race of life. In the essay that follows, Doris Anderson uses words to send the same message through the same logic. Though of course there are similarities between the lives of women and men, it is the differences, the *contrasts*, that build Anderson's point that women, though a "majority" in numbers, are a "minority" in power.

When using the logic of comparison and contrast in your own essays, you, too, may find both similarities and differences. Though it is possible to explore both, the need to focus means that using one is often better—and the choice is often the more dramatic one: *contrast.*

You have experienced contrast if you have ever known culture shock. As you enter a new country, the look of the buildings and streets, the smells in the air, the sounds, the language and customs, all seem strange—because you are contrasting them to what you just left. And if you stay a long time, the same happens in reverse when you return: home seems strange because you are contrasting it to the place where you've just been. The cars may seem too big, the food too bland, the pace of life too fast. Travel is one of the great educational experiences: through contrast, one place puts another in perspective.

In a comparison and contrast essay, it is essential to choose two subjects *of the same general type:* two countries, two sports, two poems, or two solutions to unemployment. For example, a person who knows both Vancouver and Montreal might choose to compare and/ or contrast these two cities: their cuisine, their night life, cost of rent, traffic, air pollution, crime, level of unemployment, level of multiculturalism, etc. By the end of the essay—whether or not we agree with the author's point of view or preference of city—we would have the impression of reading a logical argument. After all, Vancouver and Montreal are in the same category: major Canadian cities.

But suppose that instead of comparing two cities, the author had compared a city and an anthill. After all, there are similarities: both are crowded, both are highly organized, both have housing with many rooms located off corridors, etc. But no matter how much fun she might have had or what insights she might have got across, she would prove nothing—for the simple reason that people are not insects. The essay would be an *analogy,* a more imaginative but less logical kind of argument, which we will explore in the next chapter.

Once you have chosen your two subjects of the same general type, you face another choice: how to arrange them. There are two basic ways:

DIVIDE THE ESSAY INTO HALVES, devoting the first half to Vancouver and the second to Montreal. This system is natural in a short essay, because your reader remembers everything from the first half while reading the second half. It is also natural when for some reason the items are more clearly discussed as a whole than in parts.

DIVIDE THE SUBJECTS INTO SEPARATE POINTS. First compare the cuisine in both cities, then the night life, then the cost of rent, and so on through your whole list of points. This system is most natural in long essays: putting related material together helps the reader to grasp comparisons or contrasts without the strain of recalling every detail from ten pages back.

Although "halves" are often best for short papers and "separate points" are often best for long papers, be open to the needs of your particular subject, treatment and purpose. Choose the approach that will most strongly deliver your message.

For example, Catherine Pigott, in her essay "Chicken-Hips" in this chapter, uses halves. This fits the chronology of her subject, since she spends time first in Africa, then in Canada. More importantly, it fits her subject, which is cultural. We appreciate more easily the many cultural aspects of life in Gambia that lead to Pigott's new idea of body image, since they are all presented together. Later we have the same experience with aspects of Canada's culture, which drag her back to her old ideas of body image. Finally, Pigott's essay is fairly short, so the halves are not too long to master.

By contrast, "Apocalypse Soon," by Jon Evans, is a much longer essay, which might already suggest a point-by-point approach, to make things easier for the reader. Indeed, Evans places his contrasts of the paper book and its electronic competitors throughout the essay, as the many different subpoints come up, ranging from the economics of publishing, to physical comfort in reading, to the decline of the newspaper, to environmental implications of paper books, to commercial and moral implications of downloading. It is difficult to imagine readers mastering all this material if it were not presented in pieces small enough to digest.

Finally, the very act of comparing or contrasting means you need *examples*—either a large number of short ones or a small number of long ones. If these do not make up at least half the content of your essay (as they do in both Pigott and Evans), you are probably losing power. Add more.

To generate your examples and points, why not draw a line down the middle of a blank page and put the name of your subjects at the top of each column? Now brainstorm a list of points under each heading. Connect related items from left to right with lines, and, seeing relationships, decide on your thesis statement. Is cash better than credit? Is income tax fairer than sales tax? Are motorcycles more dangerous than cars? Whatever you believe is the truth, now write your essay, letting the many examples show your reader why.

Note: Many essays in other chapters use comparison and contrast to help make their point. See especially these:

Crisanta Sampang, "Trading Motherhood for Dollars," p. 176
Samantha Bennett, "It's Not Just the Weather That's Cooler in Canada," p. 264
Martin Hocking, "Capping the Great Cup Debate," p. 354
Kildare Dobbs, "The Scar," p. 361
Joy Kogawa, "Grinning and Happy," p. 373
Margaret Atwood, "Letter to America," p. 392

DORIS ANDERSON

The 51-Per-Cent Minority

Doris Anderson (1921–2007) was always a "rebel daughter" (to use the title of her autobiography). From a prairie childhood, with a tyrannical father but an independent mother, Anderson went on to teachers' college and taught in rural Alberta till she could put herself through university. With a B.A. from the University of Alberta, she then went to Toronto and began her career in journalism. From copy editor and researcher, she moved in 1951 to Chatelaine, *where she rose through the ranks to become editor-in-chief in 1957, the same year she married lawyer David Anderson. Years before the rise of feminism, she was shaking up her readers with articles on legalization of abortion, battered babies, divorce law reform, female sexuality and practical advice for working women. Soon a million and a half women were reading* Chatelaine *every month, and in the process gaining a taste for new rights. As early as the sixties, Anderson agitated for a Royal Commission on the Status of Women. When it was created, with herself as chair, she scored the biggest achievement of her career: while the government debated the content of its new constitution, she saw there was nothing in it for women. So she suddenly resigned in 1981 from the Royal Commission; this sparked a massive campaign by women, a crisis in the government and a result of full equal rights for women being enshrined in the new Constitution. Anderson went on to head the National Action Committee on the Status of Women, as well as the Ontario Press Council. She also published novels,* Two Women *in 1978,* Rough Layout *in 1981 and* Affairs of State *in 1988. In addition to her many editorials and articles, she also wrote two nonfiction books,* The Unfinished Revolution *(on the status of women in Europe and North America) and her 1996 autobiography. It was in 1980 that our own selection, "The 51-Per-Cent Minority," first appeared in* Maclean's.

1   In any Canadian election the public will probably be hammered numb with talk of the economy, energy and other current issues. But there will always be some far more startling topics that no one will talk about at all.

2   No one is going to say to all new Canadians: "Look, we're going through some tough times. Three out of four of you had better face the fact that you're always going to be poor. At 65 more than likely you'll be living below the poverty level."

3   And no one is going to tell Quebeckers: "You will have to get along on less money than the rest of the country. For every $1 the rest of us earn, you, because you live in Quebec, will earn 70 cents."

4   I doubt very much that any political party is going to level with the Atlantic provinces and say: "We don't consider people living there serious prime workers. Forget about any special measures to make jobs for you. In fact in future federal-provincial talks we're not even going to discuss your particular employment problems."

5   And no politician is going to tell all the left-handed people in the country: "Look, we know it looks like discrimination, but we have to save some money somewhere. So, although you will pay into your company pension plan at the same rate as everyone else, you will collect less when you retire."

6   And no one is going to say to Canadian doctors: "We know you do one of the most important jobs any citizen can perform, but from now on you're going to have to get along without any support systems. All hospital equipment and help will be drastically reduced. We believe a good doctor should instinctively know what to do—or you're in the wrong job. If you're really dedicated you'll get along."

7   As for blacks: "Because of the color of your skin, you're going to be paid less than the white person next to you who is doing exactly the same job. It's tough but that's the way it is."

8   As for Catholics: "You're just going to have to understand that you will be beaten up by people with other religious beliefs quite regularly. Even if your assailant threatens to kill you, you can't do anything about it. After all, we all need some escape valves, don't we?"

9   Does all of the above sound like some nihilistic nightmare where Orwellian forces have taken over? Well, it's not. It's all happening right now, in Canada.

It's not happening to new Canadians, Quebeckers, residents of the   10
Atlantic provinces, left-handed people, doctors, blacks or Indians. If
it were, there would be riots in the streets. Civil libertarians would be
howling for justice. But all of these discriminatory practices are being
inflicted on women today in Canada as a matter of course.

Most women work at two jobs—one inside the home and one out-   11
side. Yet three out of four women who become widowed or divorced
or have never married live out their old age in poverty.

Women workers earn, on an average, only 70 cents for every $1 a   12
man gets—even though on an average, women are better educated
than men.

And when companies base pension plans on how long people live,   13
women still pay the same rates as men but often collect less.

What politician could possibly tell doctors to train each other and get   14
along without all their high technology and trained help? Yet a more
important job than saving lives is surely creating lives. But mothers get
no training, no help in the way of a family allowance, inadequate day-
care centres, and almost nonexistent after-school programs.

No politician would dream of telling blacks they must automatically   15
earn less than other people. But women sales clerks, waitresses and
hospital orderlies often earn less than males doing the same jobs. It
would be called discrimination if a member of a religious group was
beaten up, and the assailant would be jailed. But hundreds of wives
get beaten by their husbands week in and week out, year after year.
Some die, yet society still tolerates the fact that it's happening.

Women make up 51 per cent of the population of this country.   16
Think of the kind of clout they could have if they used it at the polls.
But to listen to the political parties, the woman voter just doesn't exist.
When politicians talk to fishing folk they talk about improved processing plants and new docks. When they talk to wheat farmers they talk
of better transportation and higher price supports. When they talk to
people in the Atlantic provinces they talk about new federal money
for buildings and more incentives for secondary industry. When they
talk to ethnic groups they talk about better language training courses.
But when they think of women—if they do at all—they assume women
will vote exactly as their husbands—so why waste time offering them
anything? It's mind-boggling to contemplate, though, how all those

discriminatory practices would be swept aside if, instead of women, we were Italian, or black, or lived in Quebec or the Atlantic provinces.

EXPLORATIONS:

Doris Anderson,
>   *The Unfinished Revolution*
>   *Rebel Daughter: An Autobiography*

Simone de Beauvoir, *The Second Sex*

Naomi Wolf, *The Beauty Myth: How Images of Beauty Are Used Against Women*

Margaret Atwood, *The Handmaid's Tale* (novel)

http://www.cddc.vt.edu/feminism/can.html

http://www.cbc.ca/lifeandtimes/anderson.html

STRUCTURE:

1. Is this essay mainly a *comparison* or a *contrast*?
2. Does Anderson argue "point by point" or by "halves"?
3. Point out the passage of TRANSITION between Anderson's discussion of minorities and her discussion of women.
4. Why does this feminist essay never mention women until halfway through? How does this tactic help Anderson reach the potentially unreceptive 49% of her AUDIENCE that is male?
5. If you have read *1984* or *Animal Farm,* tell how the reference to George Orwell in paragraph 9 helps make Anderson's point.
6. Why does the closing offer a series of new *examples*? Why are they so short?

STYLE:

1. How important is the title of an essay? What should it do? How effective is this one, and why?
2. Anderson's essay first appeared in *Maclean's,* a magazine for the general reader. Name all the ways in which her essay seems designed for that person.

IDEAS FOR DISCUSSION AND WRITING:

1. Explain the IRONY of Anderson's claim: in what sense are women, 51% of the population, a "minority" in Canada?

2. Anderson states in paragraph 11, "Most women work at two jobs— one inside the home and one outside." Suppose that someday you and your partner both have full-time jobs. How much of the housework will you expect your partner to do? Defend your view with reasons.

3. When "The 51-Per-Cent Minority" first appeared in 1980 in *Maclean's,* Doris Anderson reported that women made only 61 cents for every dollar a man made. Almost three decades later, as this book was being revised for its eighth edition, a federal Department of Justice report showed that, according to the latest census figures (2000), women in Canada still make only 71 cents for every dollar a man makes (see http://www.justice.gc.ca/en/ payeqsal/6026.html). Tell all the reasons you can think of why there has been only a dime per hour of improvement in all this time.

4. In paragraph 16 Anderson writes, "Women make up 51 per cent of the population of this country. Think of the kind of clout they could have if they used it at the polls." Do you agree that women have not yet used their votes to best advantage? If so, why not? How could they begin to?

5. PROCESS IN WRITING: *Write an essay that* contrasts *the way society trains girls to be women with the way society trains boys to be men. First divide a page into halves, one for each sex, and fill each half with* examples. *Now from these notes choose contrasting pairs. Decide whether to organize the pairs by "halves" or "point by point," then write a rapid discovery draft. In your next version strengthen the* TRANSITIONS, *especially signals such as "but," "on the other hand," "however" and "yet," which point out contrast. Share a version with classmates in small groups to see if all parts work. Revise any that do not. Finally, read your best version aloud to the whole class, and be ready to answer questions asked from other points of view.*

Note: See also the Topics for Writing on the Online Learning Centre at www. mcgrawhill.ca/olc/conrad.

CATHERINE PIGOTT

Chicken-Hips*

How does a piece of writing begin? Here is an example. Seeing a documentary film about eating disorders, The Famine Within, *and interviewing its director Katherine Gilday for a magazine article, Catherine Pigott recalled her own time in Africa. It was several years earlier, while teaching English at a teachers' college, that she had shared the home and culture of a Gambian family. Then returning to Canada, she suffered culture shock: through African eyes she now saw North American ideas of eating and bodily appearance as cruel and misguided. In response to this mix of new experience and earlier memories, she wrote the essay that follows (Globe and Mail,* March 20, 1991*), a celebration of the natural life she knew in Africa. Not only is its message cross-cultural but also its form: Pigott says "I was aware of speaking as I wrote," as in the oral tradition of African narrative. Now she applies this philosophy daily in her profession. After her return she worked for a time in print journalism, then entered the world of radio: first the* CBC Radio News, *then the CBC'S celebrated* Morningside, *where she found guests for host Peter Gzowski, and researched and developed a broadcast a day. From there she moved on to* Sunday Morning, *then to CBC Radio's national program* This Morning. *At present she is a producer for the CBC in Yellowknife. Pigott thinks of her writing for radio as "not for the eye but the ear." It is direct, simple, natural. She offers similar advice to students writing essays: "Write for the ear as well as the eye."*

*Editor's title.

The women of the household clucked disapprovingly when they saw me. It was the first time I had worn African clothes since my arrival in tiny, dusty Gambia, and evidently they were not impressed. They adjusted my head-tie and pulled my *lappa*, the ankle-length fabric I had wrapped around myself, even tighter. "You're too thin," one of them pronounced. "It's no good." They nicknamed me "Chicken-hips."

I marvelled at this accolade, for I had never been called thin in my life. It was something I longed for. I would have been flattered if those ample-bosomed women hadn't looked so distressed. It was obvious I fell far short of their ideal of beauty.

I had dressed up for a very special occasion—the baptism of a son. The women heaped rice into tin basins the size of laundry tubs, shaping it into mounds with their hands. Five of us sat around one basin, thrusting our fingers into the scalding food. These women ate with such relish, such joy. They pressed the rice into balls in their fists, squeezing until the bright-red palm oil ran down their forearms and dripped off their elbows.

I tried desperately, but I could not eat enough to please them. It was hard for me to explain that I come from a culture in which it is almost unseemly for a woman to eat too heartily. It's considered unattractive. It was even harder to explain that to me thin is beautiful, and in my country we deny ourselves food in our pursuit of perfect slenderness.

That night, everyone danced to welcome the baby. Women swivelled their broad hips and used their hands to emphasize the roundness of their bodies. One needed to be round and wide to make the dance beautiful. There was no place for thinness here. It made people sad. It reminded them of things they wanted to forget, such as poverty, drought and starvation. You never knew when the rice was going to run out.

I began to believe that Africa's image of the perfect female body was far more realistic than the long-legged leanness I had been conditioned to admire. There, it is beautiful—not shameful—to carry weight on the hips and thighs, to have a round stomach and heavy, swinging breasts. Women do not battle the bulge, they celebrate it. A body is not something to be tamed and moulded.

7   The friends who had christened me Chicken-hips made it their mission to fatten me up. It wasn't long before a diet of rice and rich, oily stew twice a day began to change me. Every month, the women would take a stick and measure my backside, noting with pleasure its gradual expansion. "Oh Catherine, your buttocks are getting nice now!" they would say.

8   What was extraordinary was that I, too, believed I was becoming more beautiful. There was no sense of panic, no shame, no guilt-ridden resolves to go on the miracle grape-and-water diet. One day, I tied my *lappa* tight across my hips and went to the market to buy beer for a wedding. I carried the crate of bottles home on my head, swinging my hips slowly as I walked. I felt transformed.

9   In Gambia, people don't use words such as "cheating," "naughty," or "guilty" when they talk about eating. The language of sin is not applied to food. Fat is desirable. It holds beneficial meanings of abundance, fertility and health.

10   My perception of beauty altered as my body did. The European tourists on the beach began to look strange and skeletal rather than "slim." They had no hips. They seemed devoid of shape and substance. Women I once would have envied appeared fragile and even ugly. The ideal they represented no longer made sense.

11   After a year, I came home. I preached my new way of seeing to anyone who would listen. I wanted to cling to the liberating belief that losing weight had nothing to do with self-love.

12   Family members kindly suggested that I might look and feel better if I slimmed down a little. They encouraged me to join an exercise club. I wandered around the malls in a dislocated daze. I felt uncomfortable trying on clothes that hung so elegantly on the mannequins. I began hearing old voices inside my head: "Plaid makes you look fat.... You're too short for that style.... Vertical stripes are more slimming.... Wear black."

13   I joined the club. Just a few weeks after I had worn a *lappa* and scooped up rice with my hands, I was climbing into pink leotards and

aerobics shoes. The instructor told me that I had to set fitness goals and "weigh in" after my workouts. There were mirrors on the walls and I could see women watching themselves. I sensed that even the loveliest among them felt they were somehow flawed. As the aerobics instructor barked out commands for arm lifts and leg lifts, I pictured Gambian women pounding millet and dancing in a circle with their arms raised high. I do not mean to romanticize their rock-hard lives, but we were hardly to be envied as we ran like fools between two walls to the tiresome beat of synthesized music.

We were a roomful of women striving to reshape ourselves into   14
some kind of pubertal ideal. I reverted to my natural state: one of yearning to be slimmer and more fit than I was. My freedom had been temporary. I was home, where fat is feared and despised. It was time to exert control over my body and my life. I dreaded the thought of people saying, "She's let herself go."

If I return to Africa, I am sure the women will shake their heads in   15
bewildered dismay. Even now, I sometimes catch my reflection in a window and their voices come back to me. "Yo! Chicken-hips!"

EXPLORATIONS:

Joan J. Brumberg, *Fasting Girls: The History of Anorexia Nervosa*
Richard Gordon, *Anorexia and Bulimia: Anatomy of a Social Epidemic*
Jean Kilbourne, *Slim Hopes: Advertising and the Obsession with Thinness* (video, 1995, 30 min.)
Naomi Wolf, *The Beauty Myth: How Images of Beauty Are Used Against Women*
Joetta Schlabach, *Extending the Table: A World Community Cookbook*
http://home3.inet.tele.dk/mcamara/gam.html
http://www.phac-aspc.gc.ca/publicat/miic-mmac/chap_6_e.html
http://ca.dir.yahoo.com/Health/Diseases_and_Conditions/ Anorexia_Nervosa
http://www.pbs.org/wgbh/nova/thin/program.html# (several short online videos about eating disorders)

STRUCTURE:

1. "Chicken-Hips" is mainly a *contrast* of ideals of beauty in Gambia and Canada. Point out at least two other things that the essay *compares*.

2. Does Pigott organize her *contrast* mainly "point by point" or by "halves"?

3. How selectively does the author choose details from her year in Africa? In paragraph 1, for example, has she told anything at all that is not vital to her theme?

4. What classic techniques of organization does Pigott exploit in her opening and closing?

STYLE:

1. The Gambian women nicknamed our author "Chicken-hips" because of her relative thinness. Create five other METAPHORS they could have used to say the same thing.

2. Where do SENSE IMAGES most strongly help us "see" the author's point?

3. Judging by Pigott's vocabulary, what sort of *audience* is she aiming at in her essay?

IDEAS FOR DISCUSSION AND WRITING:

1. Review "My Body Is My Own Business" (p. 149), then *compare* and/or *contrast* the struggles of Naheed Mustafa and of Catherine Pigott with body image. Has either writer found a solution to the problem?

2. How important to you is the appearance of your body? Are you trying for an ideal size or shape? Describe it to the class. And what sources gave you this ideal?

3. Why, in Canada, is it mostly women who go on diets, and mostly women who suffer and die from anorexia nervosa?

4. In paragraph 5 thinness reminds Gambians of "things they wanted to forget, such as poverty, drought and starvation." On the other hand, the Duchess of Windsor once remarked, "Never too rich

and never too thin." How do *you* see thinness? *Compare* or *contrast* your view to one of the above, and give reasons.

5. Have you, like Pigott, lived in another country? Tell the class one major thing the other culture taught you about life. Now that you are here, are you remembering or forgetting the lesson?

6. Many Canadians go abroad, as Pigott did, to teach in developing countries. But imagine her Gambian friends coming to your school to teach you. What might some of their "lessons" be?

7. In paragraph 10, watching the "skeletal" Europeans at the beach, Pigott states "My perception of beauty altered." Examine the illustrations in a book of art history, taking notes on how our current view of human beauty differs from those of past periods. Report these differences to the class, showing illustrations as examples.

8. PROCESS IN WRITING: *Remember a time when you set out to change your body through a diet, athletics, aerobics, bodybuilding or other means. On a blank piece of paper draw a vertical line. Entitle the left column "BEFORE" and the right column "AFTER," then brainstorm to develop the* contrast. *Now looking at these notes, decide on your thesis: In which version of yourself did you actually feel happier, the before or after? Now write a rapid first draft, proceeding either by "halves" or "point by point." The next day look it over: Do images help your audience "see" you? If not, add. Is your draft at least 50% examples? If not, add. Are any words wasted? If so, cut. Finally, edit for things like grammar and spelling, then produce your good version.*

Note: See also the Topics for Writing on the Online Learning Centre at www. mcgrawhill.ca/olc/conrad.

STEPHANIE NOLEN

Regine Mamba

As Africa correspondent for the Toronto Globe and Mail, *Stephanie Nolen has a special mission to inform the world about the HIV/AIDS pandemic in Africa. Having lived now for several years in Johannesburg, South Africa, and having reported from some 40 countries around the world, including two dozen in Africa, and being able to speak seven languages, Nolen has built a formidable background of knowledge and of contacts to pursue her goal. She has long garnered journalism awards, such as the 2003 National Newspaper Award for International Reporting, then the same award in 2004 for her writings about the genocide in Rwanda. Nolen has won the Amnesty International Award for Human Rights Reporting three times. It was in 2007, though, that she stunned readers around the world with her book 28: Stories of AIDS in Africa. (The title refers to her profiles of 28 Africans, one for each million people living with HIV/AIDS in Africa.) While the book conveys statistics that amply define the challenge, it is Nolen's anecdotal portraits of AIDS victims that opens the eyes of her readers. She took substantial risks gathering her information, for example travelling with a long-distance trucker to see first-hand the lifestyle, and all the prostitution, that have so quickly spread the pandemic. Our selection comes from this volume, which Stephen Lewis, former Canadian ambassador to the U.N., has called "the best book ever written about AIDS."*

1   In the natural order of things, these would be quiet days for Regine Mamba. She would sit in the shade of the large neem tree in her swept dirt yard in Malala in southern Zambia. She

might sift through a basket of beans in her lap, picking out the stones and twigs, and she might keep an eye on a pudgy baby just learning to totter. They should be peaceful, these days at the end of her life.

Instead, Regine works. She is up before the sun to start a fire for the maize porridge the children eat, and still up well after the sun has set, trying to comfort them with a story or a hymn when they sit by the embers of that fire. And although she is exhausted, she often lies awake long after the children have fallen asleep all crammed together in two round mud houses—there is much to occupy her mind. Instead of the quiet twilight of old age that should be hers, Regine has work and worries and children.

A huge number of children: so many that when I arrived at her house, on a walk through Malala, I thought at first that it was a primary school. There were children peeping around the doors of the houses and children sitting in the shade of the thatch-roof overhang, children tussling by the kindling pile and children beneath the tree.

"These children, their mothers and fathers died," Regine said by way of introduction.

We sat beneath that tree and Regine told me about the past few years, how it came to be that they are all her children now. As a young woman, she had given birth to seven who survived, most of whom went off to the capital, Lusaka, to work as teachers and clerks and maids. There they got married and had children of their own. In the usual way of things in a place like Malala, those children would have come home every few months, bringing their own families—they might time their visit to help with the planting, and bring a sweater or a fluffy new Chinese-made blanket as a gift. Regine would have sat on a rough wood chair and listened to the stories from the city. Her children would have stayed for a couple of days, and then they would have gone home again, taking their own children with them.

It didn't work out that way. In 1998, one of her daughters died in Lusaka, and she took a rickety shared taxi into the city. "I went and assessed the situation. Their father did not have much life left in him. According to our tradition, as the grandmother you are responsible. You cannot just disregard your grandchildren." So she brought those children home to Malala. Then a second daughter and son-in-law died, and their children were sent to Regine. Then her third daughter, Lovegirl, lost her husband and came home, bringing her one surviving child and two orphans from another daughter. Before long there were more than a dozen children, in city clothes rapidly starting to fray, and at the age of seventy-four, Regine's days of sitting in the shade were over.

7   In Zambia today, basic demographics are horribly skewed. One in three children is an orphan. One in five people has HIV/AIDS. In a country of eleven million, at least 600,000 people have already died, almost all of them young adults. They have left behind a good part of a generation of children without parents. And in so many cases those children have wound up, after a few detours to aunts or neighbours, with their grandmothers.

8   Nearly two-thirds of orphans in southern and eastern Africa are in the care of grandparents. One in three heads of household in Zambia is over fifty years of age; two-thirds of them are female. In other words, grandmothers. It is the grannies, more than any other group, who carry this burden. Regine was already widowed and long past the days of sexual activity when the virus took hold in Zambia—women her age have largely escaped it. They remain healthy as their children waste away by the age of thirty. When I met her in 2003, Regine had lived to twice a Zambian woman's life expectancy, by then reduced to just thirty-seven years because of AIDS.

9   Regine and her family live at the end of a winding dirt track on a low hill. There is one big rondavel, about two metres across with smooth mud-plastered walls, where she sleeps with the little ones; one rough rondavel where they cook and keep their small store of maize; a third, small rondavel where the older children sleep; and one last round hut. Regine led me inside this one and introduced her youngest daughter, Jacqueline, who was then exactly my age, thirty-two. She was lying on the floor on a fresh grass mat, and dying. Every hour or two her toddler daughter crept up to the door and peered around it to where her mother lay. Sometimes Jacqueline gave her a little wave.

10   Regine has a constant struggle to care for this brood, ranging from one lanky fifteen-year-old boy to several grubby babies. Lovegirl, the

only other adult in the family, is fifty-one, has grandchildren of her own and could also reasonably expect to be retiring. Instead she had moved back home to help her mother.

"It's trying, it's difficult—the only way I manage is that what little I get, I give them," Regine said. "Even if it's not very nice food—as long as it helps them to live. The biggest problem is that I have to till the land, and I have no animals to help me plant a big maize field." Her back aches, and it pains her to hoe and plow, but she has no cash to hire labourers from the village and must rely on the work of the older children. Her worries have given her high blood pressure; after she slowly lowered herself to the ground, to sit and rest for a minute or two, she rubbed her swollen calves with gnarled hands.

The children were dust-smeared and grimy, wearing short trousers made out of feed sacks. It is a source of some shame for Regine, who knows that her grandchildren are less well off than her own children were. The newest child in the house that day was an infant a few weeks old, born to a fourteen-year-old granddaughter. Regine said, looking pained and embarrassed, that she was surprised by the pregnancy, but then, it isn't uncommon for orphaned village girls to have sex with older men for cash or food.

She wants the children to go to school, but in Zambia it costs 8,850 kwacha per year per child, or about $2.50—a huge burden. On the holidays and between terms, the oldest children go out to hoe the fields of better-off farmers near town to earn a few kwacha; thus far, it had been enough to keep them all enrolled for another term. Sometimes there is a bit left over for a new shirt or a pair of shoes, shoes that are worn only to school and church and otherwise kept stored away.

Regine's situation, the sheer quantity of children she has inherited, should be extraordinary. And yet in Malala, this story—of the young people dying and their wide-eyed children turning up back in the village—has become the norm. In 1999, the old women decided to organize, to pool their resources. They made a registry, and came up with 376 orphans, out of a total population of four thousand in Malala and two villages nearby. In other words, nearly one of every ten people in these villages is a child whose parents have died of AIDS. The grandmothers made a plan: committee members set out to visit each family with orphans, to see how they were coping. That chance to talk is important, Regine said—it gives the guardians an opportunity to share their worries, and the children time to air their grievances. The local branch of the Salvation Army said it would help, with blankets, food parcels and pens and notebooks. But there wasn't enough money for the one thing every grandmother wanted: money to pay the fees and keep all the children in school.

15   As I sat with Regine that day, several of her neighbours, elderly ladies dressed, as she was, in a print wrap and blouse, scarves knotted round their heads, walked slowly up over the hill. They joined us in the shade of the neem tree, stretching out callused bare feet. The grannies said they could cope with the young orphans, but the pain of their parents' deaths makes the older ones a handful. "There's a problem with teenagers," one neighbour confided, while Regine slowly nodded in agreement. "With younger children you can manage, but teenagers say, 'You are not my mother or father.' Like any teenager, they go out and we are afraid they will be infected themselves, by the older men in the drinking places." Regine glanced toward her teenage granddaughters, one with the new baby on her back.

16   Regine was keeping the children fed and clothed—in itself something of a miracle—but she worried a great deal about their spirits. "I try by all means to make the children happy; because if I look sad they will worry and wonder what is happening, so I must tell them jokes. In the evenings when we sit around the cooking fire, I tell them stories, I sing them songs. I wish them happiness."

17   She and the other grandmothers listed off the people who were sick in Malala; they could name almost two dozen children who would lose their parents in the coming year. What, I asked, would happen to those children? Someone will take them in, the women said. We will continue to take care of them until all of us are dead.

18   But that, of course, was Regine's predominant worry. She was acutely conscious of her age. What will happen if she dies? If Lovegirl gets sick or can't manage? She told me that her great fear is that if the children are orphaned again, they will be separated, each one parcelled out to a different family; no one, she knows, could be expected to take all thirteen. "I worry. I think the children will suffer … I am old now, but we thank God that I can still manage."

She was sitting with her back against the tree trunk, and one by one the smaller children had crept forward to listen to the visitors. First one, then a second, jostled for space in her lap; she moved her legs so that a couple more could cuddle up beside her. An impish girl of about four wanted to drape around her granny's neck, and Regine made room for her too.   19

"I never imagined it this way," she said.   20

EXPLORATIONS:

Stephanie Nolen, *28: Stories of AIDS in Africa*
Stephen Lewis, *Race Against Time* (2nd ed.)
Albert Camus, *The Plague*
http://www.theglobeandmail.com/special/aidsinafrica
http://www.cbc.ca/thehour/video.php?id=1549
http://www.stephenlewisfoundation.org
http://en.wikipedia.org/wiki/AIDS

STRUCTURE:

1. Stephanie Nolen starts her essay off with a vivid *contrast*. Point it out. And point out the THESIS STATEMENT to which it leads.
2. In developing her essay of *contrast*, why does Nolen devote more space to the way life has turned out for Regine Mamba than to the way it would have turned out if the pandemic of HIV/AIDS had not hit?
3. What widely used device of closing does Nolan place in her final sentence?
4. To what extent does Nolen also exploit patterns of *cause and effect*? Point out several examples.

STYLE:

1. Why does Nolen put a section break between paragraphs 9 and 10? Does it serve an organizational purpose?

2. Read paragraph 3 aloud. Why does the word "children" appear four times in these two lines—not to mention more times in the paragraphs before and after? Is this *repetition* accidental or deliberate?

3. How well has Stephanie Nolen given us a picture in words of Regine Mamba's family and surroundings? Can you picture yourself there? Where are her best passages of *description*?

IDEAS FOR DISCUSSION AND WRITING:

1. In her book from which our selection comes, Stephanie Nolen portrays a stunning change in the demographics of Sub-Saharan Africa: vast numbers of parents have died of AIDS because they are at a sexually active age, while most of the children have survived because they are young, and the grandparents because they are old. According to Nolen, what are the main *effects* on society of this disappearance of a generation?

2. Would you mostly *compare* or *contrast* the lifestyle of your own grandparents to that of 74-year-old Regine Mamba in Zambia? Do your grandparents still work hard taking care of their descendants, or are they now at ease, experiencing travel and leisure? To what extent is their lifestyle determined by economics, and to what extent by culture?

3. Why do some employees wish to retire earlier, and others later? What *effects* does choice of retirement age have on the individual? On society? And what do you see as the ideal age to retire? Defend your answer with reasons.

4. Nolen says the average woman in Zambia can expect to live 37 years (half the age of Regine Mamba), and tells how almost all Regine Mamba's children have died. Yet in the developed world HIV/AIDS has become more of a chronic than a fatal disease. People are now "living with AIDS" for decades. How have these improvements taken place here? And why have they mostly not taken place in Zambia?

5. In paragraph 13 Nolen tells how the $2.50 a year it costs for a child to go to school is "a huge burden" barely affordable to Regine Mamba's family. What does your own tuition cost in Canada? Look over the web sites of some nonprofit agencies that work in

Africa. Find one you like. Describe it to the class. If there is interest, mount a fundraising project to help the agency do its work in
education or health.

6. PROCESS IN WRITING: *Which kind of home is better to grow up in, the
   "nuclear" family of parents and children, or the "extended" family that
   may also include grandparents, uncles, aunts and cousins? Close your
   eyes as you think of this topic. Then write an essay of* contrast. *First draw
   a line down the middle of a page, and write "nuclear" at the top left and
   "extended" at the top right. Now jot down many notes on both sides. Next
   develop a clear* THESIS STATEMENT *that tells your viewpoint on the question.
   Decide whether to develop your topic by "halves" or by "separate points,"
   then write a quick draft, using many* EXAMPLES *on both sides. Later look
   it all over. Does every example contribute to your point? Do* TRANSITION
   words speed your argument? Is the language CONCISE? *Finally check the
   punctuation and spelling, and print your best version. Bring it to class to
   read aloud, and be ready to defend your point of view.*

*Note: See also the Topics for Writing on the Online Learning Centre at www.
mcgrawhill.ca/olc/conrad.*

MICHAEL CRUMMEY

The Fish, the Fish

Poet and novelist Michael Crummey was born in 1965 in Buchans, Newfoundland, a mining town where his father had come to work after finding it impossible to make a living in the Newfoundland fishery. After high school Crummey earned an Arts degree at Memorial University, then moved to Ontario, where at Queen's he completed an M.A. and wrote poetry. Crummey soon began to publish in The Fiddlehead, The Malahat Review, Prism International *and other little magazines, then in 1996 published his first book of poems,* Arguments with Gravity. *Others followed, then in 1998 his book of short stories* Flesh & Blood, *and in 2001 his first novel,* River Thieves, *about the indigenous Beothuk people of Newfoundland and their tragic encounters with the Europeans. It quickly became a bestseller, enabling Crummey to move back to Newfoundland. In 2004 he co-authored* Newfoundland: Journey into a Lost Nation, *with photographer Greg Locke. Then in 2005 appeared his second novel,* The Wreckage. *Our own selection, "The Fish, The Fish," is a free-standing essay that was published in 2006 in the anthology* Writing Life, *edited by Constance Rooke. Whether writing poetry or prose, Crummey is serious about his craft: he polishes language till it shines.*

¹ The wind was up that morning, sweeping in over the bay, lifting a heavy lop on the water. I wore jeans, sneakers, two sweaters under a life jacket. Dad had on steel-toed rubber boots, an old pair of coveralls. Mom shook her head as we headed

down to the stage,° unlikely looking fishermen, the both of us. "Don't catch a whale," she said.

"If I don't throw up," I told her, "I'll be happy."

Eric, a family friend, was taking us out in his open eighteen-footer. He'd made his living off the cod before the government-imposed moratorium ended the commercial fishery in Newfoundland due to the cod stock's near-total collapse. He drives the local school bus now, but still has his boat and the stage just below his house in North Bay.

He kept the skiff to the calmer water close to shore as we headed out, the bow slapping above the waves, the spray blown back at us bitter, salt and cold. Halfway to open ocean he turned parallel to the troughs, gunning then easing off the motor as we rolled over each successive crest, before cutting the engine altogether in the middle of the bay and throwing out a grapple to hold us steady in the pitch.

We were there to hand-line for cod, during the one weekend a year set aside for the "food fishery." Fathoms of nylon threading through our fingers over the gunnel. I sat facing Dad, Eric standing behind him in the stern, each of us jigging our lines. Dad looked up occasionally to watch me, something like a grin on his face.

I had never caught a fish in my life. Grew up in a mining town in the interior of Newfoundland, hundreds of miles from salt water. I was also afflicted with a susceptibility to seasickness, which has always felt like a personal failure, a laughable weakness. And which might have accounted, I thought, for my father's grin.

Dad started in the fishery as a boy of nine, spending the summer months of his youth on the Labrador coast with his father. Working in all but the worst weather, out to the cod traps in open boats before first light, all day then at the splitting table to clean and salt the fish. Often just making ends meet after settling the crew's wages and what was owed the merchant at season's end. When his father died, Dad quit school to take over the crew, sixteen years old then and he fell quickly into debt. Took a job at the mine intending to pay it off and go back to fishing, but wound up working in Buchans thirty years and more.

°stage: A wooden platform near the water, where cod were split, salted and put in the sun to dry.

8　　After half an hour we had only the one small cod brought up by Eric and he decided to move us farther out, a small crowd of gulls chasing the boat to the mouth of the bay. The wind and waves heavier out there, the rise and fall like flying through turbulence but steady, a false kind of soothe to it. I stood in the bow, legs braced against the wood, letting out my line. The first hint of nausea was an odd niggle in the gut, a heat that was almost pleasurable, and I ignored it, hoping it would pass. Tried to will myself not to succumb. Left it nearly too long, raced to get the line up, the blood draining from my face. Sat just in time to hold down the surge of vomit.

9　　"You sick?" Eric asked, surprised.

10　　Dad just shook his head, that grin on his face again. Not mean at all. Bemused.

11　　Sitting down settled my stomach some, but I still felt miserable. The foul acid in my mouth and I spat repeatedly into the water, wanting only to get ashore. But I wouldn't ask. Let them go on fishing.

12　　This was the summer of 2001, just before my first novel was published. Dad was already sick then with the cancer that would kill him a little over a year later. I know he worried about me. He was never sure what to make of the writing exactly, why I did it, or what it did for me. I was thirty years old before I published my first book, a slender volume of poetry after nearly a decade of slogging it out in the little magazines. I remember telling Dad the news when the manuscript was accepted.

13　　"How much are they paying you?" he asked. And after we'd laughed off that question he wanted to know what the book was called.

14　　"*Arguments with Gravity.*"

15　　An abbreviated nod as he tried to take it in. "That's a queer fucking title," he said finally.

16　　Even that summer when we took our one and only fishing trip together, after I'd sold the novel, making enough money to quit my day job and move home to Newfoundland for good, he worried. "Who's going to take care of him?" he asked my mother when they lay in bed at night. After they were gone, he meant. To his mind writing was something more uncertain and mercurial than the whereabouts of the cod, an occupation to rival fishing for its insecurity, its monumental unpredictability. He never said as much but he must have expected, as I often do, that it might leave me someday, migrate somewhere else or simply dry up.

They had no better luck after the fish in the mouth of the bay. When Eric gave up and took in his line, he gutted the single cod, heaving out bloody handfuls of offal that the waiting gulls screeched and fought over. Washed the split fish over the side of the boat. Finally, mercifully, started the outboard.   17

I was still pale and clammy-cold as we headed back in. Still without a cod to my name. Dad and I were facing each other where we sat on the tauts, him smiling at me. "Better to be a poet," he said then.   18

And at that moment I could not disagree with him.   19

EXPLORATIONS:

Michael Crummey,
> *Arguments with Gravity* (poems)
> *The River Thieves* (novel)
> *Flesh & Blood* (novel)

Constance Rooke, ed., *Writing Life: Celebrated Canadian and International Authors on Writing and Life*

http://www.library.utoronto.ca/canpoetry/crummey/index.htm

http://en.wikipedia.org/wiki/Michael_Crummey

http://www.heritage.nf.ca/arts/michaelcrummey.html

http://www.randomhouse.ca/readmag/page5_author_interview.htm

http://www.stemnet.nf.ca/cod/home1.htm

http://faculty.marianopolis.edu/c.belanger/nfldhistory/
NewfoundlandHistory.htm

STRUCTURE:

1. Read paragraph 1 aloud. How does this opening already begin to introduce the *comparison and contrast* on which "The Fish, The Fish" is built?

2. "The Fish, The Fish" is really a double *comparison and contrast*: it brings face to face two vastly different ways of making a living (or,

more probably, of failing to make a living), and brings face to face the two family members who represent these opposites. Which paragraphs examine mostly the life of the father, and which examine mostly the life of the son? Is the argument arranged mostly by *halves*, or *point by point?*

3. In this *contrast* of father and son, are there also *comparisons*, ways in which they are alike? Give examples.

4. Why is the dad's conclusion that it is "better to be a poet" placed right at the end?

5. Crummey's *comparison and contrast* is framed in a *narrative* (the day's outing to fish cod). How has he integrated his topic with this format? Give examples.

STYLE:

1. Do you know the nautical terms, such as "skiff," "fathoms" and "gunnel," that are used in this selection? Are they just vocabulary to look up, or do they somehow play a larger role in our appreciation of this topic?

2. Crummey sometimes writes partial sentences. For example, point out all the ones you see in paragraph 7. Are these errors? Or do they have some role to play? Would you see partial sentences in a more academic essay?

3. More than almost any selection in this book, "The Fish, The Fish" bristles with IRONY. Point out five strong examples of it.

IDEAS FOR DISCUSSION AND WRITING:

1. In one poem from his first book *Arguments with Gravity*, Michael Crummey writes:

> A father can be as difficult a love
> as an adopted country,
> how part of him always remains a stranger....

In "The Fish, The Fish," what evidences do you see of the "difficulty" and what evidences of the "love"? Give reasons why parent/

child relationships are not always easy. Do you have a complex relationship with your own father? Or your own mother? And if so, is this the exception or the norm?

2. "That's a queer fucking title," the father says of his son's book mentioned above. Explain the power of this example.

3. "I was thirty years old before I published my first book," says the son in paragraph 12. "How much are they paying you?" asks the father in the next lines. How much, indeed, do writers make? Enough to starve on, or enough to live on? In 2001 Michael Crummey went on to publish a bestselling novel, *The River Thieves*. Does this mean he is now on easy street?

4. Cod off Newfoundland were once legendary for their size and numbers. But after a disastrous decline, in 1992 the federal government issued a moratorium against further cod fishing. The resulting layoff, the largest in Canada's history, changed Newfoundland forever. The situation is not promising: on July 1, 2007, *CanadaEast* journalist Tara Brautigam actually reported that "offshore cod stocks are one per cent of what they were in 1977." Do some research, trying to answer these questions: Why did the cod disappear? And how might they ever come back?

5. What measures have Newfoundlanders taken to make a living, after the disappearance of the cod?

6. PROCESS IN WRITING: *What is the occupation of your own father, or your own mother? And what career are you, yourself, planning to enter? Now think of all the main comparisons and contrasts you can make between the two. Take a page of notes, and decide whether your essay will be a comparison, a contrast, or both. Now develop a THESIS STATEMENT that announces your main point (such as why you prefer your own career choice). Write a quick draft of your argument, arranged either by halves or point by point. Later look it over. Are there plenty of examples? Do they all support your main point? Is the language concise? Do TRANSITIONS join the parts? Finally, check spelling and punctuation before you print off your best version.*

Note: See also the Topics for Writing on the Online Learning Centre at www. mcgrawhill.ca/olc/conrad.

DREW HAYDEN TAYLOR

This Boat Is My Boat

An Ojibway from the Curve Lake Reserve in Ontario, Drew Hayden Taylor has become one of Canada's most prolific Native writers. Whether in his fiction, his newspaper columns or his many stage plays, Taylor's trademark is a zany, satirical wit that leaves his audience both laughing and thinking. A time as Playwright-in-Residence, then Artistic Director for Native Earth Performing Arts, confirmed Taylor's love of theatre. Since then there have been over 60 professional productions of his plays, such as Bootlegger Blues *(1991),* Someday *(1993),* AlterNatives *(2000),* The Boy in the Treehouse *(2001),* Girl Who Loved Her Horses *(2001), and* The Buz'Gem Blues *(2002). Taylor has also been a satirical columnist for the* Peterborough Examiner, *with his best pieces collected in a book,* Funny, You Don't Look Like One: Observations of a Blue-Eyed Ojibway *(1998). He has also written for* Maclean's, *the* Globe and Mail, Now Magazine *and other periodicals; has written scripts for television series such as* The Beachcombers, Street Legal *and* North of Sixty; *and has directed documentaries on native themes. In 1992 his anthology* Voices: Being Native in Canada *(with Linda Jaine) was published, and in 1998* Fearless Warriors, *a collection of short stories. In 2005 he published* 400 Kilometres, *a novel about Native identity, and also in 2005 a nonfiction book about Native humour,* Me Funny. *In one of its sections Taylor humorously attempts to prove that Cree is the funniest of all languages. Our own essay selection, comic in tone but serious in theme, first appeared in the July/ August 2004 issue of* This Magazine.

F. Scott Fitzgerald once wrote "The rich are different from you and I,"° to which everybody usually responds, "Yeah, they've got more money." On a similar theme, it's been my Ojibway-tainted observation over the years that "middle-class white people are different from you and I." Yeah. They're insane.

Much has been written over the years about the differences between native people and non-native people, and the way they view life. I think there's no better example of this admittedly broad opinion than in the peculiar world of outdoor recreational water sports and the death wish that inspires them.

As a member of Canada's indigenous population, I've cast a suspicious glance at all these waterlogged enthusiasts for several reasons. The principal one is the now familiar concept of cultural appropriation—this time of our methods of water transportation. On any given weekend, Canadian rivers are jam-packed with plastic and fibreglass kayaks and canoes, hardly any of them filled with authentic Inuit or First Nations people, all looking to taunt death using an aboriginal calling card.

Historically, kayaks and canoes were the lifeblood of Inuit and native communities. They were vital means of transportation and survival, not toys to amuse bored weekend warriors. To add insult to injury and further illustrate my point, there is a brand of gloves used by kayakers to protect their hands from developing calluses. They are called Nootkas. To the best of my knowledge, the real Nootka, a West Coast First Nation, neither kayaked nor wore gloves.

Perhaps my argument can best be articulated with an example of the different ways these two cultural groups react to a single visual stimulus. A group of native people and white people sit in two separate canoes before a long stretch of roaring rapids—with large pointy rocks and lots and lots of turbulent white water. Watch the different reactions.

°"The rich are different from you and I": This best-known of all lines from the American novelist F. Scott Fitzgerald has been quoted in many slightly different forms. Probably the most accurate is "The rich are different from you and me," to which his friend Ernest Hemingway replied, in a memorable putdown, "Yes, they have more money."

6   Granted, I'm generalizing, but I think I can safely say the vast majority of native people, based on thousands of years of travelling the rivers of this great country of ours, would probably go home and order a pizza. Or possibly put the canoe in their Ford pickup and drive downstream to a more suitable and safe location. And pick up pizza on the way. Usually, the only white water native people enjoy is in their showers. Hurtling toward potential death and certain injury tends to go against many traditional native beliefs. Contrary to popular assumption, "portage" is not a French word—it is Ojibway for "Are you crazy? I'm not going through that! Do you know how much I paid for this canoe?"

7   Now put some sunburned Caucasian canoeists in the same position, and their natural inclination is to aim directly for the rapids, paddling as fast as they can toward the white water. I heard a rumour once that Columbus was aiming his three ships directly at a raging hurricane when he discovered the Bahamas. I believe I have made my point.

8   I make these observations based on personal experience. Recently, for purely anthropological reasons, I risked my life to explore the unique subcultures of white water canoeing and sea kayaking. There is also a sport known as white water kayaking, but I have yet to put that particular bullet in my gun. So for three days, I found myself in the middle of Georgian Bay, during a storm, testing my abilities at sea kayaking. I, along with a former Olympic rower, a Quebecois lawyer who consulted on the Russian constitution, one of Canada's leading diabetes specialists, and a six-foot-seven ex-Mormon who could perform exorcisms, bonded over four-foot swells and lightning. All in all, I think a pretty normal crosscut of average Canadians. The higher the waves, the more exciting they found the experience.

9   Still, I often find these outings to be oddly patriotic in their own way. I cannot tell you the number of times I've seen people wringing out their drenched shirts, showing an array of tan lines, usually a combination of sunburned red skin and fishbelly-white stomachs. It reminds me of the red-and-white motif on the Canadian flag. Maybe that's where the federal government got its inspiration, back in the 1960s, for our national emblem.

10   But this is only one of several sports originated by various indigenous populations that has been corrupted and marketed as something

fun to do when not sitting behind a desk in a highrise office building. The Scandinavian Sami, otherwise known as Laplanders, were instrumental in the development of skiing. Though I doubt climbing to the top of a mountain and hurling themselves down as fast as gravity and snow would allow was a culturally ingrained activity. The same could be said of bungee jumping. Originally a coming-of-age ritual in the South Pacific, young boys would build platforms, tie vines to their legs and leap off to show their bravery and passage into adulthood. I doubt the same motivation still pervades the sport, if it can be called a sport.

I have brought up the issue of recreational cultural appropriation   11
many times with a friend who organizes these outdoor adventures. The irony is she works at a hospital. And she chews me out for not wearing a helmet while biking. She says there is no appropriation. If anything, her enthusiasm for the sports is a sign of respect and gratefulness.

That is why I think people should pay a royalty of sorts every time   12
they try to kill themselves using one of our cultural legacies. I'm not sure if any aboriginal group has ever sought a patent or copyright protection for kayaks or canoes—that probably was not part of the treaty negotiations. But somebody should definitely investigate the possibility. Or better yet, every time a non-native person white water canoes down the Madawaska River, or goes kayaking off Tobermory, they should first take an aboriginal person to lunch. That is a better way of showing respect and gratefulness. And it involves much less paperwork.

EXPLORATIONS:

Drew Hayden Taylor,
>   *The Buz'Gem Blues*
>   *Funny, You Don't Look Like One: Observations of a Blue-Eyed Ojibway*
>   *Voices: Being Native in Canada* (co-edited with Linda Jaine)
Ronald Wright, *Stolen Continents: Conquest and Resistance in the Americas*

http://www.ammsa.com/classroom/CLASS3appropriation.html
http://www.ipl.org/div/natam/bin/browse.pl/A185
http://www.athabascau.ca/writers/dhtaylor.html
http://www.doollee.com/PlaywrightsT/TaylorDrewHayden.htm
http://wildernesscanoe.ca/index.htm

STRUCTURE:

1. Taylor's essay title is an ALLUSION to Woody Guthrie's well-known 1956 song "This Land Is My Land." Do you know the lyrics? (If not, find them at http://www.arlo.net/lyrics/this-land.shtml.) How does the meaning of Guthrie's song lead into Taylor's topic of cultural appropriation (par. 3)?

2. In paragraph 1 the common device of a quotation opens the essay. Where do you find good quotations for your own essays? How does the Fitzgerald quotation lead into Taylor's topic?

3. Identify Taylor's *thesis statement.*

4. Is Taylor's argument a *contrast* only, or does it also have elements of *comparison*? And is it done *point by point*, or by *halves*? Identify each main contrast that supports his overall argument.

STYLE:

1. In this essay Taylor is his usual zany and satirical self—as in paragraph 6 where the natives go for pizza while the Caucasians hurtle "toward potential death and certain injury," or where the word "portage" is said to be Ojibway for "'Are you crazy? I'm not going through that! Do you know how much I paid for this canoe?'" Does all his humour prevent Taylor from mounting a real argument against cultural appropriation? Or does it just make that argument more appealing?

2. Here and there Taylor uses conversational language, for example "Yeah. They're insane" (par. 1), or "chews me out" (11). Is this informal TONE appropriate to his essay? Why or why not?

3. How ABSTRACT or CONCRETE is Taylor's STYLE? Give examples. Has he attained the recommended 50% or more of *example* content?

IDEAS FOR DISCUSSION AND WRITING:

1. Do you admire thrill-seekers who skydive, scramble mountain peaks, do acrobatics on snowboards, run class-five rapids in canoes and kayaks or ski two months over ice to the North Pole? Why or why not? Why do people perform acts such as these? Have you attempted an extreme sport? Tell the class about it.

2. As an Ojibway, Taylor argues against "cultural appropriation." Do you agree with this view of many Native people that outsiders are not qualified to write about them and their lives? To make films about them? Even to attempt their sports? Or is making this subject matter off limits to others an attack on their personal liberties?

3. According to Ronald Wright in his book *Stolen Continents*, an estimated 100 million people, a fifth of the human race, were already living in the Americas when Columbus "discovered" the New World. Within decades military conquest and epidemics of new diseases had killed most of them. The European invaders sacked cities, destroyed great works of art, shipped huge amounts of gold to Europe and took the land. Was any of this "appropriation" justified? In our time what are the implications for land claim settlements with native groups in Canada? To what extent can we and should we as a society make up for past wrongs?

4. PROCESS IN WRITING: *Think of any two sports that you play. First draw a line down the middle of a blank page, then make notes on sport A on the left and sport B on the right. Do you see mostly similarities or differences, or both? Let this help you decide whether to write a* comparison, *a* contrast, *or both. And does one sport emerge as better, more difficult, more dangerous, or what? Devise a* THESIS STATEMENT *that expresses this overall main idea. Now draw lines from left to right connecting related items, and when you are ready, organize these notes* point *by* point *into an argument. Write the first draft, and the next day look it over. Does every part develop the overall main idea in the* thesis statement? *Are there plentiful examples, as in Drew Hayden Taylor's essay? Do transitional expressions such as "on the other hand," "by contrast," "however" and "but" highlight the logic? Is there flabby language to trim? Finally, check the punctuation and print your best version.*

Note: See also the Topics for Writing on the Online Learning Centre at www. mcgrawhill.ca/olc/conrad.

CATHARINE PARR TRAILL

Remarks of Security of Person and Property in Canada

Catharine Parr ("Kate") Traill (1802–1899) exemplifies the best of Canadian pioneering life. She spent her early years in England, where she enjoyed the refinements of her father's estate near Southwold and published several books for children. But a reversal of family fortunes and her marriage to a retired half-pay officer meant immigration. In 1832 the Traills joined Catharine's brother Samuel Strickland (who would later write Twenty-Seven Years in Canada West) *near present-day Lakefield, Ontario, and soon they were joined by their sister Susanna Moodie and her husband (Moodie would go on to write a classic of pioneer life,* Roughing It in the Bush). *Catharine also wrote about Upper Canada. A collection of letters to her mother was published in 1836 as* The Backwoods of Canada, *and in 1854 appeared* The Female Emigrant's Guide, *her handbook of advice and techniques. Traill also wrote more books for children, and her professionalism as a botanist was widely recognized when in 1868 she published* Canadian Wild Flowers, *and in 1885* Studies of Plant Life in Canada. *Kate Traill's writing reflects her sunny personality: she was curious, observant, self-reliant—and above all optimistic about life in the New World. These qualities shine through our selection, from* The Female Emigrant's Guide.

1   There is one thing which can hardly fail to strike an emigrant from the Old Country, on his arrival in Canada. It is this,— The feeling of complete security which he enjoys, whether in his own dwelling or in his journeys abroad through the land. He

sees no fear—he need see none. He is not in a land spoiled and robbed, where every man's hand is against his fellow—where envy and distrust beset him on every side. At first indeed he is surprised at the apparently stupid neglect of the proper means of security that he notices in the dwellings of all classes of people, especially in the lonely country places, where the want of security would really invite rapine and murder. "How is this," he says, "you use neither bolt, nor lock, nor bar. I see no shutter to your windows; nay, you sleep often with your doors open upon the latch, and in summer with open doors and windows. Surely this is fool-hardy and imprudent." "We need no such precautions," will his friend reply smiling; "here they are uncalled for. Our safety lies neither in bars nor bolts, but in our consciousness that we are among people whose necessities are not such as to urge them to violate the laws; neither are our riches such as to tempt the poor man to rob us, for they consist not in glittering jewels, nor silver, nor gold."

"But even food and clothes thus carelessly guarded are temptations."   2

"But where others possess these requisites as well as ourselves, they are not likely to steal them from us."   3

And what is the inference that the new comer draws from this statement?   4

That he is in a country where the inhabitants are essentially honest, because they are enabled, by the exertion of their own hands, to obtain in abundance the necessaries of life. Does it not also prove to him that it is the miseries arising from poverty that induce crime.—Men do not often violate the law of honesty, unless driven to do so by necessity. Place the poor Irish peasant in the way of earning his bread in Canada, where he sees his reward before him, in broad lands that he can win by honest toil, and where he can hold up his head and look beyond that grave of a poor man's hope—the parish work house—and see in the far-off vista a home of comfort which his own hands have reared, and can go down to his grave with the thought, that he has left a name and a blessing for his children after him:—men like this do not steal.   5

Robbery is not a crime of common occurrence in Canada. In large towns such acts will occasionally be committed, for it is there that   6 poverty is to be found, but it is not common in country places. There you may sleep with your door unbarred for years. Your confidence is rarely, if ever, abused; your hospitality never violated.

7   When I lived in the backwoods, out of sight of any other habitation, the door has often been opened at midnight, a stranger has entered and lain down before the kitchen fire, and departed in the morning unquestioned. In the early state of the settlement in Douro, now twenty years ago, it was no uncommon occurrence for a party of Indians to enter the house, (they never knock at any man's door,) leave their hunting weapons outside, spread their blankets on the floor, and pass the night with or without leave, arise by the first dawn of day, gather their garments about them, resume their weapons, and silently and noiselessly depart. Sometimes a leash of wild ducks hung to the door-latch, or a haunch of venison left in the kitchen, would be found as a token of gratitude for the warmth and shelter afforded them.

8   Many strangers, both male and female, have found shelter under our roof, and never were we led to regret that we had not turned the houseless wanderer from our door.

9   It is delightful this consciousness of perfect security: your hand is against no man, and no man's hand is against you. We dwell in peace among our own people. What a contrast to my home, in England, where by sunset every door was secured with locks and heavy bars and bolts; every window carefully barricaded, and every room and corner in and around the dwelling duly searched, before we ventured to lie down to rest, lest our sleep should be broken in upon by the midnight thief. As night drew on, an atmosphere of doubt and dread seemed to encompass one. The approach of a stranger we beheld with suspicion; and however great his need, we dared not afford him the shelter of our roof, lest our so doing should open the door to robber or murderer. At first I could hardly understand why it happened that I never felt the same sensation of fear in Canada as I had done in England. My mind seemed lightened of a heavy burden; and I, who had been so timid, grew brave and fearless amid the gloomy forests of Canada. Now, I know how to value this great blessing. Let the traveller seek shelter in the poorest shanty, among the lowest Irish settlers, and he need fear no evil, for never have I

heard of the rites of hospitality being violated, or the country disgraced by such acts of cold-blooded atrocity as are recorded by the public papers in the Old Country.

Here we have no bush-rangers, no convicts to disturb the peace   10
of the inhabitants of the land, as in Australia. No savage hordes of Caffres to invade and carry off our cattle and stores of grain as at the Cape; but peace and industry are on every side. "The land is at rest and breaks forth into singing." Surely we ought to be a happy and a contented people, full of gratitude to that Almighty God who has given us this fair and fruitful land to dwell in.

EXPLORATIONS:

Catharine Parr Traill,
> *The Female Emigrant's Guide*
> *The Backwoods of Canada*

Susanna Moodie, *Roughing It in the Bush*
Margaret Atwood, *The Journals of Susanna Moodie* (poems)
Marian Fowler, *The Embroidered Tent: Five Gentlewomen in Early Canada*
http://www.uwo.ca/english/canadianpoetry/eng%20274e/pdf/traill.pdf
http://en.wikipedia.org/wiki/Catharine_Parr_Traill
http://www.trentu.ca/admin/library/archives/zwomtrli.htm

STRUCTURE:

1. The long first paragraph states all the main ideas of this essay. What, then, does the rest of the essay do?
2. In this *contrast* between the dangers of life in England and the security of life in Canada, why is so much more of the argument devoted to Canada than to England?
3. The main contrast, between Canada and England, occurs in paragraphs 7–9. Why is this detailed contrast followed, in the last paragraph, by very brief contrasts to Australia and the Cape?

STYLE:

1. Catharine Parr Traill published *The Female Emigrant's Guide* in 1854. How different does her STYLE in this selection seem from the style of today's writers? Discuss the following:

   A.   Word choice
   B.   Sentences
   C.   Paragraphs
   D.   TONE

2. Discuss the meaning of "want" in the phrase "want of security" (middle of par. 1). Do you see other words in this essay that have changed meaning since 1854?

3. In paragraph 7, Traill writes that the Native people "never knock at any man's door." In paragraph 9 she states that "your hand is against no man, and no man's hand is against you." In fact, she mentions men so often that only once does she specifically refer to women—yet she entitled her book *The Female Emigrant's Guide*. Why in the past could "man" represent everyone? And why today have we rejected this usage?

4. In exactness, in vividness, and in poetic power, has our language improved or deteriorated since the time of Catharine Parr Traill?

IDEAS FOR DISCUSSION AND WRITING:

1. Does the Canada of today more closely resemble the new land that Traill describes in this essay, or the old land she left behind?

2. If you have moved to Canada from another country, as Traill did, have you experienced the benefits she describes?

3. Traill says "it is the miseries arising from poverty that induce crime" (par. 5). Do you agree? Or does crime have other causes as well?

4. Traill states, "I, who had been so timid, grew brave and fearless amid the gloomy forests of Canada" (par. 9). The frontier has always been seen as a place to make a new start, leaving old problems in the past. In our increasingly crowded and industrialized world, do frontiers remain?

5. Can a "frontier" exist in the city? Are there new ways of living in old places, by which people can free themselves from problems of the past?

6. In paragraph 9 Traill refers to "the lowest Irish settlers." Then in paragraph 10 she refers to "bush-rangers" and "convicts" (who were brought from England to help colonize Australia, but many of whom went on to form outlaw bands). Then she refers to "savage hordes of Caffres" ("Caffre," a very negative term, referred to some groups of black Africans in what is now South Africa). Why did Traill feel so free to use racist language in 1854? Why would she not feel free to do so today?

7. PROCESS IN WRITING: *Write an essay that compares and/or contrasts life in two countries, provinces, cities, towns or neighbourhoods. First divide a page in half with a vertical line; jot down facts about item A on the left and item B on the right. Looking over these notes, decide now on your THESIS STATEMENT and choose either the "halves" or the "point by point" method of organizing. After a rapid first draft, fine-tune your organization and add more concrete detail. Now read your paper aloud, to detect repetition and any other flaws of style, before doing the final version.*

Note: See also the Topics for Writing on the Online Learning Centre at www. mcgrawhill.ca/olc/conrad.

LAWRENCE HILL

Black + White = Black

In 2001 Maclean's *published an excerpt from Lawrence Hill's book of the same year,* Black Berry, Sweet Juice: On Being Black and White in Canada. *In the* Maclean's *version reprinted here, Hill tells much of his life story. But there is more. Not only did his African-American father become Director of the Ontario Human Rights Commission, and later the province's ombudsman, but his brother Dan Hill became a noted singer/songwriter of the 70s and 80s. Lawrence himself moved from his upper-middle-class white suburb of Toronto to Quebec City, where in 1980 in French he completed a B.A. in economics from Université Laval. In 1992 he went on to an M.A. in writing from Johns Hopkins University in Baltimore. Having lived and worked abroad, Hill is fluent in French and Spanish. In 1982 he began reporting for the* Toronto Globe and Mail, *then moved to* The Winnipeg Free Press. *Eventually he went on to write for ministries of the Ontario government. Meanwhile his own writing career took shape. In 1992 appeared Hill's first novel,* Some Great Thing, *then two nonfiction books about being black in Canada. His second novel,* Any Known Blood, *was published in 1997, and his third,* The Book of Negroes, *in 2007. It spent 13 weeks in the top-ten fiction list, won the best book award for the Commonwealth Writers' Prize (for Overall Best Book) and won the Rogers Writers' Trust Fiction Prize. Also in 2007 Hill collaborated with Joshua Key, a young American seeking refugee status in Canada, in writing* The Deserter's Tale: The Story of an Ordinary Soldier Who Walked Away from the War in Iraq. *To learn more about Lawrence Hill, read* Black Berry, Sweet Juice, *and see Hill's excellent website at http://www.lawrencehill.com.*

My childhood was punctuated with sayings about black people. My father's relatives sometimes said, "The blacker the berry, the sweeter the juice." On one level, the meaning is obvious: a raspberry or strawberry that is full and dark and pregnant with its own ripeness is sweeter than its pink, prematurely plucked counterpart. But there is also a sexual undertone to the saying, a suggestion of the myth of the overcharged, overheated, high-performing black body. Presumably, the blacker berry tastes richer, more full and is juicier. The trouble with this expression is that it has always struck me as a limp-wristed effort to help black people believe that it was OK to be black. It seemed to me sad and pathetic that we even felt a need to pass around a saying like that.

But I wasn't the only one who found that the words itched more than they tickled. My father bombed the pious saying to smithereens with his own sarcastic version: "The blacker the berry/The sweeter the juice/But if you get too black/It ain't no use." I absolutely loved that variation. Why? Because it turned self-affirmation on its head with a mere 10 additional words, offering a bittersweet reminder of the hopelessness of being black in a society that doesn't love—or even like—black people. There were many other sayings, such as "If you're white/You're all right/If you're brown/Stick around/If you're black/Stay back." Black people said these words and laughed. All the sayings underscored the utter futility of being black.

I discovered, very early, that some people had strange ideas about the children of interracial unions, and seemed inclined to believe that life for us would be miserable. When I was 12, my best friend was a white girl, Marilyn (as I shall name her), whose mother would embarrass the dickens out of me by singing my praises to her own children. "Look how well Larry does in school. Why can't you be like that, Marilyn?" Astoundingly, this same mother who thought I was doing so well once took me aside and said, "Frankly, Larry, don't you think it is terrible, mixing races like that? It ruins the children! How are they to make their way in life?"

As a child, my own experience of race, including my concept of my own racial identity, was shaded quite differently from that of my parents. They were both born and raised in the United States, and their racial identities were clearly delineated all their lives. The America of their youth and early adulthood was replete with laws that banned interracial marriages and upheld segregation in every domain of public life. One of the most telling details came to me from my mother, who was working as a secretary for a Democratic senator when she met my father in Washington in 1953: "When I started dating your father, even the federal government cafeterias were segregated." In the United States, there was never any doubt that my father was first and foremost a black man. Or that my mother was a white woman. And there is no question that, had my siblings and I been raised in the United States, we would have been identified—in school, on the street, in community centres, among friends—as black.

5   But my parents threw their unborn children a curveball. They came to Toronto right after they married, had us and we all stayed here. They had had enough of racial divisions in their country of birth. And although they spent their lives at the forefront of the Canadian human-rights movement, they were also happy and relieved to set up in suburban, white, middleclass Toronto, where race faded (most of the time) into the background.

6   When I was growing up, I didn't spend much time thinking about who I was or where I fit in. I was too busy tying my shoelaces, brushing my teeth, learning to spell, swinging baseball bats and shooting hockey pucks. But once in a while, just as my guard was down, questions of my own identity would leap like a cougar from the woods and take a bite out of my backside.

7   I found that race became an issue as a result of environmental factors. The average white kid growing up in a white suburb didn't have to think of himself as white. Gradually, my environment started talking to me and making me aware that I could never truly be white. There's nothing like being called "nigger" to let you know that you're not white.

8   Learning that I wasn't white, however, wasn't the same as learning that I was black. Indeed, for the longest time I didn't learn what I was—only what I wasn't. In the strange and unique society that was Canada, I was allowed to grow up in a sort of racial limbo. People knew what I wasn't—white or black—but they sure couldn't say what I was. I have black American cousins, of both lighter and darker com-

plexions, who attended segregated schools and grew up in entirely black communities. They had no reason to doubt their racial identity. That identity was wrapped around them, like a snug towel, at the moment of birth.

In 1977, when I decided to take a year off university, I went to visit my cousins in Brooklyn before flying to Europe, which must have appeared to them a quintessentially white thing to do. My cousin Richard Flateau took me under his wing, and was patient until I asked if he liked to play squash. An indignant retort exploded from his lips: "Larry! That's a white folks' game!" Today, looking back, I find irony in that memory. There I was, son of a black American Second World War veteran and a white American civil-rights activist, playing squash, a sport virtually unknown to inner-city blacks in the United States.

These days, I think of the factors that contributed to my sense of identity, and of how malleable that sense of identity was and still is. There were days when I went straight from my exclusive, private boys' high school to family events populated by black relatives or friends who idolized the icons and heroes of my childhood—Angela Davis, with her intelligence and her kick-ass Afro; sprinters Tommie Smith and John Carlos, with their black-gloved fists raised on the Olympic podium in Mexico City; Muhammad Ali, who stood up to the white man and spoke the words that moved the world: "I ain't got no quarrel with the Viet Cong." I bounced back and forth between studying Latin, playing squash and revering black American cultural icons, but who exactly was I?

Lately, I have been looking at some family photos and mulling over what they mean to me. In my home office, I have some 30 framed shots of relatives. There are my three children, running, cavorting, picking apples. The eldest, Geneviève, is 11, and I wonder how she will come to see herself, racially, as she moves into adolescence. She has been a ballerina for six years, and you don't find a world much whiter than that, not even in Oakville, where we live. She knows who she is, and has had much contact with the black side of her family— but the girl has blue eyes and skin even lighter than mine, and I can see that if she is going to assert her own blackness one day, she may have to work hard at it. Nine-year-old Caroline, the middle child, is the darkest of my three, and has that uncanny middle-child ability to relate to anybody of any age. I have noticed that she already bonds vigorously with black women. Andrew, who is 7, is about as interested in race as he would be in nuclear physics. Interestingly, though, he has already called out a few times, "I'm not black, I'm white," and shot a look my way to test for a reaction. He looks white, too.

12   Would you like to know how my children would once have been categorized, racially? Quadroons. They have a father who is supposedly half-black and a mother who is white, and that parentage, according to the traditional racial definition blender, would have made them quadroons. Quadroons, of course, were most definitely black, and enslaved like the rest of us in Canada and the United States. Quadroon women were favoured by slave owners for features deemed exotic and sexy but not too black, thank you very much. I shudder to imagine children who looked just like mine dancing in the infamous Quadroon Balls in New Orleans, where hot-looking young women were bought and consumed until they were no longer young or beautiful.

13   Today in Canada, black people still contend with racism at every level of society. And yet, the way my children will define themselves, and be defined by others, remains up for grabs. Racial identity is about how you see yourself, about how you construct a sense of belonging, community, awareness and allegiance.

14   To this date, I have mostly seen myself as black. My black American relatives, who lived in Brooklyn, Washington, Baltimore and North Carolina, were much closer to us and much easier to visit than my mother's family. Apart from her twin, Dottie, whom we all adore, we never really got to know my mother's relatives. My mother spoke negatively of her brothers when we were young, describing how they gave her a hard time—one even questioned her sanity—when she announced that she would be marrying a black man. As a result, as a child I came to nourish a minor grudge against some of these relatives. On my father's side, however, family was like an extension of my own body and psyche.

15   My first sense of blackness, sprang from warm places. Our house boomed with jazz and blues on weekends. Dan, Karen and I watched—entranced, intrigued—as our parents danced in the living room to

Ella Fitzgerald, Billie Holiday and Duke Ellington. Dad has an amazing voice. When he sang, he waltzed up and down the tunes with a playfulness and irreverence that we found absolutely infectious.

I remember being laid up with the flu when I was 5. My father 16 asked: "Any musical requests, sir?" And I said, "Put on Joe Williams." *Every Day I Have the Blues* began to jump off the record player. I listened to my dad and Williams nailing the notes as Basie hammered the piano, and trumpets, trombones and saxophones erupted with glee. It's one of the happiest songs I've heard—even if it is about the blues. *Nobody loves me/nobody seems to care/between bad luck and trouble/ well you know I've had my share.* Just about any words could have flown from Joe Williams's lips and soared, ecstatically, as if to prove that nothing could keep this man from living and loving. Jazz and blues were already showing me the sweet alchemy of trouble and joy that defined black musical expression, and black people themselves.

I don't recall early moments with family members that gave me 17 a negative sense of race, but my siblings do. Perhaps because he was the firstborn, Dan had a rockier time with our father. Dan has no doubt that our father gave us mixed racial messages. When my brother was 11 or so, Dad gave him a stocking to wear on his head at night. The idea was to straighten out Dan's hair while he slept, or at the very least to keep it from getting too curly on the pillow. I asked Dan if Dad had told him why he had to wear it.

"It wasn't good to have curly hair. He'd pull a hair out of my head 18 and put it on the table and say, 'See? This is curly. It's not good to have curly hair.' And I remember feeling extremely hurt and ashamed, and I started wearing the stocking cap. I remember feeling very concerned that my hair was curly, and I remember being frantic about straightening it."

Dan now attributes the incident to the strange paradoxes of 19 human nature. "I think that kind of behaviour is common among people like our father, who have worked in the field of human rights. Very often, people go into these fields as compensation for their own feelings of inadequacy. That way, they can still bring those feelings of inadequacy and self-hatred—self-racial-hatred—into the house."

Dan, Karen and I learned early that you can have a white parent 20 and still be considered black, but you can never have a black parent and be considered white. It ain't allowed. You'll be reminded of your "otherness" more times than you can shake a stick at it. This is one of the reasons why I self-identify as black. Attempts at pleasant symmetry, as in "half-white, half-black," trivialize to my eye the meaning of being black. This doesn't mean I don't love my mother. I love her as profoundly as I love any person on earth. But I just don't see myself as being the same race as she is. I raised this issue with my mother recently. "Listen," she told me, "when I married your father, I knew that our children would be black. I would have been an idiot to fail to see that. Look where we came from."

21   However, the suburb of Don Mills in which they eventually settled became as suffocating for their children as D.C. had been for them. There were no blacks in my school, on my street. Because I looked so different from everyone else, I feared that I was ugly. I worried about having frizzy hair, big ears, a big nose and plump lips. When I looked in the mirror, I felt disgust. None of the people I admired looked the least bit like me. Listening to stories of my father's working world instilled in us a measure of black pride. We also derived a sense of connection from family moments around the television, which is odd because we weren't that interested in TV. But the late 1960s and the early 1970s featured big stand-up comedy numbers by Bill Cosby and Flip Wilson. When I watched these shows, I felt alive. I felt that there were people in the world who were speaking to me.

22   I had to find other ways to connect with them. So I ate up every bit of black writing that I could find. Langston Hughes, Ralph Ellison, Richard Wright—whom I approached gingerly because my mother confessed that *Native Son* had upset her so much, it had made her vomit. James Baldwin. Eldridge Cleaver—now that cat fascinated me, especially when, in *Soul on Ice*, he speculated as to why black men and white women end up together. I read Alex Haley's *Autobiography of Malcolm X*, and had to struggle through the section of Malcolm X's life when he ardently believed that white people were the devil incarnate. I knew this to be false. My mother was white, and she was no devil.

23   Without knowing exactly what I was doing, I was forming my own sense of blackness and my own connection to the black diaspora. Soon, this exploration blossomed into creative writing. Every time I wrote, my mind wandered into the lives of black characters. Slowly, I

was developing a sense of myself. These days, when I'm invited into schools with black students, I feel a tinge of nostalgia for a past not lived. I can't help wondering what it would have been like to have black people around me when I was young. I can't help wondering what it would have been like to go out with black girls, or to drift into a friend's home and find myself surrounded by black people. What a different life that would have been.

EXPLORATIONS:

Lawrence Hill,
> *Black Berry, Sweet Juice: On Being Black and White in Canada*
> *Any Known Blood* (novel)

George Elliott Clarke, ed., *Eyeing the North Star: Directions in African-Canadian Literature* (anthology)

Frances Henry, *The Caribbean Diaspora in Toronto: Learning to Live with Racism*

Henry Gates and Nellie McKay, eds., *The Norton Anthology of African American Literature*

Arnold Rampersad, ed., *The Oxford Anthology of African-American Poetry*

Richard Wright, *Native Son* (novel)

Toni Morrison, *Beloved* (novel)

http://www.lawrencehill.com

http://www.wier.ca/lhill.html

http://www.quillandquire.com/authors/profile.cfm?article_id=7654

http://www.cbc.ca/arts/books/book_of_negroes.html

STRUCTURE:

1. How do you interpret the equation in Hill's title, "Black + White = Black"? Is it a good start to the essay? What does it do? Compare another mathematical title in this book, Doris Anderson's "The 51-Per-Cent Minority."

2. Like many essayists, Hill opens with a quotation. Point out all the ways it moves us into his topic. Do you ever use this technique? If you don't have the right quotation to start your essay, where do you look for it?

3. Is Hill's argument all *contrast* between his black roots and white roots, or is there also *comparison*? If so, where?

4. In this argument of *contrast*, Hill organizes not by "halves" but "point by point." As a class, split into ten groups, each choosing a passage listed below. Examine your section in your small group, then report to the class what aspect of the total subject it analyzes through *contrast*: paragraphs 1–2, 3, 4–8, 9, 10, 11–12, 14–19, 20, 21–22, and 23.

STYLE:

1. Why do you think Hill's paragraphs are longer than those of many other writers in this book? Are they too long? Are your own ever too short? What is a good typical length, and why?

2. In paragraph 8 Hill describes his American cousins growing up in black communities where "that identity was wrapped around them, like a snug towel, at the moment of birth." Where else does Hill use strong METAPHORS?

IDEAS FOR DISCUSSION AND WRITING:

1. Do you, too, have roots in two or more races or cultures? Do you, like Hill, identify more with one than with the others(s)? Try to explain why, giving examples.

2. With a father who was Director of the Ontario Human Rights Commission and later the province's ombudsman, Lawrence Hill had a privileged upper-middle-class childhood. Do working-class people have a different experience of racial issues? Give examples.

3. Canada—especially in its big cities—is said to be the most cosmo-politan, multicultural country in the world. Do you agree? Is your own neighbourhood multicultural? If so, name all the places where its different population groups have their roots.

4. *Contrast* the American and Canadian examples of racism that Hill gives. Was Canada the more open society when Hill's parents were young? Is it now? Give examples.

5. Do interracial couples, like Hill's parents, still face extra challenges in society, or by now has fairness been achieved?

6. *Compare* or *contrast* Lawrence Hill's portrayal of racism in society with those of George Gabori (p. 26), Carol Geddes (p. 45), Goran Simic (p. 84), Naheed Mustafa (p. 149) or Joy Kogawa (p. 373).

7. PROCESS IN WRITING: *If, like most Canadians, you have roots in more than one geographical area, language, culture or race, draw a line down the middle of a page. At the top left and right, name the two most important components of your own roots (such as "Iran" and "Germany," or "Mandarin" and "English"). Make sure that both items, as in these pairs, are from the same category: two countries, two languages, etc. Below them, on each side, make many notes on their characteristics. Now look over what you have produced: What* contrasts *do you see? Draw lines across the page to link the contrasting items. Next put your overall point in a* THESIS STATEMENT, *then write a discovery draft using your* examples. *(Choose to organize your contrast either by "halves" or "point by point.") When this version has cooled off, look it over. Is it filled with* examples, *like Hill's essay? If not, add. Does it use transition signals like "but," "on the other hand," "however" and "by contrast" to heighten your* contrast? *If not, add. Finally, edit for correctness and conciseness before printing out your best version. Share it with the class.*

Note: See also the Topics for Writing on the Online Learning Centre at www. mcgrawhill.ca/olc/conrad.

JON EVANS

Apocalypse Soon

Veteran traveller, backpacker, software and Internet specialist, Jon Evans also finds time to author adventure novels set in the kinds of faraway places he explores himself. Born in 1973 in Waterloo, Ontario, Evans completed a degree in electrical and computer engineering at the University of Waterloo in 1996. Eight months of software design in California followed, then Evans began the first of his major travels, spending four months in West Africa. There followed short periods of computer-related employment in New York City, Toronto and other places, always punctuated by trips to destinations like India, Nepal, the Balkans, Egypt, Australia, New Guinea, South America and Haiti. Meanwhile he published his first novel Dark Places *(which he refers to in our essay) in 2004, then* Blood Price *(2005),* Invisible Armies *(2006), and* The Night of Knives *(2007). Reviewers remark on the level of suspense he creates, the vividness of his settings and the authentic way he portrays his own world of backpackers. He writes on other subjects as well, in essays for* The Walrus, Wired, *and the* Globe and Mail. *As a computer engineer, Evans is especially qualified to analyze the subject of our own essay: the coming changes to the way we will publish and the way we will read. "Apocalypse Soon" first appeared in* The Walrus *of September 2007.*

1 A few years ago, my first novel was published. It did pretty well, won an award, was translated and sold around the world; the movie rights were even optioned. Now I want to put it online—no charge, no hook, no catch. My motivation is simple: greed.

My publishers are resolutely opposed to this idea. They fear it   2
will "devalue the brand" and set a dangerous precedent. They fear,
intuitively but wrongly, that fewer people will buy a book that is also
given away for free. But most of all, they fear the future—and with
good reason. Book publishing is a dinosaur industry, and there's a
big scary meteor on the way.

Newspapers, with their readerships and profit margins being ham-   3
mered by television, free dailies, and the Internet (Yahoo! News and
Craigslist, among others), have been forced to adapt or die. Even the
august *New York Times* now has more readers online than "onpaper"
(for the moment a neologism). The broadsheet's publisher, Arthur
Sulzberger Jr., has speculated that in five years' time it might stop
producing a print edition. Magazines are way ahead of him. Many scientific journals don't bother printing physical copies. *Premiere*, once
one of Hollywood's mightiest arbiters, recently announced that it will
henceforth exist only online. *Slate*, an online mag covering politics
and current events, is turning a profit, and long-established titles like
the *Atlantic* and the *New Yorker* give selected content away for free,
using the web to drive subscriptions. If you thought the Internet
revolution ended with the dot-com flame-out in 2001, think again.
We are witnessing the beginnings of a massive tectonic shift.

Book publishers, however, stand apart, aloof, shielded perhaps by   4
the dismal failure of electronic books. After a decade of hype and
development, e-book sales have achieved the dizzying market share
of 0.2 percent for full-length books. It seems that books, unlike newspapers and magazines, are protected from the encroaching digital
revolution by some kind of moat. Let's examine that divide—but first,
let's take a closer look at what it guards. What exactly is a book?

From the time of Gutenberg° until about twenty years ago, any non-   5
academic could have answered this question without hesitation: a
book is a bound sheaf of pages. If the pages are blank, it's a notebook; if they're full of factual information, it's a reference book; if

---

°Gutenberg: Around 1439 Johannes Gutenberg of Germany invented moveable type, making possible the
modern book.

they tell a made-up story, it's a novel. The bound sheaf of paper is not just an artifact, it's an icon of civilization.

6   Enter the Internet, muddying definitions everywhere. Enter Project Gutenberg, which puts out-of-copyright classics online. Enter book-length blogs and online literary experiments. Enter reference works that "live" online, constantly changing and grow-ing, but that occasionally also result in paper editions—works such as *The Java Tutorial,* a technical manual that explains the intricacies of an Internet programming language. A book is the text, not the form in which the text is rendered—we'll leave to literary theorists the implications of non-linear hyperlinked texts—and the online version of a book can be the "master copy," the bound sheaf a mere textual snapshot, already stale when printed. Online reference works can make use of endless space for appendices, unlimited full-colour graphics, examples that run on the user's screen, discussion boards, and chat rooms. Given this interactivity and timeliness, why would anyone want to buy, say, *The Java Tutorial* onpaper?

7   And yet people do. The book is a worldwide bestseller for tech-nical manuals. The physical *Java Tutorial* is, compared to what's freely available and downloadable online, limited in scope and out of date; but its readers—overwhelmingly web programmers—purchase the bound sheaf version anyway. What is going on here? What is keep-ing the big bad twenty-first century from the publishing industry's nineteenth-century castle walls?

8   Both e-books and sheaves of paper have pros and cons. Sheaves never lose battery power; you can flip through them quickly, use them as bricks, or take them to the bath; and they are still relatively cheap. On the other hand, digital readers can store hundreds of e-books, including those available for free, and their contents can be updated, searched, and annotated. In the near future, the num-ber of digital readers will skyrocket, and making copies for friends will be simple. All things being equal, you'd expect e-books to have grabbed a significant share of the book market by now. So why haven't they?

The answer is simple, and if you're a publisher, not at all comfort- 9
ing. The enormous and lasting success of ink on paper is almost
entirely due to one thing: contrast. Ink on paper has almost perfect
contrast, allowing the average eye to make out small shapes such as
letters with little strain. Luminescent pixels on LCD screens represent a tougher challenge. The eye has to work for its input, a slow
and subtle strain. This is no big deal if you're reading a few pages
over the course of several minutes, but if you're devoting yourself to
tens of thousands of words—in other words, if you're devoting yourself to a book—reading from an LCD screen is a physical burn.

Of course, many say there's more to it than contrast, that there's 10
something special about paper, something sacred; that people like
the feel of paper, the smell, the cover art. All of which is true, and
similar arguments were once made about vinyl records. Until a few
months ago, I was a great champion of the "tactile experience," of
holding the thing and its art in your hands. Then I went browsing
through a Borders bookstore in California, where I saw and experienced a Sony Reader.

The Reader isn't a revolution in and of itself. For $300 all you get 11
is a tiny display and a clumsy interface. Reading a book on this would
be deeply annoying—but it wouldn't be a strain. Instead of an LCD
screen, it boasts "electronic paper," the ink highlighted in soothing
contrast, as if it were onpaper. As I stared down at the Sony Reader,
for the first time in my life I could envision myself abandoning paper
for digital books. It was a revelation.

Suppose Apple released an electronic paper iTome, I thought, 12
and suppose it was easy to use, reasonably priced, and allowed one
to switch between text and audio book on demand. Suppose, further,
that it was convenient, even sexy. Would there still be something
sacred and special about bound sheaves of paper? Or would we soon
see them supplanted by iTome on the subway, in the classroom, even
curled up beside the fireplace?

Doesn't sound so bad to me. But the idea is like a can of poisonous 13
snakes to most book publishers, and it's easy to see why when you
consider what's happening to the music industry. Go to limewire.
com, home of "the fastest file sharing program on the planet." Take

a couple of minutes to download and install the LimeWire client, *et voilà.* Despite the best efforts of the Recording Industry Association of America, you have access to nearly every song of the modern era, all downloadable free of charge.

14   This is piracy, clearly illegal and wildly popular despite lawsuit after lawsuit, despite increasingly desperate and mostly failed copyright-protection schemes. If and when e-books and digital readers become ubiquitous, the same thing will happen. The change winds have already begun to blow. Pirated audiobooks and "cracked" e-books, converted to easily shared text, are already available online, if you know where and how to look. Imagine if people could download any book they wanted, for free, onto a digital reader with contrast as good as ink and paper. The entire publishing industry would collapse.

15   The "free content" folks argue, "information wants to be free." This sounds good; maybe it even sounds right. But like many slogans it makes no sense. Information is an abstract noun, and for itself it doesn't want anything. Information is what we do with it, but what if we decide we want it for free? You can't compete with free. Or can you?

16   While most publishers tremble and fret, some authors actually want to put their work online. Many in this group are from the forward-looking field of science fiction. If you're so inclined, you can go online right now and read (for free) highly acclaimed science fiction novels such as Charles Stross's *Accelerando*, Peter Watts's *Blindsight*, and the entire oeuvre of Cory Doctorow. Science fiction publisher Baen Books has made available a "library" of copyrighted-but-free novels. You may be wondering why these authors and publishers have cut their own commercial throats. But the evidence to date indicates that releasing a book online actually increases offline sales. Readers try and then they buy.

17   Caveats apply. Such releases are still unusual, and thus they receive unusual publicity. Many readers will begin a book online, decide they like it, and buy a paper copy rather than fight their way through 100,000 low-contrast words.

18   (And, indeed, sales and publicity are the two reasons I want to put my own book online immediately, before the iTome emerges as a replacement force.) But there's also a growing body of evidence that

people often buy paper copies of books *after* reading them online for free, that many readers actually want to pay authors. I find this reassuring because, scary as it might sound, in the long run it's the publishing industry's only hope.

The music business has moved to voluntary payment already. 19 Virtually every song available on Apple's iTunes store is also available on LimeWire at the same quality, with fewer restrictions, and at no cost. Listeners can download these songs without fear of legal repercussions from any Internet café or public access Wi-Fi hotspot— and yet iTunes's business is booming. Literally billions of songs have been sold. It seems that an enormous number of people are willing to pay for what they can get for free.

Digital books have huge advantages. Printing and distributing 20 bound sheaves of paper is expensive and not exactly environment friendly. In fact, it's very strange, in this Internet era, to be shipping text on trucks and railcars. If publishers can cut out those costs and pass the savings on to their readers, basic economics dictates that more books will be purchased and profits will grow.

Unfortunately, once a book is an e-book, once a text has been turned 21 into pure information, then all the copyright-protection schemes and intellectual-property lawyers in the world won't keep it from being made available for free. It's simply too easy to share text across servers, nations, and individual computers. And if publishers don't convert their paper books to e-books, pirates will. In the not-too-distant future, *all* books will be freely available, just as essentially all popular music is right now. Readers will decide whether books are worth buying, and if so for how much, often after they've read them.

I'm not thrilled about this inevitability. I want to put my first novel 22 online for free to hook readers, who will, I hope, go on to purchase my subsequent work. And I want to do it now, while it's still a perverse and hence noteworthy thing to do, to get physical sales while there's still a reason to buy bound sheaves of paper. That's why I'm so frustrated by my publishers' demurral. They may not like this future, but to fight it is to play King Canute.° It's better by far to try to swim.

°King Canute: To cure his courtiers of their flattery (they had claimed he was so great a king he could command the tides), Canute placed his throne at the ocean's edge. When the tide came in, disobeying his command to stay back, all the court learned a lesson.

23   Books have always been available for free: libraries, used books, friends' copies. For the time being, they retain their decorative value, and a house lined with books suggests a well-read owner. But LPs were once a staple of living room decor as well. That space was overtaken by cassettes and CDs, if ever so briefly, but now a computer terminal is often the only thing on display. The question is, will anyone still buy books when payment is purely voluntary? iTunes and the music-industry precedent indicate that the answer is yes—for now.

24   (One argument for how to save traditional book publishing is to only publish superb books. In 2004, in English alone, roughly 450,000 titles were published. Many of them, perhaps most of them, were, well, quite unnecessary. For books to gain back cultural cachet, the argument goes, a counter-revolution based on quality is necessary.)

25   If enough people grow accustomed to reading without paying, then authors will have to go back to being financed by wealthy patrons, publishers will wither away, and readers will find themselves trying to sift gems from an ever-growing mountain of self-published dreck. If readers do choose to pay, they will be able to send their money directly to authors, cutting out publishers entirely, and encouraging successful writers to self-publish rather than settle for a percentage. Either way, a revolution is on the horizon.

26   A new industry will eventually emerge from the chaos. Books aren't going away, and even bound sheaves of paper will survive in some form. Readership may actually increase—I think it's safe to say the digital generation doesn't read as many books as the paper generation, and e-books might change that. But the oncoming digital meteor will hit today's publishing industry hard, and its dinosaurs are going to die.

EXPLORATIONS:

Jon Evans,
> *Dark Places* (adventure novel)
> *Invisible Armies* (adventure novel)

http://en.wikipedia.org/wiki/E-book
http://www.rezendi.com/aboutauthor.htm

http://www.harpercollins.ca/trailers/trailer000200769X.html
http://www.booked.tv/html/shop/books/authors/evans_jon.htm
http://www.walrusmagazine.com/articles/2007.09-jon-evans-
   invisible-armies

STRUCTURE:

1. How are John Evans' INTRODUCTION and CLOSING coordinated? What effects do they achieve together?
2. Identify Evans' THESIS STATEMENT.
3. Roughly what proportion of Evans' argument is devoted to *examples*? Do you use enough? Can there be too many?
4. "Apocalypse Soon" is an overall *contrast* of the paper book and the electronic book in its various forms so far. Point out the differences that strike you as the most dramatic.
5. Identify Evans' main points of *contrast* between paper and electronic books in paragraphs 8 and 9. Which is his main point in this passage?
6. In paragraph 20, where do we also see a strong *comparison?*

STYLE:

1. What FIGURE OF SPEECH does Evans use when in paragraph 4 he writes of "moats" and in paragraph 7 he writes of "castle walls"? Why does he choose these images?
2. How does Evans employ IRONY in paragraph 4?

IDEAS FOR DISCUSSION AND WRITING:

1. Have you seen or used an e-book? Describe it. Are you one of those who feel there's something "sacred" about the traditional book: "the feel of paper, the smell, the cover art" (par. 10)? Or do you look forward to its replacement, a device that stores hundreds of books and that permits easy file sharing?
2. Jon Evans wants to put his book online and offer it for free, because of "greed" (par. 1). Explain how he believes this would make him

money. Do you agree that it would? Why or why not? And can you believe that in five years the *New York Times* might do better by abandoning its paper format for digital (3)? Why or why not?

3. Evans points out that "it's very strange, in this Internet era, to be shipping text on trucks and railcars" (19). *Contrast* the book as a physical object with the book as electronic text. Include environmental and economic implications, as well as personal.

4. In one year, 2004, some 450,000 books were published in English alone (par. 23). Do you suppose all these books were worth publishing? Can there be this many good authors? Or, in fact, are publishing standards too low? Are there too many books? Give examples from your own experience.

5. If the "oncoming digital meteor" soon hits, as Evans imagines, will it kill the dinosaurs? Will the "book," in whatever form it takes, then be produced through self-publishing? Argue why or why not?

6. Suppose you wished to self-publish a book you had written. *Contrast* how you might do so in paper and ink format, with how you might do so in a digital format.

7. **PROCESS IN WRITING:** *In our time almost every topic, including publishing, has environmental implications. If the e-book is about to replace the paper and ink "sheaf," then is the e-car about to replace vehicles that burn fossil fuels? Think about this* contrast *of vehicles. Do some research, then make notes: Draw a vertical line on a page, and at the top left write "conventional car" and at the top right "e-car." Now fill both sides with notes. Next develop a* THESIS STATEMENT *that announces your topic and your own view of it (for example, that in a decade the e-car will replace the fossil fuel car). Decide whether to proceed by "halves" or by "separate points." Now write a quick draft of your argument, supplying* examples *from your research. Highlight the* contrasts *with* TRANSITION SIGNALS *such as "by contrast," "on the other hand," "however," "but," etc. Now read your draft aloud to detect wordiness or other weak style. Finally check the spelling and punctuation before printing out your best version to share in class.*

Note: See also the Topics for Writing on the Online Learning Centre at www. mcgrawhill.ca/olc/conrad.

Process in Writing: Guidelines

Follow at least some of these steps in writing your essay of comparison and contrast (your teacher may suggest which ones).

1. Spend enough time with the topic list to choose the item that best fits your interest and experience.
2. Draw a line down the middle of a blank page. Brainstorm: Jot down notes for subject "A" on the left and for subject "B" on the right. Now join related items with lines, then take stock of what you have: Is A better than B? Is it worse? Similar? Opposite? Or what? Express their relationship to each other in a THESIS STATEMENT.
3. Now choose either "halves" or "separate points" to organize your argument, depending on the nature and size of your subject, then work your notes into a brief outline.
4. Write a rapid first draft, not stopping now to revise or edit.
5. Later analyze what you have produced: Does it follow your outline? If not, is the new material off-topic, or is it a worthwhile addition, an example of "thinking in writing"? Revise accordingly.
6. Try your prose aloud, to test the style. Cut all deadwood. Sharpen word choice. Add any missing examples. Strengthen TRANSITIONS.
7. Now edit for spelling and punctuation before printing out your good copy.

CP (Chuck Stoody)

"Yet as fast as the woodsmen cut, as much as they cut, it was never fast enough. The quantity always fell short of the expectations of the weendigoes, their masters."

—*Basil Johnston, "Modern Cannibals of the Wilds"*

ANALOGY
AND RELATED
DEVICES

IN A WAY, IT'S LIKE....

One student wrote this childhood memory:

> I heard and felt a rumbling from the ground, looked up and saw a huge red metallic monster with a tail on the end approach us. "Run, run," I said, "before it eats us." My mother reassured me that no fear was necessary. The monster slowly rolled up beside us, opened its mouth, and we went in.

As adults, we know monsters have not roamed Canada for millions of years, and we know they were not red but probably green! We also know that monsters and streetcars have little in common. Yet who would say this *analogy* does not clearly express the child's first encounter with a streetcar? It may even help us, as adults, to view with new eyes something we had taken for granted. *(A caution, though: as explained below, what an analogy will* not *do for us is prove anything at all logically. An essay based on this device is more in the realm of creative writing than of factual argumentation.)*

In this chapter Basil Johnston describes another monster—the weendigo of Native American legend that eats humans who wander outside at night. In its new version the weendigo consumes not humans but pine, spruce, cedar and the wildlife that lives there. Though we know the forest industry is not staffed by monsters but by decent men and women trying to make a living, we cannot help but see, through Johnston's eyes, the "monstrous" destruction of clearcutting.

In the last chapter we discussed how two items from the same category—say, two cities—can be explained logically through comparison and contrast. By seeing how Vancouver and Montreal are alike or unlike, we gain a clearer understanding of both. An *analogy*, though, brings together two apparently *unlike* items from *different* categories (such as a monster and a modern industry). Instead of using the two to explain each other, it more often uses one as a device to explain the other. It is not the monsters we investigate, but the monstrous aspects of the streetcar or the forest industry.

In the last chapter we speculated whether, instead of comparing two cities, we could compare a city and an anthill. To those of us who live in chambers along the corridors of apartment buildings or who each day crowd into holes in the ground to take the subway, the similarities may be all too clear. We do see right away that such an argument is hardly logical, for the very good reason that people are not insects. And we would certainly not want to base a factual paper, such as a research essay, on this device. Yet in a very informal or humorous paper, an analogy may be a fresh, thought-provoking way to express aspects of city life.

Topics that are unfamiliar or abstract almost cry out for analogies to explain them. Thus, a generation ago the term "computer virus" swept the world. These electronic "diseases" "infect" computer programs, "spreading" an "epidemic" of "contagion." The "outbreaks" of various "strains" feature names such as AIDS.II, Amoeba A, Anthrax, BW.Hepatitis, Cancer.2528, Cholera.A, Ebola 3000, Encephalitis, Leprosy, Measles.212 and Plague.2647.

These plagues "contaminate" programs, erase memory and even attack hardware. Of course "antiviral" software to "vaccinate" the patient was soon developed, with brand names like "Flu Shot +," "Data Physician," "Antidote," "AntiVirus," "Virus RX," "ViruSafe" and "Vaccine 1.0." In addition, "safe computing practices" have been recommended to avoid infection by viruses such as AIDS.II.

Have we already seen the first big analogy of the new millennium? In a 2005 *Globe and Mail* article, business reporter Andrew Willis wrote, "Spurned suitors, unrequited passion. A final, joyful union. The latest round of takeovers is the stuff of romance novels.

"Just look at the flirting going on before Gillette finally fell into Procter & Gamble's waiting arms, and before SBC Communications got a ring on the finger of AT&T.... for years, chief executives at these companies met in secret spots or whispered into their phones late into the night. We've also learned they contemplated walking down the aisle with any number of other partners."

Apparently an optimist, Willis says nothing of divorce. But he has already exploited the power of the analogy. It comes not so much from its originality as its breadth, especially the heavy borrowing of vocabulary from the one item (romance) to the other (corporations). The further you develop such links between your two items, the stronger the analogy.

Yet even a brief statement, such as "A corporate merger is like a wedding," can have value. As a *simile* it is not much of an argument in itself, but is a concrete statement that can be used in support of another argument. While a *simile* states that one thing is *like* another, a *metaphor* states that one thing *is* another ("A corporate merger is a wedding"). Both devices occur often in poetry and fiction, and also occur in essays. Review Nathalie Petrowski's selection "The Seven-Minute Life of Marc Lépine," in Chapter 4. It offers a wealth of these devices, especially from paragraph 9 through the end. These carry a strong load of emotion, as the author struggles to make sense of a recent event, the worst mass murder in Canadian history. The images may not prove anything logically, but they convey a strong sense of the author's consternation, and they vividly express the violence not only of Lépine's story, but all too likely the stories of many others feeling the same pressures from our society.

In closing, again a caution: *Do not confuse the pleasures of the analogy with the logic of argumentative devices such as comparison and contrast, or cause and effect. Of course a brief figure of speech or a small analogy can help explain a point in other kinds of arguments; but the full analogy, a device on which a whole paper is based, is best saved for personal essays, humorous pieces, and satires, where its freewheeling poetic nature is most appropriate.*

Note: For more examples of analogy and related devices, see these essays in other chapters:

Analogy:
Nathalie Petrowski, "The Seven-Minute Life of Marc Lépine," p. 169
Kildare Dobbs, "The Scar," p. 361
Lt.-Gen. Roméo Dallaire, "*Cri de coeur*," p. 414

Simile, metaphor and other figures of speech:
Emily Carr, "D'Sonoqua," p. 117
Nathalie Petrowski, "The Seven-Minute Life of Marc Lépine," p. 169
Dr. Mark Bernstein, "Yes, It Is Brain Surgery," p. 311
Joy Kogawa, "Grinning and Happy," p. 373

DR. VINCENT LAM AND
DR. COLIN LEE

Dr. Lam's Perspective:
Go on a Canoe Trip

Vincent Lam is an emergency doctor at Toronto East General Hospital, practises expedition medicine on Arctic and Antarctic ships and lectures in the University of Toronto's Faculty of Medicine. Born in London, Ontario, and descended from the Chinese expatriate community of Vietnam, he completed his medical training at the University of Toronto in 1999. Like Dr. Mark Bernstein in Chapter 8 ("Yes, It Is Brain Surgery"), Lam has mastered the pen as well as the scalpel. In 2006 his book of short fiction, Bloodletting and Miraculous Cures, *created a sensation with its harrowing accounts of the SARS epidemic in Toronto (Lam had joined the fight, as a medical student). It won the Giller Prize. The same year Lam co-authored with colleague Colin Lee* The Flu Pandemic and You, *a guide to surviving the next pandemic. And in 2007 appeared his first novel,* Cholon, *set in Vietnam.*

Colin Lee is a staff emergency physician at the Royal Victoria Hospital of Barrie, Ontario, and is a specialist in pandemic influenza planning. He was born in Malaysia. After completing his M.D. at the University of Toronto (1998), Lee went on to postgraduate work at the University of Toronto and McGill. Having also an M.S. degree in Public Health in Developing Countries, Lee consults extensively with international agencies, especially as to malaria and HIV/AIDS. He has worked in Bénin, Burkina Faso, India, Kenya, Mali, Niger and South Africa. As mentioned above, it was in 2006 that he co-authored with Vincent Lam The Flu Pandemic and You, *from which our selection comes.*

1   If you want to prepare for a pandemic, or for any other disaster, think about the first time you went on a canoe trip. If you've never been, go on one. The tasks of a canoe trip are basic, and so are its lessons. The idea is to paddle and portage from one place to another, find shelter, make food, and enjoy the scenery. One lesson is that things don't happen exactly the way they always do in your regular life, or even the way you expect them to happen while canoeing. That can be all right. While portaging, you may sink into a bog and fill your boot with mud. While paddling, you may go the wrong way and end up in an unexpected (though hopefully scenic) part of the lake. You may accidentally light your dinner on fire. All these occurrences can be dealt with. Dry out your boot, consult your map, and scrape the burnt bits off your dinner. An unusual event like a pandemic is similar: things may not proceed in their usual fashion, but that in itself is probably no cause for panic. Many people may be sick. Most will recover. Everyone still needs to eat, drink, and wash their hands.

2   The first time you went on a canoe trip, you probably went with someone who knew how to do things like rescue people who fall out of canoes and tie up food high in a tree to keep it away from bears. A pandemic is the same way. Some people spend their entire careers studying public health and infectious disease so that they can tell you what to do when something like an influenza pandemic arrives. What they tell you may not be perfect, but it's a good bet that it'll help you. If you don't believe me, just try to get back into a canoe after falling out without someone telling you how to do it.

3   Another lesson of camping is that you should prepare for your trip so that really dangerous things are less likely to turn out very badly. There will always be bears in the woods, which doesn't mean you shouldn't go canoeing; it just means that you should know something about bears. Wear good boots so you're less likely to break your ankle when you go over. Know which part of the lake drains into a waterfall so that you don't get lost heading in that direction. Don't cook your dinner inside your tent. During a pandemic or another troublesome time, life may throw you a few twists and turns. Having some things prepared—a closet of food, a flu shot in your arm, and some basic supplies—is just common sense. A bear may decide to

investigate your campsite, and you may catch influenza, and since you can't entirely control whether this happens, it's not a bad idea to consider what you will do with a bear in your campsite, or a fever and a cough during a pandemic.

EXPLORATIONS:

Dr. Vincent Lam and Dr. Colin Lee, *The Flu Pandemic and You: A Canadian Guide*

Dr. Vincent Lam, *Bloodletting and Miraculous Cures* (interrelated short stories)

John M. Barry, *The Great Influenza: The Epic Story of the Greatest Plague in History*

Albert Camus, *The Plague* (novel)

Daniel Defoe, *A Journal of the Plague Year* (fictionalized reporting)

http://en.wikipedia.org/wiki/Bubonic_plague

http://www.influenza.gc.ca/index_e.html

http://www.archives.gov/exhibits/influenza-epidemic

http://www.avert.org/worldstats.htm

http://www.vincentlam.ca/about.php

http://www.vincentlam.ca/articles-030419-sars-from-behind-the-mask.php

http://wildernesscanoe.ca

STRUCTURE:

1. Point out Lam and Lee's THESIS STATEMENT. Is it unusual? Did its message surprise you? If so, why?

2. Suppose the authors knew nothing of canoeing. Could they have used some other *analogy* to describe how to survive a pandemic? Suggest one, based on some activity you know well. Suggest to the class several points you might make in developing it.

3. The three paragraphs of this short essay each support a different aspect of the overall point. Identify the main message of each, and how it contributes to the whole.

STYLE:

1. This essay has long paragraphs, but short sentences and mostly small words. What is the overall effect: a STYLE that is more FORMAL or more INFORMAL? And is this style appropriate to the AUDIENCE that you believe this selection was originally intended for?

IDEAS FOR DISCUSSION AND WRITING:

1. Have you gone on a canoe trip? Did it rain? Did you dump the boat? Did you encounter bears? Did they steal your food? Did you burn supper? Did mosquitoes and blackflies attack? Did you get lost? Or, on the other hand, was the swimming great? Did the fish bite? Was the food delicious? Were the sunsets spectacular? Tell all to the class. Why do people go canoeing in the back country?

2. If you do not go to the wilds to canoe, kayak, ski, hike or backpack, do you seek urban adventures? What are they? Tell both the good and the bad.

3. The world has long experienced pandemics. In the 14th century the Bubonic Plague wiped out a third of Europe's population. The so-called "Spanish Flu" of 1918 to 1919 killed an estimated 40 to 100 million people around the world, and in our own time HIV/AIDS has killed over 25 million. Do you agree with those experts who say another pandemic of some kind is inevitable? If so, what do you believe it might be? Or do you believe modern medicine can now prevent disaster? Defend your viewpoint with reasons.

4. You probably remember the 2003 outbreak of SARS (severe acute respiratory syndrome), which took 774 lives worldwide. It began in Asia, then showed up in Vancouver and Toronto, where our authors, Drs. Lam and Lee, took part in the fight against it. In the end, 43 Canadians died. Read Dr. Vincent Lam's book of short fiction, *Bloodletting and Miraculous Cures*, much of which describes the epidemic. Report what you find to the class, and answer these questions: Was the SARS outbreak a pandemic? Why or why not? Could it have become one? How well did Canadian public health programs and personnel work to contain the problem?

5. If you have not already read "Regine Mamba," by Stephanie Nolan, look back to Chapter 5 and read it now. She portrays a

Zambia where HIV/AIDS has killed 600,000 people, among them many parents, leaving a vast population of orphans to be raised by their grandmothers. What can more fortunate countries such as ours do at this point to help?

6. HIV/AIDS has scared the world for the last couple of decades, but it is thought that malaria has plagued the human race for at least 50,000 years. It kills between one million and three million persons every year, averaging one death every 30 seconds. Since it is spread by mosquitoes, a huge proportion of these deaths could be avoided if enough mosquito nets were made available. These cost a few dollars each, as aid organizations tell us. Write up a proposal for such a project. Share it with the class. If there is interest, mount a fundraising campaign, in cooperation with an existing nonprofit aid organization.

7. PROCESS IN WRITING: *If the challenge of a pandemic is like the challenge of a canoe trip, consider another pair of challenges: completing a postsecondary education as climbing a mountain, or as backpacking in the wilderness, or as running a marathon. Close your eyes and think for a while about your chosen* analogy. *Then draw a vertical line down the middle of a page. Write "college" or "university" above the left column, and "mountain" or "trail" or "marathon" above the right. Fill both sides with notes. Later connect items in the two columns by drawing lines between the ones that have similarities. Now write a very clear THESIS STATEMENT, like that of Drs. Lam and Lee, then produce your first draft. Look it over: Are there enough points of similarity? If not, add. Do TRANSITION signals such as "like," "as," "similarly" and "likewise" signal the likenesses? If not, add. Is your language CONCISE, like that of our authors? If not, prune. Finally, check the punctuation and spelling, then print out your best version.*

Note: See also the Topics for Writing on the Online Learning Centre at www. mcgrawhill.ca/olc/conrad.

BASIL JOHNSTON

Modern Cannibals of the Wilds

Basil Johnston is well known as a writer, storyteller and teacher of Ojibway (Anishinabe) language, mythology and history for 25 years in the Department of Ethnology of Toronto's Royal Ontario Museum. Born in 1929 on the Parry Island Reserve in Ontario, he attended Cape Croker public school, then at the Spanish Residential School lived the cultural dislocations of the residential school system which he later described in his book Indian School Days *(1988). He completed his education at Loyola College in Montreal and the Ontario College of Education. Fluent in his original language and culture, Johnston has long been a strong voice of First Nations People in Canada. Though he lectures widely on Ojibwa history, culture and language, it is his books that reach the largest audience:* Ojibway Heritage *(1976),* How the Birds Got Their Colours *(1978),* Moose Meat and Wild Rice *(1978),* Tales the Elders Told *(1981),* Ojibway Ceremonies *(1982),* By Canoe and Moccasin *(1986),* Tales of the Anishinaubaek *(1993),* The Manitous: The Spiritual World of the Ojibway *(1995),* The Bear-Walker and Other Stories *(1995),* The Star Man and Other Tales *(1997),* Mermaids and Medicine Women *(1998),* Crazy Dave *(1999) and* Honour Mother Earth *(2003). Our selection is from the August 1, 1991 Toronto* Globe and Mail. *In it Johnston goes beyond his usual role of imparting Ojibway culture; his portrait of the new "weendigo" cuts right to the heart of modern Canadian values.*

1   Woods and forest once mantled most of this land, this continent. It was the home of the Anishinabek (Ojibway, Ottawa, Potowatomi, Algonquin), their kin and their neighbours. It

was also the home of the moose, the deer, the caribou, the bear, their kindred and their neighbours. It was as well the home of the thrushes, the sparrows, the hawks, the tanagers, the ravens, the owls, their cousins and their neighbours. Mosquitoes, butterflies, caterpillars, ants, moths, their kin and their neighbours had a place therein.

Not only was it home, but a wellspring from which all drew their sustenance, medicine and knowledge.   2

Also dwelling in the woods and forests were weendigoes, giant cannibals who fed upon human flesh to allay their perpetual hunger. They stalked villages and camps, waiting for, and only for, the improvident, the slothful, the gluttonous, the promiscuous, the injudicious, the insatiable, the selfish, the avaricious and the wasteful, to be foolish enough to venture alone beyond the environs of their homes in winter.   3

But no matter how many victims a single weendigo devoured raw, he could never satisfy his hunger. The more he ate, the larger he grew, and the larger he grew, the greater his hunger. The weendigo's hunger always remained in proportion to his size.   4

Even though a weendigo is a mythical figure, he represents real human cupidity. What the old-time storyteller meant to project in the image of the weendigo was a universal and unchanging human disposition. But more learned people declared that no such monster ever existed, that he was a product of superstitious minds and imaginations.   5

As a result, the weendigo was driven from his place in Anishinabe traditions and culture, ostracized through disbelief and skepticism. It was assumed, and indeed it appeared as if, the weendigo and his brothers and sisters had passed into the Great Beyond, like many North American Indian beliefs and practices and traditions.   6

Actually, the weendigoes did not die out; they have only been assimilated and reincarnated as corporations, conglomerates and multinationals. They have taken on new names, acquired polished manners and renounced their craving for human flesh for more refined viands. But their cupidity is no less insatiable than their ancestors'.   7

One breed subsists entirely on forests. When this breed beheld forests, its collective cupidity was stirred as it looked upon an endless, boundless sea of green—as in greenbacks. They saw beyond,   8 even into the future. Money. Cash. Deposits. Bank accounts. Interest. Reserves. Investments, securities, bonds, shares, dividends, capital gains, assets, funds, deals, revenue, income, prosperity, opulence, profits, riches, wealth, comfort.

 9   They recruited woodsmen with axes, crosscut saws and Swede saws, sputters, shovels, cant hooks, grapples, chains, ropes, files and pikes, and sent them into the woods to fell, hew, saw, cut, chop, slash and level. The forests resounded with the clash of axes and the whine of saws as blades bit into the flesh of spruce, pine, cedar, tamarack and poplar to fill the demands of the weendigoes in Toronto, Montreal, Vancouver, New York, Chicago, Boston, wherever they now dwelt. Cries of "Timber!" echoed across the treetops, followed by the rip and tear of splintering trees, and thundering crashes.

10   And as fast as woodsmen felled the trees, teamsters delivered sleigh-load after sleighload to railway sidings and to the rivers. Train after train, shipload after shipload of logs were delivered to the mills.

11   Yet as fast as the woodsmen cut, as much as they cut, it was never fast enough. The quantity always fell short of the expectations of the weendigoes, their masters.

12   "Is that all? Should there not be more? We demand a bigger return for our risks and our investments. Only more will satisfy us. Any amount will do, so long as it's more, and the more the better."

13   The demands were met for more speed and more pulp, more logs and more timber. Axes, saws, woodsmen, horses and teamsters were replaced, and their blows and calls no longer rang in the forest. In their place, chainsaws whined, Caterpillar tractors with huge blades bulled and battered their way through the forest, uprooting trees to clear the way for automatic shearers that topped, limbed and sheared the trunks. These mechanical weendigoes gutted and desolated the forests, leaving death, destruction and ugliness where once there was life, abundance and beauty.

14   Trucks and transports operated day and night delivering cargo with a speed and quantity that the horses and sleighs could never have matched.

15   Yet the weendigoes wanted still more, and it didn't matter if their policies and practices of clear-cutting their harvest of timber and

pulp resulted in violations of North American Indian rights or in the further impairment of their lives.

Nor does it matter to them that their modus operandi perma- 16 nently defiles hillside and mountainside by erosion. They are indifferent to the carnage inflicted upon bears, wolves, rabbits, thrushes, sparrows, warblers. Who cares if they are displaced? What possible harm has been done? Nor does it seem as if these modern weendigoes have any regard for the rights of future generations to the yield of Mother Earth.

The new, reincarnated weendigoes are little different from their 17 forebears. They are more omnivorous than their ancestors, however, and the modern breed wears elegant clothes and comports itself with an air of cultured and dignified respectability.

Profit, wealth, comfort, power are the ends of business. Anything 18 that detracts from or diminishes the anticipated return, be it taking pains not to violate the rights of others, or taking measures to ensure that the land remains fertile and productive for future generations, must, it seems, be circumvented.

And what has been the result of this self-serving, self-glutting 19 disposition? In 10 short decades, these modern weendigoes have accomplished what at one time seemed impossible; they have laid waste immense tracts of forest that were seen as beyond limit as well as self-propagating, and ample enough to serve this generation and many more to come.

Now, as the forests are in decline, the weendigoes are looking at a 20 future that offers scarcity. Many others are assessing the weendigoes' accomplishments not in terms of dollars but in terms of damage— the damage they have inflicted on the environment and the climate and on botanical and zoological life.

EXPLORATIONS:

Basil Johnston,
> *How the Birds Got Their Colours*
> *Indian School Days*

Agnes Grant, ed., *Our Bit of Truth: An Anthology of Canadian Native Literature*

Linda Jaine and Drew Hayden, eds., *Voices: Being Native in Canada*
Elizabeth May, *At the Cutting Edge: The Crisis in Canada's Forests*
M. T. Kelly, *A Dream Like Mine* (novel)
Margaret Atwood, *Strange Things: The Malevolent North in Canadian Literature*
http://www.nativewiki.org/Basil_Johnston
http://www.turtle-island.com/rolemodels.html
http://www.whetung.com/basil.html
http://www.ipl.org/div/natam/bin/browse.pl/A41
http://archives.cbc.ca/IDD-1-75-679/science_technology/clearcutting

STRUCTURE:

1. "Modern Cannibals of the Wilds" is a FABLE. (See this book's glossary.) How do fables work? How does this one?
2. Why does Johnston open by listing so many animals, birds and insects whose "home" was once most of this continent?
3. Point out the paragraph of TRANSITION where we move from the old weendigo to the new one. Point out the THESIS STATEMENT.
4. Analyze how paragraphs 15 and 16 employ *cause and effect*.
5. Point out all the ways Johnston portrays the forestry industry as a monster and cannibal. How fully has he developed the *analogy*? Now invent an *analogy* for those who support the forestry industry, and tell it to the class.

STYLE:

1. In what kind of writing do we more often see words like "mantled," "kindred," "improvident" and "slothful"? Describe Johnston's TONE. Why do you think he chose it for this subject?
2. Read paragraph 9 aloud to the class, with feeling, so all can experience its ONOMATOPOETIC language. Which words sound like what they mean? What is the overall effect?

3. How CONCISE is Johnston's analogy? What techniques make it so?

4. Why is the METAPHOR "flesh" of paragraph 9 appropriate to Johnston's portrayal of the weendigoes?

IDEAS FOR DISCUSSION AND WRITING:

1. If our human forestry industry is a "cannibal," then in what sense is it "eating" us as well as trees?

2. "The more he ate, the larger he grew, and the larger he grew, the greater his hunger" (para. 4). What if one day the monster's "food" runs out? When our forestry industry can no longer "eat" and "grow," will it "starve"? What can we do now to either reduce its appetite or extend its food supply?

3. Defend or attack the clearcutting of forests that continues in British Columbia and most other provinces. Defend or attack the actions of environmentalists in convincing many European companies not to buy Canadian paper made through clearcutting.

4. Conservationists often say that in Canada we do not "harvest" but "mine" the forests. Extend these images into *analogies*, by giving parallels. *Contrast* the philosophies behind both.

5. What particularly qualifies Basil Johnston, a First Nations person, to write on this subject?

6. PROCESS IN WRITING: *In paragraph 16 Johnston refers to our "Mother Earth." Expand this widespread metaphor into an essay of analogy. First write the term "Mother Earth" in the centre of a page, then fill the surrounding space with other words it brings to mind. Connect related items with lines. Determine your main point. Now draw upon this cluster outline as you do a rapid first draft. When it has "cooled off," look it over. Do examples always help the reader "see" your point? If not, add. Does your TONE fit this important subject? If not, adjust. Is everything on topic? If not, cut. Finally, revise for spelling and punctuation as you produce your best version.*

Note: See also the Topics for Writing on the Online Learning Centre at www. mcgrawhill.ca/olc/conrad.

SAMANTHA BENNETT

It's Not Just the Weather
That's Cooler in Canada

When Samantha Bennett chose to write about Canada in her Pittsburgh
Post-Gazette *column of July 30, 2003, she had no idea what was about
to happen. Once her essay somehow got to Canada, and Canadians started
e-mailing it across the country, she experienced what she calls "one of the more
surreal and wonderful experiences I have ever had in my life. I got a marriage
proposal. I made friends in Kingston, Ontario who put me up.... I have been
offered more free beer, dinners, hotel rooms, city tours and guest beds than I
could ever use. I feel like an unofficial national heroine." By the time the piece
came out in the* Toronto Star, *the* Montreal Gazette *and the* Vancouver
Sun, *Bennett was receiving "several e-mails an hour from places as distant
as Newfoundland, Yellowknife, Northern Quebec and Vancouver Island."
She says, "People would actually call me up from Toronto or even Vancouver
just to ask if I was a real American journalist who really wrote that column.
And to thank me."*

*Not all the attention was positive. Some of the 1200 who replied were
"furious Canadian patriots who didn't realize it was satire and thought I
was bashing them." Quebeckers were miffed at a poor translation, and a few
Westerners said their country was "going to hell in a handbasket...." But the
American lifestyle columnist—with a B.A. in English from Yale and an M.A.
in professional writing from Carnegie Mellon University—is still wondering
how she so totally "struck a chord." Every week Bennett still writes her popular
humour column for the* Post-Gazette, *and now also broadcasts as online
liaison for the Features department.*

You live next door to a clean-cut, quiet guy. He never plays loud   1
music or throws raucous parties. He doesn't gossip over the
fence, just smiles politely and offers you some tomatoes. His
lawn is cared-for, his house is neat as a pin and you get the feeling
he doesn't always lock his front door. He wears Dockers. You hardly
know he's there.

And then one day you discover that he has pot in his basement,   2
spends his weekends at peace marches and that guy you've seen
mowing the yard is his spouse.

Allow me to introduce Canada.   3

The Canadians are so quiet that you may have forgotten they're up   4
there, but they've been busy doing some surprising things. It's like
discovering that the mice you are dimly aware of in your attic have
been building an espresso machine.

Did you realize, for example, that our reliable little tag-along   5
brother never joined the Coalition of the Willing? Canada wasn't
willing, as it turns out, to join the fun in Iraq. I can only assume
American diner menus weren't angrily changed to include "freedom
bacon,"° because nobody here eats the stuff anyway.

And then there's the wild drug situation: Canadian doctors are   6
authorized to dispense medical marijuana. Parliament is considering
legislation that would not exactly legalize marijuana possession, as
you may have heard, but would reduce the penalty for possession of
under 15 grams to a fine, like a speeding ticket. This is to allow law
enforcement to concentrate resources on traffickers; if your garden
is full of wasps, it's smarter to go for the nest rather than trying to
swat every individual bug. Or, in the United States, bong.

Now, here's the part that I, as an American, can't understand.   7
These poor benighted pinkos are doing everything wrong. They
have a drug problem: Marijuana offenses have doubled since 1991.
And Canada has strict gun control laws, which means that the criminals must all be heavily armed, the law-abiding civilians helpless and
the government on the verge of a massive confiscation campaign.

°freedom bacon: When France refused to join the U.S. invasion of Iraq, American fast-food restaurants
changed the term "French fries" to "freedom fries." "Freedom bacon" is Bennett's humorous play on "Canadian
bacon."

(The laws have been in place since the '70s, but I'm sure the government will get around to the confiscation eventually.) They don't even have a death penalty!

8   And yet … nationally, overall crime in Canada has been *declining* since 1991. Violent crimes *fell* 13 percent in 2002. Of course, there are still crimes committed with guns—brought in from the United States, which has become the major illegal weapons supplier for all of North America—but my theory is that the surge in pot-smoking has rendered most criminals too relaxed to commit violent crimes. They're probably more focused on shoplifting boxes of Ho-Hos from convenience stores.

9   And then there's the most reckless move of all: Just last month, Canada decided to allow and recognize same-sex marriages. Merciful moose, what can they be thinking? Will there be married Mounties (they always get their man!)? Dudley Do-Right° was sweet on Nell, not Mel! We must be the only ones who really care about families. Not enough to make sure they all have health insurance, of course, but more than those libertines up north.

10   This sort of behavior is a clear and present danger to all our stereotypes about Canada. It's supposed to be a cold, wholesome country of polite, beer-drinking hockey players, not founded by freedom-fighters in a bloody revolution but quietly assembled by loyalists and royalists more interested in order and good government than liberty and independence.

11   But if we are the rugged individualists, why do we spend so much of our time trying to get everyone to march in lockstep? And if Canadians are so reserved and moderate, why are they so progressive about letting people do what they want to?

12   Canadians are, as a nation, less religious than we are, according to polls. As a result, Canada's government isn't influenced by large, well-organized religious groups and thus has more in common with those of Scandinavia than those of the United States, or, say, Iran.

13   Canada signed the Kyoto global warming treaty, lets 19-year-olds drink, has more of its population living in urban areas and accepts more immigrants per capita than the United States.

°Dudley Do-Right: From a 1961 television animation that spoofed early melodramatic portrayals of the RCMP. In 1969–70 this animation was the lead feature of ABC's *The Dudley Do-Right Show.*

These are all things we've been told will wreck our society. But I   14
guess Canadians are different, because theirs seems oddly sound.

Like teenagers, we fiercely idolize individual freedom but really   15
demand that everyone be the same. But the Canadians seem more
adult—more secure. They aren't afraid of foreigners. They aren't
afraid of homosexuality. Most of all, they're not afraid of each
other.

I wonder if America will ever be that cool.   16

EXPLORATIONS:

Michael Adams, *Fire and Ice: The United States, Canada and the Myth of
     Converging Values*
Margaret Atwood, *The Handmaid's Tale* (novel)
Ian and Will Ferguson, *How to Be a Canadian, Even If You Already Are
     One*
Douglas Coupland, *Souvenir of Canada*
http://www.post-gazette.com/columnists/bio_bennett.asp
http://www.lexingtonfilm.com/samanthabennettinterview.htm
http://www.post-gazette.com/columnists/bennett.asp
http://www.parl.gc.ca/information/library/idb/forsey/can_am_
     gov_01-e.asp

STRUCTURE:

1. Who was Bennett's original AUDIENCE? Why did it need such a dramatic introduction (pars. 1–3) to the subject of Canada?
2. Point out all the ways in which paragraphs 1–3 work as an ANALOGY.
   How strong an introduction does the analogy make to the essay?
   Point out at least five places later in the argument where Bennett's
   points develop the generalizations that the analogy first makes.
3. In paragraph 5 Canada is "our reliable little tag-along brother."
   Where else does Bennett use METAPHORS? Where do you see
   SIMILES? And how do all these FIGURES OF SPEECH contribute to the
   argument?

4. To what extent is Bennett's argument a *comparison and contrast?* Cite examples. Is it organized *by halves* or *point by point?*

STYLE:

1. Zany humour fills this essay and most of Samantha Bennett's other columns for the *Post-Gazette.* Yet this essay, like most of hers, examines serious issues and comes to significant conclusions. Does her mix of light and serious work? Would it be acceptable in classroom essays? Why or why not?

2. Samantha Bennett received e-mails from "dozens of furious Canadian patriots who didn't realize it was satire and thought I was bashing them." When she makes observations such as "These poor benighted pinkos are doing everything wrong" (par. 7), did you at first mistake her meaning? Why is it sometimes hard to recognize IRONY?

IDEAS FOR DISCUSSION AND WRITING:

1. To what extent is Bennett's essay about Canada also about the United States? What messages does it have for its American readers?

2. Paragraph 5 looks at the "reliable little tag-along brother" who was however not willing to join "the fun in Iraq." Whether you were for or against that decision, how important do you feel it was in our history as a nation? Give reasons.

3. "It's supposed to be a cold, wholesome country of polite, beer-drinking hockey players ...," Bennett writes in paragraph 10. What other common STEREOTYPES of Canadians come to mind? Of Americans? Is there any truth here, or is it all image?

4. In paragraph 11 Bennett calls Americans "rugged individualists" and Canadians "reserved and moderate"—yet the former try to have everyone "march in lockstep" while the latter are "progressive about letting people do what they want to." How would you explain this PARADOX? Do you agree or disagree with her verdict? Give *examples.*

5. Though Samantha Bennett's essay was first published in a newspaper, it was also massively circulated by e-mail, and can still be

found on websites. How has digital technology changed the whole idea of "publication"? How would you, yourself, go about publishing an essay electronically?

6. **PROCESS IN WRITING:** *Samantha Bennett has discussed many things that Canada could teach her own country. Now do the reverse: brainstorm to think of things the United States could teach Canada. Begin as she does, with an analogy portraying the next-door nation as a person—then lead from this introduction to your points. Once you know those points, arrange them in increasing order of importance, with the strongest at the very end. The next day look over your draft. Does it have at least 50% example content, as hers does? Does it sparkle with SIMILES and METAPHORS, those little cousins of the analogy? Whether humorous or serious, is the TONE consistent? Do TRANSITIONS link the parts? Finally, check sentence structure and punctuation, before printing off your best version.*

Note: See also the Topics for Writing on the Online Learning Centre at www. mcgrawhill.ca/olc/conrad.

C. B. MACKINTOSH

Moss Campion

C. B. "Christy" Mackintosh was born and raised in Walkerton, Ontario, but since 1994 has lived in Alberta's mountain resort town of Banff. There she has pursued rugged outdoor sports, spending much time in the high Rockies, and, with her husband, is now raising two young girls. Mackintosh has written articles and book reviews for Western publications, has written for The Walrus, *and in 2006 published our essay "Moss Campion" in Marjorie Anderson's anthology* Dropped Threads 3: Beyond the Small Circle. *Though she says her writing life is "in hibernation" for now, because of family and business commitments, she has written 275 pages of a memoir that, as she puts it, explores in greater detail "that hard yet exhilarating climb called Motherhood." "Moss Campion" is the seed for this larger work. Comparing her writing to her outdoor pursuits, she adds that "writing is, and has always been, my trail through the wilderness."*

1   High on the ridge of Cascade Mountain, far from the swarm of tourists on Banff Avenue a thousand metres below, lives one of my perennial heroes. She makes her home in open, alpine spaces. She thrives, small and determined and hopeful, in a windswept, barren landscape of talus° and scree.° Where grey-weathered slabs of limestone pierce the sky with their jagged teeth, she flaunts her softness and her colour. Her name is *Silene acaulis* and she is a member of the pink family.

°talus: Mass of broken rock below a cliff.
°scree: Rubble of rocks and stones slanting up to a cliff or summit.

I first met Silene in 1994, when I came to Banff to work for the   2
summer and fell in with some local kids, a group of fun-loving, competitive cross-country skiers who went for three-hour bike rides after
work and climbed mountains every weekend. They asked me along
and, naively, I went, which was how I often found myself, weak-kneed
and light-headed, on Silene's terrain.

They called her moss campion, her common name, and they   3
warned me early on to watch for her. Though she is one of the
faster-growing alpine plants, her existence is delicate: her first
flower won't bloom for ten years, and a single misplaced human
step could destroy her. As my new friends led me into the back-
country, stepping from rock to rock to avoid landing on living
things, I could see that they cared for Silene; they respected her
tenuous hold on the ground they walked on, and they taught me
to do the same.

Most young people come to Banff to leave their cares behind. I   4
suppose the truth is I came to Banff that summer to get away from
my mother. Some part of me believed that, with only a sleeping bag,
my hiking boots and a plane ticket, I could save myself from drowning in her quicksand moods; I could sever her hold on me and rise
to the surface, three thousand kilometres from home, buoyant and
happily sputtering.

There were other things too, other reasons to flee: poor job pros-   5
pects, a failed relationship. But my mother's depression was a dark
shadow, a wall of snow moving up the valley toward me, threatening
to obliterate the landscape and turn the rocks beneath my feet all
slick and untrustworthy.

I stayed in Banff. I learned to dress for extreme weather. Following   6
the heels of the person in front of me up the eight steep kilometres
to Cascade's natural amphitheatre, I ignored my body's objections,
my face burning, my arms heavy, my heart pounding in my ears,
drowning out the sound of my friends' easy banter. As their voices
drifted farther up the trail away from me, my head swam with slogans
and clichés: *One step at a time. Just do it!* I kept my head down so I
couldn't see how steep the path was ahead of me, and measured each
breath to keep from hyperventilating.

7   If I kept moving, I had a purpose. At the end of an eight-hour hike, life's big questions were diverted to the comforting dilemma over which to do first: sleep, shower or eat.

8   Altitude became my therapy. When I stood on a mountaintop, there was so much *space*, it absorbed me, carried me out into the dizzying gulf between Mount Rundle and Cascade, and wove me into the sky-strewn landscape. I was so small, and yet I felt so *mighty* to be part of all that lives and grows at the tops of those lofty peaks.

9   In Banff, people were always leaving. I could try on a whole new version of myself each time the ski season ended, each time the air turned sharp, the days shortened and the summer staff returned to school in the East. Even the mountains, my steadfast sentinels, bathed in sunset or clutched by clouds, never looked the same.

10   I moved a lot. I changed jobs a lot. Boyfriends, co-workers, roommates, even my cat, came and went. I went back to Ontario, but only to visit. My mother was in and out of the hospital, taking too many, or not enough, pills. Everything there was the same. Suffocating.

11   I lived alone in an apartment above the bookstore: one small windowless room, surrounded by slamming doors and an alley that erupted with garbage-truck noise every morning at 7:00 a.m. This was not home to me. Home was the river's edge, where I would break from my run to watch the water pucker and swirl, its mirrored surface mountain-deep. Home was the beating of ravens' wings, and moonlight casting a tangle of tree shadows on the forest floor; the swish-scuttle of stone on ice, and the other-worldly call of elk rutting. Home was that moment outside time when the sound of rocks falling meant the rocks had already fallen.

12   Relationships were steep, sliding slopes of scree. After a string of boyfriends who either wanted too much or too little of me, I began a year-long, self-imposed moratorium on dating. I bought myself Bernard Callebaut chocolate. I lit candles and drank wine with dinner. I carried my notebook and pen to the sun-drenched tip of Mount Fairview, in Lake Louise. I travelled alone, overseas. I went to work. At night, if I needed company, I wrote, or read, or watched TV. Ten months later I met Lach.

13   We met in January. In February, we lay in each other's arms, huddled beneath a nylon sleeping bag in his shivery basement suite,

naming our children. Being with him was like being in the back-country, beyond the trappings of civilization, outside the constructs of time and productivity. He was my hard-earned destination, a place of rest and beauty where I could allow myself to just *be.*

Love happened like a windstorm, a sudden gust felling trees, thin- 14 ning the forest to reveal a path of limitless possibility. We moved in together. We hiked, played tennis, went to concerts, went to Paris, got married, bought a house, moved to Canmore. Making a life together, and making a child together: that was our dream.

Jerked upright in bed, like a marionette. *By what?* Silence. Drenched 15 in sweat. My T-shirt clinging to my body. My ears straining for the sound of her while the house holds its breath. I wait. *Nothing.* The clock glows 3:00 a.m.

Two hours since the last feed, she'll be waking soon, God. Should try to 16 *get more sleep. Need to shower. Change my clothes.* Dark wet circles dilate across my chest; my breasts are full, throbbing. I get up, shivering in the nighttime coolness of the house and cross the hall to where she sleeps in her bassinet. She's on her back. Her arms are bent up by the sides of her head in a body builder's pose, her little hands forming fists. *So strong, so beautiful.* Her face turned sideways is peaceful, her features delicate. I want to pick her up and hold her to me, smell her baby smell, nose pressed to the top of her head. Then: *What if I pick her up and throw her out the window? ... That's crazy. It's just ... I don't know ... I'm so tired, my incision hurts, everything hurts ...*

My mind plays these tricks, creeps up on me when my guard is 17 down. Like yesterday, on my way downstairs to the laundry room, past the side door, a thought, a cat-like pouncing in my head: *I could just walk out ...*

I leave the baby's room, turn into the bathroom and strip off my 18 clothes, stare at the body in the mirror, at the long scar across the pubis and the bulging flesh above and below, at the staple marks. The breasts are twice their normal size, pale and luminous and marbled with veins. The face is pallid, the eyes abandoned, like vacant windows. *Who is this woman?*

19   I hear the shower door close, feel hot water pouring down my face, neck, breasts. Cold air shocks the parts of me the water can't cover. Afterwards the towel is sandpaper on my nipples. I peer down to examine them and cringe at the angry red slashes I will soon be offering her hungry mouth. *Will life ever feel normal again?*

20   My mother has come. While I weather this storm of postpartum depression, she beams with a love for my baby that I cannot feel. She is strong now, thriving on the hope that sprouts from new life, new beginnings. As I cling to her lifeline of clean counters and folded laundry, I reach for her hard-earned understanding of what it means to survive.

21   It is April 2004. I am alone, now. While my husband goes off to work each day, I crouch in the corner of the living-room sofa, my baby balanced in my arms, the sun beaming like an alien spaceship behind the closed blinds. I have survived the first six weeks.

22   Mostly I stay indoors, topless, my nipples smeared with lanoline, or air-drying in breast milk. A soundtrack of screaming Oprah fans accompanies my scenery of failures and foreign objects—dirty dishes, stuffed animals, scattered laundry, an electric breast pump, a vibrating bouncy chair.

23   Venturing into the world outside my living room is an exhausting feat of logistics squeezed in between sleeps and feeds. Against a backdrop of world-class-tourist-destination peaks, I push our all-terrain stroller slowly around the neighbourhood, wary of bumps, fending off the slightest breeze with binder clips and a receiving blanket.

24   Back inside I cling to the couch, my mind held hostage by the weeds growing in our yard; the dust-streaked windows; the empty flower boxes. I sit motionless, watching the neighbours industriously cutting and watering their lawns, planting their gardens, paving their driveways.

25   I have forgotten what wilderness is. I have forgotten Silene, who among the arid, ancient-seabed shards, with no soil or water within a human arm's reach, sprouts her cushion of tiny, bright green leaves.

26   Ten years ago, as the wind whipped my hair into my face and I looked for a safe place to plant my feet, Silene showed me the strength and beauty of her vulnerability. Like grass growing up through a crack in the concrete, she showed me how, one tender green shoot at a time, Nature reclaimed the old mining town of Bankhead, at the foot of Cascade. And as I climbed higher up the

ridge, my lungs aching, my heart beating its way out of my chest, it occurred to me that *I* might belong to the same glorious, vital, and yes, obstinate life force.

It has been ten years since I first saw myself in Silene, and in my stillness—immobilized on the couch, my baby latched to my breast—I can't see that I am blooming. I can't see that in this new wilderness of motherhood, my roots are growing deep; that my roots will sustain me.

When Amanda is three months old, I order a backpack carrier from Mountain Equipment Co-op. After inspecting and adjusting all the straps and clasps, I snap her in, hoist her onto my back, and check us out in the bathroom mirror. We look happy.

I decide to take her for a test run up Cougar Creek. It's June. All spring, the sun's rays have been gathering strength, and a steady trickle of water winds its way down the creekbed toward the highway. I hear the sound of it, like laughter rippling through a crowd, gently dissipating. Summer is coming.

Pavement turns to gravel, and gravel gives way to a worn path through rocks and boulders, where Silene waits. Hoodoo° sentinels guard the cliff side on my left, while across the creek, on my right, the bright red roof of a modern ranch house gleams against its backdrop of evergreens. I pause and crane my neck around, trying to catch sight of Amanda in the carrier behind me. All I want is to watch her, my tiny, triumphant pink flower, seeing everything for the first time.

°hoodoos: Tall, tower-like spires of soft rock, eroded on the sides but protected on top by a layer of harder rock. Found usually in badlands.

EXPLORATIONS:

Cori Howard, ed., *Between Interruptions: Thirty Women Tell the Truth About Motherhood*

Marjorie Anderson, ed., *Dropped Threads 3: Beyond the Small Circle*

http://en.wikipedia.org/wiki/Moss_campion

http://www.mooddisorderscanada.ca/depression/ppd.htm
http://www.pc.gc.ca/pn-np/ab/banff/index_E.asp

STRUCTURE:

1. In her opening paragraph, why does Mackintosh refer to the moss campion plant as "she"? And how does this designation of gender begin to develop "Moss Campion" as an essay of *analogy*?
2. Point out Mackintosh's THESIS STATEMENT.
3. Why does Mackintosh insert a break between paragraphs 14 and 15, then another between paragraphs 27 and 28? How do these breaks help organize the essay?

STYLE:

1. "Moss Campion" is built on an *analogy* between plant and human. But the essay also contains many *metaphors*, those smaller cousins to the analogy. For example in paragraph 4, the mother's depression is a "wall of snow." Point out at least five more vivid metaphors in this selection.
2. In paragraphs 15 through 19, why are certain parts put into *italics*?
3. Why does the word "I" appear so many times in paragraph 12? Is this repetition accidental, or does it have some purpose?

IDEAS FOR DISCUSSION AND WRITING:

1. *"What if I pick her up and throw her out the window?"* thinks our author in paragraph 16. Is postpartum depression common? Does it occur even to mothers who are normally well balanced? Do parents automatically love their new baby, or does the love sometimes need to be learned?
2. Our author seems happier outdoors than indoors. Is nature a healer? Has it healed you? If so, tell one example of such healing.
3. Do you go to the back country, as our author does? Do you hike, backpack, climb, ski, canoe or kayak? If so, why? If not, why not?

4. Paragraph 1 contrasts the harsh surroundings of Cascade Mountain to the softness and colour of *Silene acaulis*, the moss campion, which lives there. She is delicate yet strong: she could be killed by a single footstep, yet survives rock, wind, cold and snow to bloom after ten years. Point out all the ways that C. B. Mackintosh builds her *analogy* between this plant and herself—and between this plant and her new baby daughter.

5. PROCESS IN WRITING: *Most people experience crises in their lives. Think of some you have experienced. Could you develop one of them into an analogy that sees the crisis in terms of a mountain? A river? A cliff? A swamp? A desert? An ocean? Or some other natural feature? Once you have chosen the outdoor feature that best explains your experience, fill a page with notes. Like Mackintosh, write an introduction that presents the analogy, then quickly execute a first draft, using the best of your notes. Later look it over. Does it have enough parallels to make the analogy strong? Is it filled with images, like Mackintosh's essay? Does the personal crisis incorporate vocabulary from the outdoor feature in the analogy? Finally, check the punctuation and spelling, then print out your best version.*

Note: See also the Topics for Writing on the Online Learning Centre at www. mcgrawhill.ca/olc/conrad.

Process in Writing: Guidelines

Follow at least some of these steps in writing your essay of analogy (your teacher may suggest which ones).

1. Choose or devise a topic you really like, because motivation is the single greatest factor in writing performance.

2. If you complete one of the Topics for Writing numbered 16 to 30 for this chapter on the Online Learning Centre (www.mcgrawhill. ca/olc/conrad), be sure to invent an analogy (with two items from different categories), not a comparison and contrast (with two items from the same category). Know which item is your real subject, and which one exists merely to explain the other.

3. Now freewrite on your topic, to achieve the spontaneity and originality that spark a good analogy.

4. Incorporate the best of this freewriting into your first draft. Let the ideas flow, not stopping now to revise or edit.

5. In your next version add any more points of comparison that come to you (a strong analogy is fully developed). Read your prose aloud to detect awkward passages, and revise. Trim deadwood. Heighten TRANSITIONS.

6. Now edit for things like spelling and punctuation, before printing out your best version.

JupiterImages

"The scurry of feet grew louder as more sailors began to pour out through the hatches onto the deck."

—Hugh MacLennan, *"A Sound Beyond Hearing"*

CLASSIFICATION

THERE ARE THREE KINDS OF THEM....

Our world is so complex that without classification we are lost. To make a phone call we use an alphabetized phone book. To find oranges in the supermarket we head for the fruit section. To buy a used canoe we go to the *classified* section of the newspaper. Putting things into categories is one of our most common methods of thought. Who would search the whole dictionary when the word in question begins with "T"? What student, *classified* into grade five, would look for the grade six *class*room?

For the essayist, classifying can be a powerful way of organizing. Tackling a large or detailed subject, for example, is a real challenge. One way to start making sense of it is to see it as several parts, so that, instead of thinking about everything at once, the writer can focus on one section, then focus on the next section, and so on. Of course this is also true of a comparison and contrast essay, whether developed by halves or point by point. Do remember, though, that a comparison and contrast involves only two items of the same general type, while a classification involves at least three, with a maximum of perhaps 5 or 6.

Read Ian and Will Ferguson's essay in this chapter, "Theatre." See how it presents six categories to explain its subject of theatre in Canada. This is no doubt close to the upper limit of sections we might want in a short essay, but the argument seems of reasonable size because the sections are compressed and short. Notice, by the way, how the Fergusons actually number their points, to be super-clear in their organization.

Read also "Pulling Together" by former British Columbia Governor General David Lam. In examining the ways for the province's citizens to "pull together," Lam presents three categories: "acceptance," "belonging" and "contribution" (abbreviated as A, B and C). This minimum number of categories for a classification works well here, because the sections are somewhat longer than those of the Fergusons. Thus Lam is able to give many examples to support his points.

A classification, which has more parts than a comparison and contrast, requires a somewhat larger system of logic. Observe the following guidelines:

CLASSIFY ALL ITEMS BY THE SAME PRINCIPLE. An essay on kinds of cars might be organized by any one of several different principles: size, quality, safety level, cost, fuel economy, performance, body type, engine type, etc. The important thing, though, is to work with only one of these major criteria at a time, not diluting your focus across categories. For example a focus on *size* might include the large (or "full-size") car, the midsize car, the compact car and the small car. But it certainly would not include the diesel, which concerns a fuel type and engine technology found in cars of all sizes. Neither would it include the sports car, which comes in many sizes, or the pickup truck, which is not a car at all.

DO NOT LEAVE OUT AN OBVIOUS CATEGORY. Suppose you had reasons to classify cars by the *number of cylinders* in the engine. You would probably want to have as your categories the 4, the 6 and the 8. It is true that other configurations exist: there have been cars with 1 cylinder, and others with 2, or 3, or 5, or even 12 or 16. How many of those are on the road, though? If they are rarities, they would only clutter up an argument about the engine types that do power almost all cars driven today. Just as illogical would be an argument that left out the 8-cylinder engine. It may be falling out of favour because of high fuel prices and environmental concerns, but there are millions of them still on the road. Ignoring these would leave the argument incomplete.

DO NOT LET CATEGORIES OVERLAP. A classification of cars by *quality level* might reasonably feature the categories of high quality, medium quality and low quality. After all, do these choices not cover the whole spectrum of quality? But you would not want to add the hatch-back, the station wagon or the crossover utility vehicle—because each of these represents a kind of body type, rather than any aspect of quality.

Classifying is not easy; it's a real exercise in logic. Keep applying the guidelines.

Also observe the main principle of any essay: *Know your purpose.* Exactly *why* are you comparing, say, the three kinds of parents or the four kinds of teachers or the five kinds of friends? Is it because you have a vision of what a good parent or teacher or friend is, and want to share it with others? Is it because bad experiences have led you to warn against certain kinds of parents or teachers or friends? Like any argument, an essay of classification makes a point; otherwise it is "pointless." Try freewriting or brainstorming for five or ten minutes to get thoughts flowing and ideas out in the open. Then look these over. Let them help you decide not only what the content of your classification will be, but also its overall point, its thesis statement. Since thinking is not easy, you need all the help you can get—and some of the best help comes from your own pen or computer: while it is writing, you are thinking.

THE HONOURABLE
DAVID LAM

Pulling Together

The Honourable David See-Chai Lam, born in Hong Kong in 1923, has had a long career in business and public life, culminating in his term from 1988 to 1995 as Lieutenant-Governor of British Columbia. With a B.A. from Lingnam University and an M.B.A. from Temple University, he became in 1960 the CEO of Ka Wah Bank Ltd. of Hong Kong. Then, immigrating to the "golden mountain" which he celebrates in his essay, he became in 1968 the president of Canadian International Properties Limited. When Dr. Lam was invited ten years later to be the Lieutenant-Governor of his new home, British Columbia, he underwent the uncertainties described in his essay below, at first declining because he was "living in a province with a history of discrimination against Chinese," because he was "getting old," and because English was not his first language. Reconsidering, though, he did accept the post, and, with the aid of his much-loved wife Dorothy Lam, found great fulfillment in the job through "building bridges" among the many population groups of British Columbia. Our selection, published in Maclean's *of January 30, 1995, reflects this experience in acceptance, belonging and contribution. Now retired from government, Dr. Lam lives in Vancouver, where he directs a charitable foundation that gives grants to universities, hospitals and other public institutions.*

1   Once, Asians came to North America for jobs, albeit somewhat menial ones. Particularly in the West, there was ready work on the railway, in laundries and in chop suey houses.

With the gold rush and its opportunity to strike it rich, this continent became known in China as the "golden mountain."

Today, Canada continues to attract Asians, although the lure is no longer gold. Instead, they come for things that a lot of us in Canada take for granted: stability, a peaceful life, law and order, education, generally friendly and understanding people.

As one of those who chose to settle in Canada over 28 years ago, I would like to offer a brief ABC for others hoping to make a new home here.

The A is for acceptance. And that goes two ways. Prospective immigrants must be accepted by the federal immigration department. But even if the government accepts you, your peace of mind and happiness will depend very much upon how you are accepted in your community.

Of course, newcomers could reject the broader Canadian community and choose to live only among their own people. But that choice is self-defeating: one becomes inward-looking, cut away from the mainstream of society. There is really no way to enjoy what Canada has to offer if one lives in either a physical or psychological ghetto. So, it is a duty of sorts to strive for acceptance.

There are always difficulties arising from different value systems, a different cultural style. Speaking loudly, getting things done in the quickest manner, bragging about accomplishments and wealth—all might be commonplace in Hong Kong and totally acceptable in many other parts of the world. But they are not so in Canada.

Here, we try to minimize friction between people. We downplay displays of wealth. We respect good manners. Such simple courtesies as saying good morning and thank you are daily expressions of respect for others.

The B represents belonging. This is a very important feeling. People who do not belong always feel impermanent. As with people who reside in a hotel, no matter how beautiful it may be, they are constantly reminded that they are transients.

People who divide their time between Canada and another country become "astronauts"—flying too high and fast to put down real roots or to feel a sense of belonging. They are not found just among Chinese immigrants. Some Canadians who spend half of their time in California or in Florida might also be considered astronauts. When they are asked to become involved in community services, many say: "Ah, but in a couple of months I will return to Canada ...," or, "... I'll be leaving for the States."

10   If you want to feel that you belong, ask yourself: how much do I care about what happens in my community and related issues such as crime, a clean neighborhood, volunteering to pitch in.

11   The C stands for contribution. And this is the easiest thing of all to achieve. In this new country, in this new community, in this new neighborhood in which we have started to take root, commitment makes a strong statement that you belong. You can give without loving; but you cannot love without giving.

12   When I was initially approached to consider being nominated as lieutenant-governor of British Columbia, I turned it down. My negative side told me: "You are living in a province with a history of discrimination against Chinese. You are getting old. You speak English as a second language. Don't do it."

13   Fortunately, however, my positive side saw an opportunity to build bridges among people of different cultures, different ethnic backgrounds and different races. After 6½ years, I have experienced tremendous love and respect from the people of Canada as a whole, and particularly from those in British Columbia. I feel proud to be a Canadian, because I truly appreciate the quality of its people.

14   I was brought up in Hong Kong to be so conscious of racial differences that we had derogatory nicknames for everyone. That is no way to go through life. It is like carrying a little bit of poison in the mind. And the world is changing. The day is quickly coming when people with only one culture will find it difficult to compete, let alone to prosper.

15   Don't talk to me about "tolerance." Tolerating someone is like holding your breath: you are telling the world that you can hold your breath longer than anyone else. I say, let us celebrate differences— not tolerate them.

16   I believe in multiculturalism because it adds to our strength. The Asia-Pacific region is the fastest-growing region in the world. And it is

just across the ocean from British Columbia. Let us turn the people of all the races living in Canada into partners. Let us build a "golden mountain" for all of us.

EXPLORATIONS:

Reginald H. Roy, *David Lam: A Biography*
Bennett Lee and Jim Wong-Chu, eds., *Many-Mouthed Birds: Contemporary Writings by Chinese-Canadians*
Wayson Choy, *Paper Shadows: A Chinatown Childhood* (memoir)
Sky Lee, *Disappearing Moon Cafe* (novel)
Amy Tan, *The Joy Luck Club* (novel; also made into a feature film and DVD)
Peter S. Li, *The Chinese in Canada* (2nd ed.)
http://www.fccbc.ca/NewsletterArticles/DavidLam.htm
http://archives.cbc.ca/IDD-1-69-1433/life_society/chinese_immigration
http://en.wikipedia.org/wiki/Chinese_Canadian
http://www.asian.ca/community
http://www.ccnc.ca/toronto/history/timeline.html

STRUCTURE:

1. Why does David Lam both open and close his essay with the same expression, "golden mountain"? What effect does this repetition achieve?

2. How do you rate Lam's "brief ABC" as a *classification*? Are its three categories enough? Is any obvious category left out? Are all *classified* by the same principle? Do you think the organizational device of the "ABC" is a good fit for Lam's categories?

3. How does the device of *comparison and contrast* heighten the power of paragraph 9?

4. Why does Lam wait almost till the end to describe his own decision to become Lieutenant-Governor of British Columbia?

STYLE:

1. How easy or hard is the vocabulary of "Pulling Together"? How short or long are its sentences? Its paragraphs? Who do you see as its intended AUDIENCE?

IDEAS FOR DISCUSSION AND WRITING:

1. While stating "I believe in multiculturalism because it adds to our strength" (par. 16), Lam also advises New Canadians not to live "in either a physical or psychological ghetto" (par. 5). What is your view? Do you prefer the traditional American "melting pot" which is supposed to assimilate immigrants, or the Canadian "mosaic," in which New Canadians are encouraged, even funded, to retain their first language and culture? Which path is better for the individual? For the nation?

2. David Lam's adopted home of British Columbia is part of the Asia Pacific rim, and is itself one of the most multicultural spots on earth. If you live there, describe how the cosmopolitan mix of its population has influenced your own life. Or if you live in Toronto, Montreal or another cosmopolitan place, apply this topic to your own city.

3. Lam says "The day is quickly coming when people with only one culture will find it difficult to compete, let alone to prosper" (par. 14). Do you think this is true for your own intended profession? Why or why not? If so, what have you done to prepare? If your family has immigrated, what are you doing to keep your first language and culture? If your family has earlier roots in Canada, what other languages, if any, have you learned to speak? And what experiences have you had to make yourself feel at home with other cultures?

4. **PROCESS IN WRITING:** *Whether you have immigrated, yourself, or only know others who have, think about the main challenges that face immigrants to Canada. Fill a page with brainstorming on this topic, then look it over. Circle or highlight the main points, choose your THESIS STATEMENT, then rearrange these thoughts into a short conventional outline that classifies the challenges. Are there at least three categories in your classification? Are any main ones missing? Are all classified by the same principle? Do*

any seem to overlap? Now write a rapid version of your essay of classification. *The next day look it over. Does it have enough* examples? *If not, add. Do* TRANSITIONS *move the argument from one point to the next? If not, add. Finally, check the punctuation and spelling before printing out your best version.*

Note: See also the Topics for Writing on the Online Learning Centre at www. mcgrawhill.ca/olc/conrad.

IAN AND WILL FERGUSON

Theatre

Brothers Ian and Will Ferguson, writers of zany and colourful books about Canada, grew up in a family of seven children in the rugged fur-trapping town of Fort Vermilion in northern Alberta. Years later, Ian's book Village of the Small Houses *(Stephen Leacock Medal for Humour, 2004) would chronicle their childhood of material poverty but rich experience—such as the day their father drove their mother in a race against time, over logging roads to reach the hospital in Peace River, where she would give birth to the author himself. Ian went on to become a playwright, author of almost 20 works such as* Elephant Shoes *(1990),* Uncle Joe Again *(1991) and* Bonecrack *(1997). He also originated live improvised soap operas* Sin City *and* Die-Nasty, *and the CBC TV comedy show* Liquid Soapz. *Meanwhile his brother Will joined the Canadian volunteer program Katimavik, and in 1990 graduated from the York University Film Program. Stints of travel and teaching followed in Peru, Japan, Korea, Malaysia and China. He now lives in Calgary. Will has published many books of humour, such as* Why I Hate Canadians *(1997),* Bastards & Boneheads: Our Glorious Leaders, Past and Present *(1999),* Happiness *(a novel, 2001) and* Beauty Tips from Moose Jaw: Travels in Search of Canada *(2004). Our selection comes from* How to Be a Canadian, Even If You Already Are One, *written by both brothers. Published in 2001, it has sold over 100,000 copies.*

1   In Canada, there are six different types of theatre company for you to choose from:

290

1. COMMERCIAL THEATRE

Located in Toronto, Vancouver and Montreal only. Not to be con- 2
fused with some of the larger non-profit theatres, which, despite
their not-for-profit designation, are equally interested in making
money. Commercial theatres offer epic musicals full of special effects
and spectacle. Here's how to tell. If a helicopter lands onstage or
a chandelier crashes from the ceiling at a key dramatic moment,
chances are you are attending a commercial theatre production.
If, however, the helicopter is portrayed by an actor running around
frantically beating his fists against his chest or the falling chandelier
occurs offstage with the actors pointing to the wing and shouting,
"Look! A giant chandelier has fallen to the ground … just offstage!",
you are probably at a smaller, non-profit theatre.

The tickets to commercial theatre cost a lot of money, more than 3
the cost of an actual helicopter ride, in fact. But the good part is that
you get to feel very patriotic by saying things like "Wow, did you know
that with the exception of the playwright, the composer, the director,
the choreographer, the designer and the two lead actors, the rest of
the cast and crew are completely Canadian?"

2. GOVERNMENT-FUNDED REGIONAL THEATRE, LARGE

Every big city has one, and they can usually be found in a conve- 4
nient downtown location where parking costs—well, about as much
as a helicopter ride. Large government-funded regional theatres
function like big industrial bakeries. They're in the bulk business,
and they present a consistent, if predictable, recipe of Neil Simon,
Noel Coward, the odd musical and assorted plays that were hot on
Broadway or in the West End four or five seasons ago. Tickets will
cost you almost as much as you'd pay at a commercial theatre, but
everybody involved in the show will be Canadian. Except the artistic
director. He will be from England.

3. GOVERNMENT-FUNDED REGIONAL THEATRE, SMALL

Similar to above, only "edgier." And what, per chance, does "edgier" 5
mean? It means they will build their season around a single play—
that was hot off-Broadway four or five seasons ago. In Canada, this is
considered cutting-edge. These theatres also commission new works

by Canadian writers. By law, these plays will be set in the prairies. And they will have titles like *The Wheat Is High* or *42 Short Plays about Gabriel Dumont*. Tickets will be half the price of those at the larger theatres, and the artistic director will be Canadian and easily recognized. He (or she) will be the person who has to unplug the toilet during intermission.

4. FESTIVALS, LARGE

6   These are, effectively, huge repertory theatre companies that specialize in the works of one particular playwright and related writings from around the same era. William Shakespeare or George Bernard Shaw. That kind of thing. Tickets cost an arm and a leg, but they're worth every limb, we say, if only because you'll be able to shout, "Hey! That guy from the Canadian Tire ad is playing Polonius."° The artistic directors will be of British origin, but most of them will have taken out Canadian citizenship by now. Get them to autograph your copy of this book. They'll sign anything, including their life. Away. You will find them at the bar during interval, in a festive Faustian° funk, drinking with a certain raw desperation.

5. FESTIVALS, SMALL

7   These are also called "fringe" festivals (as in "lunatic" or "benefits"). Fringe festivals are spreading across the country faster than fungus in a locker room. Low ticket prices, independent productions, and lots of first-time playwrights, actors and directors: basically this type of festival functions like a farm team for the bigger houses. The artistic director of the festival will be a woman, and you will recognize her by the huge bags under her eyes and the constant use of her cell phone to deal with yet another emergency.

8   A warning. The quality and content of fringe shows can vary widely (and wildly). Necrophilia and the true nature of love, that sort of thing. So don't attend if you're easily shocked and/or bored. Indeed, at many fringe shows you can be both—*at the very same time.* "I was never so shocked in my life! Or so bored!"

°Polonius: A minor character in Shakespeare's *Hamlet*.

°Faustian: Referring to Faust, who in works by both Christopher Marlowe and Goethe gains earthly power by selling his soul to the Devil.

6. SO-CALLED DINNER SO-CALLED THEATRE

Here, for around the same ticket price that a large government-
funded regional theatre would charge, you not only get a show, you
also get "food." (Note the use of quotation marks.) The play itself
is probably going to be a tired old British farce with a title like *Ooh,
That's Me Bum, Guv'ner!,* and it's going to feature some washed-up
American sit-com star in the lead role, but hey … have you checked
out the buffet? Some dinner theatres also have the actors waiting on
tables "in character," which seems sensible, since most of the best
waiters tend to be actors. And vice versa.

So get out there and become a regular theatregoer. If you don't
believe that the arts should be subsidized, then spend your money at a
dinner theatre or go to your local fringe festival. Chances are nobody
involved is making any money. Or, if you prefer to support individual
artists, at the very least you can give the waiter a decent tip.

EXPLORATIONS:

Ian Ferguson, *Village of the Small Houses: A Memoir of Sorts*
Will Ferguson,
    Canadian History for Dummies (2nd ed.)
    Beauty Tips from Moose Jaw: Travels in Search of Canada
    Happiness (novel)
Ian and Will Ferguson, *How to Be a Canadian, Even If You Already Are*
    One
Paul Hiebert, *Sara Binks*
http://www.willferguson.ca
http://www.leacock.ca/win2004.html
http://www.cbc.ca/wordsatlarge/blog/2007/12/will_ferguson_
    interview.html
http://www.banffcentre.ca/press/contributors/def/ferguson_w
http://www.banffcentre.ca/press/contributors/def/ferguson_i
http://www.theatrecanada.com/centres/theatres.shtml

STRUCTURE:

1. "Theatre" is one of the mostly clearly organized selections in this book. Point out all the techniques that make it so.
2. Have the Ferguson brothers reached the recommended 50% of *example* content?
3. In "Theatre" are all the categories *mutually exclusive*, or is there significant *overlap*?

STYLE:

1. In paragraph 7, "Fringe festivals are spreading across the country faster than fungus in a locker room." Point out five more vivid IMAGES in this selection. What do they achieve?
2. Point out five passages where the authors use IRONY to make their point.

IDEAS FOR DISCUSSION AND WRITING:

1. Have you ever acted in a student play, or served on the stage crew, built sets, done lighting or sound effects, done costumes or makeup, or done publicity and tickets? Describe your experience to the class.
2. Everyone has seen high school plays, but have you ever attended live professional theatre? Which of the Fergusons' categories did the most recent production fit into? Give reasons for your answer. Did you like the work and the performance? Why or why not?
3. As a playwright, should Ian Ferguson be poking fun at theatre in Canada? Why do you think he's doing so?
4. Can you afford live theatre? How much do movies cost these days? Rock concerts? NHL hockey admissions? Did you know that many theatre productions are subsidized so highly, by government and by rich patrons, that you pay as little as one third of the real cost, especially at the student rate? Find three nearby theatre companies listed in the website http://www.theatrecanada.com/centres/theatres.shtml, and report to the class what the cheapest seats go for at each.

5. In paragraph 3 the Fergusons write of commercial theatre productions, "Wow, did you know that with the exception of the playwright, the composer, the director, the choreographer, the designer and the two lead actors, the rest of the cast and crew are completely Canadian?" Are these satirical allegations true? And are the five other categories of theatre dominated by foreigners?

6. What percentage of the movies you see are Canadian, and what percentage are foreign? What percentage of the TV you watch is Canadian, and what percentage is foreign? Why?

7. In recent years Canada has become internationally known for its comedians and recording stars. Name some names.

8. Perhaps Canada's most striking success in the performing arts has been *Cirque du Soleil.* (See http://en.wikipedia.org/wiki/Cirque_du_Soleil.) Have you seen it? How and where did it begin? How has it redefined the idea of a circus? How big is it in the world now?

9. PROCESS IN WRITING: *Write an essay* classifying *one of the following: films, rock concerts, or classical concerts (focus your choice down as far as you wish—for example, to kinds of action films or love films). First do a page of brainstorming, then from these notes make an outline classifying the categories of your subject. Look it over: Are there are least three categories? (Only two would be a* comparison and contrast.*) Do they overlap? If so, revise. Are they all* classified *by the same principle? Now devise a* THESIS STATEMENT *that makes your overall main point. Write a quick first draft, then the next day look it over. Have you supplied plenty of concrete* examples, *as Ian and Will Ferguson have? Is your language* CONCISE, *as theirs is? Do* TRANSITIONS *move your argument from one point to the next? Finally, check the sentence structure and punctuation before printing out your best version.*

Note: See also the Topics for Writing on the Online Learning Centre at www. mcgrawhill.ca/olc/conrad.

HUGH MacLENNAN

A Sound Beyond Hearing*

Hugh MacLennan (1907–1990), one of Canada's best-loved novelists and essayists, authored over a dozen books and won a total of five Governor-General's Awards. Born in Glace Bay, Cape Breton, he studied at Dalhousie, Oxford and then at Princeton, where he earned a Ph.D. in classics. From 1951 to his retirement in 1982 he taught in the English Department of McGill University in Montreal. Over the years MacLennan published several widely read books of essays, among them Cross-Country *(1949),* Scotchman's Return and Other Essays *(1960) and* The Other Side of Hugh MacLennan *(1978). Among his novels are* Each Man's Son *(1951),* The Watch That Ends the Night *(1959) and* Voices in Time *(1980).* Two Solitudes *(1945), which contrasts the French- and English-Canadian cultures, is his most widely read novel, but* Barometer Rising *(1941), from which our selection comes, is thought by some to be his best. "A Sound Beyond Hearing," MacLennan's account of an event he witnessed in person at age 10, may be the best-known passage in all of Canadian literature: it describes the explosion that, on December 6, 1917, levelled much of Halifax, obliterating 1600 buildings and severely damaging 12,000 more, killing some 1500 people and injuring another 9000. In the days that followed, natural disaster added to human-made disaster as a terrible blizzard froze many people who had survived the blast and fires.*

*Editor's title.

The *Mont Blanc* was now in the Narrows and a detail of men   1
went into her chains to unship the anchor. It would be
dropped as soon as she reached her appointed station in
the Basin. A hundred yards to port were the Shipyards and another
hundred yards off the port bow was the blunt contour of Richmond
Bluff; to starboard the shore sloped gently into a barren of spruce
scrub. During the two minutes it took the *Mont Blanc* to glide
through this strait, most of Bedford Basin and nearly all its flotilla
of anchored freighters were hidden from her behind the rise of
Richmond Bluff.

Around the projection of this hill, less than fifty fathoms off   2
the port bow of the incoming *Mont Blanc*, another vessel suddenly
appeared heading for the open sea. She flew the Norwegian flag,
and to the startled pilot of the munitioner the name *Imo* was plainly
visible beside the hawse. She was moving at half-speed and listing
gently to port as she made the sharp turn out of the Basin to strike
the channel of the Narrows. And so listing, with white water surging
away from her fore-foot, she swept across the path of the *Mont Blanc*,
exposing a gaunt flank labeled in giant letters BELGIAN RELIEF.
Then she straightened, and pointed her bow directly at the fore-
quarter of the munitioner. Only at that moment did the men on the
Imo's bridge appear to realize that another vessel stood directly in
their path.

Staccato orders broke from the bridge of the *Mont Blanc* as the two   3
ships moved toward a single point. Bells jangled, and megaphoned
shouts came from both bridges. The ships sheered in the same direction, then sheered back again. With a violent shock, the bow of the
Imo struck the plates of the *Mont Blanc* and went grinding a third of
the way through the deck and the forward hold. A shower of sparks
splashed out from the screaming metal. The canisters on the deck
of the *Mont Blanc* broke loose from their bindings and some of them
tumbled and burst open. Then the vessels heeled away with engines
reversed and the water boiling out from their screws as the propel-
lers braked them to a standstill. They sprawled sideways across the

Narrows, the *Mont Blanc* veering in toward the Halifax shore, the *Imo* spinning about with steerageway lost entirely. Finally she drifted toward the opposite shore.

4   For a fraction of a second there was intense silence. Then smoke appeared out of the shattered deck of the *Mont Blanc*, followed by a racing film of flame. The men on the bridge looked at each other. Scattered shouts broke from the stern, and the engine-room bells jangled again. Orders were half-drowned by a scream of rusty metal as some sailors amidships followed their own inclination and twisted the davits around to lower a boat. The scurry of feet grew louder as more sailors began to pour out through the hatches onto the deck. An officer ran forward with a hose, but before he could connect it his men were ready to abandon ship.

5   The film of flame raced and whitened, then it became deeper like an opaque and fulminant liquid, then swept over the canisters of benzol and increased to a roaring tide of heat. Black smoke billowed and rolled and engulfed the ship, which began to drift with the out-going tide and swing in toward the graving-dock of the Shipyards. The fire trembled and leaped in a body at the bridge, driving the captain and pilot aft, and there they stood helplessly while the tarry smoke surrounded them in greasy folds and the metal of the deck began to glow under their feet. Both men glanced downward. Underneath that metal lay leashed an incalculable energy, and the bonds which checked it were melting with every second the therm-ometers mounted in the hold. A half-million pounds of trinitro-toluol° and twenty-three hundred tons of picric acid lay there in the darkness under the plates, while the fire above and below the deck converted the hollow shell of the vessel into a bake-oven.

6   If the captain had wished to scuttle the ship at that moment it would have been impossible to do so, for the heat between decks would have roasted alive any man who tried to reach the sea-cocks. By this time the entire crew was in the lifeboat. The officers followed, and the boat was rowed frantically toward the wooded slope opposite Halifax. There, by lying flat among the trees, the sailors hoped they would have a chance when their ship blew up. By the time they had beached the boat, the

---

°trinitrotoluol: TNT.

foredeck of the *Mont Blanc* was a shaking rampart of fire, and black smoke pouring from it screened the Halifax waterfront from their eyes. The sailors broke and ran for the shelter of the woods.

By this time men were running out of dock sheds and warehouses and offices along the entire waterfront to watch the burning ship. None of them knew she was a gigantic bomb. She had now come so close to the Shipyards that she menaced the graving-dock. Fire launches cut out from a pier farther south and headed for the Narrows. Signal flags fluttered from the Dockyard and the yardarms of ships lying in the Stream, some of which were already weighing anchor. The captain of the British cruiser piped all hands and called for volunteers to scuttle the *Mont Blanc*; a few minutes later the cruiser's launch was on its way to the Narrows with two officers and a number of ratings. By the time they reached the burning ship her plates were so hot that the seawater lapping the plimsoll line was simmering.

The *Mont Blanc* had become the center of a static tableau. Her plates began to glow red and the swollen air inside her hold heated the cargo rapidly towards the detonation point. Launches from the harbour fire department surrounded her like midges and the water from their hoses arched up with infinite delicacy as they curved into the rolling smoke. The *Imo*, futile and forgotten, was still trying to claw her way off the farther shore.

Twenty minutes after the collision there was no one along the entire waterfront who was unaware that a ship was on fire in the harbor. The jetties and docks near the Narrows were crowded with people watching the show, and yet no warning of danger was given. At that particular moment there was no adequate centralized authority in Halifax to give a warning, and the few people who knew the nature of the *Mont Blanc*'s cargo had no means of notifying the town or spreading the alarm, and no comfort beyond the thought that trinitrotoluol can stand an almost unlimited heat provided there is no fulminate or explosive gas to detonate it.

Bells in the town struck the hour of nine, and by this time nearly all normal activity along the waterfront had been suspended. A tug had managed to grapple the *Mont Blanc* and was towing her with imperceptible movement away from the Shipyards back into the channel of the Narrows. Bluejackets from the cruiser had found the bosun's ladder left by the fleeing crew, and with flesh shrinking from the heat, were going over the side. Fire launches surrounded her. There was a static concentration, an intense expectancy in the faces of the firemen playing the hoses, a rhythmic reverberation in the beat of the flames, a gush from the hose-nozzles and a steady hiss of scalding water. Everything else for miles around seemed motionless and silent.

11   Then a needle of flaming gas, thin as the mast and of a brilliance unbelievably intense, shot through the deck of the *Mont Blanc* near the funnel and flashed more than two hundred feet toward the sky. The firemen were thrown back and their hoses jumped suddenly out of control and slashed the air with S-shaped designs. There were a few helpless shouts. Then all movement and life about the ship were encompassed in a sound beyond hearing as the *Mont Blanc* opened up....

12   Three forces were simultaneously created by the energy of the exploding ship, an earthquake, an air-concussion, and a tidal wave. These forces rushed away from the Narrows with a velocity varying in accordance with the nature of the medium in which they worked. It took only a few seconds for the earthquake to spend itself and three minutes for the air-expansion to slow down to a gale. The tidal wave traveled for hours before the last traces of it were swallowed in the open Atlantic.

13   When the shock struck the earth, the rigid ironstone and granite base of Halifax peninsula rocked and reverberated, pavements split and houses swayed as the earth trembled. Sixty miles away in the town of Truro windows broke and glass fell to the ground, tinkling in the stillness of the streets. But the ironstone was solid and when the shock had passed, it resumed its immobility.

14   The pressure of the exploding chemicals smashed against the town with the rigidity and force of driving steel. Solid and unbreathable, the forced wall of air struck against Fort Needham and Richmond Bluff and shaved them clean, smashed with one gigantic blow the North End of Halifax and destroyed it, telescoping houses or lifting them from their foundations, snapping trees and lamp posts, and twisting iron rails into writhing, metal snakes; breaking buildings and

sweeping the fragments of their wreckage for hundreds of yards in its course. It advanced two miles southward, shattering every flimsy house in its path, and within thirty seconds encountered the long, shield-like slope of the Citadel which rose before it.

Then, for the first time since it was fortified, the Citadel was able to defend at least a part of the town. The airwall smote it, and was deflected in three directions. Thus some of its violence shot skyward at a twenty-degree angle and spent itself in space. The rest had to pour around the roots of the hill before closing in on the town for another rush forward. A minute after the detonation, the pressure was advancing through the South End. But now its power was diminished, and its velocity was barely twice that of a tornado. Trees tossed and doors broke inward, windows split into driving arrows of glass which buried themselves deep in interior walls. Here the houses, after swaying and cracking, were still on their foundations when the pressure had passed.

Underneath the keel of the *Mont Blanc* the water opened and the harbor bottom was deepened twenty feet along the channel of the Narrows. And then the displaced waters began to drive outward, rising against the town and lifting ships and wreckage over the sides of the docks. It boiled over the shores and climbed the hill as far as the third cross-street, carrying with it the wreckage of small boats, fragments of fish, and somewhere, lost in thousands of tons of hissing brine, the bodies of men. The wave moved in a gigantic bore down the Stream to the sea, rolling some ships under and lifting others high on its crest, while anchor-chains cracked like guns as the violent thrust snapped them. Less than ten minutes after the detonation, it boiled over the breakwater off the park and advanced on McNab's Island, where it burst with a roar greater than a winter storm. And then the central volume of the wave rolled on to sea, high and arching and white at the top, its back glossy like the plumage of a bird. Hours later it lifted under the keel of a steamer far out in the Atlantic and the captain, feeling his vessel heave, thought he had struck a floating mine.

But long before this, the explosion had become manifest in new forms over Halifax. More than two thousand tons of red hot steel, splintered fragments of the *Mont Blanc*, fell like meteors from the sky into which they had been hurled a few seconds before. The ship's anchor soared over the peninsula and descended through a roof on the other side of the Northwest Arm three miles away. For a few seconds the harbor was dotted white with a maze of splashes, and the decks of raddled ships rang with reverberations and clangs as fragments struck them.

18   Over the North End of Halifax, immediately after the passage of the first pressure, the tormented air was laced with tongues of flame which roared and exploded out of the atmosphere, lashing downwards like a myriad blowtorches as millions of cubic feet of gas took fire and exploded. The atmosphere went white-hot. It grew mottled, then fell to the streets like a crimson curtain. Almost before the last fragments of steel had ceased to fall, the wreckage of the wooden houses in the North End had begun to burn. And if there were any ruins which failed to ignite from falling flames, they began to burn from the fires in their own stoves, onto which they had collapsed.

19   Over this part of the town, rising in the shape of a typhoon from the Narrows and extending five miles into the sky, was poised a cloud formed by the exhausted gases. It hung still for many minutes, white, glossy as an ermine's back, serenely aloof. It cast its shadow over twenty miles of forest land behind Bedford Basin.

EXPLORATIONS:

Hugh MacLennan,
>   *Barometer Rising*
>   *Two Solitudes*
>   *Scotchman's Return and Other Essays*
>   *The Rivers of Canada*

Elspeth Cameron, *Hugh MacLennan: A Writer's Life*

Shattered City: The Halifax Explosion (a fictionalized CBC television miniseries, 2005)

http://www.mcgill.ca/about/history/pioneers/maclennan

http://digital.library.mcgill.ca/maclennan

http://www.cbc.ca/halifaxexplosion

http://www.halifaxexplosion.org/intro.html

STRUCTURE:

1. In paragraph 12 MacLennan states, "Three forces were simultaneously created by the energy of the exploding ship, an earthquake, an air-concussion, and a tidal wave." Why does MacLennan *classify* the explosion's effects into these parts? Where does the first begin? The second? The third? Why is the middle section the longest? And why does earth come first, air second, and water third?

2. To what extent does this selection trace the *causes* and *effects* of the great Halifax explosion? Could it even have appeared in our earlier chapter, "Cause and Effect"?

3. To what extent is this selection also a *narrative*? Could it have served well in our first chapter, "Narration"? And to what extent is it a *description*? Could it have served also in that chapter?

4. Does MacLennan's use of *narration, description, cause and effect,* and *classification,* all in the same selection, create confusion? Or do these modes of development go smoothly together? Do you think MacLennan consciously planned all these interlocking methods? Or might most of this have happened naturally?

STYLE:

1. This explosion scene, from MacLennan's novel *Barometer Rising,* is one of the most vivid passages in all of Canadian literature. One reason is the profusion of SENSE IMAGES. Point out one striking example each of appeals to sight, hearing, touch and smell.

2. In paragraph 3, MacLennan uses the image of "screaming metal," and in paragraph 18, the image of "tongues of flame." Point out three other examples of PERSONIFICATION, in which a non-human object is described in human terms.

3. In paragraph 17 MacLennan writes that fragments of red-hot steel "fell like meteors." Point out at least five other SIMILES, figures of speech in which one thing is said to be *like* another.

4. In paragraph 15 MacLennan writes that "windows split into driving arrows of glass." Point out at least five other METAPHORS, figures of speech in which one thing is said to *be* another.

5. What do "port," "starboard," "hawse," "scuttle" and all the other nautical terms do for this selection? Would a reader's unfamiliarity

with some of these specialized words detract from the effect? Why or why not?

IDEAS FOR DISCUSSION AND WRITING:

1. Name all the novels and films you can think of that are about disasters. Why is this kind of entertainment so popular? Do we like to be frightened? Why or why not?

2. The blast that, on December 6, 1917, killed 1600 people and wounded another 9000 in Halifax was the world's biggest human-made explosion before the atomic bomb. Look ahead to read "The Scar," by Kildare Dobbs (in the last chapter of this book), which describes the 1945 atomic blast over Hiroshima. Compare the two events in their magnitude and their effects upon the inhabitants. Report your findings to the class.

3. Do you sense moments of beauty in MacLennan's description of the Halifax disaster? Give examples. Is it appropriate or even moral to see beauty in destruction?

4. PROCESS IN WRITING: *In our era of climate change, we see more and more natural disasters. Ironically, most would fit the same categories Hugh MacLennan develops in his* classification *of the Halifax human-made disaster: effects by earth, air and water. Brainstorm this topic, jotting down different kinds of natural disasters. Now put them into groups, by earth, air and water. Develop a* THESIS STATEMENT *that expresses your point of view (for example, is one category more dangerous or less dangerous than the others, more avoidable or less avoidable, easier or harder to predict, etc.?). Now arrange your points in order and write a quick draft of your argument. Does it have enough* examples? *Are they all in the* category *to which they belong? Does their order make sense? Now read your essay of* classification *aloud to find and fix things like wordiness, repetition of vocabulary, or weakness in grammar and punctuation. Print out your best version and share with the class.*

Note: See also the Topics for Writing on the Online Learning Centre at www. mcgrawhill.ca/olc/conrad.

PROCESS IN WRITING: GUIDELINES

Follow at least some of these steps in writing your essay of classification (your teacher may suggest which ones).

1. Write a short outline, since the logic of classifying is difficult. Once you have chosen the principle on which to classify your topic, decide on the categories. Then ask: Do all relate to the same principle? If not, revise. Do any categories overlap? If so, revise. Is an obvious category missing? Add it.
2. Write your THESIS STATEMENT. Make it a significant point worth discussing.
3. Now arrange the categories in some climactic order that supports your thesis statement: smallest to largest, least important to most important, worst to best, etc.
4. Write a rapid first draft, not stopping now to revise or edit.
5. When this draft has cooled off, look it over. Does it follow the outline? If not, do the changes make sense? Does every part support the thesis statement? If not, revise the parts, the thesis, or both.
6. Now sharpen word choice. Add missing IMAGES or examples. Heighten TRANSITIONS. Cut deadwood.
7. Finally, check for things like spelling and punctuation before you print out your best version.

CP/Toronto Star (Andrew Stawicki)

"*I look up at the clock on the wall. Three hours and 20 minutes have passed since we cut skin. It seems like 15 minutes. I feel exhilarated and at the same time spent—emotionally and physically.*"

—Dr. Mark Bernstein, "Yes, It Is Brain Surgery"

8 PROCESS ANALYSIS

HERE'S HOW IT'S DONE....

Whenever you enter a large bookstore, it won't be long before you notice titles like these: *Success Without College, How to Make People Like You in 90 Seconds or Less, Think and Grow Rich, Massage Made Easy,* and *The Complete Snowboarder.* Look a little further and you might see *Awaken the Giant Within,* or *Secrets of Power Persuasion,* or *Parenting Your Out-of-Control Teenager.* Then there are the "Idiot" and "Dummy" books: *The Complete Idiot's Guide to Plumbing, The Complete Idiot's Guide to Grandparenting,* and *Italian Cooking for Dummies*—not to mention *Norton for Dummies* and all the other computer titles for still more dummies. Clearly many people want to do things, and there is a great need to learn how. But the writer who tells how has some serious thinking and organizing to do.

Consider the last time you bought something in kit form and tried to assemble it. Maybe you were lucky and everything fit together. But more likely, you were sweating to make out tiny diagrams, to understand terminology you had never heard of and to follow vague directions with spelling errors that left out steps or got them in the wrong order. With your new exercise machine or computer desk or amplifier lying in parts on the floor, you wondered if you would *ever* get it together. And when you finally did, mysterious parts were left over.

It doesn't have to be this way. We are not "dummies," but we do need explanations that are clear and easy to follow. And so does your own reader. Writing that tells *how* to do things is often called *process analysis*. Sometimes we write an essay that gives what could be called a **directional** process analysis. It is a sort of *narrative*, taking readers from the beginning to the end of a task, usually in the time order required to grow tomatoes, write a résumé, tune up a car, or do whatever else readers set out to do. It includes every step, for each is vital to the success of the project. And unless it is written for the specialist, it includes all the details right down to the spacing and depth of seeds in the soil, the order of items in your résumé, or the size of the paintbrush.

Did you ever eat something so good that you just had to have the recipe? An experienced cook has a hard time explaining. Instead of giving quantities, temperatures and measurements of time that we can actually apply, the old pro will say things like "add some yeast" or "now put in a little salt" or "take it out of the oven when it's done." The writer of recipes in a book, though, puts his or her own experience in the background and thinks instead about what the *audience* needs to know. The result is a set of directions so exact that, even if we have never cooked before, the product is likely to turn out.

If you are an "old pro" at other tasks, the challenge will be the same. Suppose you have a digital camera and regularly order prints online. The process may seem easy and transparent to you, but what about your parents or even grandparents? Imagine all the details you would have to explain about matters such as choice of website, access to it and uploading digital photos first to the computer, and from there to the website. Then there are photographic improvements to make such as editing out the "red-eye" factor, turning images to different orientations, cropping to get the best picture, etc. Then there are still more steps: recording your choice of prints (how many, what sizes, what texture, etc.), not to mention the matter of paying online. Imagine in your mind's eye the less technically sophisticated person you might be instructing, and the ways you will need to put things so they are clear.

When you are writing directions, on whatever topic, this is the main challenge: keeping your *audience* in mind. You may try to take shortcuts, skipping details you assume anyone would know. But respect the person you are writing for; remember your own encounters with procedures you have not yet learned yourself. If you estimate your reader's level of knowledge and explain accordingly, your directions—whether verbal or written—will very likely succeed.

Another kind of process analysis could be called **informational**, for it satisfies not our practical needs but our curiosity. We may wish to know how airliners are hijacked, how stockholders are swindled, how the greenhouse effect causes tornadoes and tsunamis or how the Second World War was won—knowing we will never do these things ourselves. Not every detail is given in this kind of armchair reading: only as many as it takes to inform and interest the reader. In this chapter Dr. Mark Bernstein tells how he saved a patient's life with a brain operation. His account is not a how-to-do-it set of directions, with the dose of every medication spelled out to the milligram—because he knows we're not going to operate on someone ourselves. But he does relate all the main points, and describes what happens with an almost scary vividness of imagery. He knows his *informational* process analysis will succeed if it keeps us on the edges of our seat.

Another writer in this chapter, Christie Blatchford, depicts the long process through which her mother became an alcoholic. Obviously Blatchford is not explaining to us how to do the same; she is generating an *informational* process analysis of how people fall into one of life's worst traps. The implied lesson is clear: Avoid alcoholism. At the same time, she also offers directions: in portraying her loving and heroic father, who never stops trying to help his wife, Blatchford shows readers how they, too, might help others in this dilemma.

Occasionally a writer will use the format of process analysis not really to instruct or inform, but as a means to other ends. When Stephen Leacock tells us "How to Live to Be 200," he advises us to eat cement—which seems a strange way to reach the goal, until we realize that his goal is not really longevity but laughs.

Whether you aim to help the reader accomplish a task, to satisfy the reader's curiosity, or even just to entertain, your process analysis will work only if you realize *why* you are writing it: Are you giving directions? Then follow all the advice above, so your reader's efforts will be successful. Are you explaining a task that only specialists perform? Then interest the reader with a multitude of examples. Are you even just writing humour, like Leacock? Then do anything that is fun. But even then, you will probably be making a serious point—like Leacock who advises us to enjoy life.

*Note: For more examples of **informational** process analysis, see these essays in other chapters:*

Patrick Lane, "There Is a Season," p. 37
Crisanta Sampang, "Trading Motherhood for Dollars," p. 176
Martin Hocking, "Capping the Great Cup Debate," p. 354

*For more examples of **directional** process analysis, see these essays in other chapters:*

Dr. Vincent Lam and Dr. Colin Lee, "Dr. Lam's Perspective: Go on a Canoe Trip," p. 253
Hon. David Lam, "Pulling Together," p. 284

DR. MARK BERNSTEIN

Yes, It Is Brain Surgery

Dr. Mark Bernstein is a well-known neurosurgeon, and author of over 200 medical papers and a book on brain tumours. Former head of the Division of Neurosurgery at Toronto Western Hospital, he is also Professor of Surgery at the University of Toronto, where he has won awards for his teaching of medical students and neurosurgery residents. He is charismatic as a surgeon, as a teacher—and, as we will see in the essay that follows, as a writer. Though Bernstein's main area of clinical interest is neuro-oncology (brain tumours), he is also concerned with the ethical side of medicine. In 2003 he completed a Masters of Health Science in Bioethics; his main interests in that field are medical error, ethical issues in surgical education, surgical innovation, research ethics and neuroethics. Bernstein also promotes the advancement of neurosurgery in the developing world, spending time each year teaching and operating in Southeast Asia. In addition to his many medical publications, a few years ago he began writing "popular" pieces, by now has published about 100 of them, and in 2006 in San Francisco actually gave an invited lecture to 3000 other brain surgeons on the topic of non-medical writing. (Our own selection is certainly on a medical topic, but it is "popular" in its everyday vocabulary and vivid appeal. It first appeared in the Maclean's *of October 14, 2002.) Reading this fast-paced and gripping account of how he and his team saved a life on the operating table, we can begin to share in what Bernstein calls "the unbelievable thrill of brain surgery."*

Mike is enjoying his son's Saturday morning soccer game 1
and kidding with the other soccer dads on the sideline
when he falls over with a sudden headache, as if someone

had hit him over the head with a baseball bat. An ambulance takes Mike (for the purposes of this article, a composite of typical aneurysm patients) to a local hospital. There a CT scan confirms a subarachnoid hemorrhage—a bubble on a blood vessel deep in his brain has popped. When he fully comes to, Mike discovers he's been taken to the neurosurgery unit at Toronto Western Hospital. As his neurosurgeon, I try to be as positive as possible as I tell him that an aneurysm that has ruptured in his brain has to be fixed. It's very risky surgery, but it has to be done.

2 Mike's wife sneaks away from the bedside and cries quietly. What would she and the three kids do without Mike, who's just three weeks shy of his 35th birthday? Called in on a Saturday for this emergency, I discuss the situation with my senior resident and the anaesthesiologist, and let the nurses in the OR know to get things set up. The thin blister on the blood vessel deep in the brain lies in wait for us like a bomb ready to explode and take the patient's life with it. We suit up in our riot gear.

3 The patient has been anaesthetized and his head fixed in a metal clamp attached to the operating table. The left side of the scalp has been shaved, cleansed and draped in sterile sheets. The operation begins just after noon with a long, curved incision from in front of the ear to above the eye. Then the resident and I cut and peel the scalp and underlying muscle off the bone. Using an air-powered drill and saw, we remove a window of bone the size of a playing card. The brain is tense as we open the dura, the wet, leathery covering. The fluid surrounding the brain is stained from the blood that escaped from the aneurysm when it exploded a few short hours ago.

4 We peer at the arachnoid membrane, a wispy, translucent skin covering the brain like Cellophane. We can see the Sylvian fissure, cleft between the temporal and frontal lobes. We move the operating microscope into position on its ceiling track and the resident and I adjust our eyepieces. Focusing on the brain's surface, we use small forceps, dissecting tools and scissors to open the Sylvian fissure progressively down to two inches below the surface. Then we use the metal blades of retractors to pull the lobes apart, exposing the optic nerve and, just beside it, the internal carotid artery, one

of the large vessels carrying blood to the brain. We have found our blood vessel highway, along which we will gently navigate in search of the enemy.

Step by step we dissect the brain off the carotid artery and exert more retraction. I hear one of the nurses talking about a social commitment she has this evening with her husband. I have been unaware of time and space for the last little while. I quickly wonder what my wife and daughters are doing on this beautiful weekend. 5

As we get about an inch along the carotid artery, we come to the place where it divides into the anterior cerebral and the middle cerebral arteries. The preoperative angiogram has shown us that the culprit aneurysm is on the middle cerebral. After more painstaking dissection under the operating microscope, we come to the point where that artery divides into many daughter branches. Now we can see the object of our pursuit. The aneurysm, the size of a small olive, is embraced by three good-sized daughter arteries which snake by to fulfill their vital task of providing oxygenated blood to the brain. 6

An aneurysm is a thin-walled blister that pouches out from the side of an artery because of a defect in its wall. The defect is present at birth, but it usually takes decades for the blister to expand and rupture. The dome of the aneurysm has a thin, transparent wall through which we can see the blood swirling violently. Viewed through the microscope, this is a frightening sight. 7

The object is to place a spring-loaded metal clip across the base of the aneurysm to exclude it from the general blood circulation and thus prevent rebleeding. If a patient is fortunate enough to survive the first rupture of an aneurysm, the second time is usually fatal. The challenge is to avoid leaving any of the aneurysm wall behind to collect blood, enlarge and bleed again, and to do so without pinching off any other arteries, some the size of a hair, because that could produce a devastating stroke for the patient. 8

So with delicate dissecting instruments we start to define the neck of the aneurysm, the narrow area where the bulb rises out of the artery. We do this by gently getting between the daughter arteries plastered to the aneurysm and the aneurysm itself with fine metal probes. The dissection goes slowly because if you're too rough or too fast, you can rip a hole in the aneurysm, instantly converting a controlled situation into a horrifying, potentially disastrous crisis. Your heart pounds, your eyes strain and every muscle in your body tenses 9 to place your head and hands in a perfect position. Apart from the "beep-beep" of the anaesthetic machine, there is silence in the operating room as we work away.

10   The safest way to get the arteries off the aneurysm, we decide, is to be a bit rougher. First, though, we want to place a temporary clip across the trunk of the middle cerebral artery to decrease the pressure on the aneurysm and to ensure that bleeding would be non-catastrophic if it did rupture during our manipulations. We put the clip on and ask a nurse to monitor the time. Generally one only has a few minutes to work with a clip in place without risking a stroke. We continue to try to dissect off the daughter arteries, but it's tough going—it's like they were glued on. "One minute," announces the nurse. We continue, trying to establish a good enough slot for the clip to cut off the entire aneurysm but spare vital vessels around it. "Two minutes," says the nurse.

11   I'm not happy with our progress and decide to withdraw the temporary clip from the middle cerebral trunk. I become aware of my heart thumping painfully against my breast bone. My throat is dry as a chip as I whisper to my senior assistant, "I guess we'll have to take the bull by the horns and just do this without a temporary clip." I'm really seeking her endorsement and support, rather than dictating strategy.

12   We get up for a moment and walk over to the X-ray viewing monitor to look at the angiogram. We both know this is a stalling tactic to allow us to catch our breath. We return to our posts on either side of the microscope and pick up our weapons. I decide the only way to get a good look at one of the daughter arteries as it passes behind the aneurysm is to move the aneurysm dome with a flat, spatula-like dissector.

13   I picked this technique up from one of my senior, now-retired colleagues who helped me and many other neurosurgeons learn to do aneurysm surgery. It is a risk that has to be taken if we want to get on and clip this aneurysm. I start to gently but firmly retract the aneurysm—and then it happens. The beautiful, crystal-clear but surrealistic view of aneurysm, middle cerebral artery trunk, daughter vessels and brain disappears in a swirling sea of red that rises rapidly toward us. The aneurysm has ruptured.

14   Blood rushes into our operative field. Although not an uncommon occurrence during this type of surgery, it is truly frightening, something akin to the horror when your car hits a patch of ice and

starts to slide at 100 km/h. There are some corrective measures you can take, but the outcome is unpredictable. At this pace of bleeding, the patient could die from blood loss alone in about 60 seconds, yet if we stop the flow too quickly, we could irreversibly injure the brain by damaging vital small arteries. My heart skips a few beats.

With two suckers vacuuming the blood, the resident and I work to compress the aneurysm with a bit of cloth about one centimetre square. "You better just put the clip across the aneurysm neck," I say, "and then we'll look around and make sure it's safe." After a few runs with the applicator forceps at different angles, she deftly slips the clip into place. I take the cloth off and there is no bleeding. We then retract the aneurysm to check whether the artery on the other side is free, only to find it squished in the blades of the clip. My heart skips a few more beats.

15

If we left it like this, the patient would have a serious stroke with speech problems and weakness of the right arm and leg. So again I press the cloth back on the aneurysm dome with a sucker tip to prevent bleeding, and the resident removes the clip and repositions it at a slightly different angle. Inspection now reveals that no vital artery has been trapped. The job is done.

16

I gasp and allow my muscles to relax a bit. I ask the anaesthesiologist how the patient is doing and he replies, "Solid as a rock." My head and the resident's move away from the eyepieces of the microscope and we make eye contact. Our brows are furrowed and our faces too stiff to move, but our eyes smile.

17

I look up at the clock on the wall. Three hours and 20 minutes have passed since we cut skin. It seems like 15 minutes. I feel exhilarated and at the same time spent—emotionally and physically. We remove pooled blood from the brain, make sure there are no active bleeding points, remove the retractors, stitch together the dura, replace the bone flap with little metal plates, and close the scalp.

18

Mike was cured. He woke up in fine shape and went on to be discharged a few days later. As he had slept through it all, and his wife did not witness this little war we waged in the operating room, they will never know just how close to death this husband and father had been.

19

EXPLORATIONS:

Tilda Shalof, *A Nurse's Story: Life, Death and In-Between in an Intensive Care Unit*

Ashish Goel, *Doctors Do Cry*

Oliver Sacks, *The Man Who Mistook His Wife for a Hat and Other Clinical Tales*

http://healthlink.mcw.edu/article/921177260.html

http://www.ninds.nih.gov/disorders/cerebral_aneurysm/cerebral_aneurysm.htm

STRUCTURE:

1. Not many readers of this essay will ever do brain surgery. So is Dr. Bernstein's *process analysis* any less interesting because it is *informational*, not *directional*? What can an account like this do for the reader? What gives it value? Name a process *you* could write about that probably none of your own readers would attempt, and tell why the piece could be worthwhile for those readers.
2. To what extent is this essay of process analysis also a *narrative*? Point out five TRANSITIONS that speed the action on.
3. How much concrete *description* does Dr. Bernstein give us? What are its effects? Point out five good examples of it.
4. What purposes does the introduction to this essay (pars. 1 and 2) accomplish? What does the closing (pars. 17–19) accomplish?

STYLE:

1. If the operation has taken place some time ago, why does Dr. Bernstein write in present tense?
2. A few years ago Dr. Bernstein wrote a medical article entitled "Practice Parameters in Adults with Suspected or Known Supratentorial Non-Optic Pathway Glioma." Do you know what this means? Why does he not use language like this in "Yes, It Is Brain Surgery"? What AUDIENCE does he have in mind for his *Maclean's* essay?

3. In paragraph 9 Dr. Bernstein writes, "Your heart pounds, your eyes strain and every muscle in your body tenses...." Find five more good examples of SENSE IMAGES meant to put us into the scene.

4. In paragraph 2 the author writes, "The thin blister on the blood vessel deep in the brain lies in wait for us like a bomb ready to explode and take the patient's life with it. We suit up in our riot gear." Do you use SIMILES and METAPHORS like these in your own writing? What do they achieve? Point out at least five more good FIGURES OF SPEECH in this selection.

IDEAS FOR DISCUSSION AND WRITING:

1. Do we often think specialists or experts lack emotion when they go about their work? How do you react to Dr. Bernstein's showing his own emotions? Do you see it as a good sign for the health care system?

2. The author shows us a very positive example of our health care system in action. What has been your own experience with Canadian health care? Describe one example to the class.

3. A major point of debate in Canada is whether our health care system should remain universal, or whether a two-tier system should be allowed, so that those who have the money can buy faster or better care from private sources. What is your view, and why?

4. **PROCESS IN WRITING:** *Think of something you know how to do well (such as a technical procedure, an athletic move, a social task, etc.). Now decide if the act is too difficult for the average person to learn (like brain surgery), or whether it is easy enough. Now accordingly, write the draft of an* informational *OR a* directional *process analysis. Next day look it over. Is the terminology too difficult? If so, revise for your* audience. *Have you shown vivid* images, *as Mark Bernstein does, to spark interest? If not, add. Do time signals speed the chronological steps of your process analysis? If not, add. And if your piece is actual instructions to be followed, have you given every step? Now edit for conciseness and punctuation, then share your* process analysis *with the class.*

Note: See also the Topics for Writing on the Online Learning Centre at www. mcgrawhill.ca/olc/conrad.

ALBERT KOEHL

Hockey Etiquette for the Beginner

*Albert Koehl is many things: a Maple Leafs fan, a fluent speaker of several lan-
guages, a wilderness canoeist and hiker, a lover of the arts, and a lawyer who
hunts down and prosecutes corporate polluters. After graduating from Queen's
Law School in 1987, Koehl spent six years as a prosecutor for the Ontario
Ministry of the Environment, served in Guatemala as a volunteer human
rights observer and United Nations investigator and worked in Toronto community legal clinics. Then in 2001 he joined Sierra Legal Defence (now called
Ecojustice), a powerful Canadian environmental group that studies existing
legislation to find new ways of bringing polluters to justice. As if this were not
enough, Koehl has found time to join the boards of civic organizations for the
poor; has run for political office; has travelled across Africa by box car, bush
taxi and barge; has studied Mandarin in China; is fluent in French, German,
Spanish and English; and also writes. (The essay that follows appeared in the*
Globe and Mail *of April 21, 2004.) Asked what changes he would like to see
in his lifetime, Koehl replied, "We need to change our focus from a right to pol-
lute, to a right to clean air, water, and land. I believe a clean environment is as
crucial to a child as a good education and good health care."*

1   It is a common mistake, especially for theatre, opera, and symphony lovers, to conclude from the casual attire, beverage
choice, and boisterous conduct of hockey fans that watching
a game is a cultural event of a lower social order. In reality, the etiquette expected of ice hockey aficionados is quite refined. Ignorance
of this etiquette risks turning an invitation to watch an NHL playoff
game at the home of a friend, colleague or business associate, into a

social disaster. Fortunately, even the novice can avoid embarrassing blunders by learning a few simple rules:

Arrive on time for the start of a game. Hockey fans may not make you wait on the porch for the intermission, but if a goal is scored while you are being greeted your punctuality faux pas may prejudice a future invitation.   2

Cheer for the host's team unless you have announced a contrary affiliation in advance, much like a vegan properly reveals a dietary preference before attending a pig-roast fundraiser for the opera. And cheering for the other team simply because you like the colour of their jerseys is considered uncouth.   3

Remember, each hockey fan considers his or her role as important to the team's success as that of the players on the ice. Some fans contribute to their team by a complex set of superstitions. While guests may not believe in the power of the hockey gods, they are nonetheless expected to participate. For instance, if the opposing team takes a lead you may be asked to change seats. If you refuse, you can be blamed for the team's loss. In a recent game, our team was winning until my brother sent his toddlers to bed. Soon we were down by two goals. It turned out that the children's presence had been key to the team's lead and perhaps the reason they had so vigorously resisted bedtime. "I'll go wake up the kids," I volunteered.   4

Other fans contribute to the team by intensely concentrating on the game. It would be rude to mock this intensity, much like telling a mesmerized opera lover, "Relax, it's just singin' and yellin'." Hockey fans are willing to suffer tremendous anxiety for their team, even to pay the ultimate price. A recent study found that the anxiety suffered by fans during games sometimes brings on fatal heart attacks. At least the players have the chance to work off their nervous energy—a luxury the fan does not enjoy, except for the odd sprint to greet late arrivals at the door.   5

If the opposing team scores, quietly gauge the host's reaction. At the very least, allow the host to move uninterrupted through feelings of guilt, denial, anger, and acceptance. Later, it is always helpful to blame the referee, the seating arrangement or bad luck for the team's misfortune. On the other hand, remarking on the skill of the opposing team's scorer can be dangerous and is in any case considered déclassé, like hooting at a sexy stagehand at the theatre.   6

7   However, when the home team scores there are few rules to the proper conduct of the celebration, although damaging walls, smashing light fixtures (unless your host is a tenant) or interfering with the electrical cord to the TV are frowned upon. The euphoric mood of the host is also a perfect opportunity for a business associate or friend to bring up a delicate subject, such as the loss of a major contract or running over the family dog on the rush into the driveway to avoid being late.

8   Conversation during a game is properly limited to superficial topics. Generally, matters that can be answered with "yes" or "no" are acceptable, except during commercial breaks. Attempting to engage the host in a discussion about the war in Iraq, for example, would be like phoning your stockbroker during a symphony. It is worthwhile noting, however, that hockey fans are eager to share their extensive repertoire of trivial statistics. A fan may not remember his wife's birthday but would be happy to field a question such as, "Hey, do you know how much [Maple Leafs Captain] Mats Sundin weighs?" or "How tall is [Calgary star] Jerome Iginla?"

9   Similarly, telephone calls to a hockey fan during the playoffs are best kept to a minimum and, of course, restricted to the intermission. Never phone a hockey fan after 9:30 p.m. during the playoffs, since an overtime period may be in progress. If in doubt, do not call during evening hours until late June, when the playoffs end.

10   If the host's team is eliminated from the playoffs, behaviour that is appropriate at a funeral home is expected. For instance, you would never say "Look on the bright side, you still have other relatives." By the same token, clichés like "There's always next season" are not appreciated. Instead they expect the passing of their team from competition to be marked with profound solemnity. In fact, intimacy that might otherwise raise eyebrows is perfectly acceptable. A tender hug, even for a business associate, is remembered with fondness.

11   It is even acceptable for men to weep on the demise of their team. As one caller to a hockey talk show recently admitted, "I have cried only twice in my life, each time when the Maple Leafs were eliminated from the playoffs." To belittle a man at such a time is like mocking a person moved to tears by fair Juliet's plight.

12   By mastering these simple rules, a playoff game can become an enjoyable, even rewarding, cultural experience.

EXPLORATIONS:

Ken Dryden, *The Game*
Dave Bidini, *Tropic of Hockey*
Brian McFarlane, *Brian McFarlane's World of Hockey*
Hockey: A People's History (a six-disk DVD set of the CBC television series)
http://www.hhof.com/index.htm
http://en.wikipedia.org/wiki/Ice_hockey

STRUCTURE:

1. If Albert Koehl's essay is a process analysis, why does he begin paragraph 1 with a *comparison and contrast*?
2. Point out where else, throughout this selection, Koehl uses comparison and contrast.
3. Where is Koehl's thesis statement?
4. Is Koehl's essay a *directional* or an *informational* process analysis?
5. Does Koehl give his process analysis in the usual chronological order?
6. What common technique of closing does Koehl employ?

STYLE:

1. Parts of this piece are formal (big words, big sentences, big paragraphs), while other parts are informal ("'Relax, it's just singin' and yellin'"). What is Koehl doing through this contrast of styles?

IDEAS FOR DISCUSSION AND WRITING:

1. One fan in paragraph 11 admits, "I have cried only twice in my life, each time when the Maple Leafs were eliminated from the playoffs." Why do spectator sports move us? Tell of the time when you were most deeply affected by watching a sport.

2. Which does more for us, watching a sport or playing it ourselves? Give reasons.

3. Ken Dryden, one of the greatest goalies of all time, played for the Montreal Canadiens from 1971 to 1979, when they won six Stanley Cups. He also did a law degree (like Albert Koehl), wrote four bestselling books, became president of the Toronto Maple Leafs, then went on to be a federal MP and cabinet minister. Is his a rare story, or do sports build a character and ability that help athletes later in life?

4. Do high salaries, high ticket prices and labour-management conflicts mean NHL hockey is in trouble? Suggest long-term solutions to strengthen this favourite Canadian sport. And do you think hockey will remain our favourite?

5. Paragraph 4 describes typical superstitions of sports fans. Why, in an age of science, do we still believe things like these? Tell your own strongest superstition, and give evidence whether it works or not.

6. Do you prefer watching sports, or going to the symphony, theatre or opera? Or, like Albert Koehl, do you like them all? Argue why or why not.

7. PROCESS IN WRITING: *Write a humorous process analysis, like Koehl's, entitled "Concert Etiquette for the Beginner." (The concert may be of any kind, from classical to heavy metal.) Start with a page of notes, then put them in time order and select the best. Are there plenty of actual techniques? How do concertgoers do each thing? (Include such acts as obtaining tickets, entering the hall, finding one's place, enjoying the event, dealing with annoying neighbours, showing appreciation for the performance, etc.). Now do a quick draft. The next day look it over. Are words wasted? Then cut. Do examples fill at least half the essay? If not, add. Is word choice exact? If not, see your thesaurus. Do you move the reader on with transitions such as "first," "then," "next," "at last" and "finally"? Is the punctuation accurate? If not, edit. Finally, read your process analysis, with feeling, to the class.*

Note: See also the Topics for Writing on the Online Learning Centre at www. mcgrawhill.ca/olc/conrad.

CATHERINE FORD

Yahoo, It's Calgary

Catherine Ford has had a long career as a Western Canadian journalist. Raised in Calgary and Edmonton, she went on to the University of Alberta, where she majored in English. In 1964 she joined the Calgary Herald *as a reporter, later becoming an editorial page columnist and then associate editor. The winner of ten Western Ontario Newspaper Awards, Ford has also written for* En Route *magazine,* Apple *and* Calgary Magazine. *In 2005 appeared her book* Against the Grain: An Irreverent View of Alberta. *As its title suggests, Ford has sometimes been critical of public policy in Alberta, as well as celebrating the things she loves about her home province. From* Against the Grain *comes our selection, a playful set of instructions for enjoying the Calgary Stampede.*

T o an outsider, the ten days of the Stampede look like may-   1
hem, but it is actually controlled chaos. And there is a difference between the two. Visitors just need to know the
following Seven Highly Effective Rules for Stampede Enjoyment:

1. The cowboy: Everyone is a cowboy during Stampede. "Cowpoke"   2
   is the gender-neutral term. You will be able to tell the difference
   between the two. But you might not be able to tell the file clerk
   and the CEO apart. The man in the ratty hat and jeans could be
   the owner of the biggest oil company in the city. So remember
   cowboy manners and be polite to everyone. Take no chances.
   Dance with everyone.
2. The food: Stampede meals consist of five important food groups: 3
   beef, beans, beer, and before noon, pancakes with sausages or

bacon. You need only remember the colour brown. If it isn't brown, it doesn't qualify as Stampede food. Black—as in grilled to the consistency and colour of charcoal—is passably acceptable. Greens are what you feed your horse. If you're eating fusion or other sissy food, get out of town. The only "exotic" food that is authentic is Chinese, the historic staple of Western towns. Beer is optional in the morning, although liquor is indeed served at 8 a.m. The official meal of the Stampede is breakfast. Don't miss it, because breakfast is the base for a day that might include a substantial number of liquid refreshments and other meals of such fleeting sustenance as donut holes and corn dogs.

4   3. The dress: Western, of course. Open to wide interpretation. Jeans and shirt as a minimum. Boots, hats, string ties, and all the other paraphernalia of cowboy culture is at your discretion. Newcomers may think they can avoid dressing Western, because they see no use for this stuff the other fifty-and-a-half weeks of the year. But this is Calgary, pardner. Cowboy shirts and vests, hats and boots, will appear like magic in your closet. You might as well give in as soon as you move here. The good news is that the longer you wear cowboy boots, the better they feel.

5   4. The hat: Not mandatory (this is a July event, after all) but should you want to complete your ensemble with a genuine hat, in Calgary it isn't a Stetson, it's a Smithbilt, made right here by a company started by my husband's uncle, Morris Schumiatcher/ Smith. (After Morris started Smithbilt Hats he switched its name from Smith to Schumiatcher and back again, until settling on the family's real name.)

6   Once you've purchased a fancy felt number and put it on, don't take it off. (It is the only type of headgear acceptable indoors.) A real cowboy doesn't take his hat off for a variety of reasons, but we drugstore cowboys don't take our hats off for a very specific reason: hat head. If your hat flaunts feathers, beading, sequins, or comes in any colour other than brown or black—white if you are the Stampede Queen or one of her two princesses—you are a tenderfoot. You will be considered fair game by the barkers on the midway.

7   5. The language: The official Stampede cry is "yahoo" or "ee-haw." Feel free to burst into either version anytime the mood strikes, regardless of venue. (Except, maybe, church.) "Howdy" is also acceptable.

6. The real stampede: This comprises the infield rodeo, nightly   8
chuckwagon races, crafts and art shows and competitions, the
wonderful animals and the evocative rich smells of the horse
barns, the Indian village, and anything that celebrates this city's
agricultural and ranching heritage.
7. The not-real stampede: Here's where you'll find cacti, Texas   9
longhorns, Navaho blankets, and turquoise jewellery, Weadickville
and Nashville North, although both offer the kind of West
people not steeped in Canadian history actually believe. Why
would something as blatantly fake as shootouts be featured at the
Stampede? That's simple: more than $125 million from 1 million
visitors by the end of these ten days.

The whole idea is to have fun, as long as you remember it isn't real.   10

EXPLORATIONS:

Catherine Ford, *Against the Grain: An Irreverent View of Alberta*
http://www.vueweekly.com/article.php?id=2545
http://cs.calgarystampede.com/clf_menu.html
http://corporate.calgarystampede.com
http://en.wikipedia.org/wiki/Cowboy
http://www.civilization.ca/media/docs/fsjosh01e.html

STRUCTURE:

1. To organize her *process analysis*, Ford chooses the very simple and
direct structure of a numbered list. Does this method work for
her? Give examples.
2. Are Ford's points arranged in a progression? Give examples to
illustrate your answer.
3. Do you believe that Ford's lighthearted *process analysis* is also factual enough to help visitors enjoy the Calgary Stampede? What
are the several most useful points she makes in her "Seven Highly
Effective Rules for Stampede Enjoyment"?

STYLE:

1. At what point did you first recognize the comic TONE of this selection?
2. Point out five of the funniest passages, and tell why they are funny.
3. Have you read Stephen Leacock's essay "How to Live to Be 200," in this chapter? If not, do so. Point out similarities between the ways he makes us laugh and the ways Catherine Ford makes us laugh.

IDEAS FOR DISCUSSION AND WRITING:

1. Why do we have fairs, festivals and celebrations like the Calgary Stampede? What does the Stampede do for those who attend? If you do not live in Alberta, name celebrations or festivals that occur in your own region. What do they do for you?
2. Do you wear blue jeans? Do you drive a pickup truck? Is it only Westerners who demonstrate "cowboy culture," as Ford calls it? Or is it seen right across the country? And if so, why? Give examples.
3. Alberta is sometimes called the most American of the provinces. Do you think this idea is true? If so, give examples. Then give reasons. And what implications might this all have for the future?
4. Lately Alberta has been on a roll, gaining wealth and power within Confederation, while Ontario is starting to become a have-not province. Give all the reasons you can for this reversal of earlier roles.
5. PROCESS IN WRITING: *Think of the time you were a stranger in some other province or country. What techniques did you employ to enjoy your visit? Take notes, then arrange your points in a* process analysis. *Write a quick draft, not stopping now to fix the little things. Later look it over. Are your directions clear enough to help your readers? Have you given plenty of examples? Are the points in the right order? Now read your essay aloud to detect flaws such as wordiness or grammatical errors. Finally check for spelling and punctuation, and print off your best version to share in class.*

Note: See also the Topics for Writing on the Online Learning Centre at www. mcgrawhill.ca/olc/conrad.

CHRISTIE BLATCHFORD

Mother's Milk

Christie Blatchford is one of the nation's most high-profile journalists. Born in Rouyn-Noranda, Quebec, she went to high school in Toronto and then studied journalism at Ryerson University. There her vivid columns written for an alternative campus newspaper, The Eyeopener, *already began to attract attention. Even before graduating, Blatchford went to work as a sports reporter (a rare move then for a woman) at the Toronto* Globe and Mail. *Later she moved to the* Toronto Star, *writing a regular column, and then the* Toronto Sun. *She stayed there some 20 years as a lifestyle columnist, then city columnist. Next came a time with the* National Post, *and then she took the position she holds today, columnist at the* Globe and Mail. *Blatchford reports in the old style: sparing no gory details as she covers crimes and trials, leaving no emotion untouched as she brings stories to life for her readers. Not everyone is a fan. Bloggers have criticized what they call her sensationalism in reporting, and her conservatism politically. But her readers keep on reading. After three trips to Afghanistan, interviewing soldiers and scrambling to survive with them on the battlefield, she published in 2007 a hard-hitting book about Canadian forces in the Afghan war:* Fifteen Days: Stories of Bravery, Friendship, Life and Death from Inside the New Canadian Army. *Our own selection, "Mother's Milk," appeared in Sandra Martin's anthology* The First Man in My Life: Daughters Write About Their Fathers *(2007). While the father is memorable, it is the mother and her descent into alcohol that are the focus of this frank and honest memoir.*

I was in my second year at college when my father mentioned—for the first, last and only time—that he was thinking of leaving my mother.

2   I was by then out of the house, or, as I assumed my dad thought of it, safely out of the house, living on my own in a small, ramshackle basement apartment in downtown Toronto. My brother, almost a decade older than I am, had long since fled the nest. Our parents were alone with one another in a way they had not been since they were first married, and since I could not conceive of being trapped at home with the woman my mother had become, I wasn't surprised that he might not be able to stand it, either.

3   I had always imagined that my father stayed with her as long as he did only because of me. She was such an enormous presence that even in a story supposedly about my dad, my mother figures as large in my memory as she did in our lives.

4   My mother was an alcoholic who started drinking as a teenager to allay her social nervousness. At first it worked and she was able to function—a cigarette in one hand and a drink in the other. Pictures from those days show a striking and confident-looking young woman, hair glamorously upswept in one of those big-shouldered, nipped-waist 1940s suits that so flattered her athletic frame. But as the years wore on, it was as though the booze, once a lubricant that allowed her to beat her acute self-consciousness into submission, thickened as soon as it hit her bloodstream, becoming so viscous that it all but paralyzed her.

5   Her drinking would not have been so noticeable, probably not even to my father, in the small northwestern Quebec town where I was born and raised and where my folks lived for about twenty years. Rouyn-Noranda was a hard-drinking mining town with a frontier mentality as rough as the wooden sidewalks that were in place when my parents and my brother, then just a little boy, moved there after the Second World War.

6   My parents' social life centred around bridge games at our house and their friends' homes, casual parties at the local curling or golf club and nights out at the Canadian Corps or the Moose Lodge. In this milieu, where it seemed everyone drank a lot, my mother's drinking would not have drawn any particular scrutiny, and indeed, perhaps it didn't warrant any then.

7   Her natural athleticism and competitiveness would have masked her incipient alcoholism, and the time she devoted to sports would have placed arbitrary limits on how much she could drink and still play the games she loved, at a high level. I am not the best reporter

here, for obvious reasons. My story is pieced together from my parents' recollections, and my own observations, once I was old enough to make them.

Certainly, in Noranda, my mother was still playing badminton—she was once nationally ranked—tennis and golf, clobbering the ball off the tee as far as most men, and showing the same trademark impatience on the greens as she did on the rare occasions when she lost a badminton match and she'd throw herself onto the gym floor and beat her fists in frustration. My brother told a story at her funeral about the time when, as she was walking by the field where he and his friends were playing baseball, she picked a long ball out of the air and, without breaking stride, casually hurled it right to home plate, just about tearing off the recipient's arm—and impressing the hell out of my brother's friends.   8

No accident she was known as "Babe" in her heyday.   9

But at some point after I was born—a surprise, relatively late-in-life   10
child—her drinking changed, or rather, she began to do more of it. I was still small, maybe in grade one or two, when I first picked up the glass that was always by the kitchen sink, filled it with water and spat it out because of the yechy taste. It was my mother's rye glass. It was the glass she used when I was at school and my father at work; it was the glass she kept at the ready when she made dinner; it was the glass she took to bed every single night until she was about eighty, when she finally quit booze because it had become clear to her that if she didn't, she would die. Frequently, in the last years of drinking, her potassium levels would plummet dangerously, and she would end up hospitalized for a week or so. Finally, she was scared straight.

But long before then, she morphed from party drinker to stealth   11
drinker, sipping at that damn little glass all day long so that by dinnertime, she was, as they said in those days, well-oiled, keeping mickeys of rye in her lingerie drawer, under the kitchen sink, and in her bedside table. I'm not sure who would have noticed except my father, or how long it took him to notice. It was the kind of town where kids went home for lunch, and so did fathers. My mom was still fine at lunch, cheerful and functional: Egg-salad sandwiches would be waiting for me; toasted cheese for my father; big glasses of milk for us both. I don't remember what, if anything, my mother had.

My suspicion is that even this far back, she may not have been eat-   12
ing much. I wonder now if she also had an eating disorder, or if her

appetite loss and vomiting was part and parcel of her alcoholism. By the time I was in high school, she was vomiting after almost every meal. I have no memory of ever seeing her eat, but vivid ones of the acrid smell of vomit in the bathroom after she used it. Is it even possible that she could have been throwing up what I don't remember ever seeing her swallow?

13   The awful alchemy, for that's what it was, would happen in the afternoons.

14   By dinner—and dinner was always served at five-thirty sharp—the woman from lunch had disappeared, and in her place was this sharp-tongued, sometimes vicious, almost unrecognizable person. I remember always being very worried if my dad was even five minutes late getting home for dinner, because my mother would turn on him and berate him, such that it was almost unbearable to watch; I remember knowing it was better to talk about anything important with my mom at lunch; I remember being nervous about having my friends over at night.

15   Like many children of alcoholics, I knew far too much about my parents' married life. One story alone will illustrate that. One Christmas Eve, when I was maybe thirteen, I heard my mother crying for help, and ran to the bedroom where they had their separate single beds. I can't remember what she said when I got there, but I knew my dad had gone in search of some intimacy or comfort, that she had used me to avoid it, and that he was mortified with shame by my presence. Not long after that, he moved into his own small room.

16   Still, had we never left Noranda, her decline probably would have been slower, or less remarkable. But, in 1967, when I was about fifteen, we moved to Toronto because my father thought life would be better there for all of us after the political situation changed in Quebec. My mother had lived in Toronto as a teenager with her own family, but this turned out to be an adjustment beyond her diminishing abilities.

17   My dad was a hockey rink manager, so my folks were never rich, though they spent—particularly on me—as though they were. In Toronto, they couldn't afford to join a golf or tennis club, as they had done in Noranda, so my mother's sporting outlet was effectively gone, and where my father and I made friends at work and school respectively, my mother in the main remained at home, alone. She only ever worked part-time, as a typist or secretary, and her shyness and insecurities would have rendered her difficult to get to know.

Her drinking grew heavier, or at least its effects became more pronounced, and so did her neuroses.

In Noranda, though an immensely capable driver, she was always 18 a nervous passenger; in Toronto, she drove only within a six-block area of our apartment (mostly to the Dominion store and the liquor store, and back) and refused to go on the expressways, no matter who was behind the wheel. In Noranda, she had avoided big crowds, but there, that meant only the local movie theatre; in Toronto, it meant she hardly left the house. In Noranda, she was afraid of elevators, but there were almost none because the buildings were all one or two storeys tall. In Toronto, the dentist's office was on a high floor, as was the doctor's, so she just stopped going.

And where in Noranda, she was afraid of bugs, in Toronto, it 19 seems she was frightened of people, and the places they went— shopping malls, public squares, business functions, baby showers. Even staying with family, on my parents' occasional out-of-town trips, was unsettling for her: Was it only that she was afraid that, at my brother's house in Montreal for instance, she wouldn't be able to bring her mickeys, or get enough to drink? Or was she, as it sometimes seemed, no longer able to be comfortable with her own family? Instead my parents stayed at motels, where at least my mom could be assured of having a ready supply and unrestricted access to it.

Periodically, we began having little family talks, our own version 20 of an intervention, where my dad and I would broach the problems her drinking was creating, or the idea of her joining Alcoholics Anonymous, or even having her go to a treatment centre. No, no, no, she'd say; I don't need that; I can quit any time.

And she would, too, cold turkey, all on her own, bringing her still 21 tremendous will to bear. The storm clouds that seemed perpetually to hang over the house would lift, day by day, and soon enough she'd be back, healthy-seeming, happier, sober. She would gain weight; the red in her eyes would clear up; even her hair seemed shinier, though perhaps that was my imagination. And there would be no more of that terrible meanness, no more of the small cruelties from the razor blades she seemed to take in with each sip from her rye glass and then hide in her mouth.

During one of these phases, my father even had her convinced to 22 try going on the subway, which encapsulated so many of her fears—it was underground; it was enclosed; it was often crowded and busy. I remember the day they set off, hand in hand, for Eglinton station, and how they returned, not long after, failure written on my mother's face and disappointment on my dad's. A few times, they'd go to a matinee showing of a film—the theatre would be almost empty, he figured—but my mom would flee halfway through the show.

23   Once, we drove her to an AA meeting; when we picked her up, she was full of faux-scorn for the people there, who needed this crutch. "It's not for me," she said. "I can do it on my own." At least twice, my dad arranged for her to attend a thirty-day program at a rehab centre, but the problem with that was, when push came to shove, my mom had to sign the forms herself and agree to go. She never would.

24   These sober periods never lasted longer than a month. We always knew she was drinking again long before she would tearfully confess to having "just one," or before we found the evidence in one of her drawers.

25   The clue was always the same: the viciousness would return. Once, I remember, my father had volunteered to let Angelo, one of his nice young staffers from the rink, then newly married and with a baby and no money, use our cottage (the only piece of property my parents ever owned) for a week when my folks weren't planning to go.

26   "You don't mind, do you?" my dad asked, "if Angelo uses it?"

27   "Fuck Angelo," snapped my mother. "I don't want them there."

28   Where she once reserved her sharpest comments for my dad, constantly belittling him, with me her next-favourite target, she now broadened the circle to include her grandchildren, my brother's two kids, on their increasingly infrequent visits. She would be outright drunk by eight o'clock at night, and wander about the cottage in her nightie, demanding that the children, who were then just little, be still, or quiet. An ordinary card game, the very kind she used to love, if it went any later than that, would have her stumble into the main room in a rage and demand that everyone go to bed.

29   Were my father and I enablers, as AA calls those who inadvertently, or deliberately, make it easy for drinkers to keep on drinking, or at least difficult for them to stop? I don't think so, though I've worried the point for years. My gentle, generous father's life would have been so immeasurably better if his wife had just been kinder to him. I can't imagine him sabotaging her efforts to stop drinking.

But at some point, I suppose, my dad and I gave up: There seemed   30
little we could do to make her want to stop drinking, and the drinker
who doesn't want to stop can't be made to stop.

It was easier for me, because I moved out, and was of that age   31
where for a few fleeting years, you strike out on your own and barely
pay attention to your parents. But I remained dose to them both
always, and saw them frequently even during this period.

I believe that for the rest of their life together, things remained   32
much the same, or worse. The woman who in her twenties was physically so strong, and vibrant, became increasingly neurotic and it
seemed to me that her alcoholism had turned her into a gaping maw
of exposed needs—imagined and insatiable.

And yet, after that one remark about leaving her—he told me in   33
the car, as we were returning to their apartment for dinner, and self-
ishly, I remember thinking that this was bad news for me, as I would
now have to bear more of the load he shouldered on his own—
nothing happened.

He would have been fifty-six or fifty-seven then. He would have had   34
time to meet someone new, or at least try. Even so, a life alone would
not have loomed as a terrifying possibility, but rather, I imagine, as
a relief. My dad was still working. He had many friends. He was a
voracious reader, of newspapers, novels and non-fiction. As ever, he
enjoyed the occasional drink, and he could still pound down a few at
a party, but he never needed booze the way my mother did. He had
always quit drinking whenever she tried to stop.

I didn't wonder why he never left her. I was just relieved, I suppose,   35
that he didn't, because it meant less worry and work for me. I don't
think I ever asked him about it; he just stayed, and I was glad, less for
my mother, I'm ashamed to say, than for myself.

I used to think he had stayed with her because of me, afraid that   36
if he left, I would be exposed to too much of that relentless criticism
and have my confidence permanently undermined, the very way that
hers had been. I always thought he saved my life.

But then, even when I was an adult, establishing a career and mar-   37
ried, he stayed.

Now, I believe, he stayed because he loved her. He may not have   38
loved what was left of her, but he loved the essence of who she still
was, and he could see that person still; he could see past the alcoholism and the years of damage it had done to them both.

39 Their final years together were quiet. I know because I saw them at least once a week—I could no more abandon my dad to the un-tender mercies of my mother than he could abandon me to them. And perhaps he knew, too, that I would have my turn looking after her. His lung cancer was discovered when, feeling perfectly healthy and bullet-proof, he asked his doctor what his life expectancy was, and to answer the question, the doctor took X-rays of his chest and they found the shadow there. My dad always joked that he would live forever, but I think he knew in his bones he would die sooner rather than later, and sooner than she.

40 They had the cottage in summer, where my father would count the trees on his property and tend his garden (he knew them all by their Latin names), and my mother would sit in the sun. They played cards or Scrabble, went out for dinner occasionally and took little day trips in the country. In the winters, he worked part-time until just a few years before his death. Aside from me and my ex-husband, they had few visitors, and went out infrequently.

41 Every Christmas, he bought her something red to wear, because he loved her in red. He always beamed when she got dressed up, told her she was still beautiful, that her legs still went all the way up. He told great, warm stories about her as a young woman, throwing a tantrum whenever she lost a badminton game, throwing her golf clubs when she blew a shot. He bragged of her long-gone athleticism as though she were still able to throw a baseball the way she had that day when my brother saw her in action.

42 When he entered hospital for the final time, my mother was drinking a lot. His room was on an upper floor, and she could neither force herself into the elevator nor take the stairs with any ease, so she hardly came to see him. The night he died, my ex and I were with him, and at the behest of a nurse, erring on the side of caution, I took her advice and called my mother and told her to come.

43 She was drunk when she arrived with my brother, and belligerent. Restless, she stayed perhaps twenty minutes, and furiously insisted that they leave. She complained in the hall that I had called her there needlessly. "If Daddy dies tonight," she said, and I will never forget either the words or the inflection, "don't call me again. The morning will do."

44 He did die, a few hours later.

I thought I'd never forgive her for that, and for a time, I didn't, though I always took care of her. But over the next fifteen or so years, for she lived that much longer than he did, I got at least most of the way to forgiveness. And in the last months of her own life, as she battled illness and her own enormous fear, my mother was as brave and as tough as my dad had been, and I too could see past the glass of rye, to the girl she had once been.

45

EXPLORATIONS:

Christie Blatchford, *Fifteen Days: Stories of Bravery, Friendship, Life and Death from Inside the New Canadian Army*
Sandra Martin, ed., *The First Man in My Life: Daughters Write About Their Fathers*
http://www.theglobeandmail.com/opinions/columnists/ Christie+Blatchford.html
http://www.cbc.ca/thehour/video.php?id=1787
http://en.wikipedia.org/wiki/Christie_Blatchford
http://www.thecanadianencyclopedia.com/index.cfm?PgNm=TCE &Params=A1ARTA0000126
http://alcoholism.about.com
http://www.mayoclinic.com/health/alcoholism/DS00340

STRUCTURE:

1. Clearly "Mother's Milk" is an *informational* process analysis, showing how one person became an alcoholic. But to what extent, and how, is it also a *directional* process analysis?
2. Point out all the main stages of Blatchford's *process analysis*, as the mother declines into alcoholism.
3. In chronicling her mother's slide into alcoholism, Blatchford supplies many TRANSITIONS, for example in paragraph 10 where she writes, "But at some point after I was born … her drinking changed, or rather, she began to do more of it." Point out at

least three other clear transitions that move us from one stage to another.

4. Read paragraph 18 aloud in class. Is the *repetition* that you hear accidental or deliberate? Also point out how this passage is based on *contrast*.

5. To what extent is this reading also based on *cause and effect* logic? What actual *causes* are given for the mother's alcoholism, and what *effects* does the disease cause?

STYLE:

1. In paragraph 5 Blatchford writes of Rouyn-Noranda's "frontier mentality as rough as the wooden sidewalks." What FIGURE OF SPEECH is she using here? Study this topic in the glossary at the end of the book, and then locate and name five other good figures of speech in this essay.

2. Read paragraph 10 aloud in class. What phrase is repeated time after time? What is the effect? Is this *repetition* an error made by accident, or is it deliberate and does it have a purpose?

3. Hold your book at arm's length, and look at it: Is Blatchford's *process analysis* built mostly of large words or small words? Has she made a good choice? Why or why not?

IDEAS FOR DISCUSSION AND WRITING

1. Christie Blatchford set out to write a piece for Sandra Martin's anthology *The First Man in My Life: Daughters Write About Their Fathers*. Why, then, is the title "Mother's Milk"? Who is this essay mostly about?

2. In her career as journalist, Blatchford spends most of her time reporting on murders, following sensational trials and, with the Canadian military forces, trying to survive on the battlegrounds of Afghanistan. Is the subject of "Mother's Milk" less dramatic? Less important? Why or why not?

3. Do you personally know an alcoholic? What similarities to his or her case do you most clearly recognize in this reading? How much

drinking takes place among the students of your school? What are some reasons for it? What are the effects?

4. Addictive behaviour is of course not limited to substance abuse. Do you know workaholics? What are their behavioural traits? What are the causes, and what are the results, of their addiction?

5. Some addictions are said to be "positive"—for example, addiction to exercise. Think of others as well. Do they share any of the same causes, or any of the same results, as addiction to substances such as alcohol or drugs?

6. In her closing paragraph, Blatchford writes that "over the next fifteen or so years ... I got at least most of the way to forgiveness." Review June Callwood's essay "Forgiveness," in Chapter 4 of this book. Then point out several examples from Blatchford's essay in which the daughter and the father are able to offer forgiveness.

7. PROCESS IN WRITING: *Question 4 above mentions workaholism. Think for a while on this topic, and maybe do some research, identifying the steps through which a person develops the disease. Make brief notes on this* process, *including plenty of* examples. *Next write a quick draft, covering the main steps in the process one by one. Later look it over. Does every* example *contribute to the overall* process? *If not, revise. Do* TRANSITIONS *speed your prose? If not, add. Finally read your paper aloud; wherever it sounds weak, it probably* is *weak, so do some special editing in those places. After checking punctuation and spelling, print out your best version to share in class. Another group activity can be role-playing a typical scene in the life of a workaholic.*

Note: See also the Topics for Writing on the Online Learning Centre at www. mcgrawhill.ca/olc/conrad.

STEPHEN LEACOCK

How to Live to Be 200

During his lifetime Stephen Leacock became the world's best-known humorist writing in English, a Canadian successor to the American writer Mark Twain. Reading in person, Leacock was so funny that once a member of his audience literally died laughing. Though he was for decades Canada's favourite author, Leacock has slipped into neglect. Born in England in 1869, at age six he came with his family to Ontario. He studied at Upper Canada College, the University of Toronto and the University of Chicago, where in 1903 he received a Ph.D. That year McGill hired him to teach economics and political science, and from 1908 till his retirement in 1936, he served as head of his department. He died in 1944. Leacock wrote over 60 books, many on academic subjects, but of course it is for his books of humour that he is remembered. The best-loved have been Literary Lapses *(1910),* Nonsense Novels *(1911),* Sunshine Sketches of a Little Town *(1912),* Arcadian Adventures with the Idle Rich *(1914) and* My Remarkable Uncle and Other Sketches *(1942). Our selection, from a later version of* Literary Lapses, *is vintage Leacock: through exaggeration and incongruities, it reduces to absurdity a topic that many people, today as in Leacock's time, take seriously. It may be worth noting that Leacock himself shunned the "health mania" to spend large amounts of time enjoying his favourite brandies in the McGill Faculty Club.*

1   Twenty years ago I knew a man called Jiggins, who had the Health Habit.

2   He used to take a cold plunge every morning. He said it opened his pores. After it he took a hot sponge. He said it closed the pores. He got so that he could open and shut his pores at will.

3   Jiggins used to stand and breathe at an open window for half an hour before dressing. He said it expanded his lungs. He might, of course, have had it done in a shoe-store with a boot stretcher, but after all it cost him nothing this way, and what is half an hour?

4   After he had got his undershirt on, Jiggins used to hitch himself

up like a dog in harness and do Sandow exercises. He did them forwards, backwards, and hind-side up.

He could have got a job as a dog anywhere. He spent all his time ⁵ at this kind of thing. In his spare time at the office, he used to lie on his stomach on the floor and see if he could lift himself up with his knuckles. If he could, then he tried some other way until he found one that he couldn't do. Then he would spend the rest of his lunch hour on his stomach, perfectly happy.

In the evenings in his room he used to lift iron bars, cannon-balls, ⁶ heave dumb-bells, and haul himself up to the ceiling with his teeth. You could hear the thumps half a mile.

He liked it. ⁷

He spent half the night slinging himself around the room. He said ⁸ it made his brain clear. When he got his brain perfectly clear, he went to bed and slept. As soon as he woke, he began clearing it again.

Jiggins is dead. He was, of course, a pioneer, but the fact that he ⁹ dumb-belled himself to death at an early age does not prevent a whole generation of young men from following in his path.

They are ridden by the Health Mania. ¹⁰

They make themselves a nuisance. ¹¹

They get up at impossible hours. They go out in silly little suits ¹² and run Marathon heats before breakfast. They chase around barefoot to get the dew on their feet. They hunt for ozone. They bother about pepsin. They won't eat meat because it has too much nitrogen. They won't eat fruit because it hasn't any. They prefer albumen and starch and nitrogen to huckleberry pie and doughnuts. They won't drink water out of a tap. They won't eat sardines out of a can. They won't use oysters out of a pail. They won't drink milk out of a glass. They are afraid of alcohol in any shape. Yes sir, afraid. "Cowards."

And after all their fuss they presently incur some simple old-fashioned illness and die like anybody else. ¹³

Now people of this sort have no chance to attain any great age. ¹⁴ They are on the wrong track.

Listen. Do you want to live to be really old, to enjoy a grand, green, ¹⁵ exuberant, boastful old age and to make yourself a nuisance to your whole neighbourhood with your reminiscences?

Then cut out all this nonsense. Cut it out. Get up in the morning at ¹⁶ a sensible hour. The time to get up is when you have to, not before. If your office opens at eleven, get up at ten-thirty. Take your chance on ozone. There isn't any such thing anyway. Or, if there is, you can buy a Thermos bottle full for five cents, and put it on a shelf in your cupboard. If your work begins at seven in the morning, get up at ten minutes to, but don't be liar enough to say that you like it. It isn't exhilarating, and you know it.

17   Also, drop all that cold-bath business. You never did it when you were a boy. Don't be a fool now. If you must take a bath (you don't really need to), take it warm. The pleasure of getting out of a cold bed and creeping into a hot bath beats a cold plunge to death. In any case, stop gassing about your tub and your "shower," as if you were the only man who ever washed.

18   So much for that point.

19   Next, take the question of germs and bacilli. Don't be scared of them. That's all. That's the whole thing, and if you once get on to that you never need to worry again.

20   If you see a bacilli, walk right up to it, and look it in the eye. If one flies into your room, strike at it with your hat or with a towel. Hit it as hard as you can between the neck and the thorax. It will soon get sick of that.

21   But as a matter of fact, a bacilli is perfectly quiet and harmless if you are not afraid of it. Speak to it. Call out to it to "lie down." It will understand. I had a bacilli once, called Fido, that would come and lie at my feet while I was working. I never knew a more affectionate companion, and when it was run over by an automobile, I buried it in the garden with genuine sorrow.

22   (I admit this is an exaggeration. I don't really remember its name; it may have been Robert.)

23   Understand that it is only a fad of modern medicine to say that cholera and typhoid and diphtheria are caused by bacilli and germs; nonsense. Cholera is caused by a frightful pain in the stomach, and diphtheria is caused by trying to cure a sore throat.

24   Now take the question of food.

25   Eat what you want. Eat lots of it. Yes, eat too much of it. Eat till you can just stagger across the room with it and prop it up against a sofa cushion. Eat everything that you like until you can't eat any more. The only test is, can you pay for it? If you can't pay for it, don't eat it. And listen—don't worry as to whether your food contains starch, or albumen, or gluten, or nitrogen. If you are a damn fool enough to want these things, go and buy them and eat all you want of them. Go to a laundry and get a bag of starch, and eat your fill of it. Eat it, and take a good long drink of glue after it, and a spoonful of Portland cement. That will gluten you, good and solid.

If you like nitrogen, go and get a druggist to give you a canful of it 26
at the soda counter, and let you sip it with a straw. Only don't think
that you can mix all these things up with your food. There isn't any
nitrogen or phosphorus or albumen in ordinary things to eat. In any
decent household all that sort of stuff is washed out in the kitchen
sink before the food is put on the table.

And just one word about fresh air and exercise. Don't bother with 27
either of them. Get your room full of good air, then shut up the
windows and keep it. It will keep for years. Anyway, don't keep using
your lungs all the time. Let them rest. As for exercise, if you have to
take it, take it and put up with it. But as long as you have the price of
a hack° and can hire other people to play baseball for you and run
races and do gymnastics when you sit in the shade and smoke and
watch them—great heavens, what more do you want?

°hack: A kind of horse-drawn carriage.

EXPLORATIONS:

Stephen Leacock,
   Sunshine Sketches of a Little Town
   Literary Lapses
   My Remarkable Uncle and Other Sketches
Robertson Davies, *Stephen Leacock*
D. Staines, *Stephen Leacock: A Reappraisal*
http://www.athabascau.ca/writers/leacock.html
http://archives.cbc.ca/IDD-1-41-615/sports/fitness
http://archives.cbc.ca/IDC-1-74-645-3540-20/that_was_then/
   people/stephen_leacock_obit

STRUCTURE:

1. This essay has two main parts. Where do they join? How do they
   differ?
2. We begin with Jiggins. How is his story organized? Were you surprised at his death in paragraph 9? Why? What literary device
   lies behind this effect? How does the death of Jiggins lead into
   Leacock's main argument?

3. Are Leacock's health tips given in order of application?
4. What is our first clue that Leacock's *process analysis* is meant more to entertain than to instruct?

STYLE:

1. Leacock writes "eat" ten times in paragraph 25. Read the passage aloud in class, with feeling. Is this repetition accidental? What effect does it have? In which other paragraph does Leacock exploit repetition?
2. Paragraph 25 states, "That will gluten you, good and solid." What effect does Leacock's unusual use of "gluten" have here?
3. Reduction to absurdity is a comic device Leacock often uses, as in the "bacilli" as insects to swat, or as a favourite dog run over by a car. Where else in this essay has he reduced something to total absurdity?

IDEAS FOR DISCUSSION AND WRITING:

1. Do you have the "Health Habit," like Jiggins, or do you prefer comfort and luxury, like our narrator? Give reasons.
2. Update Leacock's argument for our times. Which kinds of "Health Mania" would you drop? Which would you keep? Which might you add?
3. To women in the class: Why does Leacock refer only to men pursuing the "Health Mania"? Give a *process analysis* of your own actions to keep healthy and fit.
4. **PROCESS IN WRITING:** *Write a* process analysis *of how to reach old age in good health. First brainstorm or freewrite, then do a fast discovery draft. When it has cooled off, analyze it: Are the steps of your process in order? Are the instructions clear for your intended* AUDIENCE? *Have you supplied examples? Revise accordingly. Now sharpen word choice as well. Heighten* TRANSITIONS. *Cut deadwood. Finally, test the prose aloud before printing out your best version.*

Note: See also the Topics for Writing on the Online Learning Centre at www. mcgrawhill.ca/olc/conrad.

PROCESS IN WRITING: GUIDELINES

Follow at least some of these steps in writing your essay of process analysis (your teacher may suggest which ones).

1. Spend time deciding which topic you like best, so your motivation will increase your performance.
2. Visualize your audience (see step 6 below), and choose the level of terminology accordingly.
3. Fill a page with brief notes. Scan and sort them to choose the steps of your process analysis, and their order.
4. Write a rapid first draft, not stopping now to revise or edit. If you do notice a word that needs replacing or a passage that needs work, insert a signal so you can find and fix it later.
5. When this draft has cooled off, look it over. Are all steps of the process given? Do TRANSITIONS introduce them? In technical topics, have you defined terms that may puzzle your audience? Revise accordingly.
6. Now share the second draft with a group of classmates. Do they believe they could actually follow your directions? If not, revise.
7. If you have consulted books or periodicals to write this paper, follow standard practice in quoting and in documenting your sources. Remember that plagiarism is a serious offence.
8. As you produce your good copy, edit for things like spelling and punctuation before printing off your best version.

CP

"It is time that I tell the story from where I stood—literally in the middle of the slaughter for weeks on end."

    —*Lt.-Gen. Roméo Dallaire, with Major Brent Beardsley,* "Cri de coeur"

ARGUMENTATION
AND PERSUASION

THEREFORE....

So far the essays in this book have taken many paths in developing their subject. They have narrated events, they have described, they have explained, and some have entertained. But you have surely realized that in one way or another, whatever else they do, almost all the selections have tried to make a point. After all, an essay without a point is "pointless." The very use of a thesis statement implies a main idea or opinion. In this final chapter, we now focus more closely on how the writer makes that point. The process takes two complementary forms: *argumentation* and *persuasion*.

ARGUMENTATION

This word has a broad set of meanings, but here we will consider it the writer's attempt to convince the reader mostly *through logic*. This stance implies respect: it considers the reader a mature individual capable of independent thought. It assumes the reader will also respect the thoughts of the writer, if those thoughts are presented in a logical way. In summary, the writer and reader are *partners*: since the writer does not play on the reader's emotions, the reader considers the argument with a more open mind. If the logic makes sense, the reader may be convinced. Argumentation through logic takes two opposite forms, *deduction* and *induction*. Let's look at each.

DEDUCTION

Deduction accepts a general principle as true, then applies it to specific cases. For over two thousand years logicians have expressed this process in a formula called the *syllogism*. Here's a well-known example:

> *Major premise:* All men are mortal.
> *Minor premise:* Socrates is a man.
> *Conclusion:* Socrates is mortal.

This chain of reasoning is about as foolproof as any: since no human in the history of the world has yet lived much longer than a century, we feel safe in assuming that no one ever will; therefore "all men are mortal." And since all historical records about Socrates portray him as a man—not, say, as a rock or horse or tree—we accept the minor premise as well. Logic tells us that if both the major and minor premises are true, then the conclusion will inevitably be true as well.

But now let's look at a syllogism whose logic is not as clear:

> Major premise: Progress is good.
> Minor premise: The automobile represents progress.
> Conclusion: The automobile is good.

At first glance the argument may seem all right: it certainly reflects values common in our society. But let's examine the major premise, the foundation on which all the rest is built: is it true that "progress is good"? Well, how do we know until we define "progress"? Is it more jobs? More production? More cars? Higher sales? More consumption? A rising stock market? Or are all these the opposite of true "progress" because our natural resources are dwindling, our highways are choked with traffic, our lakes and forests are dying of acid rain, the greenhouse effect is disrupting our climate and around the world several species of life per hour are becoming extinct? Our values will determine our response.

If we cannot agree on what "progress" is, how can we say it is "good"? And how could we go on to our minor premise, saying that "the automobile represents progress"? How could we build even further on this shaky foundation, claiming in our conclusion that "the automobile is good"? Within its own framework the argument may be "valid" (or logical), but only those who accept the original premise will view the conclusion as true. Those who do not will reject it as false.

And that is the problem with deduction: not always can we agree on premises. A thousand years ago society ran almost entirely on deduction: the King or the Church or our parents told us what to believe, and we simply applied those principles to any case that came up. But in our millennium many of us do not accept being told what to think. Not only do many people now question systems of belief such as Marxism or codes of religion, but scientists even question the previously accepted "laws" of nature. How is a person to know what is true? It is therefore no coincidence that most contemporary essays argue not through deduction but through induction.

INDUCTION

We have discussed how deduction applies a general rule to explain particular cases. Induction is the opposite: it first observes particular cases, then from them formulates a general rule. This is the basis of the scientific way, the procedure that enables humans to conquer disease, multiply food production and travel to the moon. It can produce faulty results, just like deduction, but the open mind required to use it appeals to our modern sensibilities. Let's take an example:

> After a summer in the factory Joan thought she could afford a car, so the week before school began she bought a sporty red three-year-old Japanese model. Speeding around town with the stereo turned up was

so much fun that she didn't mind the $350-a-month payments. But when the insurance company hit her for $2800 as a new driver, her savings took a dive. Each month she found herself paying $150 for gas and $200 for parking. A fall tuneup set her back $180, and new tires $500. Then came the repairs: $250 for brakes, $325 for a clutch, $225 for an exhaust system, and $380 for a timing belt. In desperation Joan took a part-time job selling shoes. That helped her bank book but took her study time. Two weeks after exams, holding a feeble grade report in her hand, Joan decided to sell the car. Nobody could have told her to, since, like most people, she likes to make up her own mind. But the long string of evidence did the teaching: now Joan knows, through *induction*, that as a student she cannot afford a car.

Induction is not infallible. Conceivably Joan's next car might never need a repair. Next year insurance might somehow drop from $2800 to, say, $75. Gas stations might sell premium for 10 cents a litre, and on Boxing Day a good tire might cost $1.99. Anything is possible. But Joan feels that the consistency of her results—the steady high cost of her car ownership—will *probably* not change. Likewise, the scientist believes that her or his years of research have yielded results that will not be disproved by the very next experiment. But in all humility both Joan and the scientist must consider the new principle not a fact, not an unchangeable law, but simply an idea with a very high probability of being true.

Finally, suppose that Joan analyzes her experience in an essay. If she sets up her paper as most essayists do, we will read her thesis statement near the beginning—even though the principle it states is the *result* of the evidence still to come. This positioning is not a flaw of logic: Joan simply *introduces* the main idea so we can see where we are going, then tells us how she arrived at it, letting her evidence lead inductively toward the main point which will be restated at the end. You will find this pattern at work in several of this chapter's inductive essays, for example the one by Martin Hocking.

You will also find that, although deduction and induction represent opposite methods of logic, sometimes both are used in the same argument (when the writer's original opinion is confirmed by the evidence). This does not necessarily mean weakness in logic either. Another link between these opposites is that most principles which we accept as true, and upon which we base our own deductions, originated in someone else's induction. (Newton arrived inductively at his theory of gravity, through evidence such as the famous apple that fell on his head; almost all of us now believe Newton and his theory without waiting for an apple, or anything else, to fall on our own heads.) Similarly, a conclusion we derive from our own induction might become the premise of someone else's deduction—a link in an ongoing chain of logic. To keep this chain from breaking, the individual has a double task: to evaluate any links provided by others, then to make her or his own link as strong as possible.

PERSUASION

We have just seen how *argumentation* seeks to convince through logic. But, whether deductive or inductive, is logic enough? Now let's look at the complementary approach of *persuasion*, which attempts to convince through emotion. A century of inductive research into psychology has shown that we humans are seldom rational. Even when we think we are "reasoning," we are often building arguments merely to justify what we thought or felt already. It is possible to write an argumentative essay with enough restraint to be almost purely logical. But to most people the effort is difficult and unnatural, requiring a great deal of revision, and the result may seem cold and uninviting to those who have not spent years reading the almost pure argumentation of scholarly journals. Most professional writers would say that a little feeling and a little colour can help an essay. But how do we take this approach without slipping into dishonesty? Let's look now at the major techniques of *persuasion*—both their uses and abuses.

Word choice: Is a person "slim," "thin" or "skinny"? Is a governmental expenditure an "investment," a "cost," a "waste" or a "boondoggle"? Is an oil spill an "incident," an "accident," a "mistake," a "crime" or an "environmental tragedy"? Essayists tend to choose the term that reflects their feeling and the feeling they hope to encourage in the readers. While deliberate choice of words is one of the central tasks of all writers, including essayists, let's not abuse the process. Bertrand Russell once quipped, "I am firm; you are stubborn; he is pig-headed." If too many of your word choices follow the model of "pig-headed," you will alarm an alert reader and unfairly overwhelm a careless one.

Example: Although examples form the basis of logical induction, they can also add colour and feeling to a persuasive essay. Choose vivid ones. An attempt to show old people as active may be helped by the example of your grandmother who skis. But avoid dubious cases like that of the man in Azerbaijan who is rumoured to have ridden a horse at age 155.

Repetition: Although we try to cut accidental repetition from our writing (as in the case of one student who used the word "tire" 55 times in an essay about, you guessed it, tires), intentional repetition can build feeling. Stephen Leacock builds emphasis by using the word "eat" over and over in paragraph 25 of his essay (see p. 340), and in paragraphs 14–17 of her selection (see pp. 375–376) Joy Kogawa builds feeling by starting a whole string of sentences with the contraction "it's."

Hyperbole (exaggeration): A humorist can exaggerate and get away with it, as Stephen Leacock does when he tells us "How to Live to Be 200." By contrast, an essay with a serious subject should stay strictly with the truth.

Analogy and figures of speech: You have seen in Chapter 6 how we can suggest a point by comparing one thing with another from a different category, such as a monster with the forestry industry, or a flower with a new baby. Analogies, and their shorter cousins similes and metaphors, are powerful tools of persuasion; avoid abusing them through name-calling. Think twice before casting a politician as a dinosaur, entrepreneurs as piranhas or police officers as gorillas. Remember, above all, that neither analogies nor figures of speech are logical proof of anything.

Irony: When in Chapter 2 the poet Goran Simic tells of his job moving clothes in a warehouse; when in Chapter 4 Naheed Mustafa covers herself with the traditional *hijab* in order to be free; when in Chapter 5 Stephanie Nolen shows us an African grandmother who now has to raise a second generation of children; and when in this chapter Rita Schindler "thanks" her son's assailants for not killing him—we feel the power of irony. A writer can use this device for a lifetime without exhausting its emotional power; yet irony lends itself less easily to abuses than do many tools of persuasion, for both its use and its appreciation demand a certain exercise of intelligence.

Appeal to authority or prestige: Opponents of nuclear weapons love to quote Albert Einstein on their dangers; after all, since his discoveries made this hardware possible, he should know. We also invite our reader to believe what a famous economist says about money, what a judge says about law, or what an educator says about education. This approach appeals to our reader's ethical sense: he or she believes these people know the facts and tell the truth. But avoid the common abuse of quoting people on matters outside their competence—a terrorist on peace, a disgraced politician on honesty or a convicted murderer on religion.

Fright: You can be sure that a frightened reader is an interested reader, for fright is personal: what you say in your essay could be important! Avoid cheap effects, though. Frighten a reader only with facts that really are scary (such as the number of times computer error nearly launched a third World War).

Climax: Whatever your argument, don't trail off from strong to weak. After a good introduction, drop to your least important or least dramatic point, then progress upward to your strongest. This very rise produces an emotion in the reader, like that of the concertgoer who thrills to the final dramatic chords of "The Hallelujah Chorus."

Cause and Effect: Review the introduction to Chapter 4. Note how answers to the question "why?" can themselves cause emotion in the reader: the sudden resolution of our doubts can be a deep and satisfying experience.

Comparison and Contrast: Review the introduction to Chapter 5, which discusses how a strong contrast—such as culture shock—can create feeling.

PLAYING FAIR IN ARGUMENTATION AND PERSUASION

We have looked at some abuses both of argumentation and of persuasion. Now read the following communication, an actual chain letter that arrived one day in the mail. (Versions of it also circulate on the Internet; you may have seen one.) What attempts does it make at *deduction* or *induction*? Are they logical? What attempts does it make at *persuasion*? Are they fair? (For your information, the person who received this letter did not send it on. So far he has not died or been fired—but then, neither has he won a lottery!)

> **KISS SOMEONE YOU LOVE WHEN YOU GET THIS LETTER AND MAKE SOME MAGIC**
>
> This paper has been sent to you for good luck. The original copy is in New England. It has been around the world nine times. The luck has sent it to you. You will receive good luck within four days of receiving this letter, provided you send it back out. THIS IS NO JOKE. You will receive it in the mail. Send copies to people that you think need good luck. Don't send money as fate has no price. Do not keep this letter. It must leave your hands within 96 hours. An R.A.F. officer became a hero. Joe Elliot received $40,000, and lost it because he broke the chain. While in the Philippines, Gene Welch lost his wife six days after receiving this letter. He failed to circulate the letter. However, before her death she had won $50,000.00 in a lottery. The money was transferred to him four days after he decided to mail out this letter. Please send twenty copies of this letter and see what happens in four days. The chain came from Venezuela and was written in South America. Since the copy must make a tour of the world you must make copies and send them to your friends and associates. After a few days you will get a surprise. This is true even if you are not superstitious. Do note the following: Constantine Dias received the chain in 1953. He asked his

secretary to type twenty copies and send them out. A few days later he won a lottery of $2,000,000. Aria Daddit, an office employee, received the letter and forgot that it had to leave his hands within 96 hours. He lost his job. Later, finding the letter again, he mailed out twenty copies. A few days later he got a better job. Dalen Fairchild received the letter and not believing, threw it away. Nine days later he died. PLEASE SEND NO MONEY. PLEASE DON'T IGNORE THIS. IT WORKS!

Note: No essay in this chapter adopts a stance of pure logic to the exclusion of emotion, or of pure emotion to the exclusion of logic. The nine essays represent different proportions of both elements, and are arranged in approximate order from most argumentative to most persuasive.

For more examples of argumentation, see these essays in other chapters:

Karen Von Hahn, "Self-Serving Propaganda," p. 66
Jeffrey Rosenthal, "Poker Power," p. 71
Doris Anderson, "The 51-Per-Cent Minority," p. 191
Catharine Parr Traill, "Remarks of Security of Person and Property in Canada," p. 222
Lawrence Hill, "Black + White = Black," p. 228

For more examples of persuasion, see these essays in other chapters:

Nathalie Petrowski, "The Seven-Minute Life of Marc Lépine," p. 169
Drew Hayden Taylor, "This Boat Is My Boat," p. 216
Samantha Bennett, "It's Not Just the Weather That's Cooler in Canada," p. 264

MARTIN HOCKING

Capping the Great Cup Debate

Few scientists could be better equipped to investigate the subject of our selection than Martin Hocking. With a Ph.D. in organic chemistry from the University of Southampton (1963), experience as research chemist in industry, then extensive research and publication as professor of chemistry at the University of Victoria, Hocking has been a prominent voice in his field, even after his 2004 retirement. He has advised government on scientific issues; has long taught industrial and environmental chemistry; holds many patents in the fields of monomers, process chemistry and medicine; has over 70 scientific papers to his credit; and has published a major reference book: Handbook of Chemical Technology and Pollution Control *(third edition, 2005). It was his comparative analysis in the journal* Science *that in 1991 sparked debate on the environmental effects of paper cups and foam cups. Hocking concluded that, contrary to public opinion, foam was better. Some scientists questioned his emission figures and his view of paper mill energy use; others commended his open revealing of data sources, a practice not all scientists follow, and the relevance of his "cradle-to-grave" scope: from logging the raw resources to discarding the old cups in landfills. Then Hocking adapted and condensed his article for a general audience; in 1991 the* Globe and Mail *published this selection. In 2000 Hocking again made the news: circulation of fresh air is so slow in the new airliners, he announced in a report, that passengers risk exposure to colds, flu, measles, chicken pox and even tuberculosis. The air industry and the House of Lords reacted angrily, but on the BBC Hocking defended his findings with pertinent statistics.*

T he polystyrene foam cup has long suffered contempt from
       an environmentally aware public that assumes paper cups
       are ecologically friendlier. It's easy to understand why: paper
cups are made out of a wood product, a renewable resource, and
therefore would seem to be the proper conservationist choice.

In fact, foam cups are proving to be the environmentally better
choice.

For one thing, people overlook the fact that logging necessary
for the paper industry has adverse effects on the landscape that
range from the construction of roads to clear-cutting practices that
typically increase the likelihood of flood and drought in immediate
watershed areas.

In addition, a review of other factors does not support the use of
paper. A comparative analysis of paper versus polystyrene conducted
by us at the University of Victoria leads to the inevitable conclusion
that foam cups are better from a range of standpoints.

Here are the principal findings of the analysis:

HYDROCARBONS

The extraction and delivery of oil and gas hydrocarbons have a
significant impact on sensitive ecosystems. A polyfoam cup is made
entirely from hydrocarbons, but a similar amount of hydrocarbons
are also used to produce a paper cup.

Paper cups are made from bleached pulp, which in turn is
obtained from wood chips. Although bark, some wood waste, and
organic residues from chemical pulping are burned to supply part
of the energy required in papermaking, fuel oil or gas is used to provide much of the rest. Even more petroleum is needed if the paper
cup has a plastic or wax coating.

INORGANIC CHEMICALS

In the making of paper cups, relatively small amounts of sodium
hydroxide or sodium sulphate are needed for chemical pulping
makeup requirements, since the recycling of these in the kraft pulping process is quite efficient. But larger amounts of chlorine, sodium
hydroxide, sodium chlorate, sulphuric acid, sulphur dioxide and

calcium hydroxide are normally used on a once-through basis to the extent of 160 to 200 kilograms per metric ton of pulp.

9   The total non-recycled chemical requirement works out to an average of about 1.8 grams per cup.

10   Polystyrene is far superior to wood pulp for cup construction; only about one-sixth as much material is needed to produce a foam cup. Chemical requirements for the polystyrene foam cup are small because several of the stages in its preparation use catalysts that nudge the process along without being consumed themselves.

11   Alkylation of benzene with ethene (ethylene) also uses aluminum chloride catalytically to the extent of about 10 kilograms per metric ton of ethylbenzene produced.

12   The spent aluminum chloride is later neutralized with roughly the same amount of sodium hydroxide. Further small amounts of sulphuric acid and sodium hydroxide are also consumed to give a total chemical requirement of about 33 kilograms per metric ton of polystyrene.

13   This works out to 0.05 grams per cup, or about 3 per cent of the chemical requirement of the paper cup.

UTILITY CONSUMPTION

14   In terms of energy consumption, polystyrene cups also appear to come out ahead. One paper cup consumes about 12 times as much steam, 36 times as much electricity, and twice as much cooling water as one polystyrene foam cup, while producing 58 times the volume of waste water.

15   The contaminants present in the waste water from pulping and bleaching operations are removed to varying degrees, but the residuals (with the exception of metal salts) still amount to 10 to 100 times those present in the waste-water streams from polystyrene processing.

AIR POLLUTION

16   The wholesale price of a paper cup is about 2.5 times that of polyfoam since it consumes more in terms of raw materials and energy. But their respective purchase prices are not so closely linked to the environmental costs of productions and recycling or final disposal.

Air emissions total 22.7 kilograms per metric ton of bleached pulp compared to about 53 kilograms per metric ton of polystyrene.

On a per-cup basis, however, this comparison becomes 0.23 grams for paper versus 0.08 grams for polyfoam.

17

EMISSIONS

In terms of mass, the 43 kilograms of pentane employed as the blowing agent for each metric ton of the foamable beads used to make polystyrene foam cups is the largest single emission to air from the two technologies.

18

Pentane's atmospheric lifetime is estimated to be seven years or less, about a tenth that of the chlorofluorocarbons formerly used in some foamable beads. Unlike the chlorofluorocarbons, pentane would tend to cause a net increase in ozone concentrations, both at ground level and in the stratosphere.

19

However, its contributions to atmospheric ozone and as a "greenhouse effect" gas are almost certainly less than those of the methane losses generated from disposal of paper cups in landfill sites.

20

If the six metric tons of paper equivalent to a metric ton of polystyrene completely biodegrade anaerobically in a landfill, theoretically the paper could generate 2,370 kilograms of methane along with 3,260 kilograms of carbon dioxide.

21

Both are "greenhouse gases" that contribute to global warming.

22

RECYCLING

The technical side of recycle capability with polystyrene foam is straightforward. All that is required is granulation and washing, followed by hotair drying and re-extrusion of the resin for re-use. Though recycled resin may not be used in food applications, this only partially limits the many possible uses for recycled polystyrene products.

23

Such uses are in packaging materials, insulation, flotation billets, patio furniture and drainage tiles.

24

An improved collection infrastructure is all that is needed to make this option a more significant reality and convert this perceived negative aspect of polyfoam use to a positive one.

25

26   Paper cups use a non–water soluble hot melt or solvent-based adhesive to hold the parts together.

27   For this reason, cups are technically excluded from paper recycling programs because the adhesive resin cannot be removed during repulping.

28   If the paper is coated with a plastic film or wax, this too prevents recycling, at least for renewed paper products.

FINAL DISPOSAL

29   Polystyrene is relatively inert to decomposition when discarded in landfill. However, there is also increasing evidence that disposal of paper to landfill does not necessarily result in degradation or biodecomposition, particularly in arid regions.

30   In wet landfills, where degradation occurs, the paper cup produces methane, a gas which has five to 20 times greater global-warming effect than carbon dioxide. Water-soluble fragments of cellulose from the decomposition also contribute biochemical oxygen demand to leachate (any water that percolates through the land-filled waste) from the landfill.

31   Leachate may be treated to remove contaminants to control environmental impact on discharge, or may be lost to surface waters or underground aquifers (a porous rock layer that holds water) to exacerbate the oxygen demand in these raw water sources.

32   Thus, as a result of our analysis, it would appear that polystyrene foam cups are the ecologically better choice.

33   At the very least, they appear to be no worse than paper in one-use applications, contrary to the instinctive consumer impression.

EXPLORATIONS:

Peter Kruus, *Chemicals in the Environment*
Rachel Carson, *Silent Spring*
Chris Turner, *The Geography of Hope: A Tour of the World We Need*
Thomas Homer-Dixon, *The Upside of Down: Catastrophe, Creativity and the Renewal of Civilization*
http://www.ec.gc.ca/ecocycle

http://communications.uvic.ca/ring/01oct04/air.html
http://news.bbc.co.uk/1/hi/health/1523619.stm

STRUCTURE:

1. How does the opening prepare us for Hocking's argument?
2. Identify the THESIS STATEMENT.
3. Hocking's argument is a model *comparison and contrast* of paper and foam cups, organized *point by point*. Identify each of these major points.
4. Find three passages where Hocking reasons through *cause and effect*.
5. Do the subtitles help? Have you tried subtitles yourself?

STYLE:

1. What AUDIENCE does Hocking write for in this condensation of a scientific journal article? Are the many technical terms a barrier to these readers? Are they to you? Why or why not?

ARGUMENTATION AND PERSUASION:

1. Written by a scientist, "Capping the Great Cup Debate" is the most *argumentative* essay of this chapter. Can you find any passage at all that appeals to *emotion* rather than *reason*? Does all the logic reduce your interest in this essay, or does the quality of thought increase it?
2. As the introduction to this chapter suggests, science is based on *induction*. In saying "A comparative analysis ... leads to the inevitable conclusion that foam cups are better" (para. 4), Hocking in fact labels his argument as *inductive*. Is he right? How fully does he base his conclusion on evidence? Does he successfully avoid reasoning from prior values or assumptions?
3. How much of this argument consists of *examples*? How many are numeric (statistics)?
4. *Comparison and contrast, cause and effect,* massive *examples* and *process analysis* all help Hocking make his point. Do you think he planned

to use these all, or did some just appear as he wrote? How fully *should* we organize before writing?

IDEAS FOR DISCUSSION AND WRITING:

1. Did you think paper cups were better for the environment? Do you still, or did Hocking change your mind? Tell why.

2. "Think globally, act locally," say environmentalists. Consider the pollution caused by disposable pens, lighters, razors, towels and tissues, plastic wrap, diapers, paper plates—and cups, whether paper or foam. What "acts" could you perform to help "globally"?

3. Name one act you already perform to reduce pollution.

4. Is science outside the realm of values? Or are scientists responsible for the good and bad effects of their discoveries? Defend your view with examples, including Hocking.

5. Which is more important to you right now, the economy or the environment? Which will seem more important by the time you have grandchildren? What implications can you *deduce* from your answer?

6. **PROCESS IN WRITING:** *At the library, read and take notes on how vitamin C affects humans, making sure your evidence comes from the work of scientists, not health faddists. Let this collected evidence lead to your* THESIS STATE-MENT: *whether or not taking large doses of vitamin C improves our health. Now write your argument of induction, using any form(s) of organization that work, but basing your argument very heavily on evidence. (Your teacher may advise whether to document informally or use full MLA style.) Proofread any quotations word for word against the originals, and be sure to enclose them, even short phrases of two or three words, in quotation marks. Now read your draft aloud. Does its* STYLE *promote thought or does it promote feeling? Replace any loaded or very* INFORMAL *words with more* OBJECTIVE *ones. State your conclusion clearly. Finally, edit for things like spelling and punctuation as you produce the final version.*

Note: See also the Topics for Writing on the Online Learning Centre at www. mcgrawhill.ca/olc/conrad.

KILDARE DOBBS

The Scar*

Kildare Dobbs was born in Meerut, Uttar Pradesh, India in 1923, was educated in Ireland, then during the Second World War spent five years in the Royal Navy. After the war he joined the British Colonial Service in Tanganyika, then, after earning an M.A. at Cambridge, came in 1952 to Canada. Here Dobbs has been a teacher, editor for Macmillan, managing editor of Saturday Night, *and book editor of the* Toronto Star. *He was one of the founders, in 1956, of the* Tamarack Review. *He is also the author of many books, among them* Running to Paradise *(essays, 1962, winner of the Governor General's Award);* Canada *(an illustrated travel book, 1964);* Reading the Time *(essays, 1968);* Pride and Fall *(short fiction, 1981);* Anatolian Suite *(travel, 1989);* Ribbon of Highway *(travel, 1992);* The Eleventh Hour: Poems for the Third Millennium *(1997);* Casablanca, the Poem *(1997);* Historic Canada *(1998); and* Running the Rapids: A Writer's Life *(2005). Many of Dobbs' books are about faraway places, whether travel writing, serious analysis or both mixed. In a millennium project he visited 24 countries, logging over 27,000 miles, filing regular reports by satellite with the CBC. Our own selection, from* Reading the Time, *tells of an event Dobbs was not there to see, yet the vivid details that support his argument show all too clearly what that tragedy must have been like.*

*Editor's title.

1   T his is the story I was told in 1963 by Emiko Okamoto, a young Japanese woman who had come to live in Toronto. She spoke through an interpreter, since at that time she knew no English. It is Emiko's story, although I have had to complete it from other sources.

2   But why am I telling it? Everyone knows how terrible this story is. Everyone knows the truth of what von Clausewitz said: "Force to meet force arms itself with the inventions of art and science." First the bow-and-arrow, then Greek fire, gunpowder, poison-gas—and so on up the lethal scale. These things, we're told, should be considered calmly. No sweat—we should think about the unthinkable, or so Herman Kahn suggests, dispassionately. And he writes: "We do not expect illustrations in a book of surgery to be captioned 'Good health is preferable to this kind of cancer.' Excessive comments such as 'And now there is a lot of blood' or 'This particular cut really hurts' are out of place…. To dwell on such things is morbid." Perhaps the answer to Herman Kahn is that if surgeons hadn't dwelt on those things we wouldn't now have anaesthetics, or artery forceps either, for that matter.

3   To think about thermonuclear war in the abstract is obscene. To think about any kind of warfare with less than the whole of our mind and imagination is obscene. This is the worst treason.

4   Before that morning in 1945 only a few conventional bombs, none of which did any great damage, had fallen on the city. Fleets of U.S. bombers had, however, devastated many cities round about, and Hiroshima had begun a program of evacuation which had reduced its population from 380,000 to some 245,000. Among the evacuees were Emiko and her family.

5   "We were moved out to Otake, a town about an hour's train-ride out of the city," Emiko told me. She had been a fifteen-year-old student in 1945. Fragile and vivacious, versed in the gentle traditions of the tea ceremony and flower arrangement, Emiko still had an air of the frail school-child when I talked with her. Every day, she and her sister Hideko used to commute into Hiroshima to school. Hideko was thirteen. Their father was an antique-dealer and he owned a house in the city, although it was empty now. Tetsuro, Emiko's thirteen-year-old brother, was at the Manchurian front with the Imperial

Army. Her mother was kept busy looking after the children, for her youngest daughter Eiko was sick with heart trouble, and rations were scarce. All of them were undernourished.

The night of August 5, 1945, little Eiko was dangerously ill. She   6
was not expected to live. Everybody took turns watching by her bed, soothing her by massaging her arms and legs. Emiko retired at 8:30 (most Japanese people go to bed early) and at midnight was roused to take her turn with the sick girl. At 2 a.m. she went back to sleep.

While Emiko slept, the *Enola Gay*, a U.S. B-29 carrying the world's   7
first operational atom bomb, was already in the air. She had taken off from the Pacific island of Iwo Jima at 1:45 a.m., and now Captain William Parsons, U.S.N. ordnance expert, was busy in her bomb-hold with the final assembly of Little Boy. Little Boy looked much like an outsize T.N.T. block-buster but the crew knew there was something different about him. Only Parsons and the pilot, Colonel Paul Tibbets, knew exactly in what manner Little Boy was different. Course was set for Hiroshima.

Emiko slept.   8

On board the *Enola Gay* co-pilot Captain Robert Lewis was writing   9
up his personal log. "After leaving Iwo," he recorded, "we began to pick up some low stratus and before very long we were flying on top of an under-cast. Outside of a thin, high cirrus and the low stuff, it's a very beautiful day."

Emiko and Hideko were up at six in the morning. They dressed in   10
the uniform of their women's college—white blouse, quilted hat, and black skirt—breakfasted and packed their aluminum lunch-boxes with white rice and eggs. These they stuffed into their shoulder bags as they hurried for the seven-o'clock train to Hiroshima. Today there would be no classes. Along with many women's groups, high school students, and others, the sisters were going to work on demolition. The city had begun a project of clearance to make fire-breaks in its downtown huddle of wood and paper buildings.

It was a lovely morning.   11

While the two young girls were at breakfast, Captain Lewis, over   12
the Pacific, had made an entry in his log. "We are loaded. The bomb is now alive, and it's a funny feeling knowing it's right in back of you. Knock wood!"

13   In the train Hideko suddenly said she was hungry. She wanted to eat her lunch. Emiko dissuaded her: she'd be much hungrier later on. The two sisters argued, but Hideko at last agreed to keep her lunch till later. They decided to meet at the main station that afternoon and catch the five-o'clock train home. By now they had arrived at the first of Hiroshima's three stations. This was where Hideko got off, for she was to work in a different area from her sister. "Sayonara!" she called. "Goodbye." Emiko never saw her again.

14   There had been an air-raid at 7 a.m., but before Emiko arrived at Hiroshima's main station, two stops farther on, the sirens had sounded the all-clear. Just after eight, Emiko stepped off the train, walked through the station, and waited in the morning sunshine for her streetcar.

15   At about the same moment Lewis was writing in his log. "There'll be a short intermission while we bomb our target."

16   It was hot in the sun. Emiko saw a class-mate and greeted her. Together they moved back into the shade of a high concrete wall to chat. Emiko looked up at the sky and saw, far up in the cloudless blue, a single B-29.

17   It was exactly 8:10 a.m. The other people waiting for the streetcar saw it too and began to discuss it anxiously. Emiko felt scared. She felt that at all costs she must go on talking to her friend. Just as she was thinking this, there was a tremendous greenish-white flash in the sky. It was far brighter than the sun. Emiko afterwards remembered vaguely that there was a roaring or a rushing sound as well, but she was not sure, for just at that moment she lost consciousness.

18   "About 15 seconds after the flash," noted Lewis, 30,000 feet high and several miles away, "there were two very distinct slaps on the ship from the blast and the shock wave. That was all the physical effect we felt. We turned the ship so that we could observe the results."

19   When Emiko came to, she was lying on her face about forty feet away from where she had been standing. She was not aware of any pain. Her first thought was: "I'm alive!" She lifted her head slowly and looked about her. It was growing dark. The air was seething with dust and black smoke. There was a smell of burning. Emiko felt something trickle into her eyes, tasted it in her mouth. Gingerly she put a hand to her head, then looked at it. She saw with a shock that it was covered with blood.

She did not give a thought to Hideko. It did not occur to her that [20] her sister who was in another part of the city could possibly have been in danger. Like most of the survivors, Emiko assumed she had been close to a direct hit by a conventional bomb. She thought it had fallen on the post-office next to the station. With a hurt child's panic, Emiko, streaming with blood from gashes in her scalp, ran blindly in search of her mother and father.

The people standing in front of the station had been burned to [21] death instantly (a shadow had saved Emiko from the flash). The people inside the station had been crushed by falling masonry. Emiko heard their faint cries, saw hands scrabbling weakly from under the collapsed platform. All around her the maimed survivors were running and stumbling away from the roaring furnace that had been a city. She ran with them toward the mountains that ring the landward side of Hiroshima.

From the *Enola Gay*, the strangers from North America looked [22] down at their handiwork. "There, in front of our eyes," wrote Lewis, "was without a doubt the greatest explosion man had ever witnessed. The city was nine-tenths covered with smoke of a boiling nature, which seemed to indicate buildings blowing up, and a large white cloud which in less than three minutes reached 30,000 feet, then went to at least 50,000 feet."

Far below, on the edge of this cauldron of smoke, at a distance [23] of some 2,500 yards from the blast's epicentre, Emiko ran with the rest of the living. Some who could not run limped or dragged themselves along. Others were carried. Many, hideously burned, were screaming with pain; when they tripped they lay where they had fallen. There was a man whose face had been ripped open from mouth to ear, another whose forehead was a gaping wound. A young soldier was running with a foot-long splinter of bamboo protruding from one eye. But these, like Emiko, were the lightly wounded.

Some of the burned people had been literally roasted. Skin hung [24] from their flesh like sodden tissue paper. They did not bleed but plasma dripped from their seared limbs.

The *Enola Gay*, mission completed, was returning to base. Lewis [25] sought words to express his feelings, the feelings of all the crew. "I might say," he wrote, "I might say 'My God! What have we done?'"

26   Emiko ran. When she had reached the safety of the mountain she remembered that she still had her shoulder bag. There was a small first-aid kit in it and she applied ointment to her wounds and to a small cut in her left hand. She bandaged her head.

27   Emiko looked back at the city. It was a lake of fire. All around her the burned fugitives cried out in pain. Some were scorched on one side only. Others, naked and flayed, were burned all over. They were too many to help and most of them were dying. Emiko followed the walking wounded along a back road, still delirious, expecting suddenly to meet her father and mother.

28   The thousands dying by the roadside called feebly for help or water. Some of the more lightly injured were already walking in the other direction, back towards the flames. Others, with hardly any visible wounds, stopped, turned ashy pale, and died within minutes. No one knew then that they were victims of radiation.

29   Emiko reached the suburb of Nakayama.

30   Far off in the *Enola Gay*, Lewis, who had seen none of this, had been writing, "If I live a hundred years, I'll never get those few minutes out of my mind. Looking at Captain Parsons, why he is as confounded as the rest, and he is supposed to have known everything and expected this to happen...."

31   At Nakayama, Emiko stood in line at a depot where riceballs were being distributed. Though it distressed her that the badly maimed could hardly feed themselves, the child found she was hungry. It was about 6 p.m. now. A little farther on, at Gion, a farmer called her by name. She did not recognize him, but it seemed he came monthly to her home to collect manure. The farmer took Emiko by the hand, led her to his own house, where his wife bathed her and fed her a meal of white rice. Then the child continued on her way. She passed another town where there were hundreds of injured. The dead were being hauled away in trucks. Among the injured a woman of about forty-five was waving frantically and muttering to herself. Emiko brought this woman a little water in a pumpkin leaf. She felt guilty about it; the schoolgirls had been warned not to give water to the seriously wounded. Emiko comforted herself with the thought that the woman would die soon anyway.

At Koi, she found standing-room in a train. It was heading for ³² Otake with a full load of wounded. Many were put off at Ono, where there was a hospital; and two hours later the train rolled into Otake station. It was around 10 p.m.

A great crowd had gathered to look for their relations. It was a ³³ nightmare, Emiko remembered years afterwards; people were calling their dear kinfolk by name, searching frantically. It was necessary to call them by name, since most were so disfigured as to be unrecognizable. Doctors in the town council offices stitched Emiko's head-wounds. The place was crowded with casualties lying on the floor. Many died as Emiko watched.

The town council authorities made a strange announcement. They ³⁴ said a new and mysterious kind of bomb had fallen in Hiroshima. People were advised to stay away from the ruins.

Home at midnight, Emiko found her parents so happy to see her ³⁵ that they could not even cry. They could only give thanks that she was safe. Then they asked, "Where is your sister?"

For ten long days, while Emiko walked daily one and a half miles ³⁶ to have her wounds dressed with fresh gauze, her father searched the rubble of Hiroshima for his lost child. He could not have hoped to find her alive. All, as far as the eye could see, was a desolation of charred ashes and wreckage, relieved only by a few jagged ruins and by the seven estuarial rivers that flowed through the waste delta. The banks of these rivers were covered with the dead and in the rising tidal waters floated thousands of corpses. On one broad street in the Hakushima district the crowds who had been thronging there were all naked and scorched cadavers. Of thousands of others there was no trace at all. A fire several times hotter than the surface of the sun had turned them instantly to vapour.

On August 11 came the news that Nagasaki had suffered the same ³⁷ fate as Hiroshima; it was whispered that Japan had attacked the United States mainland with similar mysterious weapons. With the lavish circumstantiality of rumour, it was said that two out of a fleet of six-engined trans-Pacific bombers had failed to return. But on August 15, speaking for the first time over the radio to his people, the Emperor Hirohito announced his country's surrender. Emiko heard him. No more bombs! she thought. No more fear! The family did not learn till June the following year that this very day young Tetsuro had been killed in action in Manchuria.

38   Emiko's wounds healed slowly. In mid-September they had closed with a thin layer of pinkish skin. There had been a shortage of antiseptics and Emiko was happy to be getting well. Her satisfaction was short-lived. Mysteriously she came down with diarrhoea and high fever. The fever continued for a month. Then one day she started to bleed from the gums, her mouth and throat become acutely inflamed, and her hair started to fall out. Through her delirium the child heard the doctors whisper by her pillow that she could not live. By now the doctors must have known that ionizing radiation caused such destruction of the blood's white cells that victims were left with little or no resistance against infection.

39   Yet Emiko recovered.

40   The wound on her hand, however, was particularly troublesome and did not heal for a long time.

41   As she got better, Emiko began to acquire some notion of the fearful scale of the disaster. Few of her friends and acquaintances were still alive. But no one knew precisely how many had died in Hiroshima. To this day the claims of various agencies conflict.

42   According to General Douglas MacArthur's headquarters, there were 78,150 dead and 13,083 missing. The United States Atomic Bomb Casualty Commission claims there were 79,000 dead. Both sets of figures are probably far too low. There's reason to believe that at the time of the surrender Japanese authorities lied about the number of survivors, exaggerating it to get extra medical supplies. The Japanese welfare ministry's figures of 260,000 dead and 163,263 missing may well be too high. But the very order of such discrepancies speaks volumes about the scale of the catastrophe. The dead were literally uncountable.

43   This appalling toll of human life had been exacted from a city that had been prepared for air attack in a state of full wartime readiness. All civil-defence services had been overwhelmed from the first moment and it was many hours before any sort of organized rescue and relief could be put into effect.

It's true that single raids using so-called conventional weapons   44
on other cities such as Tokyo and Dresden inflicted far greater
casualties. And that it could not matter much to a victim whether he
was burnt alive by a fire-storm caused by phosphorus, or by napalm
or by nuclear fission. Yet in the whole of human history so savage
a massacre had never before been inflicted with a single blow. And
modern thermonuclear weapons are upwards of 1,000 times more
powerful and deadly than the Hiroshima bomb.

The white scar I saw on Emiko's small, fine-boned hand was a tiny   45
metaphor, a faint but eloquent memento.

EXPLORATIONS:

Kildare Dobbs, *Reading the Time*
John Hershey, *Hiroshima*
Ernie Regehr and Simon Rosenblum, eds., *The Road to Peace*
John Whittier Treat, *Writing Ground Zero: Japanese Literature and the
    Atomic Bomb*
Paul W. Tibbets, *The Tibbets Story*
http://www.acepilots.com/usaaf_tibbets.html
http://www.csi.ad.jp/ABOMB
http://www.dannen.com/decision
http://www.lclark.edu/~history/HIROSHIMA
http://www.doug-long.com
http://www.dannen.com/hiroshima_links.html

STRUCTURE:

1. Identify Dobbs' THESIS STATEMENT, the principle from which his
   argument is *deduced*. In what very direct way does the rest of this
   selection teach us to apply that principle?
2. "The Scar" is mostly a *narrative*, in fact two parallel narratives. How
   do the stories of Emiko and of Captain Lewis complement each
   other? How does each focus differently on nuclear war?

3. Dobbs' argument is a short essay enclosing a long narrative. Where does each part join the next? And what is the strategy behind this plan?

STYLE:

1. In his log Captain Lewis writes "it's a very beautiful day" (par. 9), and in paragraph 11 Dobbs adds "It was a lovely morning." What effect do these pleasant words have in the context of the situation? What literary device underlies their power?
2. Captain Lewis writes in his log, "There'll be a short intermission while we bomb our target" (par. 15). Do these words seem peculiar? If so, why?
3. In referring to the first operational nuclear bomb as "Little Boy" (par. 7), what does Dobbs add to the force of his narrative?
4. Paragraphs 23, 24, 27 and 36 are filled with gruesome details that show the effects of "Little Boy." Does this help Dobbs' argument? Do these details spur the reader to oppose nuclear weapons? Or, in their dreadfulness, do they lead the reader to drop the subject and think of other things?
5. What qualifies the SYMBOL of Emiko's scar to close the essay?

ARGUMENTATION AND PERSUASION:

1. Dobbs' argument is *deductive*, based on his opening premise that "To think about thermonuclear war in the abstract is obscene. To think about any kind of warfare with less than the whole of our mind and imagination is obscene. This is the worst treason" (par. 3). Identify five passages in which he shuns abstraction to dwell on the CONCRETE and personal experience of nuclear war. Does he apply his own thesis by using "the whole of [his] mind and imagination"?
2. Point out three passages where Dobbs shows Captain Lewis' abstract view of nuclear war to be "obscene." Does the *contrast* between Lewis' bird's-eye view and Emiko's ground-level view develop Dobbs' premise?

3. Does Dobbs make his point mostly through *argumentation* or *persuasion*? To what extent does he *argue* through objective logic, fact and example? To what extent does he *persuade* through IRONY, loaded words, fright or other appeals to emotion?

4. In the closing, why does Dobbs shift from specific examples to generalizations and statistics (pars. 42–44)?

IDEAS FOR DISCUSSION AND WRITING:

1. Albert Einstein, discoverer of the mathematics behind the atomic bomb, said that if he had foreseen the results of his work, he would have chosen to be a shoemaker. Do you hold Einstein and the scientists who worked on "Little Boy" responsible for the carnage in Hiroshima? Or should the scientist pursue abstract truth and leave the application to others?

2. All the rest of his life, Paul Tibbets, who had piloted the *Enola Gay* on her deadly mission, believed he had done the right thing: dropping the atomic bomb on Japan to end the war and save the lives of American soldiers. Yet in 2007 when he died at age 92, he requested that his ashes be scattered on the Atlantic Ocean, so there would be no gravesite that would give protestors a place to demonstrate. How do you explain the PARADOX in his thinking?

3. The Cold War and the arms race between East and West are said to be over. Can we stop dreading nuclear weapons and war now? How dangerous is the new post-9/11 terrorism compared to the old arms race? Give *examples*.

4. In her book *A Matter of Survival: Canada in the 21st Century*, the Canadian economist Diane Francis states, "Already a global government has formed through the auspices of the United Nations and the G-7 process." Do you believe her? Would a true global government prevent war? To what extent could you see Canada functioning as the "police" of such a global government, through its military or peacekeeping missions?

5. **PROCESS IN WRITING:** *Politicians often state that one letter received from a citizen is worth a thousand votes. Decide whether you think Canada should spend more or less on its military. Now write to the Minister of*

Defence, arguing your point deductively. *Apply your premise to a specific example or examples, such as tanks, fighter planes, submarines, destroyers, military bases, the pay rate of personnel, etc. As you look over your "discovery draft," see whether you have specialized in either* argumentation *or* persuasion. *If your treatment seems too extreme, modify it in your second draft with a dose of the other approach, to produce a combined treatment like that of Dobbs. In your final draft edit for conciseness (the best letters to politicians are short). Finally, send your e-mail or letter (you need no stamp to mail a letter to any member of Parliament).*

Note: See also the Topics for Writing on the Online Learning Centre at www. mcgrawhill.ca/olc/conrad.

JOY KOGAWA

Grinning and Happy*

*With three published books of poetry to her credit—*The Splintered Moon *(1967),* A Choice of Dreams *(1974) and* Jericho Road *(1977)—Joy Kogawa had become a respected minor poet. But in 1981 she caused a sensation with her first novel.* Obasan *represented a new step for Kogawa as a writer and as a person: in it she explored her own past and one of the most serious injustices of Canadian history. Born in Vancouver in 1935, Kogawa was a child during the Second World War when the federal government classified Japanese-Canadians as "enemy aliens." Her parents' house in Vancouver was seized, and the family was moved first to a relocation camp in Slocan, B.C., then to the sugar-beet fields of southern Alberta, which are the setting of our selection from the novel. Our narrator is modelled after Kogawa herself, Stephen is the narrator's brother, Obasan is the narrator's silent and suffering aunt and "Aunt Emily" is modelled after Muriel Kitagawa, a Japanese-Canadian activist whose letters Kogawa studied in the National Archives in Ottawa. These same characters returned in* Naomi's Road *(1986), a children's adaptation of* Obasan, *then in Kogawa's 1992 sequel for adults* Itsuka, *about the struggle of Japanese-Canadians to gain redress for the wrongs described in* Obasan. *Her third novel,* The Rain Ascends *(1995), looked to new subject matter, the unmasking of a respected Protestant minister as a sexual abuser of children. Yet its themes echo those of* Obasan *and* Itsuka, *as the sins of the fathers are visited upon new generations. Then in 2000 appeared another book of poems,* A Song of Lilith, *and in 2003 her selected poems,* A Garden of Anchors. *Though her recent work is well regarded, it is still* Obasan *that places Kogawa among our major Canadian writers.*

*Editor's title.

1   There is a folder in Aunt Emily's package containing only one newspaper clipping and an index card with the words "Facts about evacuees in Alberta." The newspaper clipping has a photograph of one family, all smiles, standing around a pile of beets. The caption reads: "Grinning and Happy."

2   **Find Jap Evacuees Best Beet Workers**
    Lethbridge, Alberta, Jan. 22.

3   Japanese evacuees from British Columbia supplied the labour for 65% of Alberta's sugar beet acreage last year, Phil Baker, of Lethbridge, president of the Alberta Sugar Beet Growers Association, stated today.

4   "They played an important part in producing our all-time record crop of 363,000 tons of beets in 1945," he added.

5   Mr. Baker explained Japanese evacuees worked 19,500 acres of beets and German prisoners of war worked 5,000 acres. The labour for the remaining 5,500 acres of Alberta's 30,000 acres of sugar beets was provided by farmers and their families. Some of the heaviest beet yields last year came from farms employing Japanese evacuees.

6   Generally speaking, Japanese evacuees have developed into most efficient beet workers, many of them being better than the transient workers who cared for beets in southern Alberta before Pearl Harbor....

7   Facts about evacuees in Alberta? The fact is I never got used to it and I cannot, I cannot bear the memory. There are some nightmares from which there is no waking, only deeper and deeper sleep.

8   There is a word for it. Hardship. The hardship is so pervasive, so inescapable, so thorough it's a noose around my chest and I cannot move any more. All the oil in my joints has drained out and I have been invaded by dust and grit from the fields and mud is in my

bone marrow. I can't move any more. My fingernails are black from scratching the scorching day and there is no escape.

Aunt Emily, are you a surgeon cutting at my scalp with your fold-   9 ers and your filing cards and your insistence on knowing all? The memory drains down the sides of my face, but it isn't enough, is it? It's your hands in my abdomen, pulling the growth from the lining of my walls, but bring back the anaesthetist turn on the ether clamp down the gas mask bring on the chloroform when will this operation be over Aunt Em?

Is it so bad?   10

Yes.   11

Do I really mind?   12

Yes, I mind. I mind everything. Even the flies. The flies and flies   13 and flies from the cows in the barn and the manure pile—all the black flies that curtain the windows, and Obasan with a wad of toilet paper, spish, then with her bare hands as well, grabbing them and their shocking white eggs and the mosquitoes mixed there with the other insect corpses around the base of the gas lamp.

It's the chicken coop "house" we live in that I mind. The uninsu-   14 lated unbelievable thin-as-a-cotton-dress hovel never before inhabited in winter by human beings. In summer it's a heat trap, an incubator, a dry sauna from which there is no relief. In winter the icicles drip down the inside of the windows and the ice is thicker than bricks at the ledge. The only place that is warm is by the coal stove where we rotate like chickens on a spit and the feet are so cold they stop registering. We eat cloves of roasted garlic on winter nights to warm up.

It's the bedbugs and my having to sleep on the table to escape the nightly attack, and the welts over our bodies. And all the swamp bugs   15 and the dust. It's Obasan uselessly packing all the cracks with rags. And the muddy water from the irrigation ditch which we strain and settle and boil, and the tiny carcasses of water creatures at the bottom of the cup. It's walking in winter to the reservoir and keeping the hole open with the axe and dragging up the water in pails and lugging it back and sometimes the water spills down your boots and your feet are red and itchy for days. And it's everybody taking a bath in the round galvanized tub, then Obasan washing clothes in the water after and standing outside hanging the clothes in the freezing weather where everything instantly stiffens on the line.

16   Or it's standing in the beet field under the maddening sun, standing with my black head a sun-trap even though it's covered, and lying down in the ditch, faint, and the nausea in waves and the cold sweat, and getting up and tackling the next row. The whole field is an oven and there's not a tree within walking distance. We are tiny as insects crawling along the grill and there is no protection anywhere. The eyes are lidded against the dust and the air cracks the skin, the lips crack, Stephen's flutes crack and there is no energy to sing any more anyway.

17   It's standing in the field and staring out at the heat waves that waver and shimmer like see-through curtains over the brown clods and over the tiny distant bodies of Stephen and Uncle and Obasan miles away across the field day after day and not even wondering how this has come about.

18   There she is, Obasan, wearing Uncle's shirt over a pair of dark baggy trousers, her head covered by a straw hat that is held on by a white cloth tied under her chin. She is moving like a tiny earth cloud over the hard clay clods. Her hoe moves rhythmically up down up down, tiny as a toothpick. And over there, Uncle pauses to straighten his back, his hands on his hips. And Stephen farther behind, so tiny I can barely see him.

19   It's hard, Aunt Emily, with my hoe, the blade getting dull and mud-caked as I slash out the Canada thistle, dandelions, crab grass, and other nameless non-beet plants, then on my knees, pulling out the extra beets from the cluster, leaving just one to mature, then three hand spans to the next plant, whack whack, and down on my knees again, pull, flick flick, and on to the end of the long long row and the next and the next and it will never be done thinning and weeding and weeding and weeding. It's so hard and so hot that my tear glands burn out.

20   And then it's cold. The lumps of clay mud stick on my gumboots and weight my legs and the skin under the boots beneath the knees at the level of the calves grows red and hard and itchy from the flap flap of the boots and the fine hairs on my legs grow coarse there and ugly.

21   I mind growing ugly.

I mind the harvest time and the hands and the wrists bound in rags   22
to keep the wrists from breaking open. I lift the heavy mud-clotted
beets out of the ground with the hook like an eagle's beak, thick and
heavy as a nail attached to the top of the sugar-beet knife. Thwack.
Into the beet and yank from the shoulder till it's out of the ground
dragging the surrounding mud with it. Then crack two beets together
till most of the mud drops off and splat, the knife slices into the beet
scalp and the green top is tossed into one pile, the beet heaved onto
another, one more one more one more down the icy line. I cannot
tell about this time, Aunt Emily. The body will not tell.

We are surrounded by a horizon of denim-blue sky with clouds   23
clear as spilled milk that turn pink at sunset. Pink I hear is the colour
of llama's milk. I wouldn't know. The clouds are the shape of our new
prison walls—untouchable, impersonal, random.

There are no other people in the entire world. We work together   24
all day. At night we eat and sleep. We hardly talk anymore. The boxes
we brought from Slocan are not unpacked. The King George/Queen
Elizabeth mugs stay muffled in the *Vancouver Daily Province*. The camera phone does not sing. Obasan wraps layers of cloth around her
feet and her torn sweater hangs unmended over her sagging dress.

Down the miles we are obedient as machines in this odd ballet   25
without accompaniment of flute or song.

"Grinning and happy" and all smiles standing around a pile of   26
beets? That is one telling. It's not how it was.

EXPLORATIONS:

Joy Kogawa,
> *Obasan*
> *Itsuka*

Barry Broadfoot, *Years of Sorrow, Years of Shame: The Story of Japanese
    Canadians in World War II*

Ken Adachi, *The Enemy That Never Was: A History of the Japanese
    Canadians.*

Ann Sunahara, *The Politics of Racism: The Uprooting of Japanese
    Canadians During the Second World War*

Joy Kogawa (video, 1998, 45 min., Sleeping Giant Productions)

http://voices.cla.umn.edu/vg/Bios/entries/kogawa_joy_nakayama.html

http://www.brocku.ca/canadianwomenpoets/Kogawa.htm

http://quarles.unbc.ca/kbeeler_html/research/kog1.html

http://www.najc.ca

http://www.lib.washington.edu/subject/Canada/internment/intro.html

Structure:

1. Why does Kogawa "frame" her argument by citing the newspaper article in both her opening and closing?
2. How does the device of *contrast* help organize this selection?
3. What percentage of *examples* has Kogawa reached in the content of this selection? Is it enough? Do you use enough?
4. How important is *description* to the success of this passage? Give examples.
5. Most THESIS STATEMENTS are placed early in an argument. Why is Kogawa's put in the very last line?

Style:

1. Until *Obasan*, Kogawa was best known as a poet. What poetical qualities do you see in this sample of her PROSE?
2. To what extent does Kogawa communicate by SENSE IMAGES? Cite one case each of appeals to sight, hearing, touch, taste and smell.
3. The poet Kogawa fills her prose with FIGURES OF SPEECH. Point out three good SIMILES and three good METAPHORS.
4. In paragraphs 14 through 17, how many times does the contraction "it's" appear at or near the beginning of a sentence? Is the *repetition* accidental or deliberate? What is its effect?
5. How many words long is the first sentence of paragraph 19? How many times does it use the word "and"? Is this run-on sentence accidental or deliberate? What is its effect?

ARGUMENTATION AND PERSUASION:

1. As a member of a persecuted minority, Kogawa's narrator rejects a *deductive* stance; she shuns the official "telling" of the newspaper article, and instead produces her own eyewitness "telling." Point out at least ten pieces of evidence that lead *inductively* to her own conclusion that the newspaper's version of the truth is "not how it was."

2. Does Kogawa rely more on *argumentation* or on *persuasion*? To what extent does she communicate through reason, and to what extent through emotion?

3. Analyze Kogawa's tools of *persuasion*: point out at least five loaded words, five SENSE IMAGES and five FIGURES OF SPEECH that build emotion. Identify one case of deliberate repetition, and one of extreme sentence length, both of which build emotion. Does all this persuasion put you on guard? Or does it convince you?

IDEAS FOR DISCUSSION AND WRITING:

1. How often are you, like Kogawa's narrator, caught between two or more views of the truth? Cite a recent case. Did you act *deductively*, accepting a view already held by yourself or others, or did you move *inductively* to a new conclusion?

2. The narrator and her family are Canadian citizens of Japanese descent, removed by our federal government from the coast of British Columbia during the Second World War for fear they would betray Canada to enemy Japan. (Not a single case of such betrayal was ever found.) Many families were separated and their property taken. Attack or defend these official actions against citizens like Kogawa's fictional family. Have such acts occurred in Canada before? Since? Can you imagine them happening in future to any group you belong to?

3. During the war the Canadian government confiscated an island off British Columbia, compensating its Japanese-Canadian owner with $2000. Two generations later his granddaughter, a university student, estimated the worth of this property at $200 million. In 1988 the Canadian government officially apologized to

the Japanese-Canadians and offered each survivor of the epoch $21,000. Has the wrong been righted? Attack or defend our government's actions.

4. You are the student in question 3 above. Write to the prime minister, arguing either *deductively* or *inductively* that the island be restored to the heirs of its original owner. *Or* you are the present owner. Write to the prime minister, arguing either *deductively* or *inductively* that your island should not be seized and given to descendants of the man who once owned it.

5. PROCESS IN WRITING: *Name a group that you believe has been badly treated by Canadian society (for example, Native people, immigrants, the disabled, the elderly, farmers, AIDS victims, single parents, etc.). Take notes, then write an* inductive argument *giving the evidence that led to your belief. In a further draft, fine-tune the balance of* argumentation and persuasion. *Now share this version with a small group of classmates, and apply their best advice. Edit. Finally, read your good version aloud to the whole class, and be ready to defend your view.*

Note: See also the Topics for Writing on the Online Learning Centre at www. mcgrawhill.ca/olc/conrad.

CANDACE SAVAGE

Stuck on the Prairies: Where Is Here?

Literary critic Northrop Frye once summed up the riddle of what Canada is in the question "Where is here?" It is no accident that in the title of our essay, Candace Savage has referred to those words, for she has spent her life immersed in the "here" of the Canadian prairies and in writing about it. Born in 1949 in Grande Prairie, Alberta, Savage completed a degree in English at the University of Alberta (winning the Governor-General's gold medal) but, as she points out, never specializing in the field of biology. Yet her arts educa-tion proved a gift. After going on to examine thousands of scholarly articles and interview many dozens of scientists, she has used her way with words to author over 20 books in the field of natural sciences. Their titles suggest the breadth of her work: Wild Mammals of Western Canada; Eagles of North America; Wolves; Grizzly Bears; Peregrine Falcons; Wild Cats; *and* Prairie: A Natural History. *Like scientist and media figure David Suzuki, Savage interprets the natural sciences to the greater public. "My goal," she states, "has always been the same: to write accurately and with feeling about real things, organisms, people and events, and to honor the magic of language." She has clearly done all this in the essay that follows. It first appeared in her book* Prairie: A Natural History *(2004), then in her 2005 collection* Curious by Nature: One Woman's Exploration of the Natural World.

There are people who think of the prairie as boring, and   1
it is hard not to pity them. We see them on the highways,
trapped inside their cars, propelled by a burning desire to

be somewhere else. But even as we wonder at their hurry, we have to admit that these disgruntled travelers are following in a grand old North American tradition. On both sides of the Canada–U.S. border, prairie bashing is as old as the written record. In 1803, for example, when the United States was contemplating the acquisition of the lands west of the Mississippi River from the French, through the Louisiana Purchase, the great orator Daniel Webster was moved to object. "What do we want with this vast, worthless area," he thundered, "this region of savages and wild beasts, of deserts of shifting sands and whirlwinds of dust, of cactus and prairie dogs?" And even after this supposedly howling wilderness had been annexed to the U.S., many observers remained unimpressed. The painter and naturalist John James Audubon was among them. In 1843, we find him traveling up the Missouri River on his first visit to the Great Plains. Forced onto the shore when his steamboat became grounded on a sandbar, he turned a disparaging eye toward the Dakota countryside. "The prairies around us are the most arid and dismal you can conceive of," he wrote. "In fact these prairies (so called) look more like great deserts."

2   Another traveler of the same era, a trader named Rufus Sage, was even more direct: "That this section of the country should ever become inhabited by civilized man except in the vicinity of large water courses, is an idea too preposterous to be entertained for a single moment." North of the border, Captain John Palliser, who crossed the Saskatchewan prairies in the late 1850s, was of much the same mind. Forget farming, he recommended. This country is just too dry.

3   It wasn't until near the end of the nineteenth century that the tide of expert opinion turned and the Great Plains were opened to agricultural settlement, now touted far and wide as the new Garden of Eden. The fact was, however, that these magnificent grasslands were neither desert nor garden but something completely new to European and Euro-American experience. So new that at first there wasn't even a name for them in either French or English. Pressed to come up with something, the early French fur traders had extended their term for a woodland meadow—*une prairie*—as a kind of metaphor for this big, wide, sparsely wooded, windswept world. But the Great Plains were far more than a meadow. What the travelers had

encountered was a vast, dynamic ecosystem, a kind of tawny, slowly evolving organism that, in a climate of constant change, had sustained itself ever since the retreat of the glaciers at the end of the Ice Age. In the presence of this strangeness and grandeur, words and vision failed.

When the newcomers looked around them, all they could see was where they weren't. This was not forest or sea coast or mountains; it was nothing but light and grass, the Big Empty in the middle of the continent. A vacant space, as they saw it, in desperate need of improvement. And this failure of vision—this inability to see and appreciate the Great Plains grasslands for what they truly are—has continued to plague our perceptions right down to the present. Flat? Boring? Lifeless? Nothing could be further from the truth. It's time to drop out of the fast lane and give the prairies, our prairies, a second, loving look.

AN EMPIRE OF GRASS

The key to everything that happens on the prairies lies trampled under our feet. Although grasses may look humble, they are actually versatile and tough, capable of growing under the widest possible range of conditions. Anywhere plants can grow, grasses are likely to be on the scene, whether coexisting with cactuses in a desert, poking up among lichens on the Arctic tundra, or hiding in the leafy understory of a forest. And when circumstances are especially favorable for them—for example, when the climate strikes just the right balance between precipitation and drought—grasses can assert themselves to become the dominant vegetation. ("Dominance," in this case, refers to the plants that contribute the most living tissue, or biomass, to the ecosystem. As trees to forest, so grasses to grassland.)

A glance at a map of the world's major grasslands suggests that these conditions are most likely to occur on a broad, landlocked plain, far from any significant body of water, somewhere near the center of a continental landmass. It is in this semiarid environment—too wet to be a desert and too dry for forest—that grasses gain the upper hand, whether it be on the steppes of central Asia, on the pampas of Argentina, on the savannas of East Africa, or in the broad heartland of North America.

7   Globally, grasslands are the largest of the four terrestrial biomes, or life zones, with a sweep that extends across roughly one-quarter of the land area of the planet, more than tundra, desert, or woodlands. (At least, that's the area over which grasses would potentially hold sway if natural conditions were allowed to prevail.) We're talking some 46 million square kilometers (18 million square miles)— almost three times the area of Russia. In North America alone, grasslands naturally extend over about 3.5 million square kilometers (1.4 million square miles), an area larger than many of the world's major nations.

8   The first European known to have set foot on this great empire of grass was a soldier and sometime explorer named Francisco Vásquez de Coronado. Dispatched from Mexico City in 1540, he was supposed to investigate rumors about a kingdom called Cíbola, somewhere to the north, and to plunder its Seven Cities of Gold. When these glittering mirages turned out to be sun-baked Zuñi pueblos in what is now New Mexico, he turned his attention to the uncharted Great Plains, where the fish were as big as horses, the people ate off golden plates, and the king was lulled to sleep at night by a tree full of golden bells. At least that's what people told him and what he chose to believe. And so off set Coronado, with a party of armed men, in the vague direction of present-day Kansas. In the end the promised golden city turned out to be village of grass thatched huts, where the people lived by hunting bison and growing gardens, each in their season.

9   Yet despite this disillusionment, Coronado and his party were astonished by what they found along their route. Here lay "a wilderness in which nothing grew, except for very small plants," but which nonetheless was teeming with million upon million of strange humpbacked cattle. "I found such a quantity of cows [bison]," Coronado reported, "that it is impossible to number them, for while I was journeying through these plains, until I return to where I first found them, there was not a day that I lost sight of them." Following along after these apparently endless herds were parties of nomadic hunters—ancestral Lipan Apaches, or Quechero Indians—who dressed in bison-skin clothing (sewn with bison sinew, drawn through a bison-bone awl), slept in bison-hide tipis, and subsisted on a diet of

bison blood and bison muscle. Even the grass in this new world was cause for amazement, as it rebounded from the conquistadors' steps and erased the trace of their presence. In this great round world, all that glittered was grass and an ecosystem of such richness and diversity that it could scarcely be credited.

But think how amazed Coronado would have been if he had somehow been able to sense the true extent and variety of North America's grasslands. Little did he know that he had set foot on a vast prairie heartland—a continent of grass—that was flanked on every side by smaller islands of grassland and prairie-to-forest transitions, or savannas. To the north, for instance, beyond his farthest imaginings, lay the Peace River Parklands, a region of rolling grass and poplars that marked the frontier between the Great Plains grasslands and the boreal forest. To the east, the Prairie-and-Oak Transition zone—a tongue of prairie interspersed with groves of hardwoods—extended to the Great Lakes and beyond, marking the interface between the grasslands and the eastern deciduous forest. To the south, the prairies merged and melted into sultry, soupy marshlands to produce the semitropical vistas of the Western Gulf Coastal Grasslands. And to the west, in the broad valleys of the western Cordillera, lay the California Grasslands—spangled in spring by lupines and yellow-orange poppies—and the arid Palouse Grasslands of the Great Basin. Dominated by scraggly stands of sagebrush and spiky, sparse grasses, the Palouse, or bunchgrass, prairie stretched along the drainage of the Columbia and Snake Rivers to intergrade with the shrubby growth of the Montana Valley Grasslands.

And in the center of everything there was the main attraction, the Great Plains Grasslands themselves, a landscape that even today invites wonderment. This truly is big sky country, with horizons that extend from the boreal forests of Alberta, Saskatchewan, and Manitoba to the deserts of the American Southwest and from the foothills of the Rockies to the Mississippi drainage. The numbers speak for themselves. Length: 2,400 kilometers (1,500 miles). Width: between 600 and 1,100 kilometers (between 400 and 700 miles). Vaguely triangular in outline, the region is broadest toward the north and narrows to its apex in the Hill Country of central Texas. Total area: 2.6 million square kilometers (1 million square miles), or roughly 14 percent of the entire landmass of Canada, Alaska, and the Lower Forty-Eight states.

THEN AND NOW

12 It is one thing to send our minds running across the contours of the Great Plains grasslands. It is quite another to bring these spaces to life, to try to perceive them in their full, natural vitality and splendor. What would it have been like to step out onto the round bowl of the southern grasslands with Coronado in 1541, aware that at any moment our progress might be blocked by a dusty, pawing, milling herd of bison? Or, precisely 150 years later, in 1691, to have traveled with Henry Kelsey and his Cree and Assiniboine guides from Hudson Bay through the northern forest and onto the prairies of the Saskatchewan River country? What emotion would have seized us when a blocky, hunched shadow gradually resolved into the form of a massive and potentially lethal grizzly bear? Or what if we could slip back in time to 1804 (a mere two hundred years ago) and join Lewis and Clark on their famous expedition up the Missouri River?

13 Imagine: Bison beyond counting. ("I do not think I exaggerate," Lewis wrote as he crossed the Dakota Plains in 1804, "when I estimate the number of Buffaloe which could be compre[hend]ed at one view to amount to 3000.") Flights of pronghorns at every turn. Elk coming up out of misty valleys to graze on the prairie at dawn. Bighorn sheep perched on the steep crumbling walls of the Little Missouri badlands. Wolves threading across the prairies, trailing the herds.

14 Two hundred years isn't very long on the geologic time scales of planet Earth. These memories lie at the very threshold of the present, so close that we half expect to be able to walk into a fold in the landscape and encounter them. And something like this still occasionally happens when we stumble across a physical trace of the past, whether it's a flaked stone tool that once belonged to a bison hunter or a shallow, saucer-shaped hollow that was worn into the dirt by generations of rolling, grunting bison. The animals have vanished, but the imprint of their flesh and blood is still on the land. It is all so mind-bogglingly recent.

15 There are not many places where the wild is as close at hand as it is on the Great Plains. In the Old World of Europe and Asia, no

one can quite remember what "natural" looked like, because the land has been successively shaped and reshaped to meet human needs for hundreds or thousands of years. But in the New World of the prairies—right up to the moment when the settlement boom began—humans had lived off the natural productivity of this vast, sun-swept expanse of grass. From the time of their arrival on the plains, some eleven thousand years before, the First Peoples had drawn their sustenance from the native animals and plants, experiencing both feast and famine as hunters and gatherers. This is not to say that they sat back passively and let nature take its course. They were active participants in the ecosystem, ready and willing to use whatever technologies they could command to improve their chances of survival. For example, they had no qualms about setting the prairies on fire to green up the grass and draw bison in for the hunt. They tilled the soil of fertile river valleys and planted gardens of sunflowers, corn, and squash. They eagerly adapted to the new culture of firearms and horses.

Yet despite these human innovations, the underlying dynamic of the ecosystem—the interplay between climate and grasses, grazers and predators—remained robust. A landscape that had evolved to support large herds of grazing animals was still doing exactly that, as life ebbed and flowed in time with the seasons. Then, in the early to mid-1800s, the pace of change accelerated. In far-off Washington and Ottawa, ambitious governments began to assert their claim to the land and resources of the Great Plains. As a prelude to agricultural settlement, Native people were confined on reserves and reservations, whether by persuasion or by brute force, and the bison on which they depended—the multitudes of "humpbacked cattle" that had darkened the plains—were virtually wiped out in a bloody orgy of killing. Tellingly, the final stages of this slaughter were motivated by the discovery that bison hides could be cut and sewn into leather belts and used to power machines in the burgeoning industrial complex in the East. (The last free-roaming bison were killed in Canada in 1883 and in the U.S. in 1891.) Modern times had arrived on the prairies.

And then came the settlers, an onrush of humanity that reached full flood in the late 1800s and early 1900s. Determined to make a stand in this new country, the incomers quickly progressed from temporary shacks and shanties into substantial homes, making them the first people ever to establish permanent, year-round dwellings on the open plains. This was a bold experiment, occasioned with far more risk than anyone at the time seemed to recognize or, at least, was prepared to admit. But whatever the hazards, the way forward was clear. The object was to assert control over the ecosystem and redirect its natural vitality into the production of commodities that could be bought and sold on the world market. Beef, not bison. Wheat and corn instead of prairie wool.

18   The result of this revolution is the landscape that we see today, a colorful patchwork of fields and rangelands, where geese feed in the stubble, foxes hunt in farmyards, and meadowlarks sing their hearts out on fence posts. These are the prairies that our generation was born to, and they are beautiful in their own right.

19   Yet the more we love this place as it is, the more we feel the pain of what it so recently was. The wild prairie ecosystem is gone. And this tragedy is compounded by the realization that we don't even know exactly what it is that we have lost. "Civilization" and "progress" over-ran the grasslands with such an urgent rush that the ecosystem was disrupted before anyone had a chance to make a systematic study of exactly what was out there or to figure out how all the pieces inter-acted with each other. The people who might have had the most to teach us—the last generation of hunters and gatherers—went to their graves largely unheeded by the newcomers, taking their knowledge of the prairie and its lifeways with them. We are left with little to guide us except for fragments of written descriptions in the journals of explorers and early settlers—partial lists of species, brief sightings, and offhand remarks—that leave many basic questions unanswered.

20   The depth of our ignorance is startling. Question: How many bison were there on the plains before the slaughter began? Answer: No one can tell us with any assurance. By working and reworking the available strands of evidence, experts have estimated the precontact population at anywhere from 12 million to 125 million animals, a variance that leaves more than 100 million bison in limbo. Although the currently accepted figure sets the herds at some 30 million, no one really knows. And if we cannot account for big things like bison, how much less do

we know about the smaller and less conspicuous organisms—little things like insects and spiders, fish and frogs, rodents and songbirds—that lived and died in their untold variety and interest and abundance? Yet if the wild past is lost to us, we can still look ahead. Despite everything that has happened, it is not too late to acknowledge the natural forces that continue to animate the prairie world and that, even today, shape the lives of all its creatures.

EXPLORATIONS:

Candace Savage, *Prairie: A Natural History*
Sharon Butala, *The Perfection of the Morning*
Frederick Philip Grove, *Settlers of the Marsh*
Paul Kane, *Wanderings of an Artist*
Margaret Laurence, *The Stone Angel*
W. O. Mitchell, *Who Has Seen the Wind*
Sinclair Ross, *As for Me and My House*
Wallace Stegner, *Wolf Willow*
http://esask.uregina.ca/entry/savage_candace_1949-.html
http://en.wikipedia.org/wiki/Canadian_Prairies
http://www.hww.ca/hww2.asp?id=97

STRUCTURE:

1. Candace Savage opens her argument with the image of travellers on the prairies "propelled by a burning desire to be somewhere else" (par. 1). How do this, and the further insulting views reported in paragraphs 1 and 2, prepare us for her celebration of the prairies? What device of organization has she used here?
2. When Savage shows us Coronado setting out with hopes of plunder, then seeing the realities of the prairies (pars. 8–10), what organizational device is she using?
3. Savage's THESIS STATEMENT is exceptionally clear and direct: "Flat? Boring? Lifeless? Nothing could be further from the truth. It's time to drop out of the fast lane and give the prairies, our prairies,

a second, loving look" (par. 4). How does this passage also function as a TRANSITION?

4. Do Savage's subheadings help you follow her argument? Have you used subheadings in your own essays? When are they most appropriate?

5. What techniques does Savage use to end this selection on a strong note?

STYLE:

1. How FORMAL or INFORMAL is the language of this selection (length of sentences and paragraphs, level of vocabulary, etc.)?

2. Read paragraph 9 aloud. Is the repetition of "bison" accidental or deliberate? What effects does it have?

3. Tell what each of the following FIGURES OF SPEECH does for your view of the prairies: "the Big Empty" (par. 4), an "empire of grass" (5), a "continent of grass" (10) and "big sky country" (11).

ARGUMENTATION AND PERSUASION:

1. Which is stronger in this essay, *argumentation* (logic) or *persuasion* (emotion)? Give examples.

2. What do all the statistics, in paragraphs 7, 11, 13 and 20, do for Savage's argument? Are they a kind of *example?* Do they serve to balance the more "persuasive" side of this essay?

3. Examine again Savage's THESIS STATEMENT at the end of paragraph 4. Does it announce an analysis that will be powered by *deduction* (applying received attitudes to the present case) or by *induction* (studying examples, then drawing conclusions from them)? Explain.

IDEAS FOR DISCUSSION AND WRITING:

1. Name as many ways as you can in which the urban lawn differs from the prairie.

2. You may have noticed the list of prairie books recommended in "Explorations" above. Why so many? What kinds of subjects

could writers develop about the place some people call "the Big Empty"?

3. During the droughts of the 1930s much of the Canadian prairie turned to swirling dust, as sod became desert. Do you expect that, in our own era of global warming, this could happen again? Might we even someday conclude that the prairies should never have been broken by the plough?

4. Imagining future Dust Bowls, and observing a steady depopulation of the prairies, Americans Frank and Deborah Popper have long proposed the creation of a "Buffalo Commons." Vast areas of prairie in the United States would be replanted in sturdy native grasses, and they would again host a vast population of bison. What is your reaction? Is such a project feasible biologically, economically, politically?

5. Savage states that "'Civilization' and 'progress' overran the grasslands with such an urgent rush that the ecosystem was disrupted before anyone had a chance to make a systematic study of exactly what was out there" (par. 19). She goes on to say that "The people who might have had the most to teach us—the last generation of hunters and gatherers—went to their graves largely unheeded by the newcomers, taking their knowledge of the prairie and its lifeways with them." Imagine a different past, in which this knowledge of the prairies was cherished and preserved. Describe it to the class.

6. PROCESS IN WRITING: *Consider the idea of a "Buffalo Commons" described in question 4 above. Visit several of the many websites on this subject, taking notes. Now sift this information, and let the evidence help you decide,* inductively, *where you stand on the issue. Devise a clear THESIS STATEMENT, either for or against the Buffalo Commons, then write a quick first version of your argument, supported by the examples you have found. Later look it over. Does every example contribute? Is your language CONCISE? Do TRANSITIONS move the argument forward? Finally check for punctuation and spelling before bringing your best version to class to share.*

Note: See also the Topics for Writing on the Online Learning Centre at www. mcgrawhill.ca/olc/conrad.

MARGARET ATWOOD

Letter to America

Novelist, poet, essayist, social and literary critic, Margaret Atwood has had a long and distinguished career, and is still at the forefront of Canadian literature. Born in Ottawa in 1939, she spent much of her childhood with her parents in the wilds of the Canadian North, where her father did biological research. After studies at the University of Toronto and at Radcliffe, she published several books of poetry that explored the inability of language to express reality, and the alienation of women in society. Then her feminist vision found even broader scope in a long series of successful novels, such as The Edible Woman *(1969),* Surfacing *(1972) and* The Handmaid's Tale *(1985), which became an international bestseller and was made into a feature film and an opera. The novel already shows her preoccupation with America. Set in Boston, it portrays a future United States, ruined by nuclear pollution, in which a right-wing theocracy has reduced women to the status of slaves. The main characters flee north toward Canada, as did slaves before the Civil War. Of Atwood's dozen novels so far,* Alias Grace *(1996), a polished work investigating a notorious murder in 19th-century Canada, has also been widely admired. By now Atwood's collected poems, stories, essays and her novels total well over 30 books, and she has been translated into more than two dozen languages. Our selection, "Letter to America," expresses an unease with recent American government and society. It first appeared April 14, 2003 in the American journal* The Nation, *then on March 28 in the Toronto* Globe *and* Mail, *and finally in the collection of Atwood's essays,* Moving Targets: Writing with Intent, 1982–2004.

1 Dear America:

2 This is a difficult letter to write, because I'm no longer sure who you are. Some of you may be having the same trouble.

I thought I knew you: we'd become well acquainted over the past fifty-five years. You were the Mickey Mouse and Donald Duck comic books I read in the late 1940s. You were the radio shows—Jack Benny, *Our Miss Brooks.* You were the music I sang and danced to: the Andrews Sisters, Ella Fitzgerald, the Platters, Elvis. You were a ton of fun.

You wrote some of my favourite books. You created Huckleberry ³ Finn, and Hawkeye, and Beth and Jo in *Little Women,* courageous in their different ways. Later, you were my beloved Thoreau, father of environmentalism, witness to individual conscience; and Walt Whitman, singer of the great Republic; and Emily Dickinson, keeper of the private soul. You were Hammett and Chandler, heroic walkers of mean streets; even later, you were the amazing trio, Hemingway, Fitzgerald, and Faulkner, who traced the dark labyrinths of your hidden heart. You were Sinclair Lewis and Arthur Miller, who, with their own American idealism, went after the sham in you, because they thought you could do better.

You were Marlon Brando in *On the Waterfront,* you were Humphrey ⁴ Bogart in *Key Largo,* you were Lillian Gish in *The Night of the Hunter.* You stood up for freedom, honesty, and justice; you protected the innocent. I believed most of that. I think you did, too. It seemed true at the time.

You put God on the money, though, even then. You had a way of ⁵ thinking that the things of Caesar° were the same as the things of God: that gave you self-confidence. You have always wanted to be a city upon a hill, a light to all nations, and for a while you were. Give me your tired, your poor, you sang, and for a while you meant it.

We've always been close, you and us. History, that old entangler, ⁶ has twisted us together since the early seventeenth century. Some of us used to be you; some of us want to be you; some of you used to be us. You are not only our neighbours: In many cases—mine, for instance—you are also our blood relations, our colleagues, and our personal friends. But although we've had a ringside seat, we've never understood you completely, up here north of the 49th parallel.

°the things of Caesar: In Luke 20:22–25 the priests said, "Is it lawful for us to give tribute unto Caesar, or no?" Jesus asked them to show a coin with the emperor's image, then said: "Render therefore unto Caesar the things which be Caesar's, and unto God the things which be God's."

We're like Romanized Gauls°—look like Romans, dress like Romans, but aren't Romans—peering over the wall at the real Romans. What are they doing? Why? What are they doing now? Why is the haruspex° eyeballing the sheep's liver? Why is the soothsayer wholesaling the Bewares?

7   Perhaps that's been my difficulty in writing you this letter: I'm not sure I know what's really going on. Anyway, you have a huge posse of experienced entrail sifters who do nothing but analyze your every vein and lobe. What can I tell you about yourself that you don't already know?

8   This might be the reason for my hesitation: embarrassment, brought on by a becoming modesty. But it is more likely to be embarrassment of another sort. When my grandmother—from a New England background—was confronted with an unsavoury topic, she would change the subject and gaze out the window. And that is my own inclination: keep your mouth shut, mind your own business.

9   But I'll take the plunge, because your business is no longer merely your business. To paraphrase Marley's ghost,° who figured it out too late, mankind is your business. And vice versa: when the Jolly Green Giant goes on the rampage, many lesser plants and animals get trampled underfoot. As for us, you're our biggest trading partner: We know perfectly well that if you go down the plughole, we're going with you. We have every reason to wish you well.

10   I won't go into the reasons why I think your recent Iraqi adventures have been—taking the long view—an ill-advised tactical error. By the time you read this, Baghdad may or may not be a pancake, and many more sheep entrails will have been examined. Let's talk, then, not about what you're doing to other people but about what you're doing to yourselves.

11   You're gutting the Constitution. Already your home can be entered without your knowledge or permission, you can be snatched away and incarcerated without cause, your mail can be spied on, your private records searched. Why isn't this a recipe for widespread business theft, political intimidation, and fraud? I know you've been told that all this is for your own safety and protection, but think about it for a minute. Anyway, when did you get so scared? You didn't used to be easily frightened.

°Gauls: The early inhabitants of what is now France, who had been conquered by the Romans.

°haruspex: A soothsayer or fortune-teller who discovered the will of the gods by reading the entrails of sacrificed animals.

°Marley's ghost: In Charles Dickens' famous story "A Christmas Carol," the ghost of Scrooge's business partner repents his former selfish ways, saying "Mankind was my business.... The dealings of my trade were but a drop of water in the comprehensive ocean of my business!"

You're running up a record level of debt. Keep spending at this rate   12
and pretty soon you won't be able to afford any big military adventures.
Either that or you'll go the way of the USSR: lots of tanks, but no air
conditioning. That will make folks very cross. They'll be even crosser
when they can't take a shower because your shortsighted bulldozing
of environmental protections has dirtied most of the water and dried
up the rest. Then things will get hot and dirty indeed.

You're torching the American economy. How soon before the   13
answer to that will be not to produce anything yourselves but to grab
stuff other people produce, at gunboat-diplomacy prices? Is the world
going to consist of a few mega-rich King Midases,° with the rest being
serfs, both inside and outside your country? Will the biggest business
sector in the United States be the prison system? Let's hope not.

If you proceed much further down the slippery slope, people   14
around the world will stop admiring the good things about you.
They'll decide that your city upon the hill is a slum and your democracy is a sham, and therefore you have no business trying to impose
your sullied vision on them. They'll think you've abandoned the rule
of law. They'll think you've fouled your own nest.

The British used to have a myth about King Arthur. He wasn't   15
dead, but sleeping in a cave, it was said; and in the country's hour of
greatest peril, he would return. You too have great spirits of the past
you may call upon: men and women of courage, of conscience, of
prescience. Summon them now, to stand with you, to inspire you, to
defend the best in you. You need them.

°King Midas: In Greek legend, the king of Phrygia who could turn all he touched into gold.

Explorations:

Margaret Atwood,
    Moving Targets: Writing with Intent, 1982–2004 (essays)
    The Journals of Susanna Moodie (poems)
    The Handmaid's Tale (novel)
    Alias Grace (novel)
Howell, Corel Ann, *Margaret Atwood*
Michael Adams, *Fire and Ice: The United States, Canada and the Myth of
    Converging Values*

http://www.owtoad.com
http://www.mscd.edu/~atwoodso
http://www.library.utoronto.ca/canpoetry/atwood

STRUCTURE:

1. The essay as a letter has a long and rich history. Does any other author in the book use this device? What advantages of this format has Atwood exploited in "Letter to America"?
2. Atwood presents a flood of *examples*. Do you put enough of them into your own essays? Is there any upper limit?
3. What gives so much power to Atwood's final words, "You need them"?

STYLE:

1. Margaret Atwood knows how to say more with less. In paragraph 6 she writes, "Some of us used to be you; some of us want to be you; some of you used to be us." Find five other examples of extreme CONCISENESS in her essay.
2. Writing shortly before the American invasion of Iraq, Atwood says, "By the time you read this, Baghdad may or may not be a pancake" (10). Does this METAPHOR make you uneasy? Does it seem sarcastic or even cruel? Or is it supposed to shock, and thus support the author's criticisms of U.S. foreign policy? Find five other META-PHORS and/or SIMILES, and comment on them as well.

ARGUMENTATION AND PERSUASION:

1. Atwood's essay both affirms and criticizes America. Are these thoughts derived mostly through DEDUCTION (applying an overall principle to specific examples) or INDUCTION (letting specific examples lead to the principle)?
2. Read paragraphs 2 and 3 aloud in class. Why are certain phrases repeated so many times? And why are the first words of paragraphs 11, 12 and 13 repetitious? Does this show weak style or strong style? What is the effect? Are we looking at ARGUMENTATION or PERSUASION here?
3. What other examples of PERSUASION do you see in this selection? (Review the list of persuasive techniques in the introduction to this chapter.) All in all, is "Letter to America" based mostly on PERSUASION or ARGUMENTATION?

IDEAS FOR DISCUSSION AND WRITING:

1. In paragraphs 2–4 Atwood admires many American singers, writers, actors, etc. who influenced her in the past. Name ten Americans you would put on your own list for today, and for each one tell why.

2. "I thought I knew you," says Atwood in par. 2. Do you agree with her that the United States has changed? And if so, what are the changes you, yourself, notice? And to what extent do these seem caused by the World Trade Center terrorist attack of September 11, 2001?

3. In paragraph 6 Atwood builds an *analogy*: "We're like Romanized Gauls—look like Romans, dress like Romans, but aren't Romans—peering over the wall at the real Romans." Is this a true portrait of Canadians? In what ways do you feel most "like" Americans? In what ways do you feel most different from them?

4. The three most specific criticisms Atwood makes are of the "recent Iraqi adventures" (par. 10), the "gutting" of the Constitution (11) and the "record level of debt" which will "torch" the U.S. economy (12–13). Study those paragraphs. Do you agree with Atwood's analysis? If not, why not? Or if so, what concrete steps do you believe the U.S. could take to begin solving each of these problems?

5. **PROCESS IN WRITING:** *Margaret Atwood writes a "Letter to America." Now imagine yourself looking north across the border and writing a "Letter to Canada." First* freewrite *or* brainstorm *for 10 or 15 minutes, then search these notes for points and a topic. (For example, is Canada getting better or worse? Fairer or less fair to minorities? Stronger or weaker economically? Greener or more wasteful environmentally? More respected or less respected internationally? And so on.) Write a first draft, then look it over. Have you lived up to the model of Atwood's letter: Do you say more with less? Are the points concrete, with* examples*? Do they all support the overall main point? Do they rise in importance to a* climax*? Now look at your logic: Is it mostly* deductive *or* inductive*? (Write which it is at the top.) Mostly* argumentative *or* persuasive*? (Write which it is at the top.) If it is* argumentative*, are your points real and fair? If it is* persuasive*, does the feeling of everything contribute to the overall tone and the overall point? If not, revise. Finally, edit for correctness and read your letter to the class.*

Note: See also the Topics for Writing on the Online Learning Centre at www. mcgrawhill.ca/olc/conrad.

NAOMI KLEIN

Local Foreign Policy

Naomi Klein, born 1970 in Montreal, is one of the most influential political commentators and activists in the world today. Growing up with the progressive ideals of her parents (Americans who had moved to Canada), then marrying into the famous Canadian political family of television host Avi Lewis, his parents Stephen Lewis (former Canadian ambassador to the UN) and Michele Landsberg (the legendary feminist newspaper columnist), Klein herself has become a prolific and hard-hitting speaker and writer. She publishes a regular column in The Guardian *and* The Nation*, speaks at antiglobalization rallies around the world, and in 2000 published an international bestseller, translated into 28 languages:* No Logo: Taking Aim at the Brand Bullies. *In it she exposed the abuses of transnational corporations such as Nike, Reebok and Disney, which pay low wages to workers in poor countries but spend fortunes in advertising to sell brand-name clothes in rich countries. From* No Logo *comes our own selection "Local Foreign Policy."* *Two years later she published* Fences and Windows: Dispatches from the Front Lines of the Globalization Debate. *Then in 2004, with Avi Lewis, she released* The Take, *her documentary film about auto workers in Argentina taking matters into their own hands: when the economy collapsed and their factory was closed, they formed a workers' cooperative and reopened it. Then in 2007 appeared another blockbuster book,* The Shock Doctrine: The Rise of Disaster Capitalism. *In it Klein explores her theory that governments take advantage of events such as 9/11 or Hurricane Katrina to push through conservative legislation that will benefit the rich, while the public, stunned by the event, does not realize what is happening.*

"**O**kay, I need people on each door. Let's go!" shouted Sean Hayes in the distinctive clipped baritone of a high-school basketball coach, which, as it happens, he is. "Let's go!" Coach Hayes bellowed again, clapping his meaty hands loud enough for the sound to bounce off the walls of the huge gymnasium of St. Mary's Secondary School in Pickering, Ontario (a town best known for its proximity to a nuclear power plant of questionable quality).

Hayes had invited me to participate in the school's first "Sweatshop Fashion Show," an event he began planning when he discovered that the basketball team's made-in-Indonesia Nike sneakers had likely been manufactured under sweatshop conditions. He's an unapologetic jock with a conscience and, together with a handful of do-gooder students, had organized today's event to get the other two thousand kids at St. Mary's to think about the clothes they wear in terms beyond "cool" or "lame."

The plan was simple: as student models decked out in logowear strutted down a makeshift runway, another student off to the side would read a prepared narration about the lives of the Third World workers who made the gear. The students would quickly follow that with scenes from *Mickey Mouse Goes to Haiti* and a skit about how teenagers often feel "unloved, unwanted, unacceptable and unpopular if you do not have the right clothes." My part would come at the end, when I was to give a short speech about my research in export processing zones, and then facilitate a question-and-answer period. It sounded straightforward enough.

While we were waiting for the bell to ring and the students to stream in, Hayes turned to me and said, with a forced smile: "I hope the kids actually hear the message and don't think it's just a regular fashion show." Having read the students' prepared narration I couldn't help thinking that his concern sounded, frankly, paranoid. True, fashion shows have become such a high-school stalwart that they now rival car washes as the prom fundraiser of choice. But did Hayes actually think his students were so heartless that they could listen to testimony about starvation wages and physical abuse and expect that the clothing in question would be on sale at a discount after the assembly? Just then, a couple of teenage boys poked their heads in the door and checked out the frantic preparations. "Yo, guys," one of them said. "I'm guessing fashion show—this should be a joke." Coach Hayes looked nervous.

5   As two thousand students piled onto the bleachers, the room came alive with the giddiness that accompanies all mass reprieves from class, whether for school plays, AIDS education lectures, teachers' strikes or fire alarms. A quick scan of the room turned up no logos on these kids, but that was definitely not by choice. St. Mary's is a Catholic school and the students wear uniforms—bland affairs that they were nonetheless working for all they were worth. It's hard to make gray flannel slacks and acrylic navy sweaters look like gangsta gear but the guys were doing their best, wearing their pants pulled down halfway to their knees with patterned boxer shorts bunched over their belts. The girls were pushing the envelope too, pairing their drab tunics with platform loafers and black lipstick.

6   As it turned out, Coach Hayes's concerns were well founded. As the hip-hop started playing and the first kids bounded down the runway in Nike shoes and workout wear, the assembly broke into cheers and applause. The moment the young woman saddled with reading the earnest voice-over began, "Welcome to the world of Nike …" she was drowned out by hoots and whistles. It didn't take much to figure out that they weren't cheering for her but rather at the mere mention of the word Nike—everyone's favorite celebrity brand.

7   Waiting for my cue, I was ready to flee the modern teenage world forever, but after some booming threats from Coach Hayes, the crowd finally quieted down. My speech was at least not booed and the discussion that followed was among the liveliest I've ever witnessed. The first question (as at all Sweatshop 101 events) was "What brands are sweatshop-free?"—Adidas? they asked. Reebok? The Gap? I told the St. Mary's students that shopping for an exploitation-free wardrobe at the mall is next to impossible, given the way all the large brands produce. The best way to make a difference, I told them, is to stay informed by surfing the Net, and by letting companies know what you think by writing letters and asking lots of questions at the store. The St. Mary's kids were deeply skeptical of this non-answer. "Look, I don't have time to be some kind of major political activist every time I go to the mall," one girl said, right hand planted firmly on right hip. "Just tell me what kind of shoes are okay to buy, okay?"

Another girl, who looked about sixteen, sashayed to the micro- 8
phone. "I'd just like to say that this is capitalism, okay, and people
are allowed to make money and if you don't like it maybe you're just
jealous."

The hands shot up in response. "No, *I'd* just like to say that you 9
are totally screwed up and just because everyone is doing something doesn't mean it's right—you've got to stand up for what you
believe in instead of just standing in front of the mirror trying to
look good!"

After watching thousands of Ricki and Oprah episodes, these kids 10
take to the talk-show format as naturally as Elizabeth Dole. Just as they
had cheered for Nike moments before, the students now cheered for
each other—dog-pound style, with lots of "you-go-girls." Moments
before the bell for next period, Coach Hayes made time for one last
question. A boy in saggy slacks sauntered across the gym holding his
standard-issue navy blue sweater away from his lanky body with two
fingers, as if he detected a foul odor. Then, he slouched down to the
mike and said, in an impeccable teenage monotone, "Umm, Coach
Hayes, if working conditions are so bad in Indonesia, then why do
we have to wear these uniforms? We buy thousands of these things
and it says right here that they are 'Made in Indonesia.' I'd just like
to know, how do you know they weren't made in sweatshops?"

The auditorium exploded. It was a serious burn. Another student 11
rushed to the mike and suggested that the students should try to
find out who makes their uniforms, a project for which there was no
shortage of volunteers. When I left St. Mary's that day, the school had
its work cut out for it.

EXPLORATIONS:

Naomi Klein,
> *No Logo: Taking Aim at the Brand Bullies*
> *The Shock Doctrine: The Rise of Disaster Capitalism*
> *The Take* (documentary film, 87 min., 2004)

Madeleine Drohan, *Making a Killing: How and Why Corporations Use
Armed Force to Do Business*

http://www.nologo.org

http://www.guardian.co.uk/Columnists/Archive/0,5673,-991,00.
  html

http://www.commondreams.org/views/092300-103.htm

http://www.thenation.com/directory/bios/naomi_klein

http://adbusters.org/home

STRUCTURE:

1. Naomi Klein's book *No Logo* often uses passages of *narration* to argue and persuade. Show how this selection does so. How does telling of the school assembly illustrate the problem of sweatshop labour, and the difficulties Canadians face in doing something about it? Where in this selection do we also see use of *example*? Of *description*? Of *cause and effect*? Of *comparison and contrast*? And of *process analysis*?

2. One of the strongest techniques of an essayist is to build the argument up to a CLIMAX. Has Klein done this? How?

STYLE:

1. Why does Klein use SLANG or COLLOQUIAL terms such as "jock" (par. 2), "cool" (2), "lame" (2), "gangsta" (5) and "a serious burn" (11)? Are these too racy for a serious argument, or do they work with Klein's subject and format?

2. What kind of AUDIENCE do you believe Klein is writing for? Give reasons.

ARGUMENTATION AND PERSUASION:

1. Is Klein's argument based mostly on *deduction* (a principle applied to specific cases) or *induction* (evidence that leads to a principle)? Support your answer with reasons.

2. To what extent does Klein base this selection on reason (*argumentation*) and to what extent on appeals to emotion (*persuasion*)? Cite examples to defend your view.

IDEAS FOR DISCUSSION AND WRITING:

1. Look at the clothing you have on right now. Tell the class whether any of it is by Adidas, Reebok, The Gap or other big name-brand

companies. Then try to explain all the factors that led you to choose each item. Cost? Durability? Performance? Or image? Now look at the labels. Where was each item made? What is your estimate of the hourly wage made by the worker in each location?

2. Review the passage on branding in the introduction to Naomi Klein. Better yet, read her book. What are your views so far on this issue? Is it exploitation for big transnational companies to pay workers in Indonesia or Malaysia a tiny fraction of what the running shoes or other clothes will sell for here? Or is it just good business? Is it fair to make them work long hours in special zones patrolled by armed guards? Or are companies doing them a favour by creating employment?

3. Elsewhere Naomi Klein has stated "People come up to me and say, 'I read your book and burned all my Nike clothes.'" Attack or defend their reaction, giving reasons.

4. In paragraph 8 a student states, "I'd just like to say that this is capitalism, okay, and people are allowed to make money and if you don't like it maybe you're just jealous." In paragraph 9 a classmate replies, "No, *I'd* just like to say that you are totally screwed up and just because everyone is doing something doesn't mean it's right— you've got to stand up for what you believe in instead of just standing in front of the mirror trying to look good!" With which student do you most agree? Defend your choice with reasons.

5. What does the title mean? How can "foreign" policy be "local"? What is a PARADOX? Is this title one?

6. PROCESS IN WRITING: *Choose one of the two students from question 4 just above as a hypothetical* AUDIENCE *for your own essay. Now brainstorm a page of notes on the topic of transnational companies producing at low wages in one country and selling at high prices in another. When you realize your own point of view on the topic, put it into a* THESIS STATEMENT. *Next decide how much reason* (argumentation) *and how much emotion* (persuasion) *are needed to reach your reader. Finally, write a discovery draft, filling it with* examples *from your own experience and reading. The next day look it over. Does everything contribute to your overall main point? Is the argument appropriate for your chosen* AUDIENCE? *Have you gone so far using emotion that you're just playing on the reader's feelings? Or is your pure logic so dry it has no life? Then adjust. Finally, edit, print, and share with the class.*

Note: See also the Topics for Writing on the Online Learning Centre at www. mcgrawhill.ca/olc/conrad.

RITA SCHINDLER

Thanks for Not Killing My Son

All we know about Rita Schindler is what she herself says in her letter. It was a student who noticed "Thanks for Not Killing My Son" in the "Have Your Say" feature of the December 30, 1990 Toronto Star. *He tore it out and brought it to his writing teacher, exclaiming what a fine argument it was. The teacher agreed. By the time the editor of this book tried to reach Ms. Schindler, though, the* Star *had discarded her address. None of the many Schindlers listed in the Toronto phone book knew her, and the hospital mentioned in her letter would not divulge information. As this new edition was being put together we tried again to find her, but could not. Finally, Access Canada, the Canadian Copyright Licensing Agency, gave permission to reprint the letter, as it can do in such cases. We sincerely believe that Ms. Schindler would want her eloquent and highly principled argument made available to more persons of her son's generation. If you happen to know her, please show her this book and ask her to contact the publisher, who will direct her to the agency office where her author's fee is waiting.*

1   I hope you will print my letter of gratitude to the strangers who have affected our lives.

2   Sometime between 1:30 p.m., Dec. 8, and 1 a.m., Dec. 9, a young man was viciously attacked—beaten and kicked unconscious for no apparent reason other than walking by you on a public sidewalk.

3   He was left lying in a pool of blood from an open head wound—in the Victoria Park-Terraview area. He was found around 1 a.m. and taken to Scarborough General Hospital where ironically his mother spent 48 hours in labor before giving him birth, 23 years earlier.

404

His mother is angry of course, but thankful for the following reasons. 4

First of all—his eye socket was shattered and hemorrhaging but his eyesight will not be affected. Thank you. 5

His ear canal was lacerated internally from a tremendous blow to the side of his head. The cut could not be stitched and the bleeding was difficult to stop. But his eardrum seems to be undamaged—thank you. 6

He required numerous stitches to his forehead, temple and face but your boots didn't knock one tooth out—thank you. His head was swollen almost twice its size—but Mom knew that his brain was intact—for he held her hand for six hours as he lay on a gurney, by the nurses station, I.V. in his arm—his head covered and crusted with dried blood—waiting for x-ray results and the surgeon to stitch him up. 7

So, thank you for this eyesight, his hearing and his hands which you could have easily crushed. 8

His hands—human hands—the most intricately beautiful and complex instruments of incredible mechanism—the result of billions of years of evolution—and you people used yours to beat another human being. Five guys and two girls to beat one person. Who do I thank? Did you know he was a talented young musician with a budding career—and that playing his keyboards and piano mean more to him than my words can say. 9

And when his friends were talking about revenge, I heard him say, "No, I don't want someone else's mother to go through what mine has." That's who you were kicking in the head. And so—I thank you for not causing the most horrible and devastating thing that can happen to any parent—that is—the untimely tragic loss of a child—at any age. 10

You could have kicked him to death but you only left him to die, thank you. A person found him and called for help. 11

I am his mother—and I have been given a second chance—thanks to you. 12

I hope that someday you'll have children and love them as much as I love mine—but I wouldn't wish on your child what you did to mine. 13

Rita Schindler 14
Scarborough 15

EXPLORATIONS:

William Golding, *Lord of the Flies*
Anthony Burgess, *A Clockwork Orange*
Dan Korem, *Suburban Gangs: The Affluent Rebels*
Frederick Mathews, *Youth Gangs on Youth Gangs*
www.bullying.org
www.cyberbullying.ca
http://www.cln.org/themes/youth_violence.html
http://www.wsd1.org/PC_LMS/pf/youthgangs.htm
http://www.ps-sp.gc.ca/prg/cp/bldngevd/2007-yg-2-en.asp
http://www.cbc.ca/news/background/bullying
http://www.cbc.ca/news/background/virk
http://en.wikipedia.org/wiki/Reena_Virk

STRUCTURE:

1. Schindler's argument is cast as a letter. For what *audience* is it meant? The youths who attacked her son? All the readers of the *Toronto Star*? How well does her "letter" work as an essay?
2. Schindler organizes her letter by examining in turn each injury inflicted on her son. Point out each. What proportion of the letter's content is given to these *examples*? Could the point have been made without them?
3. After all her ironic "thanking," Schindler ends more literally: "I wouldn't wish on your child what you did to mine." Is her closing weak because it drops the IRONY, or strong because it caps the point?

STYLE:

1. Six of Schindler's paragraphs have only one sentence. Give reasons. Is this style effective?
2. How CONCISE is this selection? Try to find a passage of deadwood that could have been cut.

3. How FORMAL or INFORMAL is Schindler's TONE? Give examples. Does the tone fit the content? Why or why not?

ARGUMENTATION AND PERSUASION:

1. "You could have kicked him to death but you only left him to die, thank you," writes the victim's mother in paragraph 11. Her letter of "thanks" is *persuasion* as strong as any in this book. Explain the IRONY of Schindler's "thanking" her son's attackers.
2. Find and explain at least ten more IRONIES in this selection.
3. The author might have called her son's attackers "thugs," "goons" or worse. Would this openly *persuasive* mode be more effective than the "thanks" she gives? Defend your answer with reasons.
4. In addition to *irony*, the introduction to this chapter lists *repetition*, *fright* and *climax* as techniques of persuasion. How does Schindler use each? Respond with examples.
5. Does Schindler make her point *deductively* (through an innate rejection of violence) or *inductively* (through the many examples she cites, leading to her point)? Can an argument go both ways at once? Would this be a failure of logic?

IDEAS FOR DISCUSSION AND WRITING:

1. Does Schindler attempt only to heap shame on her son's attackers, or do you also detect, for example in the closing, a desire for reconciliation?
2. When his friends desired revenge, the son said, "No, I don't want someone else's mother to go through what mine has" (par. 10). What would *you* have said? Defend your answer with reasons.
3. How much do techniques of nonviolent resisters such as Mahatma Gandhi and Martin Luther King have in common with the responses of Rita Schindler and her son? Is their way ultimately weaker or stronger than the way of those who defend themselves through violence? Give examples.
4. Think of a time when you witnessed bullying at school. Tell the story to the class. Was the incident resolved, and if so, how?

5. In 1997 Reena Virk, a 14-year-old student in Saanich, Vancouver Island, was brutally beaten by classmates, mostly girls, and left dead under a bridge. Review this event in the websites given in "Explorations," then give as many reasons as you can why this tragedy occurred. Now give as many ways as you can how this tragedy could have been avoided.

6. Is there violent crime at your school or campus? Give examples. Defend or attack the "zero tolerance" policy of some school boards that permanently expel students who commit violent offences. Are there other solutions?

7. Are public forums such as the letters to the editor column or blogs or Internet chatrooms good vehicles for promoting our own ideas? Do others actually read and heed what we say?

8. PROCESS IN WRITING: *Read the crime news in your newspaper or hear it on radio or TV. Choose one violent act that provokes your anger or concern. Consider how, like Rita Schindler, you can respond to it through IRONY to persuade your audience to take your side. Make notes, look them over, then write a rapid first draft of a letter to the perpetrator, or to the public, or to both. The next day look it over. Will it startle and persuade the AUDIENCE by meaning the opposite of what it says? (Remember Schindler's "thanking" the attackers, or in Chapter 8 Stephen Leacock's "advice" on how to live to be 200.) Is the ironic TONE consistent? Is the letter concise, like Schindler's? If not, revise. Finally, check the spelling and grammar. When you have produced your good draft, send it as a letter to the editor of the newspaper you read. Or post it with an appropriate discussion group on the Internet. Check either for responses. Collect them, then show them, with the original letter, to the class.*

Note: See also the Topics for Writing on the Online Learning Centre at www. mcgrawhill.ca/olc/conrad.

ROBERT CHRISTY

Life with Cerebral Palsy

In the essay that follows, from the February 5, 2001 Maclean's, *Robert ("Bob") Christy tells much of his life story. Here are a few more facts: In 1940 he was born to parents who, though he had cerebral palsy and stuttered, taught him to believe he was not disabled. He learned the lesson well, emerging as a lifelong optimist whose motto is "To Look Beyond What You See." In 1963 Christy earned a B.A. in commerce, economics and math from Queen's, and in 1965 an M.B.A. from the University of Toronto. Then during a successful 30-year career in the federal public service in Ottawa and Regina, he was a social policy researcher, analyst, advisor and writer. Now retired and a grandfather, Christy writes on issues of physical disability, while living with his wife Gail, who also has cerebral palsy and is an ordained minister in the United Church of Canada.*

Much of Christy's essay deals with a famous legal case. In 1993 Saskatchewan farmer Robert Latimer put his 12-year-old daughter Tracy, severely disabled and in pain from cerebral palsy, into the cab of his truck. He then filled the cab with exhaust fumes till she died. Always known by friends and neighbours as a loving father, Latimer said he did it to end her pain. The court cases that followed were widely covered in the news. In 1997 a judge granted Latimer a constitutional exemption in order to give him a sentence of only two years—with just one year to be served in jail. Supporters were overjoyed, while groups representing the disabled were enraged. A higher court then overturned the verdict, and in 2001 the Supreme Court of Canada upheld the second-degree murder charge with a life sentence and no chance of parole for ten years. However, day parole was finally granted in 2008. The debate continues: Who is right, the friends and neighbours who think Latimer did a kindness for Tracy, or opponents of mercy killing who guard the rights of the disabled?

M y name is Bob, and I am living a wonderful life as a son, brother, husband, father, father-in-law and grandfather. I have studied at three post-secondary institutions, received bachelor's and master's degrees from two of Canada's top universities, and had a 30-year career with the federal government. But people may want to tell me what's best for me, because I have cerebral palsy. When I was young, I was popular in the community and at school, received high grades through working hard and exercising an agile mind, and did everything other kids my age did. Yet a close relative thought I should have been "destroyed at birth," because of my condition. I'm a raging extrovert, energized by people, and humorous when I am with them. Yet those who paid my salary put me into jobs away from the public eye, doing research and policy writing, refusing me the chance to do the things I could do best. When I didn't shine or meet the potential that those who knew me thought I should achieve, people could justifiably say: "What do you expect? He has cerebral palsy."

Among the many people I know from all walks of life are a professor, now dead, who taught in a major Canadian university, an Anglican priest and her spouse, a water resources economist who is listed in *Who's Who*, and my wife, a clergywoman who is one of the leaders of the largest Protestant denomination in Canada. We all have cerebral palsy. I've travelled, stood on the Great Wall in China and cruised down the Yangtze River, through the Three Gorges. I've been on safari, swum in the Indian Ocean and played golf in Kenya. I've walked the beaches of Trinidad, stood in the main square of Lima, driven a car in England, Scotland, Ireland (north and south) and Wales, and prayed at the Western Wall of the Second Temple in Jerusalem. I paid for it all myself, through writing contracts, even though I have cerebral palsy.

But now I cry. For the plight of Robert Latimer and his family, who will suffer for 10 long years because in their frustration, ignorance and—grudgingly, I'll say—love, they followed their own pigheadedness, apparently did not listen to the wisdom of others and did not grasp the help that was there for their daughter Tracy, whom he killed because he said he could not stand her pain.

I also weep for the lack of knowledge of people in our so-called high-literacy nation that think cerebral palsy hurts. It doesn't. What hurts is atrophy when muscles are not used: as the saying goes, use them or lose them. Physiotherapy and patterning help blood flow and ease any pain. Another thing that hurts is the attitude of others. I weep for the many people who, in their ignorance, think Latimer did the "right thing"—who, think, perhaps, that murder, if committed in love to save someone from a "horrible life," is OK if it's a disabled person who dies. Would they feel that way if a person killed another out of love to save the "loved one" from a horrible life as a street person? And I cry for politicians who have forgotten the promises made in 1981, the International Year of Disabled Persons. They are the ones who could be easily tempted to listen to whoever makes the loudest noise, regardless of right or wrong.

But maybe I cry most of all for me; in spite of my cleverness, dili-   5
gence and successes now and in future, will I only be judged in a negative, non-flattering way as "Bob, the man with cerebral palsy"?

EXPLORATIONS:

Elaine Geralis, ed., *Children with Cerebral Palsy: A Parents' Guide*
http://www.cerebralpalsy.org
http://www.ofcp.on.ca/aboutcp.html
http://www.chninternational.com/default.html
http://www.cbc.ca/news/background/latimer/index.html
http://en.wikipedia.org/wiki/Euthanasia
http://www.hawking.org.uk/home/hindex.html
http://www.stevenfletcher.com/profile.php

STRUCTURE:

1. Why does Christy give his name, Bob, in both the opening and closing sentences? What are the effects?
2. Identify Christy's THESIS STATEMENT. Why is it placed towards the middle of the essay?
3. Paragraph 2 is stuffed with a series of quick and colourful *examples*. Are there enough? Is it possible to have too many? Does Christy? What are the effects?
4. Christy ends his argument with a question. Is it a real question? If not, what is its purpose?

STYLE:

1. In question 2 above, we looked at Christy's thesis statement, "But now I cry," which begins paragraph 3. Now identify every place in the rest of the essay where he writes "I cry" or "I weep." Is this *repetition* accidental or deliberate? What are its effects?

2. For what AUDIENCE do you believe Christy is writing? What challenges does he face in communicating with non-disabled readers? Point out everything he does to teach them the facts of his own condition.

ARGUMENTATION AND PERSUASION:

1. To what extent is "Life with Cerebral Palsy" *induction*, based on *examples* that lead to its author's points? Identify at least ten such examples.

2. Does Christy's essay also employ *deduction*, applying a general principle to specific cases?

3. Does Christy's essay work only through logical thought (*argumentation*) or do we also feel *persuasion*? We have already seen the large amount of evidence he presents to argue his case; now look for places where emotion is used as a tool to help us accept his views.

IDEAS FOR DISCUSSION AND WRITING:

1. In the introduction to this essay, review the case of Robert Latimer, who in 1993 killed his daughter Tracy to end her pain from cerebral palsy. Do you view this mercy killing as a crime? Did Latimer deserve the minimum ten-year prison sentence he received? Were disability organizations right in supporting this court decision, so that future disabled persons would be safer? Or do you view Latimer as a loving parent who did the best for his child, and then was unjustly punished? Defend your answers with reasons.

2. In paragraph 3, Christy "cries" for the Latimer family, despite his viewing Latimer's act as "murder." Does this attitude weaken or strengthen his overall argument?

3. One of the world's most brilliant physicists and astronomers, Stephen Hawking, is severely disabled by amyotrophic lateral

sclerosis. Visit his official home page at http://www.hawking.org.
uk/home/hindex.html. Find out how he goes about his work
despite his disability, then tell the class.

4. Are you disabled, or do you have a family member or friend who
is? Report to the class on the challenges of the disability, and how
to face them.

5. Stephen Fletcher had won Manitoba's kayaking championship,
had canoed thousands of miles of northern rivers, and was working as an engineer. Then in a highway collision with a moose, he
became a paraplegic. Visit his blog at http://www.stevenfletcher.
com/profile.php, to read how Fletcher became an MP in the 2004
federal election, and Senior Health Critic for the Conservative
Party. Report to the class on how he has achieved this success
despite a severe physical disability.

6. In Canada we often see special facilities for the disabled: elevators,
ramps, Braille signs in elevators, audible signals at traffic lights,
seeing-eye dogs, etc. Is this enough? Do you have suggestions for
what more might be done?

7. PROCESS IN WRITING: *Do an Internet search on Saskatchewan farmer
Robert Latimer, and spend a couple of hours reading and taking notes (or
printing materials) on his famous court case mentioned above. Now decide
whether you support or condemn Latimer's act of mercy killing. Write a
short outline of your argument, then do a quick discovery draft. Look it
over. Is it mostly* deduction *(beginning with a principle you believe in
strongly, then applied to make sense of the facts)? Or is it mostly* induction
*(examining the facts of the case, then using them to arrive at an overall
THESIS STATEMENT)? Examine also your TONE: Do you argue rationally,
using mostly fact to support your* argumentation? *Or has this controversial topic made you emotional, so that you in turn use emotion as your
main way to* persuade *the reader? At the top of the page, label your essay
DEDUCTION or INDUCTION, and also label it ARGUMENTATION or PERSUASION.
Now make sure your approach is consistent. Revise and polish. Finally,
join with a small group of your classmates to share each other's papers and
your reactions to them.*

*Note: See also the Topics for Writing on the Online Learning Centre at www.
mcgrawhill.ca/olc/conrad.*

LT.-GEN. ROMÉO DALLAIRE, WITH MAJOR BRENT BEARDSLEY

*Cri de coeur**

Making peace can take more courage than making war. In 1993 the United Nations named Canadian Lieutenant-General Roméo Dallaire commander of an international peacekeeping force with a tough mandate: to stop an ethnic conflict in the tiny African country of Rwanda. (The career soldier from Quebec seemed a natural choice for operations in a French-speaking nation.) Out of old resentments stemming from the Belgian colonial era, the majority Hutus had begun a persecution of their former masters, the Tutsis. Dallaire saw genocide coming. He alerted the UN, the United States, France and other key players. He requested, then demanded, more troops and weapons. When the slaughters began in spring of 1994, he hounded the major UN countries to save the Tutsis—but they all declined to help, because they saw in Rwanda no strategic value and no oil. So Dallaire and his tiny force went into action: they moved thousands of Tutsis to safety behind the front lines of a rebel Tutsi force; they used moral suasion to defy the governing Hutus; and the apparently fearless General personally intimidated members of the government to obey terms of the peace treaty they had signed. But when the dust settled after 100 days of butchery, some 800,000 men, women and children had died. Dallaire blamed himself, and sank into depression. But over the next decade the world acknowledged its own guilt, and his heroism. Almost a dozen books, documentaries and feature films now tell the story (see "Explorations"). The best of these is Dallaire's own

---

*Cri de coeur: Editor's title, in French meaning "a cry from the heart."

414

book Shake Hands with the Devil: The Failure of Humanity in Rwanda *(2003). Our selection is the book's introduction to this harrowing story. The memoir has become an international bestseller, and has been called the most important Canadian book of the decade. Though Dallaire himself seems not to believe it, these pages portray a true Canadian, and world, hero.*

I t was an absolutely magnificent day in May 1994. The blue sky was cloudless, and there was a whiff of breeze stirring the trees. It was hard to believe that in the past weeks an unimaginable evil had turned Rwanda's gentle green valleys and mist-capped hills into a stinking nightmare of rotting corpses. A nightmare we all had to negotiate every day. A nightmare that, as commander of the UN peacekeeping force in Rwanda, I could not help but feel deeply responsible for. 1

In relative terms, that day had been a good one. Under the protection of a limited and fragile ceasefire, my troops had successfully escorted about two hundred civilians—a few of the thousands who had sought refuge with us in Kigali, the capital of Rwanda—through many government- and militia-manned checkpoints to reach safety behind the Rwandese Patriotic Front (RPF) lines. We were seven weeks into the genocide, and the RPF, the disciplined rebel army (composed largely of the sons of Rwandan refugees who had lived over the border in camps in Uganda since being forced out of their homeland at independence), was making a curved sweep toward Kigali from the north, adding civil war to the chaos and butchery in the country. 2

Having delivered our precious cargo of innocent souls, we were headed back to Kigali in a white UN Land Cruiser with my force commander pennant on the front hood and the blue UN flag on a staff attached to the right rear. My Ghanaian sharpshooter, armed with a new Canadian C-7 rifle, rode behind me, and my new Senegalese aide-de-camp, Captain Ndiaye, sat to my right. We were driving a particularly dangerous stretch of road, open to sniper fire. Most of the people in the surrounding villages had been slaughtered, the few survivors escaping with little more than the clothes on their backs. In a few short weeks, it had become a lonely and forlorn place. 3

Suddenly up ahead we saw a child wandering across the road. I stopped the vehicle close to the little boy, worried about scaring him 4 off, but he was quite unfazed. He was about three years old, dressed in a filthy, torn T-shirt, the ragged remnants of underwear, little more than a loincloth, drooping from under his distended belly. He was caked in dirt, his hair white and matted with dust, and he was enveloped in a cloud of flies, which were greedily attacking the open sores that covered him. He stared at us silently, sucking on what I realized was a high-protein biscuit. Where had the boy found food in this wasteland?

5   I got out of the vehicle and walked toward him. Maybe it was the condition I was in, but to me this child had the face of an angel and eyes of pure innocence. I had seen so many children hacked to pieces that this small, whole, bewildered boy was a vision of hope. Surely he could not have survived all on his own? I motioned for my aide-de-camp to honk the horn, hoping to summon up his parents, but the sound echoed over the empty landscape, startling a few birds and little else. The boy remained transfixed. He did not speak or cry, just stood sucking on his biscuit and staring up at us with his huge, solemn eyes. Still hoping that he wasn't all alone, I sent my aide-de-camp and the sharpshooter to look for signs of life.

6   We were in a ravine lush with banana trees and bamboo shoots, which created a dense canopy of foliage. A long straggle of deserted huts stood on either side of the road. As I stood alone with the boy, I felt an anxious knot in my stomach: this would be a perfect place to stage an ambush. My colleagues returned, having found no one. Then a rustling in the undergrowth made us jump. I grabbed the boy and held him firmly to my side as we instinctively took up defensive positions around the vehicle and in the ditch. The bushes parted to reveal a well-armed RPF soldier about fifteen years old. He recognized my uniform and gave me a smart salute and introduced himself. He was part of an advance observation post in the nearby hills. I asked him who the boy was and whether there was anyone left alive in the village who could take care of him. The soldier answered that the boy had no name and no family but that he and his buddies were looking after him. That explained the biscuit but did nothing to allay my concerns over the security and health of the boy. I protested that the child needed proper care and that I could give it to him: we were protecting and supporting orphanages in Kigali where he would be

much better off. The soldier quietly insisted that the boy stay where he was, among his own people.

I continued to argue, but this child soldier was in no mood to discuss the situation and with haughty finality stated that his unit would care and provide for the child. I could feel my face flush with anger and frustration, but then noticed that the boy himself had slipped away while we had been arguing over him, and God only knew where he had gone. My aide-de-camp spotted him at the entrance to a hut a short distance away, clambering over a log that had fallen across the doorway. I ran after him, closely followed by my aide-de-camp and the RPF child soldier. By the time I had caught up to the boy, he had disappeared inside. The log in the doorway turned out to be the body of a man, obviously dead for some weeks, his flesh rotten with maggots and beginning to fall away from the bones.

As I stumbled over the body and into the hut, a swarm of flies invaded my nose and mouth. It was so dark inside that at first I smelled rather than saw the horror that lay before me. The hut was a two-room affair, one room serving as a kitchen and living room and the other as a communal bedroom; two rough windows had been cut into the mud-and-stick wall. Very little light penetrated the gloom, but as my eyes became accustomed to the dark, I saw strewn around the living room in a rough circle the decayed bodies of a man, a woman and two children, stark white bone poking through the desiccated, leather-like covering that had once been skin. The little boy was crouched beside what was left of his mother, still sucking on his biscuit. I made my way over to him as slowly and quietly as I could and, lifting him into my arms, carried him out of the hut.

The warmth of his tiny body snuggled against mine filled me with a peace and serenity that elevated me above the chaos. This child was alive yet terribly hungry, beautiful but covered in dirt, bewildered but not fearful. I made up my mind: this boy would be the fourth child in the Dallaire family. I couldn't save Rwanda, but I could save this child.

Before I had held this boy, I had agreed with the aid workers and representatives of both the warring armies that I would not permit any exporting of Rwandan orphans to foreign places. When confronted by such requests from humanitarian organizations, I would argue that the money to move a hundred kids by plane to France or Belgium could help build, staff and sustain Rwandan orphanages that could house three thousand children. This one boy eradicated all my arguments. I could see myself arriving at the terminal in Montreal like a latter-day St. Christopher° with the boy cradled in my arms, and my wife, Beth, there ready to embrace him.

11   That dream was abruptly destroyed when the young soldier, fast as a wolf, yanked the child from my arms and carried him directly into the bush. Not knowing how many members of his unit might already have their gunsights on us, we reluctantly climbed back into the Land Cruiser. As I slowly drove away, I had much on my mind.

12   By withdrawing, I had undoubtedly done the wise thing: I had avoided risking the lives of my two soldiers in what would have been a fruitless struggle over one small boy. But in that moment, it seemed to me that I had backed away from a fight for what was right, that this failure stood for all our failures in Rwanda.

13   Whatever happened to that beautiful child? Did he make it to an orphanage deep behind the RPF lines? Did he survive the following battles? Is he dead or is he now a child soldier himself, caught in the seemingly endless conflict that plagues his homeland?

14   That moment, when the boy, in the arms of a soldier young enough to be his brother, was swallowed whole by the forest, haunts me. It's a memory that never lets me forget how ineffective and irresponsible we were when we promised the Rwandans that we would establish an atmosphere of security that would allow them to achieve a lasting peace. It has been almost nine years since I left Rwanda, but as I write this, the sounds, smells and colours come flooding back in digital clarity. It's as if someone has sliced into my brain and grafted this horror called Rwanda frame by blood-soaked frame directly on my cortex. I could not forget even if I wanted to. For many of these years, I have yearned to return to Rwanda and disappear into the blue-green hills with my ghosts. A simple pilgrim seeking forgiveness and pardon. But as I slowly begin to piece my life back together, I know the time has come for me to make a more difficult pilgrimage: to travel back through all those terrible memories and retrieve my soul.

°St. Christopher: A fearless martyr of the third century, patron saint of travellers.

I did try to write this story soon after I came back from Rwanda in September 1994, hoping to find some respite for myself in sorting out how my own role as Force Commander of UNAMIR interconnected with the international apathy, the complex political manoeuvres, the deep well of hatred and barbarity that resulted in a genocide in which over 800,000 people lost their lives. Instead, I plunged into a disastrous mental health spiral that led me to suicide attempts, a medical release from the Armed Forces, the diagnosis of post-traumatic stress disorder, and dozens upon dozens of therapy sessions and extensive medication, which still have a place in my daily life.

It took me seven years to finally have the desire, the willpower and the stamina to begin to describe in detail the events of that year in Rwanda. To recount, from my insider's point of view, how a country moved from the promise of a certain peace to intrigue, the fomenting of racial hatred, assassinations, civil war and genocide. And how the international community, through an inept UN mandate and what can only be described as indifference, self-interest and racism, aided and abetted these crimes against humanity—how we all helped create the mess that has murdered and displaced millions and destabilized the whole central African region.

A growing library of books and articles is exploring the tragic events in Rwanda from many angles: eyewitness accounts, media analyses, assaults on the actions of the American administration at the time, condemnations of the UN's apparent ineptitude. But even in the international and national inquiries launched in the wake of the genocide, the blame somehow slides away from the individual member nations of the UN, and in particular those influential countries with permanent representatives on the Security Council, such as the United States, France and the United Kingdom, who sat back and watched it all happen, who pulled their troops or didn't offer any troops in the first place. A few Belgian officers were brought to court to pay for the sins of Rwanda. When my sector commander in Kigali, Colonel Luc Marchal, was court-martialled in Brussels, the charges against him were clearly designed to deflect any responsibility away from the Belgian government for the deaths of the ten Belgian peacekeepers under my command. The judge eventually threw out all the charges, accepting the fact that Marchal had performed his duties magnificently in a near-impossible situation. But the spotlight never turned to the reasons why he and the rest of the UNAMIR force were in such a dangerous situation in the first place.

18   It is time that I tell the story from where I stood—literally in the middle of the slaughter for weeks on end. A public account of my actions, my decisions and my failings during that most terrible year may be a crucial missing link for those attempting to understand the tragedy both intellectually and in their hearts. I know that I will never end my mourning for all those Rwandans who placed their faith in us, who thought the UN peacekeeping force was there to stop extremism, to stop the killings and help them through the perilous journey to a lasting peace. That mission, UNAMIR, failed. I know intimately the cost in human lives of the inflexible UN Security Council mandate, the pennypinching financial management of the mission, the UN red tape, the political manipulations and my own personal limitations. What I have come to realize as the root of it all, however, is the fundamental indifference of the world community to the plight of seven to eight million black Africans in a tiny country that had no strategic or resource value to any world power. An overpopulated little country that turned in on itself and destroyed its own people, as the world watched and yet could not manage to find the political will to intervene. Engraved still in my brain is the judgment of a small group of bureaucrats who came to "assess" the situation in the first weeks of the genocide: "We will recommend to our government not to intervene as the risks are high and all that is here are humans."

19   My story is not a strictly military account nor a clinical, academic study of the breakdown of Rwanda. It is not a simplistic indictment of the many failures of the UN as a force for peace in the world. It is not a story of heroes and villains, although such a work could easily be written. This book is a *cri de coeur* for the slaughtered thousands, a tribute to the souls hacked apart by machetes because of their supposed difference from those who sought to hang on to power. It is the story of a commander who, faced with a challenge that didn't fit the classic Cold War–era peacekeeper's rule book, failed to find an effective solution and witnessed, as if in punishment, the loss of some of his own troops, the attempted annihilation of an ethnicity, the butchery of children barely out of the womb, the stacking of

severed limbs like cordwood, the mounds of decomposing bodies being eaten by the sun.

This book is nothing more nor less than the account of a few 20 humans who were entrusted with the role of helping others taste the fruits of peace. Instead, we watched as the devil took control of paradise on earth and fed on the blood of the people we were supposed to protect.

EXPLORATIONS:

Lt.-Gen. Roméo Dallaire, with Major Brent Beardsley, *Shake Hands with the Devil: The Failure of Humanity in Rwanda*
Gerald Caplan, *Rwanda: The Preventable Genocide*
Barbara Coloroso, *Extraordinary Evil: A Brief History of Genocide*
Gil Courtemanche, *A Sunday at the Pool in Kigali* (novel)
Joseph Conrad, *Heart of Darkness* (novella)
Hotel Rwanda (feature film, 2004)
Ghosts of Rwanda (PBS documentary)
The Last Just Man (documentary film, 2002)
Shake Hands with the Devil: The Journey of Roméo Dallaire (documentary film, 2005)
Shake Hands with the Devil (feature film, starring Roy Dupuis, 2007)
http://en.wikipedia.org/wiki/Rom%E9o_Dallaire#Early_life_and_education
http://www.thirdworldtraveler.com/Heroes/Gen_Romeo_Dallaire.html
http://tanadineen.com/COLUMNIST/Columns/Dallaire.htm
http://www.pbs.org/wgbh/pages/frontline/shows/ghosts/interviews/dallaire.html

STRUCTURE:

1. Read the opening paragraph aloud. How does Dallaire prepare us for his topic, in telling of the "absolutely magnificent day," the "gentle green valleys" and the "mist-capped hills" of Rwanda?

2. The logic of *cause and effect* plays a large part in Dallaire's argument. Point out five examples of it in these pages.

3. To what extent is "*Cri de coeur*" a *narrative?*

4. In not fighting over "one small boy," the general follows military good sense. But he goes on to say, "in that moment, it seemed to me that I had backed away from a fight for what was right, that this failure stood for all our failures in Rwanda" (12). Point out all the ways in which this selection is an *analogy* to larger things.

STYLE:

1. The author's first language is French. Apart from the term *cri de coeur*, chosen from paragraph 19 as our title, do you see any effects of this fact on his style?

2. Read paragraphs 7–8 aloud, if you can. What overall technique lies behind their power to evoke horror?

ARGUMENTATION AND PERSUASION:

1. Examine the logic of this selection. Is it mostly *deduction* (extending a principle to explain individual cases) or *induction* (letting examples lead to a point)?

2. To what extent does the General's *cri de coeur* ("cry from the heart") use emotion, or *persuasion*, to make its points? Give examples. And to what extent does it work through logic, or *argumentation?* Can it draw on both at once?

IDEAS FOR DISCUSSION AND WRITING:

1. After an 11-year-old boy found his 5-year-old sister near the corpses of their parents, he said, "I will hunt the killers to the end of the world. I will kill their children when I grow up. I know the killers; even 70 years from now, I will remember how they and their children look" (*The Ottawa Citizen*, July 13, 2000). What conclusions would you draw from this *example?*

2. As this book was going to press, ten years after the events in Rwanda, another genocide had begun in the Sudan, a country with almost no central government and with no Roméo Dallaires

to intervene. Give your suggestions as to how this continuing tragedy can be ended.

3. After contemplating the downward spiral of his own mental health, the General concludes, "It is time that I tell the story from where I stood" (18). Why did it take nine years for him to put it on paper? Do you believe that writing and sharing his "story" has brought him peace? Canadian novelist Sylvia Fraser once said "Writing is healing." Do your own acts of writing lead your own conflicts toward peace?

4. At one hopeless point during the conflict, Dallaire was asked "What in the hell are you doing here? Why are you staying?" He replied, "If I can save one life, then it's worth it." "Yeah, but there are tens of thousands being slaughtered every day." The General concluded, "Then maybe if I could be a witness, maybe I'll have a chance to tell everything that we've been seeing." Now tell of the time you, too, were a "witness," and what it accomplished.

5. In her 2007 book *Extraordinary Evil: A Brief History of Genocide*, Barbara Coloroso, who writes widely on the problem of bullying in schools, states that genocide is "the most extreme form of bullying." Describe to the class the worst example of bullying that you personally have seen or experienced in school, and point out any similarities you detect between it and the tragedy Dallaire describes in his book.

6. **PROCESS IN WRITING:** *Like Roméo Dallaire, use* persuasion *to "tell the story" of the worst conflict you have ever been in. First close your eyes and remember the situation or incident, then freewrite for several minutes. Look over these notes and work the best of them into a rapid first draft. Be sure to state your* THESIS STATEMENT, *the overall main point. Later review the 11 devices of persuasion listed on pages 349–351 of our chapter introduction, and add them wherever they will strengthen your message. Add* SENSE IMAGES, *as Dallaire has, to bring the scene alive. Add* TRANSITIONS *(such as "then," "next" and "finally") to speed the narrative, and add logic signals to sharpen your thoughts. Finally, edit for* STYLE *and correctness, then read the piece aloud, with feeling, to the class. Later consider whether this act of writing has brought you peace.*

Note: See also the Topics for Writing on the Online Learning Centre at www.mcgrawhill.ca/olc/conrad.

Process in Writing: Guidelines

Follow at least some of these steps in writing your essay of argumentation and/ or persuasion (your teacher may suggest which ones).

1. Choose a good topic, if necessary customize it, then go to either 2 or 3 below.

2. ***DEDUCTION:*** Do you already know your point of view because of a moral or intellectual principle you hold? First examine that principle, the foundation of your argument: Is it extreme, or is it reasonable enough (and clear enough) that your AUDIENCE can accept it? If the latter, proceed. Make notes, then do a rapid first draft showing how the principle supports your point.

OR

3. ***INDUCTION:*** Did experience or observation teach you the point you wish to make? First generate a page of notes. Then put these experiences or observations into the order that led you to your conclusion. Now transfer this argument to a rapid first draft.

4. You have probably organized your draft through a pattern we studied in an earlier chapter. *Cause and effect* is a natural for either deduction or induction, and so is *comparison and contrast.* You have surely used *examples,* perhaps *narrating* or *describing* them. You might also have *classified* your subject, or cast your logic in a *process analysis.* Apart from *analogy,* which appeals more to emotion than to logic, all the approaches we have studied so far can serve deduction or induction. Use whatever works. If your first draft makes partial use of a major pattern, consider revising to extend the pattern and strengthen its effect.

5. As you look over your first draft, add any missing examples, especially if your argument is inductive (the more evidence, the better). Heighten your logic with signals such as "however," "therefore," "as a result" and "in conclusion."

6. Now judge how *argumentative* or *persuasive* your approach has been so far. Does your cold logic need a little colour and life? If so, add it, consulting pages 349–351 on techniques of persuasion. Or do emotions dominate your argument? Do they even encourage the audience not to think? If so, revise toward a more blended stance in your second draft.

7. Now cut all deadwood. Check for spelling and punctuation before printing out your best version.

GLOSSARY

abstract Theoretical, relying more on GENERALIZATION than on facts and examples. Abstract writing may lack interest and force, because it is hard to understand and the ideas are hard to apply. *See also* the opposite of abstract, CONCRETE.

allegory In poetry or PROSE, a passage or an entire work that has two levels of meaning: literal and symbolic (*see* SYMBOL). Like a parable, an allegory draws such numerous or striking parallels between its literal subject and its implied subject that, without ever stating "the moral of the story," it leads us to perceive a moral or philosophical truth. An allegory, though, is longer and more complex than a parable. It also differs from an analogy in that it does not openly identify and compare the two subjects.

allusion An indirect reference to a passage in literature or scripture, to an event, a person, or anything else familiar to the reader. An allusion is a device of compression in language, for in a few words it summons up the meaning of the thing to which it refers, and applies that meaning to the subject at hand. Critics of big government, for example, often *allude* to Big Brother, the personification of governmental tyranny in George Orwell's novel *1984.*

anecdote A short account of an interesting incident. An anecdote can be a joke or a true story about others or oneself, and is often used as an example to introduce an essay, close an essay or illustrate points within an essay.

audience The reader or readers. One of the essayist's crucial tasks is to match the level and strategy of an argument to the needs and qualities of the particular audience that will read it. *See* the section "Who is my audience?" in this book's introductory essay, "The Act of Writing," p. 100.

bias words Terms that, either subtly or openly, encourage strong value judgements. SUBJECTIVE language is a vital ingredient of much good writing, especially in description and in persuasion; to avoid it completely is difficult and often undesirable. The important thing is to avoid blatantly loaded language in an essay: terms like "jerk," "slob," "cretin," "geezer," "Hogtown," "Newfie," "tree hugger" or "neocon" will inflame an uncritical reader and offend a critical one. Note that many bias words are also SLANG.

cliché A worn-out expression that takes the place of original thought: "sadder but wiser," "bite the bullet," "hustle and bustle," 'been there, done that," "the bottom line," and "no pain, no gain." All clichés were once fresh, but like last year's fad in clothing or music, have lost their appeal and may even annoy.

climax In an essay, the point where the argument reaches its culmination, its point of greatest intensity or importance. The closing of an essay is normally a climax; if it is not, it may give the impression of trailing feebly off into nothingness.

colloquial Speech-like. Colloquial expressions like "cop," "guy," "kid," "nitty gritty" and "okay" are often used in conversation but are usually avoided in essays, especially FORMAL essays. Though lively, colloquialisms can be inexact: "guy," for example, can refer to a rope as well as a person, and "kid" can refer to a goat as well as a child. *See also* SLANG.

conciseness The art of conveying the most meaning in the fewest words. A concise essay does not explain its topic less fully than a wordy one; it just uses words more efficiently. Concise writers get straight to the point and stay on topic. They are well enough organized to avoid repeating themselves. They give CONCRETE examples rather than pages of ABSTRACT argument. They use a short word unless a long one is more exact. And most concise writers, to achieve these goals, revise extensively.

concrete Factual and specific, relying more on examples than on abstract theory. Concrete language makes writing more forceful, interesting and convincing by recreating vividly for the reader what the writer has experienced or thought. SENSE IMAGES, ANECDOTES, FIGURES OF SPEECH and CONCISENESS all play a part in concrete language and are usually lacking in its opposite, ABSTRACT language.

deduction A kind of logic that accepts a general principle as true, then uses it to explain a specific case or cases. *See* "Deduction," p. 346, and its opposite, "Induction," p. 347.

dialogue The quoted conversation of two or more people. Normally a new paragraph begins with each change of speaker, to avoid confusion as to who says what. A bit of dialogue can lend colour to an essay, but heavy use of it is normally reserved for fiction and drama.

economy See CONCISENESS.

epigram A short, clever, and often wise saying. The best-known epigrams are proverbs, such as "What can't be cured must be endured" and "To know all is to forgive all."

epigraph A short introductory quotation prefixed to an essay or other piece of writing.

essay Derived from the French term *essai*, meaning a "try" or "attempt," the word "essay" refers to a short composition in which a point is made, usually through analysis and example. While most essays are alike in being limited to one topic, they may vary widely in other ways. The *formal essay*, for example, is objective and stylistically dignified, while the *familiar essay* is subjective, anecdotal and sometimes colloquial.

euphemism A polite expression that softens or even hides the truth: "pass away" for "die," "senior citizens" for "old people," "low-income neighbourhood" for "slum," "gosh darn" for "God damn," "perspire" for "sweat," "terminate" for "kill," and "de-hire" or "select out" for "fire." Euphemisms have become more and more common in uses ranging from personal kindness to advertising to political repression.

fable A tale, usually about animals, that teaches a moral truth or lesson meant for humans. Examples range from the classical Greek fables of Aesop about animals such as the tortoise and the hare, to modern fables such as Basil Johnston's selection in this book, "Modern Cannibals of the Wilds."

fiction Imaginative literature written in PROSE. Consisting mainly of novels and short stories, fiction uses invented characters and plots to create a dramatic story. Most ESSAYS, by contrast, rely on literal fact and analysis to create an argument. There is of course an area of overlap: some fiction is very factual and some essays are very imaginative.

figures of speech Descriptive and often poetic devices in which meaning is concentrated and heightened, usually through comparisons:

A. **Simile**: A figure of speech in which one thing is said to be *like* another. ("With its high buildings on all sides, Bay Street is like a canyon.")
B. **Metaphor**: A figure of speech, literally false but poetically true, in which one thing is said to *be* another. ("Bay Street is a canyon walled by cliffs of concrete.")

C. **Hyperbole**: Exaggeration. ("The office buildings rise miles above the city.")

D. **Personification**: A figure of speech in which a non-human object is described as human. ("At night the empty buildings stare from their windows at the street.")

formal Formal writing is deliberate and dignified. It avoids partial sentences, most contractions, colloquial expressions and slang. Instead its vocabulary is standard and its sentences are often long and qualified with dependent clauses. It follows accepted rules of grammar and principles of style. *See also* INFORMAL.

generalization A broad statement of overall principle, as opposed to an explanation using specific examples. Although an essay needs generalizations, especially in places such as the THESIS STATEMENT and the CONCLUSION, most arguments that lack concrete examples are dull and difficult to understand.

hyperbole *See* FIGURES OF SPEECH.

image In literature, a mental picture triggered by words. Because they strongly stimulate thought and feeling, yet take little space, well-chosen images are vital ingredients of writing that is CONCRETE and has CONCISENESS. *See also* SENSE IMAGES.

induction A kind of logic that derives a general principle from the evidence of specific examples. *See* "Induction," p. 347, and its opposite, "Deduction," p. 346.

informal Informal writing resembles speech and, in fact, is often a representation of speech in writing. It may contain partial sentences, many short sentences, contractions, COLLOQUIAL expressions and sometimes SLANG. *See also* its opposite, FORMAL. Academic essays avoid almost all informal language.

irony A manner of expression in which a statement that seems literally to mean one thing actually means another. "Wonderful!" is a literal remark when said by a dinner guest enjoying the pie, but an ironic complaint when said by a driver who has backed into a tree. In a larger sense, *irony of situation* is a contrast between what is expected to happen and what does happen. It is this that creates our interest in the national leader who is impeached, the orphan who becomes a millionaire or the evangelist convicted of tax fraud. Irony is a powerful tool of argument and especially of SATIRE.

jargon Technical language or language that seeks to impress by *appearing* difficult or technical. Specialized terms can hardly be avoided in technical explanations: How could two electricians discuss a radio without words like "capacitor," "diode" and "transistor"? But these same words may need defining when put in an essay for the general reader. Other jargon uses technical-sounding or otherwise difficult words to seem important. An honest essayist will try to avoid "input," "output," "feedback," "interface," "knowledgeable," "parameters" and other ugly words of this sort when writing for the general reader.

juxtaposition The deliberate placing together of two or more thoughts, IMAGES or other elements that emphasize each other, usually by contrast.

metaphor *See* FIGURES OF SPEECH.

neologism A newly invented word. Some new terms are accepted into our standard vocabulary. For example, the word "laser" quickly became standard because we needed it to label a new and important invention. Most newly minted words are nuisances, though, meaningless to the many readers who do not know them.

objective The opposite of SUBJECTIVE. In objective writing the author relies more on hard evidence and logical proof than on intuitions, prejudices or interpretations.

onomatopoeia A poetical device in which language sounds like what it means. Some onomatopoetic words, such as "boom," "bang" and "crash," are obvious sound effects; others, such as "slither," "ooze" and "clatter," are more subtle. Onomatopoeia can be achieved not only through word choice but also through larger aspects of style. A series of short sentences, for example, gives an impression of tenseness and rapidity.

paradox A statement that seems illogical but that in some unexpected way may be true. The Bible is full of paradoxes, as in "Blessed are the meek, for they shall inherit the earth."

personification *See* FIGURES OF SPEECH.

prose Spoken or written language without the metrical structure that characterizes poetry. Conversations, letters, short stories, novels and essays are all prose.

pun A play on words. A pun is based either on two meanings of one word or on two words that sound alike but have different meanings. Often called the lowest form of humour, the pun is the basis of many jokes. (Why did the fly fly? Because the spider spider.)

quotation The words of one person reproduced exactly in the writing or speech of another person. A well-chosen quotation can add force to an argument by conveying the opinion of an authority or by presenting an idea in words so exact or memorable that they could hardly be improved upon. Quotations should be reproduced exactly, placed in quotation marks and attributed to their source. In writing research papers, there are whole systems of presenting and documenting quotations.

reduction to absurdity A technique of SATIRE in which the subject is belittled through being portrayed as absurd. A favourite device of humorists, such as Stephen Leacock.

sarcasm Scornful and contemptuous criticism, from the Greek word *sarkazein* ("to tear flesh").

satire Humorous criticism meant to improve an individual or society by exposing abuses. In TONE, satire can range from light humour to bitter criticism. Its main tools are wit, IRONY, exaggeration and sometimes SARCASM and ridicule.

sense images Descriptive appeals to one or more of the reader's five senses: sight, hearing, touch, taste and smell. Sense images are vital in helping the reader to experience, at second hand, what the writer has lived in person. CONCRETE language has many sense images; ABSTRACT language does not.

simile *See* FIGURES OF SPEECH.

slang Racy, unconventional language, often limited to a certain time, place or group. Slang is the extreme of colloquial language, terminology used in conversation but hardly ever in an ESSAY except for dialogue or special effects. One reason to avoid a slang term is that not everyone will know it: expressions like "swell," "square" and "far out" have fallen out of use, while expressions like "bug juice," "croaker," "jointman" and "rounder" are known to only one group—in this case, prison inmates. *See also* COLLOQUIAL.

stereotype An established mental image of something. Most stereotypes are of people and are based on their sex, race, colour, size or shape, economic or social class, or profession. Jokes about mothers-in-law, "Newfies," absent-minded professors, woman drivers or short people are all examples of stereotyping. While they may provoke humour, stereotypes are anything but harmless: they prevent recognition of people's individuality and they encourage prejudices which, at their extreme, can result in persecution like that of the Jews in Nazi Germany.

style In general, the *way* something is written, as opposed to *what* it is written about. Style is to some extent a matter of TONE—light or serious, INFORMAL or FORMAL, ironic or literal. It is also a matter of technique. Word choice, FIGURES OF SPEECH, level of CONCISENESS and characteristics of sentence structure and paragraphing are all ingredients of style. Although a writer should pay close attention to these matters, the idea that one deliberately seeks out "a style" is a mistake that only encourages imitation. An individual style emerges naturally as the sum of the writer's temperament, skills and experience.

subjective The opposite of OBJECTIVE. In subjective writing the author relies more on intuitions, prejudices or interpretations than on hard evidence and logical proof.

symbol One thing that stands for another, as in a flag representing a country, the crescent representing Islam or a logo representing a company. Symbols in word form appear frequently in poetry, drama, fiction and also essays.

thesis statement The sentence or sentences, usually in the introduction, that first state the main point and restrict the focus of an essay.

tone The manner of a writer toward the subject and reader. The tone of an essay can be light or serious, INFORMAL or FORMAL, ironic or literal. Tone is often determined by subject matter; for example, an essay about parties is likely to be lighter and less formal than one about funerals. An innovative writer, though, might reverse these treatments to give each of the essays an ironic tone. The identity of the reader also influences tone. An essay for specialists to read in a technical journal will tend to be more OBJECTIVE and serious than one written for the general reader. The main point for the writer is to choose the tone most appropriate to a particular essay and audience, then maintain it throughout.

transition A word, phrase, sentence or paragraph that moves the reader from one part of the essay to the next. Transitions, even ones as short as "next," "then," "as a result," "on the other hand," "in conclusion" or "finally," are crucial not only to speeding the argument along, but also to pointing out its logic.